SAGE Publications
London • Thousand Oaks • New Delhi

in association with

REPRESENTATION
Cultural Representations and Signifying Practices

Edited by STUART HALL

The Open University, Walton Hall, Milton Keynes MK7 6AA

© The Open University 1997

First published in 1997

Reprinted 1998, 1999, 2000, 2001, 2002 (twice), 2003

The opinions expressed are not necessarily those of the Course Team or of The Open University.

SAGE Publications Ltd
6 Bonhill Street
London EC2A 4PU

SAGE Publications Inc.
2455 Teller Road
Thousand Oaks
California 91320

SAGE Publications India Pvt Ltd
32, M-Block Market
Greater Kailash - I
New Delhi 110 048

British Library Cataloguing in Publication data

A catalogue record for this book is available from The British Library.

ISBN 0 7619 5431 7 (cased)

ISBN 0 7619 5432 5 (pbk)

Library of Congress catalog card number 96-071228

Edited, designed and typeset by The Open University.

Printed in Great Britain by Bath Press Colourbooks, Glasgow

REPRESENTATION
Cultural Representations and Signifying Practices

Culture, Media and Identities

The Open University Course Team

Claire Alexander, Critical reader

Maggie Andrew, Tutor panel member, Study Guide author

Melanie Bayley, Editor

Veronica Beechey, Critical reader

Robert Bocock, Author

David Boswell, Critical reader

Peter Braham, Author

David Calderwood, Project controller

Elizabeth Chaplin, Tutor panel member, Study Guide author

Lene Connolly, Print buying controller

Jeremy Cooper, BBC producer

Margaret Dickens, Print buying co-ordinator

Jessica Evans, Critical reader

Martin Ferns, Editor

Paul du Gay, Book 1 Chair, Book 4 Chair, Author

Ruth Finnegan, Author

Stuart Hall, Course Chair, Book 2 Chair, Author

Peter Hamilton, Author

Jonathan Hunt, Copublishing advisor

Linda Janes, Course manager

Siân Lewis, Graphic designer

Hugh Mackay, Book 5 Chair, Author

David Morley, Goldsmiths College, University of London, External assessor

Lesley Passey, Cover designer

Clive Pearson, Tutor panel member, Study Guide author

Peter Redman, Tutor panel member, Study Guide author

Graeme Salaman, Author

Paul Smith, Media librarian

Kenneth Thompson, Book 6 Chair, Author

Alison Tucker, BBC series producer

Pauline Turner, Course secretary

Kathryn Woodward, Book 3 Chair, Author

Chris Wooldridge, Editor

Consultant authors

Susan Benson, University of Cambridge

Paul Gilroy, Goldsmiths College, University of London

Christine Gledhill, Staffordshire University

Henrietta Lidchi, Museum of Mankind, London

Daniel Miller, University of London

Shaun Moores, Queen Margaret College, Edinburgh

Keith Negus, University of Leicester

Sean Nixon, University of Essex

Bhikhu Parekh, University of Hull

Kevin Robins, University of Newcastle upon Tyne

Lynne Segal, Middlesex University

Chris Shilling, University of Portsmouth

Nigel Thrift, University of Bristol

John Tomlinson, Nottingham Trent University

This book is part of the *Culture, Media and Identities* series published by Sage in association with The Open University.

Doing Cultural Studies: The Story of the Sony Walkman by Paul du Gay, Stuart Hall, Linda Janes, Hugh Mackay and Keith Negus

Representation: Cultural Representations and Signifying Practices edited by Stuart Hall

Identity and Difference edited by Kathryn Woodward

Production of Culture/Cultures of Production edited by Paul du Gay

Consumption and Everyday Life edited by Hugh Mackay

Media and Cultural Regulation edited by Kenneth Thompson

The final form of the text is the joint responsibility of chapter authors, book editors and course team commentators.

The books are part of The Open University course D318 *Culture, Media and Identities*. Details of this and other Open University courses can be obtained from the Course Reservations and Sales Centre, PO Box 724, The Open University, Milton Keynes MK7 6ZS. For availability of other course components, including video- and audio-cassette materials, contact Open University Educational Enterprises Ltd, 12 Cofferidge Close, Stony Stratford, Milton Keynes MK11 1BY.

REPRESENTATION: CULTURAL REPRESENTATIONS AND SIGNIFYING PRACTICES

edited by Stuart Hall

Introduction

Stuart Hall

The chapters in this volume all deal, in different ways, with the question of representation. This is one of the central practices which produce culture and a key 'moment' in what has been called the 'circuit of culture' (see **du Gay, Hall et al.**, 1997*). But what does representation have to do with 'culture': what is the connection between them? To put it simply, culture is about 'shared meanings'. Now, language is the privileged medium in which we 'make sense' of things, in which meaning is produced and exchanged. Meanings can only be shared through our common access to language. So language is central to meaning and culture and has always been regarded as the key repository of cultural values and meanings.

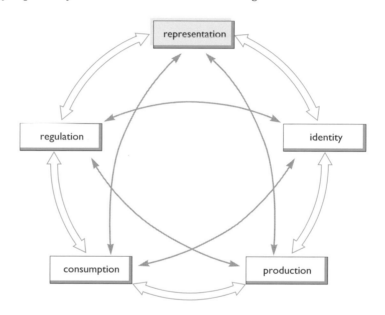

The circuit of culture

But how does language construct meanings? How does it sustain the dialogue between participants which enables them to build up a culture of shared understandings and so interpret the world in roughly the same ways? Language is able to do this because it operates as a *representational system.* In language, we use signs and symbols – whether they are sounds, written words, electronically produced images, musical notes, even objects – to stand for or represent to other people our concepts, ideas and feelings. Language is one of the 'media' through which thoughts, ideas and feelings are represented in a culture. Representation through language is therefore central to the processes by which meaning is produced. This is the basic, underlying idea which underpins all six chapters in this book. Each chapter examines 'the production and circulation of meaning through language' in different ways, in relation to different examples, different areas of social

* A reference in bold indicates another book, or another chapter in another book, in the series.

practice. Together, these chapters push forward and develop our understanding of how representation actually *works*.

'Culture' is one of the most difficult concepts in the human and social sciences and there are many different ways of defining it. In more traditional definitions of the term, culture is said to embody the 'best that has been thought and said' in a society. It is the sum of the great ideas, as represented in the classic works of literature, painting, music and philosophy – the 'high culture' of an age. Belonging to the same frame of reference, but more 'modern' in its associations, is the use of 'culture' to refer to the widely distributed forms of popular music, publishing, art, design and literature, or the activities of leisure-time and entertainment, which make up the everyday lives of the majority of 'ordinary people' – what is called the 'mass culture' or the 'popular culture' of an age. High culture versus popular culture was, for many years, the classic way of framing the debate about culture – the terms carrying a powerfully evaluative charge (roughly, high = good; popular = debased). In recent years, and in a more 'social science' context, the word 'culture' is used to refer to whatever is distinctive about the 'way of life' of a people, community, nation or social group. This has come to be known as the 'anthropological' definition. Alternatively, the word can be used to describe the 'shared values' of a group or of society – which is like the anthropological definition, only with a more sociological emphasis. You will find traces of all these meanings somewhere in this book. However, as its title suggests, 'culture' is usually being used in these chapters in a somewhat different, more specialized way.

What has come to be called the 'cultural turn' in the social and human sciences, especially in cultural studies and the sociology of culture, has tended to emphasize the importance of *meaning* to the definition of culture. Culture, it is argued, is not so much a set of *things* – novels and paintings or TV programmes and comics – as a process, a set of *practices*. Primarily, culture is concerned with the production and the exchange of meanings – the 'giving and taking of meaning' – between the members of a society or group. To say that two people belong to the same culture is to say that they interpret the world in roughly the same ways and can express themselves, their thoughts and feelings about the world, in ways which will be understood by each other. Thus culture depends on its participants interpreting meaningfully what is happening around them, and 'making sense' of the world, in broadly similar ways.

This focus on 'shared meanings' may sometimes make culture sound too unitary and too cognitive. In any culture, there is always a great diversity of meanings about any topic, and more than one way of interpreting or representing it. Also, culture is about feelings, attachments and emotions as well as concepts and ideas. The expression on my face 'says something' about who I am (identity) and what I am feeling (emotions) and what group I feel I belong to (attachment), which can be 'read' and understood by other people, even if I didn't intend deliberately to communicate anything as formal as 'a message', and even if the other person couldn't give a very logical account of how s/he came to understand what I was 'saying'. Above all, cultural meanings are not only 'in the head'. They organize and regulate social practices, influence our conduct and consequently have real, practical effects.

The emphasis on cultural practices is important. It is participants in a culture who give meaning to people, objects and events. Things 'in themselves' rarely if ever have any one, single, fixed and unchanging meaning. Even something as obvious as a stone can be a stone, a boundary marker or a piece of sculpture, depending on *what it means* – that is, within a certain context of use, within what the philosophers call different 'language games' (i.e. the language of boundaries, the language of sculpture, and so on). It is by our use of things, and what we say, think and feel about them – how we represent them – that we *give them a meaning*. In part, we give objects, people and events meaning by the frameworks of interpretation which we bring to them. In part, we give things meaning by how we use them, or integrate them into our everyday practices. It is our use of a pile of bricks and mortar which makes it a 'house'; and what we feel, think or say about it that makes a 'house' a 'home'. In part, we give things meaning by how we *represent* them – the words we use about them, the stories we tell about them, the images of them we produce, the emotions we associate with them, the ways we classify and conceptualize them, the values we place on them. Culture, we may say, is involved in all those practices which are not simply genetically programmed into us – like the jerk of the knee when tapped – but which carry meaning and value for us, which need to be *meaningfully interpreted* by others, or which *depend on meaning* for their effective operation. Culture, in this sense, permeates all of society. It is what distinguishes the 'human' element in social life from what is simply biologically driven. Its study underlines the crucial role of the *symbolic* domain at the very heart of social life.

Where is meaning produced? Our 'circuit of culture' suggests that, in fact, meanings are produced at several different sites and circulated through several different processes or practices (the cultural circuit). Meaning is what gives us a sense of our own identity, of who we are and with whom we 'belong' – so it is tied up with questions of how culture is used to mark out and maintain identity within and difference between groups (which is the main focus of **Woodward**, ed., 1997). Meaning is constantly being produced and exchanged in every personal and social interaction in which we take part. In a sense, this is the most privileged, though often the most neglected, site of culture and meaning. It is also produced in a variety of different *media;* especially, these days, in the modern mass media, the means of global communication, by complex technologies, which circulate meanings between different cultures on a scale and with a speed hitherto unknown in history. (This is the focus of **du Gay**, ed., 1997.) Meaning is also produced whenever we express ourselves in, make use of, consume or appropriate cultural 'things'; that is, when we incorporate them in different ways into the everyday rituals and practices of daily life and in this way give them value or significance. Or when we weave narratives, stories – and fantasies – around them. (This is the focus of **Mackay**, ed., 1997.) Meanings also regulate and organize our conduct and practices – they help to set the rules, norms and conventions by which social life is ordered and governed. They are also, therefore, what those who wish to govern and regulate the conduct and ideas of others seek to structure and shape. (This is the focus of **Thompson**, ed., 1997.) In other words, the question of meaning arises in relation to *all* the different moments or practices in our 'cultural circuit' – in the construction of identity and the marking of difference, in production and consumption, as well as in the regulation of social conduct. However, in all these instances, and at all these different institutional sites, one of the privileged 'media' through which meaning is produced and circulated is *language*.

So, in this book, where we take up in depth the first element in our 'circuit of culture', we start with this question of meaning, language and representation. Members of the same culture must share sets of concepts, images and ideas which enable them to think and feel about the world, and thus to interpret the world, in roughly similar ways. They must share, broadly speaking, the same 'cultural codes'. In this sense, thinking and feeling are themselves 'systems of representation', in which our concepts, images and emotions 'stand for' or represent, in our mental life, things which are or may be 'out there' in the world. Similarly, in order to *communicate* these meanings to other people, the participants to any meaningful exchange must also be able to use the same linguistic codes – they must, in a very broad sense, 'speak the same language'. This does not mean that they must all, literally, speak German or French or Chinese. Nor does it mean that they understand perfectly what anyone who speaks the same language is saying. We mean 'language' here in a much wider sense. Our partners must speak enough of the same language to be able to 'translate' what 'you' say into what 'I' understand, and vice versa. They must also be able to read visual images in roughly similar ways. They must be familiar with broadly the same ways of producing sounds to make what they would both recognize as 'music'. They must all interpret body language and facial expressions in broadly similar ways. And they must know how to translate their feelings and ideas into these various languages. Meaning is a dialogue – always only partially understood, always an unequal exchange.

Why do we refer to all these different ways of producing and communicating meaning as 'languages' or as 'working like languages' ? How do languages work? The simple answer is that languages work *through representation*. They are 'systems of representation'. Essentially, we can say that all these practices 'work like languages', *not* because they are all written or spoken (they are not), but because they all use some element to stand for or represent what we want to say, to express or communicate a thought, concept, idea or feeling. Spoken language uses sounds, written language uses words, musical language uses notes on a scale, the 'language of the body' uses physical gesture, the fashion industry uses items of clothing, the language of facial expression uses ways of arranging one's features, television uses digitally or electronically produced dots on a screen, traffic lights use red, green and amber – to 'say something'. These elements – sounds, words, notes, gestures, expressions, clothes – are part of our natural and material world; but their importance for language is not what they *are* but what they *do*, their function. They construct meaning and transmit it. They signify. They don't have any clear meaning *in themselves*. Rather, they are the vehicles or media which *carry meaning* because they operate as *symbols*, which stand for or represent (i.e. symbolize) the meanings we wish to communicate. To use another metaphor, they function as *signs*. Signs stand for or *represent* our concepts, ideas and feelings in such a way as to enable others to 'read', decode or interpret their meaning in roughly the same way that we do.

Language, in this sense, is a signifying practice. Any representational system which functions in this way can be thought of as working, broadly speaking, according to the principles of representation through language. Thus photography is a representational system, using images on light-sensitive paper to communicate photographic meaning about a particular person, event or scene. Exhibition or display in a museum or gallery can also be thought of as 'like a language', since it uses objects on display to produce certain meanings about the subject-matter of the exhibition. Music is 'like a language' in so far as it uses musical notes to communicate feelings and ideas, even if these are very abstract, and do not refer in any obvious way to the 'real world'. (Music has been called 'the most noise conveying the least information'.) But turning up at football matches with banners and slogans, with faces and bodies painted in certain colours or inscribed with certain symbols, can also be thought of as 'like a language' – in so far as it is a symbolic practice which gives meaning or expression to the idea of belonging to a national culture, or identification with one's local community. It is part of the language of national identity, a discourse of national belongingness. Representation, here, is closely tied up with both identity and knowledge. Indeed, it is difficult to know what 'being English', or indeed French, German, South African or Japanese, *means* outside of all the ways in which our ideas and images of national identity or national cultures have been represented. Without these 'signifying' systems, we could not take on such identities (or indeed reject them) and consequently could not build up or sustain that common 'life-world' which we call a culture.

So it is through culture and language *in this sense* that the production and circulation of meaning takes place. The conventional view used to be that 'things' exist in the material and natural world; that their material or natural characteristics are what determines or constitutes them; and that they have a perfectly clear meaning, *outside* of how they are represented. Representation, in this view, is a process of secondary importance, which enters into the field only after things have been fully formed and their meaning constituted. But since the 'cultural turn' in the human and social sciences, meaning is thought to be *produced* – constructed – rather than simply 'found'. Consequently, in what has come to be called a 'social constructionist approach', representation is conceived as entering into the very constitution of things; and thus culture is conceptualized as a primary or 'constitutive' process, as important as the economic or material 'base' in shaping social subjects and historical events – not merely a reflection of the world after the event.

'Language' therefore provides one general model of how culture and representation work, especially in what has come to be known as the *semiotic* approach – *semiotics* being the study or 'science of signs' and their general role as vehicles of meaning in culture. In more recent years, this preoccupation with meaning has taken a different turn, being more concerned, not with the detail of how 'language' works, but with the broader role of *discourse* in culture. Discourses are ways of referring to or constructing knowledge about a particular topic of practice: a cluster (or *formation*) of ideas, images and practices, which provide ways of talking about, forms of knowledge and conduct associated with, a particular topic, social activity or institutional site in society. These *discursive formations*, as they are known, define what is and is not appropriate in our formulation of, and our practices in relation to, a particular subject or site of social activity; what knowledge is considered useful, relevant and 'true' in that context; and what sorts of persons or 'subjects' embody its characteristics. 'Discursive' has become the general term used to refer to any approach in which meaning, representation and culture are considered to be constitutive.

There are some similarities, but also some major differences, between the *semiotic* and the *discursive* approaches, which are developed in the chapters which follow. One important difference is that the *semiotic* approach is concerned with the *how* of representation, with how language produces meaning – what has been called its 'poetics'; whereas the *discursive* approach is more concerned with the *effects and consequences* of representation – its 'politics'. It examines not only how language and representation produce meaning, but how the knowledge which a particular discourse produces connects with power, regulates conduct, makes up or constructs identities and subjectivities, and defines the way certain things are represented, thought about, practised and studied. The emphasis in the *discursive* approach is always on the historical specificity of a particular form or 'regime' of representation: not on 'language' as a general concern, but on specific *languages* or meanings, and how they are deployed at particular times, in particular places. It points us towards greater historical specificity – the way representational practices operate in concrete historical situations, in actual practice.

The general use of language and discourse as models of how culture, meaning and representation work, and the 'discursive turn' in the social and cultural sciences which has followed, is one of the most significant shifts of direction in our knowledge of society which has occurred in recent years. The discussion around these two versions of 'constructionism' – the semiotic and discursive approaches – is threaded through and developed in the six chapters which follow. The 'discursive turn' has not, of course, gone uncontested. You will find questions raised about this approach and critiques offered, as well as different variants of the position explored, by the different authors in this volume. Elsewhere in this series (in **Mackay**, ed., 1997, for example) alternative approaches are explored, which adopt a more 'creative', expressive or performative approach to meaning, questioning, for example, whether it makes sense to think of music as 'working like a language'. However, by and large, with some variations, the chapters in this book adopt a broadly 'constructionist' approach to representation and meaning.

In Chapter 1 on 'The work of representation', Stuart Hall fills out in greater depth the theoretical argument about meaning, language and representation briefly summarized here. What do we mean by saying that 'meaning is produced through language'? Using a range of examples – which it is important to work through for yourself – the chapter takes us through the argument of exactly what this entails. Do things – objects, people, events in the world – carry their own, one, true meaning, fixed like number plates on their backs, which it is the task of language to reflect accurately? Or are meanings constantly shifting as we move from one culture to another, one language to another, one historical context, one community, group or sub-culture, to another? Is it through our systems of representation, rather than 'in the world', that meaning is fixed? It is clear that representation is neither as simple nor transparent a practice as it first appears and that, in order to unpack the idea, we need to do some work on a range of examples, and bring to bear certain concepts and theories, in order to explore and clarify its complexities.

The question – 'Does visual language reflect a truth about the world which is already there or does it produce meanings about the world through representing it?' – forms the basis of Chapter 2, 'Representing the social: France and Frenchness in post-war humanist photography' by Peter Hamilton. Hamilton examines the work of a group of documentary photographers in France in the fifteen years following World War II, all of whom, he argues, adopted the representational approach, subject-matter, values and aesthetic forms of a particular practice – what he calls the 'humanist paradigm' – in French photography. This distinctive body of work produced a very specific image and definition of 'what it meant to be French' in this period, and thus helped to give a particular meaning to the idea of belonging to French culture and to 'Frenchness' as a national identity. What, then, is the status, the 'truth-claims', which these documentary photographic images are making? What are they 'documenting'? Are they to be judged by the authenticity of their representation or by the depth and subtlety of the feelings which the photographers put into their images? Do they reflect 'the truth' about French society at that time – or was there more than one kind of truth, more than one kind of 'Frenchness', depending on how it was represented? How did the image of France which emerges from this work relate to the rapid social changes sweeping through France in that period and to our (very different?) image of 'Frenchness' today?

Chapter 3, 'The poetics and the politics of exhibiting other cultures' by Henrietta Lidchi, takes up some of the same questions about representation, but in relation to a different subject-matter and a different set of signifying practices. Whereas Chapter 2 deals with the practice of photography – the production of meaning through images – Chapter 3 deals with exhibition – the production of meaning through the display of objects and artefacts from 'other cultures' within the context of the modern museum. Here, the elements exhibited are often 'things' rather than 'words or images' and the signifying practice involved is that of arrangement and display within a physical space, rather than layout on the page of an illustrated magazine or journal. Nevertheless, as this chapter argues, exhibition too is a 'system' or 'practice of representation' – and therefore works 'like a language'. Every choice – to show this rather than that, to show this in relation to that, to say this about that – is a choice about how to represent 'other cultures'; and each choice has consequences both for *what* meanings are produced and for *how* meaning is produced. Henrietta Lidchi shows how those meanings are inevitably implicated in relations of *power* – especially between those who are doing the exhibiting and those who are being exhibited.

The introduction of questions of power into the argument about representation is one of the ways in which the book consistently seeks to probe, expand and complexify our understanding of the process of representation. In Chapter 4, 'The spectacle of the "Other"', Stuart Hall takes up this theme of 'representing difference' from Chapter 3, but now in the context of more contemporary popular cultural forms (news photos, advertising, film and popular illustration). It looks at how 'racial', ethnic and sexual difference has been 'represented' in a range of visual examples across a number of historical archives. Central questions about how 'difference' is represented as 'Other', and the essentializing of 'difference' through stereotyping are addressed. However, as the argument develops, the chapter takes up the wider question of how signifying practices actually structure the way we 'look' – how different modes of 'looking' are being inscribed by these representational practices; and how violence, fantasy and 'desire' also play into representational practices, making them much more complex and their meanings more ambivalent. The chapter ends by considering some counter-strategies in the 'politics of representation' – the way meaning can be struggled over, and whether a particular regime of representation can be challenged, contested and transformed.

The question of how the spectator or the consumer is drawn into and implicated by certain practices of representation returns in Sean Nixon's Chapter 5, 'Exhibiting masculinity', on the construction of new gendered identities in contemporary advertising, magazines and consumer industries addressed especially to men. Nixon asks whether representational practices in the media in recent years, have been constructing new 'masculine identities'. Are the different languages of consumer culture, retailing and display developing new 'subject-positions', with which young men are increasingly invited to identify? And, if so, what do these images tell us about how the meanings of masculinity are shifting in late-modern visual culture? 'Masculinity', Nixon argues, far from being fixed and given biologically, accretes a variety of different meanings – different ways of 'being' or 'becoming masculine' – in different historical contexts. To address these questions, Nixon not only expands and applies some of the theoretical perspectives from earlier chapters, but adds new ones, including a psychoanalytically informed cultural analysis and film theory.

In the final Chapter 6, 'Genre and gender: the case of soap opera', Christine Gledhill takes us into the rich, narrative world of popular culture and its genres, with an examination of how representation is working in television soap opera. These are enormously popular sources of fictional narrative in modern life, circulating meanings throughout popular culture – and increasingly worldwide – which have been traditionally defined as 'feminine' in their appeal, reference and mode of operation. Gledhill unpacks the way this gendered identification of a TV genre has been constructed. She considers how and why such a 'space of representation' should have opened up within popular culture; how genre and gender elements interact in the narrative structures and representational forms; and how these popular forms have been ideologically shaped and inflected. She examines how the meanings circulated in soap operas – so frequently dismissed as stereotypical and manufactured – nevertheless enter into the discursive arena where the meaning of masculine and feminine identifications are being contested and transformed.

The book uses a wide range of examples from different cultural media and discourses, mainly concentrating on *visual* language. These examples are a key part of your work on the book – they are not simply 'illustrative'. Representation can only be properly analysed in relation to the actual concrete forms which meaning assumes, in the concrete practices of signifying, 'reading' and interpretation; and these require analysis of the actual signs, symbols, figures, images, narratives, words and sounds – the material forms – in which symbolic meaning is circulated. The examples provide an opportunity to practise these skills of analysis and to apply them to many other similar instances which surround us in daily cultural life.

It is worth emphasizing that there is no single or 'correct' answer to the question, 'What does this image mean?' or 'What is this ad saying?' Since there is no law which can guarantee that things will have 'one, true meaning', or that meanings won't change over time, work in this area in bound to be interpretative – a debate between, not who is 'right' and who is 'wrong', but between equally plausible, though sometimes competing and contested, meanings and interpretations. The best way to 'settle' such contested readings is to look again at the concrete example and to try to justify one's 'reading' in detail in relation to the actual practices and forms of signification used, and what meanings they seem to you to be producing.

One soon discovers that meaning is not straightforward or transparent, and does not survive intact the passage through representation. It is a slippery customer, changing and shifting with context, usage and historical circumstances. It is therefore never finally fixed. It is always putting off or 'deferring' its rendezvous with Absolute Truth. It is always being negotiated and inflected, to resonate with new situations. It is often contested, and sometimes bitterly fought over. There are always different circuits of meaning circulating in any culture at the same time, overlapping discursive formations, from which we draw to create meaning or to express what we think.

Moreover, we do not have a straightforward, rational or instrumental relationship to meanings. They mobilize powerful feelings and emotions, of both a positive and negative kind. We feel their contradictory pull, their ambivalence. They sometimes call our very identities into question. We struggle over them because they matter – and these are contests from which serious consequences can flow. They define what is 'normal', who belongs – and therefore, who is excluded. They are deeply inscribed in relations of power. Think of how profoundly our lives are shaped, depending on which meanings of male/female, black/white, rich/poor, gay/straight, young/old, citizen/alien, are in play in which circumstances. Meanings are often organized into sharply opposed binaries or opposites. However, these binaries are constantly being undermined, as representations interact with one another, substituting for each other, displacing one another along an unending chain. Our material interests and our bodies can be called to account, and differently implicated, depending on how meaning is given and taken, constructed and interpreted in different situations. But equally engaged are our fears and fantasies, the sentiments of desire and revulsion, of ambivalence and aggression. The more we look into this process of representation, the more complex it becomes to describe adequately or explain – which is why the various chapters enlist a variety of theories and concepts, to help us unlock its secrets.

The embodying of concepts, ideas and emotions in a symbolic form which can be transmitted and meaningfully interpreted is what we mean by 'the practices of representation'. Meaning must enter the domain of these practices, if it is to circulate effectively within a culture. And it cannot be considered to have completed its 'passage' around the cultural circuit until it has been 'decoded' or intelligibly received at another point in the chain. Language, then, is the property of neither the sender nor the receiver of meanings. It is the shared cultural 'space' in which the production of meaning through language – that is, representation – takes place. The receiver of messages and meanings is not a passive screen on which the original meaning is accurately and transparently projected. The 'taking of meaning' is as much a signifying practice as the 'putting into meaning'. Speaker and hearer or writer and reader are active participants in a process which – since they often exchange roles – is always double-sided, always interactive. Representation functions less like the model of a one-way transmitter and more like the model of a dialogue – it is, as they say, *dialogic.* What sustains this 'dialogue' is the presence of shared cultural codes, which cannot guarantee that meanings will remain stable forever – though attempting to fix meaning is exactly why *power* intervenes in *discourse.* But, even when power *is* circulating through meaning and knowledge, the codes only work if they are to some degree shared, at least to the extent that they make effective 'translation' between 'speakers' possible. We should perhaps learn to think of meaning less in terms of 'accuracy' and 'truth' and more in terms of effective exchange – a process of *translation*, which facilitates cultural communication while always recognizing the persistence of difference and power between different 'speakers' within the same cultural circuit.

References

DU GAY, P. (ed.) (1997) *Production of Culture/Cultures of Production*, London, Sage/The Open University (Book 4 in this series).

DU GAY, P., HALL, S., JANES, L., MACKAY, H. and NEGUS, K. (1997) *Doing Cultural Studies: the story of the Sony Walkman*, London, Sage/The Open University (Book 1 in this series).

HALL, S. (ed.) (1977) *Representation: cultural representations and signifying practices,* London, Sage/The Open University (Book 2 in this series).

MACKAY, H. (ed.) (1997) *Consumption and Everyday Life*, London, Sage/The Open University (Book 5 in this series).

THOMPSON, K. (ed.) (1997) *Media and Cultural Regulation*, London, Sage/The Open University (Book 6 in this series).

WOODWARD, K. (ed.) (1997) *Identity and Difference*, London, Sage/The Open University (Book 3 in this series).

THE WORK OF REPRESENTATION

Stuart Hall

CHAPTER ONE

Contents

1   Representation, meaning and language

In this chapter we will be concentrating on one of the key processes in the 'cultural circuit' (see **du Gay, Hall et al.**, 1997, and the Introduction to this volume) – the practices of *representation*. The aim of this chapter is to introduce you to this topic, and to explain what it is about and why we give it such importance in cultural studies.

The concept of representation has come to occupy a new and important place in the study of culture. Representation connects meaning and language to culture. But what exactly do people mean by it? What does representation have to do with culture and meaning? One common-sense usage of the term is as follows: 'Representation means using language to say something meaningful about, or to represent, the world meaningfully, to other people.' You may well ask, 'Is that all?' Well, yes and no. Representation *is* an essential part of the process by which meaning is produced and exchanged between members of a culture. It *does* involve the use of language, of signs and images which stand for or represent things. But this is a far from simple or straightforward process, as you will soon discover.

How does the concept of representation connect meaning and language to culture? In order to explore this connection further, we will look at a number of different theories about how language is used to represent the world. Here we will be drawing a distinction between three different accounts or theories: the *reflective*, the *intentional* and the *constructionist* approaches to representation. Does language simply reflect a meaning which already exists out there in the world of objects, people and events (*reflective*)? Does language express only what the speaker or writer or painter wants to say, his or her personally intended meaning (*intentional*)? Or is meaning constructed in and through language (*constructionist*)? You will learn more in a moment about these three approaches.

Most of the chapter will be spent exploring the *constructionist* approach, because it is this perspective which has had the most significant impact on cultural studies in recent years. This chapter chooses to examine two major variants or models of the constructionist approach – the *semiotic* approach, greatly influenced by the great Swiss linguist, Ferdinand de Saussure, and the *discursive* approach, associated with the French philosopher and historian, Michel Foucault. Later chapters in this book will take up these two theories again, among others, so you will have an opportunity to consolidate your understanding of them, and to apply them to different areas of analysis. Other chapters will introduce theoretical paradigms which apply constructionist approaches in different ways to that of semiotics and Foucault. All, however, put in question the very nature of representation. We turn to this question first.

1.1 Making meaning, representing things

What does the word **representation** really mean, in this context? What does
the process of representation involve? How does representation work?

representation

To put it briefly, representation is the production of meaning through
language. The *Shorter Oxford English Dictionary* suggests two relevant
meanings for the word:

1   To represent something is to describe or depict it, to call it up in the mind
    by description or portrayal or imagination; to place a likeness of it before
    us in our mind or in the senses; as, for example, in the sentence, 'This
    picture represents the murder of Abel by Cain.'

2   To represent also means to symbolize, stand for, to be a specimen of, or to
    substitute for; as in the sentence, 'In Christianity, the cross represents the
    suffering and crucifixion of Christ.'

The figures in the painting *stand in the place of,* and at the same time, *stand
for* the story of Cain and Abel. Likewise, the cross simply consists of two
wooden planks nailed together; but in the context of Christian belief and
teaching, it takes on, symbolizes or comes to stand for a wider set of
meanings about the crucifixion of the Son of God, and this is a concept we
can put into words and pictures.

ACTIVITY 1

Here is a simple exercise about representation. Look at any familiar
object in the room. You will immediately recognize what it is. But how
do you *know* what the object is? What does 'recognize' mean?

Now try to make yourself conscious of what you are doing – observe what
is going on as you do it. You recognize what it is because your thought-
processes decode your visual perception of the object in terms of a
concept of it which you have in your head. This must be so because, if
you look away from the object, you can still *think* about it by conjuring it
up, as we say, 'in your mind's eye'. Go on – try to follow the process as it
happens: There is the object … and there is the concept in your head
which tells you what it is, what your visual image of it *means*.

Now, tell me what it is. Say it aloud: 'It's a lamp' – or a table or a book or
the phone or whatever. The concept of the object has passed through your
mental representation of it to me *via* the word for it which you have just
used. The word stands for or represents the concept, and can be used to
reference or designate either a 'real' object in the world or indeed even
some imaginary object, like angels dancing on the head of a pin, which
no one has ever actually seen.

This is how you give meaning to things through language. This is how you
'make sense of' the world of people, objects and events, and how you are able
to express a complex thought about those things to other people, or

communicate about them through language in ways which other people are able to understand.

Why do we have to go through this complex process to represent our thoughts? If you put down a glass you are holding and walk out of the room, you can still *think* about the glass, even though it is no longer physically there. Actually, you can't think with a glass. You can only think with *the concept of* the glass. As the linguists are fond of saying, 'Dogs bark. But the concept of "dog" cannot bark or bite.' You can't speak with the actual glass, either. You can only speak with the *word* for glass – GLASS – which is the linguistic sign which we use in English to refer to objects which you drink water out of. This is where *representation* comes in. Representation is the production of the meaning of the concepts in our minds through language. It is the link between concepts and language which enables us to *refer to* either the 'real' world of objects, people or events, or indeed to imaginary worlds of fictional objects, people and events.

systems of representation So there are *two* processes, two **systems of representation**, involved. First, there is the 'system' by which all sorts of objects, people and events are correlated with a set of concepts or *mental representations* which we carry around in our heads. Without them, we could not interpret the world meaningfully at all. In the first place, then, meaning depends on the system of concepts and images formed in our thoughts which can stand for or 'represent' the world, enabling us to refer to things both inside and outside our heads.

Before we move on to look at the second 'system of representation', we should observe that what we have just said is a very simple version of a rather complex process. It is simple enough to see how we might form concepts for things we can perceive – people or material objects, like chairs, tables and desks. But we also form concepts of rather obscure and abstract things, which we can't in any simple way see, feel or touch. Think, for example, of our concepts of war, or death, or friendship or love. And, as we have remarked, we also form concepts about things we never have seen, and possibly can't or won't ever see, and about people and places we have plainly made up. We may have a clear concept of, say, angels, mermaids, God, the Devil, or of Heaven and Hell, or of Middlemarch (the fictional provincial town in George Eliot's novel), or Elizabeth (the heroine of Jane Austen's *Pride and Prejudice)*.

We have called this a '*system* of representation'. That is because it consists, not of individual concepts, but of different ways of organizing, clustering, arranging and classifying concepts, and of establishing complex relations between them. For example, we use the principles of similarity and difference to establish relationships between concepts or to distinguish them from one another. Thus I have an idea that in some respects birds are like planes in the sky, based on the fact that they are similar because they both fly – but I also have an idea that in other respects they are different, because one is part of nature whilst the other is man-made. This mixing and matching of relations between concepts to form complex ideas and thoughts is possible because our concepts are arranged into different classifying systems. In this example, the first is based on a distinction between flying/not flying and the second is based on the distinction between natural/man-made. There are other principles of organization like this at work in all conceptual systems: for example, classifying according to sequence – which concept follows which – or causality – what causes what – and so on. The point here is that we are talking about, not just a random collection of concepts, but concepts organized, arranged and classified into complex relations with one another. That is what our conceptual system actually is like. However, this does not undermine the basic point. Meaning depends on the relationship between things in the world – people, objects and events, real or fictional – and the conceptual system, which can operate as *mental representations* of them.

Now it could be the case that the conceptual map which I carry around in my head is totally different from yours, in which case you and I would interpret or make sense of the world in totally different ways. We would be incapable of sharing our thoughts or expressing ideas about the world to each other. In fact, each of us probably does understand and interpret the world in a unique and individual way. However, we are able to communicate because we share broadly the same conceptual maps and thus make sense of or interpret the world in roughly similar ways. That is indeed what it means when we say we 'belong to the same culture'. Because we interpret the world in roughly similar ways, we are able to build up a shared culture of meanings and thus construct a social world which we inhabit together. That is why 'culture' is sometimes defined in terms of 'shared meanings or shared conceptual maps' (see **du Gay, Hall et al.**, 1997).

However, a shared conceptual map is not enough. We must also be able to represent or exchange meanings and concepts, and we can only do that when we also have access to a shared language. Language is therefore the second system of representation involved in the overall process of constructing meaning. Our shared conceptual map must be translated into a common language, so that we can correlate our concepts and ideas with certain written words, spoken sounds or visual images. The general term we use for words, sounds or images which carry meaning is *signs*. These signs stand for or represent the concepts and the conceptual relations between them which we carry around in our heads and together they make up the meaning-systems of our culture.

Signs are organized into languages and it is the existence of common languages which enable us to translate our thoughts (concepts) into words, sounds or images, and then to use these, operating as a language, to express meanings and communicate thoughts to other people. Remember that the term 'language' is being used here in a very broad and inclusive way. The writing system or the spoken system of a particular language are both obviously 'languages'. But so are visual images, whether produced by hand, mechanical, electronic, digital or some other means, when they are used to express meaning. And so are other things which aren't 'linguistic' in any ordinary sense: the 'language' of facial expressions or of gesture, for example, or the 'language' of fashion, of clothes, or of traffic lights. Even music is a 'language', with complex relations between different sounds and chords, though it is a very special case since it can't easily be used to reference actual things or objects in the world (a point further elaborated in **du Gay**, ed., 1997, and **Mackay**, ed., 1997). Any sound, word, image or object which functions as a sign, and is organized with other signs into a system which is capable of carrying and expressing meaning is, from this point of view, 'a language'. It is in this sense that the model of meaning which I have been analysing here is often described as a 'linguistic' one; and that all the theories of meaning which follow this basic model are described as belonging to 'the linguistic turn' in the social sciences and cultural studies.

At the heart of the meaning process in culture, then, are two related 'systems of representation'. The first enables us to give meaning to the world by constructing a set of correspondences or a chain of equivalences between things – people, objects, events, abstract ideas, etc. – and our system of concepts, our conceptual maps. The second depends on constructing a set of correspondences between our conceptual map and a set of signs, arranged or organized into various languages which stand for or represent those concepts. The relation between 'things', concepts and signs lies at the heart of the production of meaning in language. The process which links these three elements together is what we call 'representation'.

1.2 Language and representation

Just as people who belong to the same culture must share a broadly similar conceptual map, so they must also share the same way of interpreting the signs of a language, for only in this way can meanings be effectively exchanged between people. But how do we know which concept stands for which thing? Or which word effectively represents which concept? How do I know which sounds or images will carry, through language, the meaning of my concepts and what I want to say with them to you? This may seem relatively simple in the case of visual signs, because the drawing, painting, camera or TV image of a sheep bears a resemblance to the animal with a woolly coat grazing in a field to which I want to refer. Even so, we need to remind ourselves that a drawn or painted or digital version of a sheep is not exactly like a 'real' sheep. For one thing, most images are in two dimensions whereas the 'real' sheep exists in three dimensions.

Visual signs and images, even when they bear a close resemblance to the things to which they refer, are still signs: they carry meaning and thus have to be interpreted. In order to interpret them, we must have access to the two systems of representation discussed earlier: to a conceptual map which correlates the sheep in the field with the concept of a 'sheep'; and a language system which in visual language, bears some resemblance to the real thing or 'looks like it' in some way. This argument is clearest if we think of a cartoon drawing or an abstract painting of a 'sheep', where we need a very

FIGURE 1.1
William Holman Hunt, *Our English Coasts ('Strayed Sheep')*, 1852.

sophisticated conceptual and shared linguistic system to be certain that we are all 'reading' the sign in the same way. Even then we may find ourselves wondering whether it really is a picture of a sheep at all. As the relationship between the sign and its referent becomes less clear-cut, the meaning begins to slip and slide away from us into uncertainty. Meaning is no longer transparently passing from one person to another …

So, even in the case of visual language, where the relationship between the concept and the sign seems fairly straightforward, the matter is far from simple. It is even more difficult with written or spoken language, where words don't look or sound anything like the things to which they refer. In part, this is because there are different kinds of signs. Visual signs are what are called *iconic* signs. That is, they bear, in their form, a certain resemblance to the object, person or event to which they refer. A photograph of a tree reproduces some of the actual conditions of our visual perception in the visual sign. Written or spoken signs, on the other hand, are what is called *indexical*.

FIGURE 1.2
Q: When is a sheep not a sheep?
A: When it's a work of art.
(Damien Hirst, *Away from the Flock*, 1994).

They bear no obvious relationship at all to the things to which they refer. The letters T,R,E,E, do not look anything like trees in Nature, nor does the word 'tree' in English sound like 'real' trees (if indeed they make any sound at all!). The relationship in these systems of representation between the sign, the concept and the object to which they might be used to refer is entirely *arbitrary*. By 'arbitrary' we mean that in principle any collection of letters or any sound in any order would do the trick equally well. Trees would not mind if we used the word SEERT – 'trees' written backwards – to represent the concept of them. This is clear from the fact that, in French, quite different letters and a quite different sound is used to refer to what, to all appearances, is the same thing – a 'real' tree – and, as far as we can tell, to the same concept – a large plant that grows in nature. The French and English seem to be using the same concept. But the concept which in English is represented by the word, TREE, is represented in French by the word, ARBRE.

1.3 Sharing the codes

The question, then, is: how do people who belong to the same culture, who share the same conceptual map and who speak or write the same language (English) know that the arbitrary combination of letters and sounds that makes up the word, TREE, will stand for or represent the concept 'a large plant that grows in nature'? One possibility would be that the objects in the world themselves embody and fix in some way their 'true' meaning. But it is not at all clear that real trees *know* that they are trees, and even less clear that they know that the word in English which represents the concept of themselves is written TREE whereas in French it is written ARBRE! As far as they are concerned, it could just as well be written COW or VACHE or indeed XYZ. The meaning is *not* in the object or person or thing, nor is it *in* the word. It is we who fix the meaning so firmly that, after a while, it comes to seem natural and inevitable. The meaning is *constructed by the system of representation.* It is constructed and fixed by the *code*, which sets up the correlation between our conceptual system and our language system in such a way that, every time we think of a tree, the code tells us to use the English word TREE, or the French word ARBRE. The code tells us that, in our culture – that is, in our conceptual and language codes – the concept 'tree' is represented by the letters T,R,E,E, arranged in a certain sequence, just as in Morse code, the sign for V (which in World War II Churchill made 'stand for' or represent 'Victory') is Dot, Dot, Dot, Dash, and in the 'language of traffic lights', Green = Go! and Red = Stop!

One way of thinking about 'culture', then, is in terms of these shared conceptual maps, shared language systems and the *codes which govern the relationships of translation between them.* Codes fix the relationships between concepts and signs. They stabilize meaning within different languages and cultures. They tell us which language to use to convey which idea. The reverse is also true. Codes tell us which concepts are being referred to when we hear or read which signs. By arbitrarily fixing the relationships between our conceptual system and our linguistic systems (remember, 'linguistic' in a broad sense), codes make it possible for us to speak and to hear intelligibly, and establish the translatability between our concepts and our languages which enables meaning to pass from speaker to hearer and be effectively communicated within a culture. This translatability is not given by nature or fixed by the gods. It is the result of a set of social conventions. It is fixed socially, fixed in culture. English or French or Hindi speakers have, over time, and without conscious decision or choice, come to an unwritten agreement, a sort of unwritten cultural covenant that, in their various languages, certain signs will stand for or represent certain concepts. This is what children learn, and how they become, not simply biological individuals but cultural subjects. They learn the system and conventions of representation, the codes of their language and culture, which equip them with cultural 'know-how' enabling them to function as culturally competent subjects. Not because such knowledge is imprinted in their genes, but because they learn its conventions and so gradually *become* 'cultured persons' – i.e. members of their culture. They unconsciously internalize the codes which allow them to express certain concepts and ideas through their systems of representation – writing, speech, gesture, visualization, and so on – and to interpret ideas which are communicated to them using the same systems.

You may find it easier to understand, now, why meaning, language and representation are such critical elements in the study of culture. To belong to a culture is to belong to roughly the same conceptual and linguistic universe, to know how concepts and ideas translate into different languages, and how language can be interpreted to refer to or *reference* the world. To share these things is to see the world from within the same conceptual map and to make sense of it through the same language systems. Early anthropologists of language, like Sapir and Whorf, took this insight to its logical extreme when they argued that we are all, as it were, locked into our cultural perspectives or 'mind-sets', and that language is the best clue we have to that conceptual universe. This observation, when applied to all human cultures, lies at the root of what, today, we may think of as cultural or linguistic *relativism*.

ACTIVITY 2

You might like to think further about this question of how different cultures conceptually classify the world and what implications this has for meaning and representation.

The English make a rather simple distinction between sleet and snow. The Inuit (Eskimos) who have to survive in a very different, more extreme and hostile climate, apparently have many more words for snow and snowy weather. Consider the list of Inuit terms for snow from the Scott Polar Research Institute in Table 1.1. There are many more than in English, making much finer and more complex distinctions. The Inuit have a complex classificatory conceptual system for the weather compared with the English. The novelist Peter Hoeg, for example, writing about Greenland in his novel, *Miss Smilla's Feeling For Snow* (1994, pp. 5–6), graphically describes 'frazzil ice' which is 'kneaded together into a soapy mash called porridge ice, which gradually forms free-floating plates, pancake ice, which one, cold, noonday hour, on a Sunday, freezes into a single solid sheet'. Such distinctions are too fine and elaborate even for the English who are always talking about the weather! The question, however, is – do the Inuit actually experience snow differently from the English? Their language system suggests they conceptualize the weather differently. But how far is our experience actually bounded by our linguistic and conceptual universe?

Table 1.1   Inuit terms for snow and ice

snow		ice	siku
blowing —	piqtuluk	— pan, broken —	siqumniq
is snowstorming	piqtuluktuq	— ice water	immiugaq
falling —	qanik	melts — to make water	immiuqtuaq
— is falling; — is snowing	qaniktuq	candle —	illauyiniq
light falling —	qaniaraq	flat —	qaimiq
light — is falling	qaniaraqtuq	glare —	quasaq
first layer of — in fall	apilraun	piled —	ivunrit
deep soft —	mauya	rough —	ivvuit
packed — to make water	aniu	shore —	tugiu
light soft —	aquluraq	shorefast —	tuvaq
sugar—	pukak	slush —	quna
waterlogged, mushy —	masak	young —	sikuliaq
— is turning into *masak*	masaguqtuaq		
watery —	maqayak		
wet —	misak		
wet falling —	qanikkuk		
wet — is falling	qanikkuktuq		
— drifting along a surface	natiruvik		
— is drifting along a surface	natiruviktuaq		
— lying on a surface	apun		
snowflake	qanik		
is being drifted over with —	apiyuaq		

One implication of this argument about cultural codes is that, if meaning is the result, not of something fixed out there, in nature, but of our social, cultural and linguistic conventions, then meaning can never be *finally* fixed. We can all 'agree' to allow words to carry somewhat different meanings – as we have for example, with the word 'gay', or the use, by young people, of the word 'wicked!' as a term of approval. Of course, there must be *some* fixing of meaning in language, or we would never be able to understand one another. We can't get up one morning and suddenly decide to represent the concept of a 'tree' with the letters or the word VYXZ, and expect people to follow what we are saying. On the other hand, there is no absolute or final fixing of meaning. Social and linguistic conventions do change over time. In the language of modern managerialism, what we used to call 'students', 'clients', 'patients' and 'passengers' have all become 'customers'. Linguistic codes vary significantly between one language and another. Many cultures do not have words for concepts which are normal and widely acceptable to us. Words constantly go out of common usage, and new phrases are coined: think, for example, of the use of 'down-sizing' to represent the process of firms laying people off work. Even when the actual words remain stable, their connotations shift or they acquire a different nuance. The problem is especially acute in translation. For example, does the difference in English between *know* and *understand* correspond exactly to and capture exactly the same conceptual distinction as the French make between *savoir* and *connaitre*? Perhaps; but can we be sure?

The main point is that meaning does not inhere *in* things, in the world. It is constructed, produced. It is the result of a signifying practice – a practice that *produces* meaning, that *makes things mean*.

1.4 Theories of representation

There are broadly speaking three approaches to explaining how representation of meaning through language works. We may call these the reflective, the intentional and the constructionist or constructivist approaches. You might think of each as an attempt to answer the questions, 'where do meanings come from?' and 'how can we tell the "true" meaning of a word or image?'

In the **reflective approach**, meaning is thought to lie in the object, person, idea or event in the real world, and language functions like a mirror, to *reflect* the true meaning as it already exists in the world. As the poet Gertrude Stein once said, 'A rose is a rose is a rose'. In the fourth century BC, the Greeks used the notion of *mimesis* to explain how language, even drawing and painting, mirrored or imitated Nature; they thought of Homer's great poem, *The Iliad*, as 'imitating' a heroic series of events. So the theory which says that language works by simply reflecting or imitating the truth that is already there and fixed in the world, is sometimes called 'mimetic'.

reflective or mimetic approach

Of course there is a certain obvious truth to mimetic theories of representation and language. As we've pointed out, visual signs do bear some relationship to the shape and texture of the objects which they represent. But, as was also pointed out earlier, a two-dimensional visual image of a *rose* is a sign – it should not be confused with the real plant with thorns and blooms growing in the garden. Remember also that there are many words, sounds and images which we fully well understand but which are entirely fictional or fantasy and refer to worlds which are wholly imaginary – including, many people now think, most of *The Iliad!* Of course, I can use the word 'rose' to *refer* to real, actual plants growing in a garden, as we have said before. But this is because I know the code which links the concept with a particular word or image. I cannot *think* or *speak* or *draw* with an actual rose. And if someone says to me that there is no such word as 'rose' for a plant in her culture, the actual plant in the garden cannot resolve the failure of communication between us. Within the conventions of the different language codes we are using, we are both right – and for us to understand each other, one of us must learn the code linking the flower with the word for it in the other's culture.

intentional approach

The second approach to meaning in representation argues the opposite case. It holds that it is the speaker, the author, who imposes his or her unique meaning on the world through language. Words mean what the author intends they should mean. This is the **intentional approach**. Again, there is some point to this argument since we all, as individuals, do use language to convey or communicate things which are special or unique to us, to our way of seeing the world. However, as a general theory of representation through language, the intentional approach is also flawed. We cannot be the sole or unique source of meanings in language, since that would mean that we could express ourselves in entirely private languages. But the essence of language is communication and that, in turn, depends on shared linguistic conventions and shared codes. Language can never be wholly a private game. Our private intended meanings, however personal to us, have to *enter into the rules, codes and conventions of language* to be shared and understood. Language is a social system through and through. This means that our private thoughts have to negotiate with all the other meanings for words or images which have been stored in language which our use of the language system will inevitably trigger into action.

constructionist approach

The third approach recognizes this public, social character of language. It acknowledges that neither things in themselves nor the individual users of language can fix meaning in language. Things don't *mean*: we *construct* meaning, using representational systems – concepts and signs. Hence it is called the constructivist or **constructionist approach** to meaning in language. According to this approach, we must not confuse the *material* world, where things and people exist, and the *symbolic* practices and processes through which representation, meaning and language operate. Constructivists do not deny the existence of the material world. However, it is not the material world which conveys meaning: it is the language system or whatever system we are using to represent our concepts. It is social actors who use the conceptual systems of their culture and the linguistic and other representational systems to construct meaning, to make the world meaningful and to communicate about that world meaningfully to others.

Of course, signs may also have a material dimension. Representational systems consist of the actual *sounds* we make with our vocal chords, the *images* we make on light-sensitive paper with cameras, the *marks* we make with paint on canvas, the digital *impulses* we transmit electronically. Representation is a practice, a kind of 'work', which uses material objects and effects. But the *meaning* depends, not on the material quality of the sign, but on its *symbolic function*. It is because a particular sound or word *stands for, symbolizes or represents* a concept that it can function, in language, as a sign and convey meaning – or, as the constructionists say, signify (sign-i-fy).

1.5   The language of traffic lights

The simplest example of this point, which is critical for an understanding of how languages function as representational systems, is the famous traffic lights example. A traffic light is a machine which produces different coloured lights in sequence. The effect of light of different wavelengths on the eye – which is a natural and material phenomenon – produces the sensation of different colours. Now these things certainly do exist in the material world. But it is our culture which breaks the spectrum of light into different colours, distinguishes them from one another and attaches names – Red, Green, Yellow, Blue – to them. We use a way of *classifying* the colour spectrum to create colours which are different from one another. We *represent* or symbolize the different colours and classify them according to different colour-concepts. This is the conceptual colour system of our culture. We say 'our culture' because, of course, other cultures may divide the colour spectrum differently. What's more, they certainly use different actual *words* or *letters* to identify different colours: what we call 'red', the French call 'rouge' and so on. This is the linguistic code – the one which correlates certain words (signs) with certain colours (concepts), and thus enables us to communicate about colours to other people, using 'the language of colours'.

But how do we use this representational or symbolic system to regulate the traffic? Colours do not have any 'true' or fixed meaning in that sense. Red does not mean 'Stop' in nature, any more than Green means 'Go'. In other settings, Red may stand for, symbolize or represent 'Blood' or 'Danger' or 'Communism'; and Green may represent 'Ireland' or 'The Countryside' or 'Environmentalism'. Even these meanings can change. In the 'language of electric plugs', Red used to mean 'the connection with the positive charge' but this was arbitrarily and without explanation changed to Brown! But then for many years the producers of plugs had to attach a slip of paper telling people that the code or convention had changed, otherwise how would they know? Red and Green work in the language of traffic lights because 'Stop' and 'Go' are the meanings which have been assigned to them in our culture by the code or conventions governing this language, and this code is widely known and almost universally obeyed in our culture and cultures like ours – though we can well imagine other cultures which did not possess the code, in which this language would be a complete mystery.

Let us stay with the example for a moment, to explore a little further how, according to the constructionist approach to representation, colours and the 'language of traffic lights' work as a signifying or representational system. Recall the *two* representational systems we spoke of earlier. First, there is the conceptual map of colours in our culture – the way colours are distinguished from one another, classified and arranged in our mental universe. Secondly, there are the ways words or images are correlated with colours in our language – our linguistic colour-codes. Actually, of course, a *language* of colours consists of more than just the individual words for different points on the colour spectrum. It also depends on how they function in relation to one another – the sorts of things which are governed by grammar and syntax in written or spoken languages, which allow us to express rather complex ideas. In the language of traffic lights, it is the sequence and position of the colours, as well as the colours themselves, which enable them to carry meaning and thus function as signs.

Does it matter which colours we use? No, the constructionists argue. This is because what signifies is not the colours themselves but (a) the fact that they are different and can be distinguished from one another; and (b) the fact that they are organized into a particular sequence – Red followed by Green, with sometimes a warning Amber in between which says, in effect, 'Get ready! Lights about to change.' Constructionists put this point in the following way. What signifies, what carries meaning – they argue – is not each colour in itself nor even the concept or word for it. It is *the difference between Red and Green* which signifies. This is a very important principle, in general, about representation and meaning, and we shall return to it on more than one occasion in the chapters which follow. Think about it in these terms. If you couldn't differentiate between Red and Green, you couldn't use one to mean 'Stop' and the other to mean 'Go'. In the same way, it is only the difference between the letters P and T which enable the word SHEEP to be linked, in the English language code, to the concept of 'the animal with four legs and a woolly coat', and the word SHEET to 'the material we use to cover ourselves in bed at night'.

In principle, any combination of colours – like any collection of letters in written language or of sounds in spoken language – would do, provided they are sufficiently different not to be confused. Constructionists express this idea by saying that all signs are 'arbitrary'. 'Arbitrary' means that there is no natural relationship between the sign and its meaning or concept. Since Red only means 'Stop' because that is how the code works, in principle any colour would do, including Green. It is the code that fixes the meaning, not the colour itself. This also has wider implications for the theory of representation and meaning in language. It means that signs themselves cannot fix meaning. Instead, meaning depends on *the relation between* a sign and a concept which is fixed by a code. Meaning, the constructionists would say, is 'relational'.

ACTIVITY 3

Why not test this point about the arbitrary nature of the sign and the importance of the code for yourself? Construct a code to govern the movement of traffic using two different colours – Yellow and Blue – as in the following:

When the yellow light is showing, …

Now add an instruction allowing pedestrians and cyclists only to cross, using Pink.

Provided the code tells us clearly how to read or interpret each colour, and everyone agrees to interpret them in this way, any colour will do. These are just colours, just as the word SHEEP is just a jumble of letters. In French the same animal is referred to using the very different linguistic sign MOUTON. Signs are arbitrary. Their meanings are fixed by codes.

As we said earlier, traffic lights are machines, and colours are the material effect of light-waves on the retina of the eye. But objects – things – can also function as signs, provided they have been assigned a concept and meaning within our cultural and linguistic codes. As signs, they work symbolically – they represent concepts, and signify. Their effects, however, are felt in the material and social world. Red and Green function in the language of traffic lights as signs, but they have real material and social effects. They regulate the social behaviour of drivers and, without them, there would be many more traffic accidents at road intersections.

1.6 Summary

We have come a long way in exploring the nature of representation. It is time to summarize what we have learned about the constructionist approach to representation through language.

Representation is the production of meaning through language. In representation, constructionists argue, we use signs, organized into languages of different kinds, to communicate meaningfully with others. Languages can use signs to symbolize, stand for or reference objects, people and events in the so-called 'real' world. But they can also reference imaginary things and fantasy worlds or abstract ideas which are not in any obvious sense part of our material world. There is no simple relationship of reflection, imitation or one-to-one correspondence between language and the real world. The world is not accurately or otherwise reflected in the mirror of language. Language does not work like a mirror. Meaning is produced within language, in and through various representational systems which, for convenience, we call 'languages'. Meaning is produced by the practice, the 'work', of representation. It is constructed through signifying – i.e. meaning-producing – practices.

How does this take place? In fact, it depends on two different but related systems of representation. First, the concepts which are formed in the mind function as a system of mental representation which classifies and organizes the world into meaningful categories. If we have a concept for something, we can say we know its 'meaning'. But we cannot communicate this meaning without a second system of representation, a language. Language consists of signs organized into various relationships. But signs can only convey meaning if we possess codes which allow us to translate our concepts into language – and vice versa. These codes are crucial for meaning and representation. They do not exist in nature but are the result of social conventions. They are a crucial part of our culture – our shared 'maps of meaning' – which we learn and unconsciously internalize as we become members of our culture. This constructionist approach to language thus introduces the symbolic domain of life, where words and things function as signs, into the very heart of social life itself.

ACTIVITY 4

All this may seem rather abstract. But we can quickly demonstrate its relevance by an example from painting.

FIGURE 1.3
Juan Cotán,
Quince, Cabbage,
Melon and
Cucumber,
c. 1602.

Look at the painting of a still life by the Spanish painter, Juan Sanchez Cotán (1521–1627), entitled *Quince, Cabbage, Melon and Cucumber* (Figure 1.3). It seems as if the painter has made every effort to use the 'language of painting' accurately to reflect these four objects, to capture or 'imitate nature'. Is this, then, an example of a *reflective* or *mimetic* form of representation – a painting reflecting the 'true meaning' of what already exists in Cotán's kitchen? Or can we find the operation of certain codes,

the language of painting used to produce a certain meaning? Start with the question, what does the painting mean to you? What is it 'saying'? Then go on to ask, how is it saying it – how does representation work in this painting?

Write down any thoughts at all that come to you on looking at the painting. What do these objects say to you? What meanings do they trigger off?

READING A

Now read the edited extract from an analysis of the still life by the art critic and theorist, Norman Bryson, included as Reading A at the end of this chapter. Don't be concerned, at this stage, if the language seems a little difficult and you don't understand all the terms. Pick out the main points about the way *representation* works in the painting, according to Bryson.

Bryson is by no means the only critic of Cotán's painting, and certainly doesn't provide the only 'correct' reading of it. That's not the point. The point of the example is that he helps us to see how, even in a still life, the 'language of painting' does *not* function simply to reflect or imitate a meaning which is already there in nature, but to *produce meanings*. The act of painting is a *signifying practice*. Take note, in particular, of what Bryson says about the following points:

1   the way the painting invites you, the viewer, to *look* – what he calls its 'mode of seeing'; in part, the function of the language is to position you, the viewer, in a certain relation to meaning.

2   the relationship to *food* which is posed by the painting.

3   how, according to Bryson, 'mathematical form' is used by Cotán to *distort* the painting so as to bring out a particular meaning. Can a distorted meaning in painting be 'true'?

4   the meaning of the difference between 'creatural' and 'geometric' space: the language of painting creates its own kind of space.

If necessary, work through the extract again, picking up these specific points.

2   Saussure's legacy

The social constructionist view of language and representation which we have been discussing owes a great deal to the work and influence of the Swiss linguist, Saussure, who was born in Geneva in 1857, did much of his work in Paris, and died in 1913. He is known as the 'father of modern linguistics'. For our purposes, his importance lies, not in his detailed work in linguistics, but in his general view of representation and the way his model of language shaped the *semiotic* approach to the problem of representation in a wide variety of cultural fields. You will recognize much about Saussure's thinking from what we have already said about the *constructionist* approach.

For Saussure, according to Jonathan Culler (1976, p. 19), the production of meaning depends on language: 'Language is a system of signs.' Sounds, images, written words, paintings, photographs, etc. function as signs within language 'only when they serve to express or communicate ideas … [To] communicate ideas, they must be part of a system of conventions …' (ibid.). Material objects can function as signs and communicate meaning too, as we saw from the 'language of traffic lights' example. In an important move, Saussure analysed the **sign** into two further elements. There was, he argued, the *form* (the actual word, image, photo, etc.), and there was the *idea or concept* in your head with which the form was associated. Saussure called the first element, the **signifier**, and the second element – the corresponding concept it triggered off in your head – the **signified**. Every time you hear or read or see the *signifier* (e.g. the word or image of a *Walkman*, for example), it correlates with the *signified* (the concept of a portable cassette-player in your head). Both are required to produce meaning but it is the relation between them, fixed by our cultural and linguistic codes, which sustains representation. Thus 'the sign is the union of a form which signifies (*signifier*) … and an idea signified (*signified*). Though we may speak … as if they are separate entities, they exist only as components of the sign … (which is) the central fact of language' (Culler, 1976, p. 19).

Saussure also insisted on what in section 1 we called the arbitrary nature of the sign: 'There is no natural or inevitable link between the signifier and the signified' (ibid.). Signs do not possess a fixed or essential meaning. What signifies, according to Saussure, is not RED or the essence of 'red-ness', but *the difference between RED and GREEN*. Signs, Saussure argued 'are members of a system and are defined in relation to the other members of that system.' For example, it is hard to define the meaning of FATHER except in relation to, and in terms of its difference from, other kinship terms, like MOTHER, DAUGHTER, SON and so on.

This marking of difference within language is fundamental to the production of meaning, according to Saussure. Even at a simple level (to repeat an earlier example), we must be able to distinguish, within language, between SHEEP and SHEET, before we can link one of those words to the concept of an animal that produces wool, and the other to the concept of a cloth that covers a bed. The simplest way of marking difference is, of course, by means of a binary opposition – in this example, all the letters are the same except P and T. Similarly, the meaning of a concept or word is often defined in relation to its direct opposite – as in night/day. Later critics of Saussure were to observe that binaries (e.g. *black/white*) are only one, rather simplistic, way of establishing difference. As well as the stark difference between *black* and *white,* there are also the many other, subtler differences between *black* and *dark grey, dark grey* and *light grey, grey* and *cream* and *off-white, off-white* and *brilliant white*, just as there are between *night, dawn, daylight, noon, dusk,* and so on. However, his attention to binary oppositions brought Saussure to the revolutionary proposition that a language consists of signifiers, but in order to produce meaning, the signifiers have to be organized into 'a system of differences'. It is the differences between signifiers which signify.

Furthermore, the relation between the *signifier* and the *signified*, which is fixed by our cultural codes, is not – Saussure argued – permanently fixed. Words shift their meanings. The concepts (signifieds) to which they refer also change, historically, and every shift alters the conceptual map of the culture, leading different cultures, at different historical moments, to classify and think about the world differently. For many centuries, western societies have associated the word BLACK with everything that is dark, evil, forbidding, devilish, dangerous and sinful. And yet, think of how the perception of black people in America in the 1960s changed after the phrase 'Black is Beautiful' became a popular slogan – where the *signifier,* BLACK, was made to signify the exact opposite meaning (*signified*) to its previous associations. In Saussure's terms, 'Language sets up an arbitrary relation between signifiers of its own choosing on the one hand, and signifieds of its own choosing on the other. Not only does each language produce a different set of signifiers, articulating and dividing the continuum of sound (or writing or drawing or photography) in a distinctive way; each language produces a different set of signifieds; it has a distinctive and thus arbitrary way of organizing the world into concepts and categories' (Culler, 1976, p. 23).

The implications of this argument are very far-reaching for a theory of representation and for our understanding of culture. If the relationship between a signifier and its signified is the result of a system of social conventions specific to each society and to specific historical moments – then all meanings are produced within history and culture. They can never be finally fixed but are always subject to change, both from one cultural context and from one period to another. There is thus no single, unchanging, universal 'true meaning'. 'Because it is arbitrary, the sign is totally subject to history and the combination at the particular moment of a given signifier and signified is a contingent result of the historical process' (Culler, 1976, p. 36). This opens up meaning and representation, in a radical way, to history and change. It is true that Saussure himself focused exclusively on the state of the language system at one moment of time rather than looking at linguistic change over time. However, for our purposes, the important point is the way this approach to language *unfixes* meaning, breaking any natural and inevitable tie between signifier and signified. This opens representation to the constant 'play' or slippage of meaning, to the constant production of new meanings, new interpretations.

However, if meaning changes, historically, and is never finally fixed, then it follows that 'taking the meaning' must involve an active process of **interpretation**. Meaning has to be actively 'read' or 'interpreted'. Consequently, there is a necessary and inevitable imprecision about language. The meaning we take, as viewers, readers or audiences, is never exactly the meaning which has been given by the speaker or writer or by other

interpretation

viewers. And since, in order to say something meaningful, we have to 'enter language', where all sorts of older meanings which pre-date us, are already stored from previous eras, we can never cleanse language completely, screening out all the other, hidden meanings which might modify or distort what we want to say. For example, we can't entirely prevent some of the negative connotations of the word BLACK from returning to mind when we read a headline like, 'WEDNESDAY – A BLACK DAY ON THE STOCK EXCHANGE', even if this was not intended. There is a constant *sliding of meaning* in all interpretation, a margin – something in excess of what we intend to say – in which other meanings overshadow the statement or the text, where other associations are awakened to life, giving what we say a different twist. So interpretation becomes an essential aspect of the process by which meaning is given and taken. The *reader* is as important as the *writer* in the production of meaning. Every signifier given or encoded with meaning has to be meaningfully interpreted or decoded by the receiver (Hall, 1980). Signs which have not been intelligibly received and interpreted are not, in any useful sense, 'meaningful'.

2.1 The social part of language

Saussure divided language into two parts. The first consisted of the general rules and codes of the linguistic system, which all its users must share, if it is to be of use as a means of communication. The rules are the principles which we learn when we learn a language and they enable us to use language to say whatever we want. For example, in English, the preferred word order is subject–verb–object ('the cat sat on the mat'), whereas in Latin, the verb usually comes at the end. Saussure called this underlying rule-governed structure of language, which enables us to produce well-formed sentences, the ***langue*** (the language system). The second part consisted of the particular acts of speaking or writing or drawing, which – using the structure and rules of the *langue* – are produced by an actual speaker or writer. He called this ***parole***. '*La langue* is the system of language, the language as a system of forms, whereas *parole* is actual speech [or writing], the speech acts which are made possible by the language' (Culler, 1976, p. 29).

For Saussure, the underlying structure of rules and codes (*langue*) was the social part of language, the part which could be studied with the law-like precision of a science because of its closed, limited nature. It was his preference for studying language at this level of its 'deep structure' which made people call Saussure and his model of language, **structuralist**. The second part of language, the individual speech-act or utterance (*parole*), he regarded as the 'surface' of language. There were an infinite number of such possible utterances. Hence, *parole* inevitably lacked those structural properties – forming a closed and limited set – which would have enabled us to study it 'scientifically'. What made Saussure's model appeal to many later scholars was the fact that the closed, structured character of language at the level of its rules and laws, which, according to Saussure, enabled it to be

langue

parole

structuralist

studied scientifically, was combined with the capacity to be free and unpredictably creative in our actual speech acts. They believed he had offered them, at last, a scientific approach to that least scientific object of inquiry – culture.

In separating the social part of language (*langue*) from the individual act of communication (*parole*), Saussure broke with our common-sense notion of how language works. Our common-sense intuition is that language comes from within us – from the individual speaker or writer; that it is this speaking or writing subject who is the author or originator of meaning. This is what we called, earlier, the *intentional* model of representation. But according to Saussure's schema, each authored statement only becomes possible because the 'author' shares with other language-users the common rules and codes of the language system – the *langue* – which allows them to communicate with each other meaningfully. The author decides what she wants to say. But she cannot 'decide' whether or not to use the rules of language, if she wants to be understood. We are born into a language, its codes and its meanings. Language is therefore, for Saussure, a social phenomenon. It cannot be an individual matter because we cannot make up the rules of language individually, for ourselves. Their source lies in society, in the culture, in our shared cultural codes, in the language system – not in nature or in the individual subject.

We will move on in section 3 to consider how the constructionist approach to representation, and in particular Saussure's linguistic model, was applied to a wider set of cultural objects and practices, and evolved into the *semiotic* method which so influenced the field. First we ought to take account of some of the criticisms levelled at his position.

2.2 Critique of Saussure's model

Saussure's great achievement was to force us to focus on language itself, as a social fact; on the process of representation itself; on how language actually works and the role it plays in the production of meaning. In doing so, he saved language from the status of a mere transparent medium between *things* and *meaning*. He showed, instead, that representation was a practice. However, in his own work, he tended to focus almost exclusively on the two aspects of the sign – *signifier* and *signified*. He gave little or no attention to how this relation between *signifier/signified* could serve the purpose of what earlier we called *reference* – i.e. referring us to the world of things, people and events outside language in the 'real' world. Later linguists made a distinction between, say, the meaning of the word BOOK and the use of the word to refer to a *specific* book lying before us on the table. The linguist, Charles Sanders Pierce, whilst adopting a similar approach to Saussure, paid greater attention to the relationship between signifiers/signifieds and what he called their *referents*. What Saussure called signification really involves *both* meaning and reference, but he focused mainly on the former.

Another problem is that Saussure tended to focus on the *formal* aspects of language – how language actually works. This has the great advantage of making us examine representation as a practice worthy of detailed study in its own right. It forces us to look at language for itself, and not just as an empty, transparent, 'window on the world'. However, Saussure's focus on language may have been too exclusive. The attention to its formal aspects did divert attention away from the more interactive and dialogic features of language – language as it is actually used, as it functions in actual situations, in dialogue between different kinds of speakers. It is thus not surprising that, for Saussure, questions of *power* in language – for example, between speakers of different status and positions – did not arise.

As has often been the case, the 'scientific' dream which lay behind the structuralist impulse of his work, though influential in alerting us to certain aspects of how language works, proved to be illusory. Language is *not* an object which can be studied with the law-like precision of a science. Later cultural theorists learned from Saussure's 'structuralism' but abandoned its scientific premise. Language remains rule-governed. But it is not a 'closed' system which can be reduced to its formal elements. Since it is constantly changing, it is by definition *open-ended*. Meaning continues to be produced through language in forms which can never be predicted beforehand and its 'sliding', as we described it above, cannot be halted. Saussure may have been tempted to the former view because, like a good structuralist, he tended to study the state of the language system at one moment, as if it had stood still, and he could halt the flow of language-change. Nevertheless it is the case that many of those who have been most influenced by Saussure's radical break with all reflective and intentional models of representation, have built on his work, not by imitating his scientific and 'structuralist' approach, but by applying his model in a much looser, more open-ended – i.e. 'post-structuralist' – way.

2.3 Summary

How far, then, have we come in our discussion of theories of *representation*? We began by contrasting three different approaches. The *reflective* or *mimetic* approach proposed a direct and transparent relationship of imitation or reflection between words (signs) and things. The *intentional* theory reduced representation to the intentions of its author or subject. The *constructionist* theory proposed a complex and mediated relationship between things in the world, our concepts in thought and language. We have focused at greatest length on this approach. The correlations between these levels – the material, the conceptual and the signifying – are governed by our cultural and linguistic codes and it is this set of interconnections which produces meaning. We then showed how much this general model of how systems of representation work in the production of meaning owed to the work of Ferdinand de Saussure. Here, the key point was the link provided by the codes between the forms of expression used by language (whether speech, writing, drawing, or other types of representation) – which Saussure called the *signifiers* – and the mental concepts associated with them – the *signifieds*. The connection between these two systems of representation produced *signs*; and signs, organized into languages, produced meanings, and could be used to reference objects, people and events in the 'real' world.

3   From language to culture: linguistics to semiotics

Saussure's main contribution was to the study of linguistics in a narrow sense. However, since his death, his theories have been widely deployed, as a foundation for a general approach to language and meaning, providing a model of representation which has been applied to a wide range of cultural objects and practices. Saussure himself foresaw this possibility in his famous lecture-notes, collected posthumously by his students as the *Course in General Linguistics* (1960), where he looked forward to 'A science that studies the life of signs within society … I shall call it semiology, from the Greek *semeion* "signs" …' (p. 16). This general approach to the study of signs in culture, and of culture as a sort of 'language', which Saussure foreshadowed, is now generally known by the term **semiotics**.

semiotics

The underlying argument behind the semiotic approach is that, since all cultural objects convey meaning, and all cultural practices depend on meaning, they must make use of signs; and in so far as they do, they must work like language works, and be amenable to an analysis which basically makes use of Saussure's linguistic concepts (e.g. the signifier/signified and *langue/ parole* distinctions, his idea of underlying codes and structures, and the arbitrary nature of the sign). Thus, when in his collection of essays, *Mythologies* (1972), the French critic, Roland Barthes, studied 'The world of wrestling', 'Soap powders and detergents', 'The face of Greta Garbo' or 'The *Blue Guides* to Europe', he brought a *semiotic* approach to bear on 'reading' popular culture, treating these activities and objects as signs, as a language through which meaning is communicated. For example, most of us would think of a wrestling match as a competitive game or sport designed for one wrestler to gain victory over an opponent. Barthes, however, asks, not 'Who won?' but 'What is the meaning of this event?' He treats it as a *text* to be *read*. He 'reads' the exaggerated gestures of wrestlers as a grandiloquent language of what he calls the pure spectacle of excess.

FIGURE 1.4 Wrestling as a language of 'excess'.

READING B

You should now read the brief extract from Barthes's 'reading' of 'The world of wrestling', provided as Reading B at the end of this chapter.

In much the same way, the French anthropologist, Claude Lévi-Strauss, studied the customs, rituals, totemic objects, designs, myths and folk-tales of so-called 'primitive' peoples in Brazil, not by analysing how these things were produced and used in the context of daily life amongst the Amazonian peoples, but in terms of what they were trying to 'say', what messages about the culture they communicated. He analysed their meaning, not by interpreting their content, but by looking at the underlying rules and codes through which such objects or practices produced meaning and, in doing so, he was making a classic Saussurean or structuralist 'move', from the *paroles* of a culture to the underlying structure, its *langue*. To undertake this kind of work, in studying the meaning of a television programme like *Eastenders*, for example, we would have to treat the pictures on the screen as signifiers, and use the code of the television soap opera as a *genre*, to discover how each image on the screen made use of these rules to 'say something' (signifieds) which the viewer could 'read' or interpret within the formal framework of a particular kind of television narrative (see the discussion and analysis of TV soap operas in Chapter 6).

In the semiotic approach, not only words and images but objects themselves can function as signifiers in the production of meaning. Clothes, for example, may have a simple physical function – to cover the body and protect it from the weather. But clothes also double up as signs. They construct a meaning and carry a message. An evening dress may signify 'elegance'; a bow tie and tails, 'formality'; jeans and trainers, 'casual dress'; a certain kind of sweater in the right setting, 'a long, romantic, autumn walk in the wood' (Barthes, 1967). These signs enable clothes to convey meaning and to function like a language – 'the language of fashion'. How do they do this?

ACTIVITY 5

Look at the example of clothes in a magazine fashion spread (Figure 1.5). Apply Saussure's model to analyse what the clothes are 'saying'? How would you decode their message? In particular, which elements are operating as *signifiers* and what concepts – *signifieds* – are you applying to them? Don't just get an overall impression – work it out in detail. How is the 'language of fashion' working in this example?

The clothes themselves are the *signifiers*. The fashion code in western consumer cultures like ours correlates particular kinds or combinations of clothing with certain concepts ('elegance', 'formality', 'casual-ness', 'romance'). These are the *signifieds*. This coding converts the clothes into *signs*, which can then be read as a language. In the language of fashion, the signifiers are arranged in a certain sequence, in certain relations to one another. Relations may be of similarity – certain items 'go together' (e.g. casual shoes with jeans). Differences are also marked – no leather belts with evening wear. Some signs actually create meaning by exploiting 'difference': e.g. Doc Marten boots with flowing long skirt. These bits of clothing 'say something' – they convey meaning. Of course, not everybody reads fashion in the same way. There are differences of gender, age, class, 'race'. But all those who share the same fashion code will interpret the signs in roughly the same ways. 'Oh, jeans don't look right for that event. It's a formal occasion – it demands something more elegant.'

You may have noticed that, in this example, we have moved from the very narrow linguistic level from which we drew examples in the first section, to a wider, cultural level. Note, also, that two linked operations are required to complete the representation process by which meaning is produced. First, we need a basic *code* which links a particular piece of material which is cut and sewn in a particular way (*signifier*) to our mental concept of it (*signified*) – say a particular cut of material to our concept of 'a dress' or 'jeans'. (Remember that only some cultures would 'read' the signifier in this way, or indeed possess the concept of (i.e. have classified clothes into) 'a dress', as different from 'jeans'.) The combination of signifier and signified is what Saussure called a *sign*. Then, having recognized the material as a dress, or as jeans, and produced a sign, we can progress to a second, wider level, which links these signs to broader, cultural themes, concepts or meanings – for example, an evening dress to 'formality' or 'elegance', jeans to 'casualness'. Barthes called the first, descriptive level, the level of **denotation**: the second level, that of **connotation**. Both, of course, require the use of codes.

FIGURE 1.5
Advertisement for Gucci, in *Vogue*, September 1995.

denotation

connotation

Denotation is the simple, basic, descriptive level, where consensus is wide and most people would agree on the meaning ('dress', 'jeans'). At the second level – *connotation* – these signifiers which we have been able to 'decode' at a simple level by using our conventional conceptual classifications of dress to read their meaning, enter a wider, second kind of code – 'the language of fashion' – which connects them to broader themes and meanings, linking them with what, we may call the wider *semantic fields* of our culture: ideas of 'elegance', 'formality', 'casualness' and 'romance'. This second, wider meaning is no longer a descriptive level of obvious interpretation. Here we are beginning to interpret the completed signs in terms of the wider realms of social ideology – the general beliefs, conceptual frameworks and value systems of society. This second level of signification, Barthes suggests, is more 'general, global and diffuse ...'. It deals with 'fragments of an ideology... These signifieds have a very close communication with culture, knowledge, history and it is through them, so to speak, that the environmental world [of the culture] invades the system [of representation]' (Barthes, 1967, pp. 91–2).

3.1 Myth today

In his essay 'Myth today', in *Mythologies*, Barthes gives another example which helps us to see exactly how representation is working at this second, broader cultural level. Visiting the barbers' one day, Barthes is shown a copy of the French magazine *Paris Match*, which has on its cover a picture of 'a young Negro in a French uniform saluting with his eyes uplifted, probably fixed on the fold of the tricolour' (the French flag) (1972b, p. 116). At the first level, to get any meaning at all, we need to decode each of the signifiers in the image into their appropriate concepts: e.g. a soldier, a uniform, an arm raised, eyes lifted, a French flag. This yields a set of signs with a simple, literal message or meaning: *a black soldier is giving the French flag a salute* (denotation). However, Barthes argues that this image also has a wider, cultural meaning. If we ask, 'What is *Paris Match* telling us by using this picture of a black soldier saluting a French flag?', Barthes suggests that we may come up with the message: '*that France is a great Empire, and that all her sons, without any colour discrimination, faithfully serve under her flag, and that there is no better answer to the detractors of an alleged colonialism than the zeal shown by this Negro in serving his so-called oppressors*' (connotation) (ibid.).

Whatever you think of the actual 'message' which Barthes finds, for a proper semiotic analysis you must be able to outline precisely the different steps by which this broader meaning has been produced. Barthes argues that here representation takes place through two separate but linked processes. In the first, the signifiers (the elements of the image) and the signifieds (the concepts – soldier, flag and so on) unite to form a sign with a simple denoted message: *a black soldier is giving the French flag a salute*. At the second stage, this completed message or sign is linked to a second set of signifieds – a broad, ideological theme about French colonialism. The first, completed meaning functions as the signifier in the second stage of the representation process, and when linked with a wider theme by a reader, yields a second, more elaborate and ideologically framed message or meaning. Barthes gives this second concept or theme a name – he calls it 'a purposeful mixture of "French imperiality" and "militariness"'. This, he says, adds up to a 'message' about French colonialism and her faithful Negro soldier-sons. Barthes calls this second level of signification the level of *myth*. In this reading, he adds, 'French imperiality is the very drive behind the myth. The concept reconstitutes a chain of causes and effects, motives and intentions ...

Through the concept ... a whole new history ... is implanted in the myth ... the concept of French imperiality ... is again tied to the totality of the world: to the general history of France, to its colonial adventures, to its present difficulties' (Barthes, 1972b, p. 119).

READING C

Turn to the short extract from 'Myth today' (Reading C at the end of this chapter), and read Barthes's account of how myth functions as a system of representation. Make sure you understand what Barthes means by 'two staggered systems' and by the idea that myth is a 'meta-language' (a second-order language).

For another example of this two-stage process of signification, we can turn now to another of Barthes's famous essays.

ACTIVITY 6

Now, look carefully at the advertisement for *Panzani* products (Figure 1.6) and, with Barthes's analysis in mind, do the following exercise:

1   What *signifiers* can you identify in the ad?

2   What do they mean? What are their *signifieds*?

3   Now, look at the ad as a whole, at the level of 'myth'. What is its wider, cultural message or theme? Can you construct one?

READING D

Now read the second extract from Barthes, in which he offers an interpretation of the *Panzani* ad for spaghetti and vegetables in a string bag as a 'myth' about Italian national culture. The extract from 'Rhetoric of the image', in *Image–Music–Text* (1977), is included as Reading D at the end of this chapter.

PATES - SAUCE - PARMESAN
A L'ITALIENNE DE LUXE

FIGURE 1.6

'Italian-ness' and the *Panzani* ad.

FIGURE 1.7

An image of 'Englishness' – advertisement for Jaguar.

Barthes suggests that we can read the *Panzani* ad as a 'myth' by linking its completed message *(this is a picture of some packets of pasta, a tin, a sachet, some tomatoes, onions, peppers, a mushroom, all emerging from a half-open string bag)* with the cultural theme or concept of 'Italianicity' (or as we would say, 'Italian-ness'). Then, at the level of the myth or meta-language, the Panzani ad becomes a message about the *essential meaning of Italian-ness as a national culture*. Can commodities really become the signifiers for myths of nationality? Can you think of ads, in magazines or television, which work in the same way, drawing on the myth of 'Englishness'? Or 'Frenchness'? Or 'American-ness'? Or 'Indian-ness'? Try to apply the idea of 'Englishness' to the ad reproduced as Figure 1.7.

4   Discourse, power and the subject

What the examples above show is that the semiotic approach provides a method for analysing how visual representations convey meaning. Already, in Roland Barthes's work in the 1960s, as we have seen, Saussure's 'linguistic' model is developed through its application to a much wider field of signs and representations (advertising, photography, popular culture, travel, fashion, etc.). Also, there is less concern with how individual words function as signs in language, more about the application of the language model to a much broader set of cultural practices. Saussure held out the promise that the whole domain of meaning could, at last, be systematically mapped. Barthes, too, had a 'method', but his semiotic approach is much more loosely and interpretively applied; and, in his later work (for example, *The Pleasure of the Text*, 1975), he is more concerned with the 'play' of meaning and desire across texts than he is with the attempt to fix meaning by a scientific analysis of language's rules and laws.

Subsequently, as we observed, the project of a 'science of meaning' has appeared increasingly untenable. Meaning and representation seem to belong irrevocably to the interpretative side of the human and cultural sciences, whose subject matter – society, culture, the human subject – is not amenable to a positivistic approach (i.e. one which seeks to discover scientific laws about society). Later developments have recognized the necessarily interpretative nature of culture and the fact that interpretations never produce a final moment of absolute truth. Instead, interpretations are always followed by other interpretations, in an endless chain. As the French philosopher, Jacques Derrida, put it, writing always leads to more writing. Difference, he argued, can never be wholly captured within any binary system (Derrida, 1981). So any notion of a *final* meaning is always endlessly put off, deferred. Cultural studies of this interpretative kind, like other qualitative forms of sociological inquiry, are inevitably caught up in this 'circle of meaning'.

In the semiotic approach, representation was understood on the basis of the way words functioned as signs within language. But, for a start, in a culture, meaning often depends on larger units of analysis – narratives, statements, groups of images, whole discourses which operate across a variety of texts, areas of knowledge about a subject which have acquired widespread authority. Semiotics seemed to confine the process of representation to language, and to treat it as a closed, rather static, system. Subsequent developments became more concerned with representation as a source for the production of social *knowledge* – a more open system, connected in more intimate ways with social practices and questions of power. In the semiotic approach, the subject was displaced from the centre of language. Later theorists returned to the question of the subject, or at least to the empty space which Saussure's theory had left; without, of course, putting him/her back in the centre, as the author or source of meaning. Even if language, in some sense, 'spoke us' (as Saussure tended to argue) it was also important that in certain historical moments, some people had more power to speak about some subjects than others (male doctors about mad female patients in the late nineteenth century, for example, to take one of the key examples developed in the work of Michel Foucault). Models of representation, these critics argued, ought to focus on these broader issues of knowledge and power.

Foucault used the word 'representation' in a narrower sense than we are using it here, but he is considered to have contributed to a novel and significant general approach to the problem of representation. What concerned him was the production of knowledge (rather than just meaning) discourse

through what he called **discourse** (rather than just language). His project, he said, was to analyse 'how human beings understand themselves in our culture' and how our knowledge about 'the social, the embodied individual and shared meanings' comes to be produced in different periods. With its emphasis on cultural understanding and shared meanings, you can see that Foucault's project was still to some degree indebted to Saussure and Barthes (see Dreyfus and Rabinow, 1982, p. 17) while in other ways departing radically from them. Foucault's work was much more historically grounded, more attentive to historical specificities, than the semiotic approach. As he said, 'relations of power, not relations of meaning' were his main concern. The particular objects of Foucault's attention were the various disciplines of knowledge in the human and social sciences – what he called 'the subjectifying social sciences'. These had acquired an increasingly prominent and influential role in modern culture and were, in many instances, considered to be the discourses which, like religion in earlier times, could give us the 'truth' about knowledge.

We will return to Foucault's work in some of the subsequent chapters in this book (for example, Chapter 5). Here, we want to introduce Foucault and the *discursive* approach to representation by outlining three of his major ideas: his concept of *discourse*; the issue of *power and knowledge*; and the question of *the subject*. It might be useful, however, to start by giving you a general flavour, in Foucault's graphic (and somewhat over-stated) terms, of how he saw his project differing from that of the semiotic approach to representation. He moved away from an approach like that of Saussure and Barthes, based on 'the domain of signifying structure', towards one based on analysing what he called 'relations of force, strategic developments and tactics':

> Here I believe one's point of reference should not be to the great model of language (*langue*) and signs, but to that of war and battle. The history which bears and determines us has the form of a war rather than that of a language: relations of power not relations of meaning ...

> (Foucault, 1980, pp. 114–5)

Rejecting both Hegelian Marxism (what he calls 'the dialectic') and semiotics, Foucault argued that:

> Neither the dialectic, as logic of contradictions, nor semiotics, as the structure of communication, can account for the intrinsic intelligibility of conflicts. 'Dialectic' is a way of evading the always open and hazardous reality of conflict by reducing it to a Hegelian skeleton, and 'semiology' is a way of avoiding its violent, bloody and lethal character by reducing it to the calm Platonic form of language and dialogue.

> (ibid.)

4.1   From language to discourse

The first point to note, then, is the shift of attention in Foucault from 'language' to 'discourse'. He studied not language, but *discourse* as a system of representation. Normally, the term 'discourse' is used as a linguistic concept. It simply means passages of connected writing or speech. Michel Foucault, however, gave it a different meaning. What interested him were the rules and practices that produced meaningful statements and regulated discourse in different historical periods. By 'discourse', Foucault meant 'a group of statements which provide a language for talking about – a way of representing the knowledge about – a particular topic at a particular historical moment. ... Discourse is about the production of knowledge through language. But ... since all social practices entail *meaning*, and meanings shape and influence what we do – our conduct – all practices have a discursive aspect' (Hall, 1992, p. 291). It is important to note that the concept of *discourse* in this usage is not purely a 'linguistic' concept. It is about language *and* practice. It attempts to overcome the traditional distinction between what one *says* (language) and what one *does* (practice). Discourse, Foucault argues, constructs the topic. It defines and produces the objects of our knowledge. It governs the way that a topic can be meaningfully talked about and reasoned about. It also influences how ideas are put into practice and used to regulate the conduct of others. Just as a discourse 'rules in' certain ways of talking about a topic, defining an acceptable and intelligible way to talk, write, or conduct oneself, so also, by definition, it 'rules out', limits and restricts other ways of talking, of conducting ourselves in relation to the topic or constructing knowledge about it. Discourse, Foucault argued, never consists of one statement, one text, one action or one source. The same discourse, characteristic of the way of thinking or the state of knowledge at any one time (what Foucault called the *episteme*), will appear across a range of texts, and as forms of conduct, at a number of different institutional sites within society. However, whenever these discursive events 'refer to the same object, share the same style and ... support a strategy ... a common institutional, administrative or political drift and pattern' (Cousins and Hussain, 1984, pp. 84–5), then they are said by Foucault to belong to the same **discursive formation**.

discursive formation

Meaning and meaningful practice is therefore constructed within discourse. Like the semioticians, Foucault was a 'constructionist'. However, unlike them, he was concerned with the production of knowledge and meaning, not through language but through discourse. There were therefore similarities, but also substantive differences between these two versions.

The idea that 'discourse produces the objects of knowledge' and that nothing which is meaningful exists *outside discourse,* is at first sight a disconcerting proposition, which seems to run right against the grain of common-sense thinking. It is worth spending a moment to explore this idea further. Is Foucault saying – as some of his critics have charged – that *nothing exists outside of discourse*? In fact, Foucault does *not* deny that things can have a real, material existence in the world. What he does argue is that '*nothing has any meaning outside of discourse*' (Foucault, 1972). As Laclau and Mouffe put it, 'we use [the term discourse] to emphasize the fact that every social configuration is *meaningful*' (1990, p. 100). The concept of discourse is not about whether things exist but about where meaning comes from.

READING E

Turn now to Reading E, by Ernesto Laclau and Chantal Mouffe, a short extract from *New Reflections on the Revolution of our Time* (1990), from which we have just quoted, and read it carefully. What they argue is that physical objects *do* exist, but they have no fixed meaning; they only take on meaning and become objects of knowledge *within discourse*. Make sure you follow their argument before reading further.

1   In terms of the discourse about 'building a wall', the distinction between the linguistic part (asking for a brick) and the physical act (putting the brick in place) does not matter. The first is linguistic, the second is physical. But *both* are 'discursive' – meaningful within discourse.

2   The round leather object which you kick is a physical object – a ball. But it only becomes 'a football' within the context of the rules of the game, which are socially constructed.

3   It is impossible to determine the meaning of an object outside of its context of use. A stone thrown in a fight is a different thing ('a projectile') from a stone displayed in a museum ('a piece of sculpture').

This idea that physical things and actions exist, but they only take on meaning and become objects of knowledge within discourse, is at the heart of the *constructionist* theory of meaning and representation. Foucault argues that since we can only have a knowledge of things if they have a meaning, it is discourse – not the things-in-themselves – which produces knowledge. Subjects like 'madness', 'punishment' and 'sexuality' only exist meaningfully *within* the discourses about them. Thus, the study of the discourses of madness, punishment or sexuality would have to include the following elements:

1   statements about 'madness', 'punishment' or 'sexuality' which give us a certain kind of knowledge about these things;

2   the rules which prescribe certain ways of talking about these topics and exclude other ways – which govern what is 'sayable' or 'thinkable' about insanity, punishment or sexuality, at a particular historical moment;

3   'subjects' who in some ways personify the discourse – the madman, the hysterical woman, the criminal, the deviant, the sexually perverse person; with the attributes we would expect these subjects to have, given the way knowledge about the topic was constructed at that time;

4   how this knowledge about the topic acquires authority, a sense of embodying the 'truth' about it; constituting the 'truth of the matter', at a historical moment;

5   the practices within institutions for dealing with the subjects – medical treatment for the insane, punishment regimes for the guilty, moral discipline for the sexually deviant – whose conduct is being regulated and organized according to those ideas;

6   acknowledgement that a different discourse or *episteme* will arise at a later historical moment, supplanting the existing one, opening up a new *discursive formation*, and producing, in its turn, new conceptions of 'madness' or 'punishment' or 'sexuality', new discourses with the power and authority, the 'truth', to regulate social practices in new ways.

4.2 Historicizing discourse: discursive practices

The main point to get hold of here is the way discourse, representation, knowledge and 'truth' are radically *historicized* by Foucault, in contrast to the rather ahistorical tendency in semiotics. Things meant something and were 'true', he argued, *only within a specific historical context*. Foucault did not believe that the same phenomena would be found across different historical periods. He thought that, in each period, discourse produced forms of knowledge, objects, subjects and practices of knowledge, which differed radically from period to period, with no necessary continuity between them.

Thus, for Foucault, for example, mental illness was not an objective fact, which remained the same in all historical periods, and meant the same thing in all cultures. It was only *within* a definite discursive formation that the object, 'madness', could appear at all as a meaningful or intelligible construct. It was 'constituted by all that was said, in all the statements that named it, divided it up, described it, explained it, traced its development, indicated its various correlations, judged it, and possibly gave it speech by articulating, in its name, discourses that were to be taken as its own' (1972, p. 32). And it was only after a certain definition of 'madness' was put into practice, that the appropriate subject – 'the madman' as current medical and psychiatric knowledge defined 'him' – could appear.

Or, take some other examples of discursive practices from his work. There have always been sexual relations. But 'sexuality', as a specific way of talking about, studying and regulating sexual desire, its secrets and its fantasies, Foucault argued, only appeared in western societies at a particular historical moment (Foucault, 1978). There may always have been what we now call homosexual forms of behaviour. But 'the homosexual' as a specific kind of social subject, was *produced*, and could only make its appearance, within the moral, legal, medical and psychiatric discourses, practices and institutional apparatuses of the late nineteenth century, with their particular theories of sexual perversity (Weeks, 1981, 1985). Similarly, it makes nonsense to talk of the 'hysterical woman' outside of the nineteenth-century view of hysteria as a very widespread female malady. In *The Birth of the Clinic* (1973), Foucault charted how 'in less than half a century, the medical understanding of disease was transformed' from a classical notion that disease existed separate from the body, to the modern idea that disease arose within and could be mapped directly by its course through the human body (McNay, 1994). This discursive shift changed medical practice. It gave greater importance to the doctor's 'gaze' which could now 'read' the course of disease simply by a powerful look at what Foucault called 'the visible body' of the patient – following the 'routes … laid down in accordance with a now familiar geometry … the anatomical atlas' (Foucault, 1973, pp. 3–4). This greater knowledge increased the doctor's power of surveillance vis-à-vis the patient.

Knowledge about and practices around *all* these subjects, Foucault argued, were historically and culturally specific. They did not and could not meaningfully exist outside specific discourses, i.e. outside the ways they were represented in discourse, produced in knowledge and regulated by the discursive practices and disciplinary techniques of a particular society and time. Far from accepting the trans-historical continuities of which historians are so fond, Foucault believed that more significant were the radical breaks, ruptures and discontinuities between one period and another, between one discursive formation and another.

4.3   From discourse to power/knowledge

In his later work Foucault became even more concerned with how knowledge was put to work through discursive practices in specific institutional settings to regulate the conduct of others. He focused on the relationship between knowledge and power, and how power operated within what he called an institutional *apparatus* and its *technologies* (techniques). Foucault's conception of the *apparatus* of punishment, for example, included a variety of diverse elements, linguistic and non-linguistic – 'discourses, institutions, architectural arrangements, regulations, laws, administrative measures, scientific statements, philosophic propositions, morality, philanthropy, etc. … The apparatus is thus always inscribed in a play of power, but it is also always linked to certain co-ordinates of knowledge. … This is what the apparatus consists in: strategies of relations of forces supporting and supported by types of knowledge' (Foucault, 1980b, pp. 194, 196).

This approach took as one of its key subjects of investigation the relations between knowledge, power and the body in modern society. It saw knowledge as always inextricably enmeshed in relations of power because it was always being applied to the regulation of social conduct in practice (i.e. to particular 'bodies'). This foregrounding of the relation between discourse, knowledge and power marked a significant development in the *constructionist* approach to representation which we have been outlining. It rescued representation from the clutches of a purely formal theory and gave it a historical, practical and 'worldly' context of operation.

You may wonder to what extent this concern with discourse, knowledge and power brought Foucault's interests closer to those of the classical sociological theories of ideology, especially Marxism with its concern to identify the class positions and class interests concealed within particular forms of knowledge. Foucault, indeed, does come closer to addressing some of these questions about ideology than, perhaps, formal semiotics did (though Roland Barthes was also concerned with questions of ideology and myth, as we saw earlier). But Foucault had quite specific and cogent reasons why he rejected the classical Marxist problematic of 'ideology'. Marx had argued that, in every epoch, ideas reflect the economic basis of society, and thus the 'ruling ideas' are those of the ruling class which governs a capitalist economy, and correspond to its dominant interests. Foucault's main argument against the classical Marxist theory of ideology was that it tended to reduce all the relation between knowledge and power to a question of *class* power and *class* interests. Foucault did not deny the existence of classes, but he was strongly opposed to this powerful element of economic or class *reductionism* in the Marxist theory of ideology. Secondly, he argued that Marxism tended to contrast the 'distortions' of bourgeois knowledge, against its own claims to 'truth' – Marxist science. But Foucault did not believe that *any* form of thought could claim an absolute 'truth' of this kind, outside the play of discourse. *All* political and social forms of thought, he believed, were inevitably caught up in the interplay of knowledge and power. So, his work rejects the traditional Marxist question, 'in whose class interest does language, representation and power operate?'

Later theorists, like the Italian, Antonio Gramsci, who was influenced by Marx but rejected class reductionism, advanced a definition of 'ideology' which is considerably closer to Foucault's position, though still too preoccupied with class questions to be acceptable to him. Gramsci's notion was that particular social groups struggle in many different ways, including ideologically, to win the consent of other groups and achieve a kind of ascendancy in both thought and practice over them. This form of power Gramsci called **hegemony**. Hegemony is never permanent, and is not reducible to economic interests or to a simple class model of society. This has some similarities to Foucault's position, though on some key issues they differ radically. (The question of hegemony is briefly addressed again in Chapter 4.)

hegemony

What distinguished Foucault's position on discourse, knowledge and power from the Marxist theory of class interests and ideological 'distortion'? Foucault advanced at least two, radically novel, propositions.

1 Knowledge, power and truth

The first concerns the way Foucault conceived the linkage between knowledge and power. Hitherto, we have tended to think that power operates in a direct and brutally repressive fashion, dispensing with polite things like culture and knowledge, though Gramsci certainly broke with that model of power. Foucault argued that not only is knowledge always a form of power, but power is implicated in the questions of whether and in what circumstances knowledge is to be applied or not. This question of the

power/knowledge

application and *effectiveness* of **power/knowledge** was more important, he thought, than the question of its 'truth'.

Knowledge linked to power, not only assumes the authority of 'the truth' but has the power to *make itself true.* All knowledge, once applied in the real world, has real effects, and in that sense at least, 'becomes true'. Knowledge, once used to regulate the conduct of others, entails constraint, regulation and the disciplining of practices. Thus, 'There is no power relation without the correlative constitution of a field of knowledge, nor any knowledge that does not presuppose and constitute at the same time, power relations' (Foucault, 1977a, p. 27).

According to Foucault, what we think we 'know' in a particular period about, say, crime has a bearing on how we regulate, control and punish criminals. Knowledge does not operate in a void. It is put to work, through certain technologies and strategies of application, in specific situations, historical contexts and institutional regimes. To study punishment, you must study how the combination of discourse and power – power/knowledge – has produced a certain conception of crime and the criminal, has had certain real effects both for criminal and for the punisher, and how these have been set into practice in certain historically specific prison regimes.

This led Foucault to speak, not of the 'Truth' of knowledge in the absolute sense – a Truth which remained so, whatever the period, setting, context – but of a discursive formation sustaining a **regime of truth**. Thus, it may or may not be true that single parenting inevitably leads to delinquency and crime. But if everyone believes it to be so, and punishes single parents accordingly, this will have real consequences for both parents and children and will become 'true' in terms of its real effects, even if in some absolute sense it has never been conclusively proven. In the human and social sciences, Foucault argued:

regime of truth

> Truth isn't outside power. ... Truth is a thing of this world; it is produced only by virtue of multiple forms of constraint. And it induces regular effects of power. Each society has its regime of truth, its 'general politics' of truth; that is, the types of discourse which it accepts and makes function as true, the mechanisms and instances which enable one to distinguish true and false statements, the means by which each is sanctioned ... the status of those who are charged with saying what counts as true.
>
> (Foucault, 1980, p. 131)

2 New conceptions of power

Secondly, Foucault advanced an altogether novel conception of power. We tend to think of power as always radiating in a single direction – from top to bottom – and coming from a specific source – the sovereign, the state, the ruling class and so on. For Foucault, however, power does not 'function in the form of a chain' – it circulates. It is never monopolized by one centre. It 'is deployed and exercised through a net-like organization' (Foucault, 1980, p. 98). This suggests that we are all, to some degree, caught up in its circulation – oppressors and oppressed. It does not radiate downwards, either from one source or from one place. Power relations permeate all levels of social existence and are therefore to be found operating at every site of social life – in the private spheres of the family and sexuality as much as in the public spheres of politics, the economy and the law. What's more, power is not only negative, repressing what it seeks to control. It is also *productive*. It 'doesn't only weigh on us as a force that says no, but … it traverses and produces things, it induces pleasure, forms of knowledge, produces discourse. It needs to be thought of as a productive network which runs through the whole social body' (Foucault, 1980, p. 119).

The punishment system, for example, produces books, treatises, regulations, new strategies of control and resistance, debates in Parliament, conversations, confessions, legal briefs and appeals, training regimes for prison officers, and so on. The efforts to control sexuality produce a veritable explosion of discourse – talk about sex, television and radio programmes, sermons and legislation, novels, stories and magazine features, medical and counselling advice, essays and articles, learned theses and research programmes, as well as new sexual practices (e.g. 'safe' sex) and the pornography industry. Without denying that the state, the law, the sovereign or the dominant class may have positions of dominance, Foucault shifts our attention away from the grand, overall strategies of power, towards the many, localized circuits, tactics, mechanisms and effects through which power circulates – what Foucault calls the 'meticulous rituals' or the 'micro-physics' of power. These power relations 'go right down to the depth of society' (Foucault, 1977a, p. 27). They connect the way power is actually working on the ground to the great pyramids of power by what he calls a capillary movement (capillaries being the thin-walled vessels that aid the exchange of oxygen between the blood in our bodies and the surrounding tissues). Not because power at these lower levels merely reflects or 'reproduces, at the level of individuals, bodies, gestures and behaviour, the general form of the law or government' (Foucault, 1977a, p. 27) but, on the contrary, because such an approach 'roots [power] in forms of behaviour, bodies and local relations of power which should not at all be seen as a simple projection of the central power' (Foucault, 1980, p. 201).

To what object are the micro-physics of power primarily applied, in Foucault's model? To the body. He places the body at the centre of the struggles between different formations of power/knowledge. The techniques of regulation are applied to the body. Different discursive formations and apparatuses divide, classify and inscribe the body differently in their respective regimes of power and 'truth'. In *Discipline and Punish*, for example, Foucault analyses the very different ways in which the body of the criminal is 'produced' and disciplined in different punishment regimes in France. In earlier periods, punishment was haphazard, prisons were places into which the public could wander and the ultimate punishment was inscribed violently on the body by means of instruments of torture and execution, etc. – a practice the essence of which is that it should be public, visible to everyone. The modern form of disciplinary regulation and power, by contrast, is private, individualized; prisoners are shut away from the public and often from one another, though continually under surveillance from the authorities; and punishment is individualized. Here, the body has become the site of a new kind of disciplinary regime.

Of course this 'body' is not simply the natural body which all human beings possess at all times. This body is *produced* within discourse, according to the different discursive formations – the state of knowledge about crime and the criminal, what counts as 'true' about how to change or deter criminal behaviour, the specific apparatus and technologies of punishment prevailing at the time. This is a radically historicized conception of the body – a sort of surface on which different regimes of power/knowledge write their meanings and effects. It thinks of the body as 'totally imprinted by history and the processes of history's deconstruction of the body' (Foucault, 1977a, p. 63).

4.4 Summary: Foucault and representation

Foucault's approach to representation is not easy to summarize. He is concerned with the production of knowledge and meaning through discourse. Foucault does indeed analyse particular texts and representations, as the semioticians did. But he is more inclined to analyse the whole *discursive formation* to which a text or a practice belongs. His concern is with knowledge provided by the human and social sciences, which organizes conduct, understanding, practice and belief, the regulation of bodies as well as whole populations. Although his work is clearly done in the wake of, and profoundly influenced by, the 'turn to language' which marked the *constructionist* approach to representation, his definition of *discourse* is much broader than language, and includes many other elements of practice and institutional regulation which Saussure's approach, with its linguistic focus, excluded. Foucault is always much more historically specific, seeing forms of power/knowledge as always rooted in particular contexts and histories. Above all, for Foucault, the production of knowledge is always crossed with questions of power and the body; and this greatly expands the scope of what is involved in representation.

The major critique levelled against his work is that he tends to absorb too much into 'discourse', and this has the effect of encouraging his followers to neglect the influence of the material, economic and structural factors in the operation of power/knowledge. Some critics also find his rejection of any criterion of 'truth' in the human sciences in favour of the idea of a 'regime of truth' and the will-to-power (the will to make things 'true') vulnerable to the charge of relativism. Nevertheless, there is little doubt about the major impact which his work has had on contemporary theories of representation and meaning.

4.5 Charcot and the performance of hysteria

In the following example, we will try to apply Foucault's method to a particular example. Figure 1.8 shows a painting by André Brouillet of the famous French psychiatrist and neurologist, Jean-Martin Charcot (1825–93), lecturing on the subject of female hysteria to students in the lecture theatre of his famous Paris clinic at La Salpêtrière.

ACTIVITY 7

> Look at Brouillet's painting (Figure 1.8). What does it reveal as a representation of the study of hysteria?

Brouillet shows a hysterical patient being supported by an assistant and attended by two women. For many years, hysteria had been traditionally identified as a female malady and although Charcot demonstrated conclusively that many hysterical symptoms were to be found in men, and a significant proportion of his patients were diagnosed male hysterics, Elaine Showalter observes that 'for Charcot, too, hysteria remains symbolically, if not medically, a female malady' (1987, p. 148). Charcot was a very humane man who took his patients' suffering seriously and treated them with dignity. He diagnosed hysteria as a genuine ailment rather than a malingerer's excuse (much as has happened, in our time, after many struggles, with other illnesses, like anorexia and ME). This painting represents a regular feature of Charcot's treatment regime, where hysterical female patients displayed before an audience of medical staff and students the symptoms of their malady, ending often with a full hysterical seizure.

FIGURE 1.8 André Brouillet, *A clinical lesson at La Salpêtrière (given by Charcot)*, 1887.

The painting could be said to capture and represent, visually, a discursive 'event' – the emergence of a new regime of knowledge. Charcot's great distinction, which drew students from far and wide to study with him (including, in 1885, the young Sigmund Freud from Vienna), was his demonstration 'that hysterical symptoms such as paralysis could be produced and relieved by hypnotic suggestion' (Showalter, 1987, p. 148). Here we see the practice of hypnosis being applied in practice.

Indeed, the image seems to capture *two* such moments of knowledge production. Charcot did not pay much attention to what the patients said (though he observed their actions and gestures meticulously). But Freud and his friend Breuer did. At first, in their work when they returned home, they used Charcot's hypnosis method, which had attracted such wide attention as a novel approach to treatment of hysteria at La Salpêtrière. But some years later they treated a young woman called Bertha Pappenheim for hysteria, and she, under the pseudonym 'Anna O', became the first case study written up in Freud and Breuer's path-breaking *Studies in Hysteria* (1974/1895). It was the 'loss of words', her failing grasp of the syntax of her own language (German), the silences and meaningless babble of this brilliantly intellectual, poetic and imaginative but rebellious young woman, which gave Breuer and Freud the first clue that her linguistic disturbance was related to her resentment at her 'place' as dutiful daughter of a decidedly patriarchal father, and thus deeply connected with her illness. After hypnosis, her capacity to speak coherently returned, and she spoke fluently in three other languages, though not in her native German. Through her dialogue with Breuer, and her ability to 'work through' her difficult relationship in relation to language, 'Anna O' gave the first example of the 'talking cure' which, of course, then provided the whole basis for Freud's subsequent development of the psychoanalytic method. So we are looking, in this image, at the 'birth' of two new psychiatric *epistemes*: Charcot's method of hypnosis, and the conditions which later produced psychoanalysis.

The example also has many connections with the question of *representation*. In the picture, the patient is performing or 'representing' with her body the hysterical symptoms from which she is 'suffering'. But these symptoms are also being 're-presented' – in the very different medical language of diagnosis and analysis – to her (his?) audience by the Professor: a relationship which involves *power*. Showalter notes that, in general, 'the representation of female hysteria was a central aspect of Charcot's work' (p.148). Indeed, the clinic was filled with lithographs and paintings. He had his assistants assemble a photographic album of nervous patients, a sort of visual inventory of the various 'types' of hysterical patient. He later employed a professional photographer to take charge of the service. His analysis of the displayed symptoms, which seems to be what is happening in the painting, accompanied the hysterical 'performance'. He did not flinch from the spectacular and theatrical aspects associated with his demonstrations of hypnosis as a treatment regime. Freud thought that 'Every one of his "fascinating lectures"' was 'a little work of art in construction and composition'. Indeed, Freud noted, 'he never appeared greater to his listeners than after he had made the effort, by giving the most detailed account of his train of thought, by the greatest frankness about his doubts and hesitations, to reduce the gulf between teacher and pupil' (Gay, 1988, p. 49).

ACTIVITY 8

Now look carefully at the picture again and, bearing in mind what we have said about Foucault's method of and approach to representation, answer the following questions:

1   Who commands the centre of the picture?

2   Who or what is its 'subject'? Are (1) and (2) the same?

3   Can you tell that knowledge is being produced here? How?

4   What do you notice about relations of power in the picture? How are they represented? How does the *form* and *spatial relationships* of the picture represent this?

5   Describe the 'gaze' of the people in the image: who is looking at whom? What does *that* tell us?

6   What do the age and gender of the participants tell us?

7   What message does the patient's body convey?

8   Is there a *sexual* meaning in the image? If so, what?

9   What is the relationship of you, the viewer, to the image?

10 Do you notice anything else about the image which we have missed?

READING F

Now read the account of Charcot and La Salpêtrière offered by Elaine Showalter in 'The performance of hysteria' from *The Female Malady*, reproduced as Reading F at the end of this chapter. Look carefully at the two photographs of Charcot's hysterical women patients. What do you make of their captions?

5   Where is 'the subject'?

We have traced the shift in Foucault's work from language to discourse and knowledge, and their relation to questions of power. But where in all this, you might ask, is the subject? Saussure tended to abolish the subject from the question of representation. Language, he argued, speaks us. The subject appears in Saussure's schema as the author of individual speech-acts (*paroles*). But, as we have seen, Saussure did not think that the level of the *paroles* was one at which a 'scientific' analysis of language could be conducted. In one sense, Foucault shares this position. For him, it is *discourse*, not the subject, which produces knowledge. Discourse is enmeshed with power, but it is not necessary to find 'a subject' – the king, the ruling class, the bourgeoisie, the state, etc. – for *power/knowledge* to operate.

On the other hand, Foucault *did* include the subject in his theorizing, though he did not restore the subject to its position as the centre and author of representation. Indeed, as his work developed, he became more and more concerned with questions about 'the subject', and in his very late and unfinished work, he even went so far as to give the subject a certain reflexive awareness of his or her own conduct, though this still stopped short of restoring the subject to his/her full sovereignty.

Foucault was certainly deeply critical of what we might call the traditional conception of the subject. The conventional notion thinks of 'the subject' as an individual who is fully endowed with consciousness; an autonomous and stable entity, the 'core' of the self, and the independent, authentic source of action and meaning. According to this conception, when we hear ourselves speak, we feel we are identical with what has been said. And this identity of the subject with what is said gives him/her a privileged position in relation to meaning. It suggests that, although other people may misunderstand us, *we* always understand ourselves because *we were the source of meaning in the first place.*

However, as we have seen, the shift towards a constructionist conception of language and representation did a great deal to displace the subject from a privileged position in relation to knowledge and meaning. The same is true of Foucault's discursive approach. It is discourse, not the subjects who speak it, which produces knowledge. Subjects may produce particular texts, but they are operating within the limits of the *episteme*, the *discursive formation,* the *regime of truth*, of a particular period and culture. Indeed, this is one of Foucault's most radical propositions: the 'subject' is *produced within discourse.* This subject *of* discourse cannot be outside discourse, because it must be *subjected to* discourse. It must submit to its rules and conventions, to its dispositions of power/knowledge. The subject can become the bearer of the kind of knowledge which discourse produces. It can become the object through which power is relayed. But it cannot stand outside power/ knowledge as its source and author. In 'The subject and power' (1982), Foucault writes that 'My objective … has been to create a history of the different modes by which, in our culture, human beings are made subjects … It is a form of power which makes individuals subjects. There are two meanings of the word *subject*: subject to someone else's control and dependence, and tied to his (*sic*) own identity by a conscience and self-knowledge. Both meanings suggest a form of power which subjugates and makes subject to' (Foucault, 1982, pp. 208, 212). Making discourse and representation more historical has therefore been matched, in Foucault, by an equally radical historicization of *the subject.* 'One has to dispense with the constituent subject, to get rid of the subject itself, that's to say, to arrive at an analysis which can account for the constitution of the subject within a historical framework' (Foucault, 1980, p. 115).

Where, then, is 'the subject' in this more discursive approach to meaning, representation and power?

Foucault's 'subject' seems to be produced through discourse in *two* different senses or places. First, the discourse itself produces 'subjects' – figures who personify the particular forms of knowledge which the discourse produces. These subjects have the attributes we would expect as these are defined by the discourse: the madman, the hysterical woman, the homosexual, the individualized criminal, and so on. These figures are specific to specific discursive regimes and historical periods. But the discourse also produces a *place for the subject* (i.e. the reader or viewer, who is also 'subjected to' discourse) from which its particular knowledge and meaning most makes sense. It is not inevitable that all individuals in a particular period will become the subjects of a particular discourse in this sense, and thus the bearers of its power/knowledge. But for them – us – to do so, they – we – must locate themselves/ourselves in the *position* from which the discourse makes most sense, and thus become its 'subjects' by 'subjecting' ourselves to its meanings, power and regulation. All discourses, then, construct **subject-positions**, from which alone they make sense.

subject-positions

This approach has radical implications for a theory of representation. For it suggests that discourses themselves construct the subject-positions from which they become meaningful and have effects. Individuals may differ as to their social class, gendered, 'racial' and ethnic characteristics (among other factors), but they will not be able to take meaning until they have identified with those positions which the discourse constructs, *subjected* themselves to its rules, and hence become the *subjects of its power/knowledge*. For example, pornography produced for men will only 'work' for women, according to this theory, if in some sense women put themselves in the position of the 'desiring male voyeur' – which is the ideal subject-position which the discourse of male pornography constructs – and look at the models from this 'masculine' discursive position. This may seem, and is, a highly contestable proposition. But let us consider an example which illustrates the argument.

5.1   How to make sense of Velasquez' *Las Meninas*

Foucault's *The Order of Things* (1970) opens with a discussion of a painting by the famous Spanish painter, Velasquez, called *Las Meninas*. It has been a topic of considerable scholarly debate and controversy. The reason I am using it here is because, as all the critics agree, the painting itself does raise certain questions about the nature of *representation*, and Foucault himself uses it to talk about these wider issues of the subject. It is these arguments which interest us here, not the question of whether Foucault's is the 'true', correct or even the definitive reading of the painting's meaning. That the painting has no one, fixed or final meaning is, indeed, one of Foucault's most powerful arguments.

The painting is unique in Velasquez' work. It was part of the Spanish court's royal collection and hung in the palace in a room which was subsequently destroyed by fire. It was dated '1656' by Velasquez' successor as court painter. It was originally called 'The Empress with her Ladies and a Dwarf'; but by the inventory of 1666, it had acquired the title of 'A Portrait of the Infanta of Spain with her Ladies In Waiting and Servants, by the Court Painter and Palace Chamberlain Diego Velasquez'. It was subsequently called *Las Meninas* – 'The Maids of Honour'. Some argue that the painting shows Velasquez working on *Las Meninas* itself and was painted with the aid of a mirror – but this now seems unlikely. The most widely held and convincing explanation is that Velasquez was working on a full-length portrait of the King and Queen, and that it is the royal couple who are reflected in the mirror on the back wall. It is at the couple that the princess and her attendants are looking and on them that the artist's gaze appears to rest as he steps back from his canvas. The reflection artfully includes the royal couple in the picture. This is essentially the account which Foucault accepts.

ACTIVITY 9

Look at the picture carefully, while we summarize Foucault's argument.

FIGURE 1.9
Diego Velasquez,
Las Meninas,
1656.

Las Meninas shows the interior of a room – perhaps the painter's studio or some other room in the Spanish Royal Palace, the Escorial. The scene, though in its deeper recesses rather dark, is bathed in light from a window on the right. 'We are looking at a picture in which the painter is in turn looking out at us,' says Foucault (1970, p. 4). To the left, looking forwards, is the painter himself, Velasquez. He is in the act of painting and his brush is raised, 'perhaps … considering whether to add some finishing touch to the canvas' (p. 3). He is looking at his model, who is sitting in the place from which we are looking, but we cannot see who the model is because the canvas on which Velasquez is painting has its back to us, its face resolutely turned away from our gaze. In the centre of the painting stands what tradition recognizes as the little princess, the Infanta Maragarita, who has come to watch the proceedings. She is the centre of the picture we are looking at, but she is not the 'subject' of Velasquez' canvas. The Infanta has with her an 'entourage of duennas, maids of honour, courtiers and dwarfs' and her dog (p. 9). The courtiers stand behind, towards the back on the right. Her maids of honour stand on either side of her, framing her. To the right at the front are two dwarfs, one a famous court jester. The eyes of many of these figures, like that of the painter himself, are looking out towards the front of the picture at the sitters.

Who are they – the figures at whom everyone is looking but whom we cannot look at and whose portraits on the canvas we are forbidden to see? In fact, though at first we think we cannot see them, the picture tells us who they are because, behind the Infanta's head and a little to the left of the centre of the picture, surrounded by a heavy wooden frame, is a mirror; and in the mirror – at last – are reflected the sitters, who are in fact seated *in the position from which we are looking*: 'a reflection that shows us quite simply what is lacking in everyone's gaze' (p. 15). The figures reflected in the mirror are, in fact, the King, Philip IV, and his wife, Mariana. Beside the mirror, to the right of it, in the back wall, is another 'frame', but this is not a mirror reflecting forwards; it is a doorway leading *backwards* out of the room. On the stair, his feet placed on different steps, 'a man stands out in full-length silhouette'. He has just entered or is just leaving the scene and is looking at it from behind, observing what is going on in it but 'content to surprise those within without being seen himself' (p. 10).

5.2 The subject of/in representation

Who or what is *the subject* of this painting? In his comments, Foucault uses *Las Meninas* to make some general points about his theory of representation and specifically about the role of the subject:

1 'Foucault reads the painting in terms of representation and the subject' (Dreyfus and Rabinow, 1982, p. 20). As well as being a painting which shows us (represents) a scene in which a portrait of the King and Queen of Spain is being painted, it is also a painting which *tells us something about how representation and the subject work*. It produces its own kind of knowledge.

Representation and the subject are the painting's underlying message – what it is about, its sub-text.

2   Clearly, representation here is *not* about a 'true' reflection or imitation of reality. Of course, the people in the painting may 'look like' the actual people in the Spanish court. But the discourse of painting in the picture is doing a great deal more than simply trying to mirror accurately what exists.

3   Everything in a sense is *visible* in the painting. And yet, what it is 'about' – its meaning – depends on how we 'read' it. *It is as much constructed around what you can't see as what you can.* You can't see what is being painted on the canvas, though this seems to be the point of the whole exercise. You can't see what everyone is looking at, which is the sitters, unless we assume it is a reflection of them in the mirror. They are both in and not in the picture. Or rather, they are present through a kind of substitution. We cannot see them because they are not directly represented: but their 'absence' is represented – *mirrored* through their reflection in the mirror at the back. The meaning of the picture is produced, Foucault argues, through this complex inter-play between *presence* (what you see, the visible) and *absence* (what you can't see, what has displaced it within the frame). Representation works as much through what is *not* shown, as through what is.

4   In fact, a number of substitutions or displacements seem to be going on here. For example, the 'subject' and centre of the painting we are looking at seems to be the Infanta. But the 'subject' or centre is also, of course, the sitters – the King and Queen – whom we can't see but whom the others are looking at. You can tell this from the fact that the mirror on the wall in which the King and Queen are reflected is also almost exactly at the centre of the field of vision of the picture. So the Infanta and the Royal Couple, in a sense, share the place of the centre as the principal 'subjects' of the painting. It all depends on where you are looking from – in towards the scene from where you, the spectator, is sitting or outwards from the scene, from the position of the people in the picture. If you accept Foucault's argument, then there are *two* subjects to the painting and *two* centres. And the composition of the picture – its discourse – forces us to oscillate between these two 'subjects' without ever finally deciding which one to identify with. Representation in the painting seems firm and clear – everything in place. But our vision, the way we *look* at the picture, oscillates between two centres, two subjects, two positions of looking, two meanings. Far from being finally resolved into some absolute truth which is *the* meaning of the picture, the discourse of the painting quite deliberately keeps us in this state of suspended attention, in this oscillating process of looking. Its meaning is always in the process of emerging, yet any final meaning is constantly deferred.

5   You can tell a great deal about how the picture works as a discourse, and what it means, by following the orchestration of *looking* – who is looking at what or whom. *Our* look – the eyes of the person looking at the picture, the spectator – follows the relationships of looking as represented in the picture.

We know the figure of the Infanta is important because her attendants are looking at her. But we know that someone even more important is sitting in front of the scene whom we can't see, because many figures – the Infanta, the jester, the painter himself – are looking at them! So the spectator (who is also 'subjected' to the discourse of the painting) is doing two kinds of looking. Looking at the scene from the position outside, in front of, the picture. And at the same time, looking out of the scene, by *identifying with* the looking being done by the figures in the painting. Projecting ourselves into the subjects of the painting help us as spectators to see, to 'make sense' of it. We take up the positions indicated by the discourse, identify with them, subject ourselves to its meanings, and become its 'subjects'.

6   It is critical for Foucault's argument that the painting does not have a completed meaning. It only means something in relation to the spectator who is looking at it. The spectator completes the meaning of the picture. Meaning is therefore constructed in the dialogue between the painting and the spectator. Velasquez, of course, could not know who would subsequently occupy the position of the spectator. Nevertheless, the whole 'scene' of the painting had to be laid out in relation to that ideal point in front of the painting from which *any* spectator must look if the painting is to make sense. The spectator, we might say, is painted into position in front of the picture. In this sense, the discourse produces a *subject-position* for the spectator-subject. For the painting to work, the spectator, whoever he or she may be, must first 'subject' himself/herself to the painting's discourse and, in this way, become the painting's ideal viewer, the producer of its meanings – its 'subject'. This is what is meant by saying that the discourse constructs the spectator as a subject – by which we mean that it constructs a place for the subject-spectator who is looking at and making sense of it.

7   Representation therefore occurs from at least three positions in the painting. First of all there is us, the spectator, whose 'look' puts together and unifies the different elements and relationships in the picture into an overall meaning. This subject must be there for the painting to make sense, but he/she is not represented in the painting.

Then there is the painter who painted the scene. He is 'present' in two places at once, since he must at one time have been standing where we are now sitting, in order to paint the scene, but he has then put himself into (represented himself in) the picture, looking back towards that point of view where we, the spectator, have taken his place. We may also say that the scene makes sense and is pulled together in relation to the court figure standing on the stair at the back, since he too surveys it all but – like us and like the painter – from somewhat outside it.

8   Finally, consider the mirror on the back wall. If it were a 'real' mirror, it should now be representing or reflecting *us*, since we are standing in that position in front of the scene to which everyone is looking and from which everything makes sense. But it does not mirror us, it shows *in our place* the King and Queen of Spain. Somehow the discourse of the painting positions us

in the place of the Sovereign! You can imagine what fun Foucault had with this substitution.

Foucault argues that it is clear from the way the discourse of representation works in the painting that it *must* be looked at and made sense of from that one subject-position in front of it from which we, the spectators, are looking. This is also the point-of-view from which a camera would have to be positioned in order to film the scene. And, lo and behold, the person whom Velasquez chooses to 'represent' sitting in this position is The Sovereign – 'master of all he surveys' – who is both the 'subject of' the painting (what it is about) and the 'subject in' the painting – the one whom the discourse sets in place, but who, simultaneously, makes sense of it and understands it all by a look of supreme mastery.

6   Conclusion: representation, meaning and language reconsidered

We started with a fairly simple definition of representation. Representation is the process by which members of a culture use language (broadly defined as any system which deploys signs, any signifying system) to produce meaning. Already, this definition carries the important premise that things – objects, people, events, in the world – do not have in themselves any fixed, final or true meaning. It is us – in society, within human cultures – who make things mean, who signify. Meanings, consequently, will always change, from one culture or period to another. There is no guarantee that every object in one culture will have an equivalent meaning in another, precisely because cultures differ, sometimes radically, from one another in their codes – the ways they carve up, classify and assign meaning to the world. So one important idea about representation is the acceptance of a degree of *cultural relativism* between one culture and another, a certain lack of equivalence, and hence the need for *translation* as we move from the mind-set or conceptual universe of one culture or another.

We call this the *constructionist* approach to representation, contrasting it with both the *reflective* and the *intentional* approaches. Now, if culture is a process, a practice, how does it work? In the *constructionist perspective*, representation involves making meaning by forging links between three different orders of things: what we might broadly call the world of things, people, events and experiences; the conceptual world – the mental concepts we carry around in our heads; and the signs, arranged into languages, which 'stand for' or communicate these concepts. Now, if you have to make a link between systems which are not the same, and fix these at least for a time so that other people know what, in one system, corresponds to what in another system, then there must be something which allows us to translate between them – telling us what word to use for what concept, and so on. Hence the notion of *codes*.

Producing meaning depends on the practice of interpretation, and interpretation is sustained by us actively using the code – *encoding*, putting things into the code – and by the person at the other end interpreting or *decoding* the meaning (Hall, 1980). But note, that, because meanings are always changing and slipping, codes operate more like social conventions than like fixed laws or unbreakable rules. As meanings shift and slide, so inevitably the codes of a culture imperceptibly change. The great advantage of the concepts and classifications of the culture which we carry around with us in our heads is that they enable us to *think* about things, whether they are there, present, or not; indeed, whether they ever existed or not. There are concepts for our fantasies, desires and imaginings as well as for so-called 'real' objects in the material world. And the advantage of language is that our thoughts about the world need not remain exclusive to us, and silent. We can translate them into language, make them 'speak', through the use of signs which stand for them – and thus talk, write, communicate about them to others.

Gradually, then, we complexified what we meant by representation. It came to be less and less the straightforward thing we assumed it to be at first – which is why we need *theories* to explain it. We looked at two versions of constructionism – that which concentrated on how *language* and *signification* (the use of signs in language) works to produce *meanings*, which after Saussure and Barthes we called *semiotics*; and that, following Foucault, which concentrated on how *discourse* and *discursive practices* produce knowledge. I won't run through the finer points in these two approaches again, since you can go back to them in the main body of the chapter and refresh your memory. In semiotics, you will recall the importance of signifier/ signified, *langue/parole* and 'myth', and how the marking of difference and binary oppositions are crucial for meaning. In the *discursive* approach, you will recall discursive formations, power/knowledge, the idea of a 'regime of truth', the way discourse also produces the subject and defines the *subject-positions* from which knowledge proceeds and indeed, the return of questions about 'the subject' to the field of representation. In several examples, we tried to get you to work with these theories and to apply them. There will be further debate about them in subsequent chapters.

Notice that the chapter does *not* argue that the *discursive* approach overturned everything in the *semiotic* approach. Theoretical development does not usually proceed in this linear way. There was much to learn from Saussure and Barthes, and we are still discovering ways of fruitfully applying their insights – without necessarily swallowing everything they said. We offered you some critical thoughts on the subject. There is a great deal to learn from Foucault and the *discursive* approach, but by no means everything it claims is correct and the theory is open to, and has attracted, many criticisms. Again, in later chapters, as we encounter further developments in the theory of representation, and see the strengths and weaknesses of these positions applied in practice, we will come to appreciate more fully that we are only at the beginning of the exciting task of exploring this process of meaning construction, which is at the heart of culture, to its full depths. What we have offered here is, we hope, a relatively clear account of a set of complex, and as yet tentative, ideas in an unfinished project.

References

BARTHES, R. (1967) *The Elements of Semiology*, London, Cape.

BARTHES, R. (1972) *Mythologies*, London, Cape.

BARTHES, R. (1972a) 'The world of wrestling' in *Mythologies*, London, Cape.

BARTHES, R. (1972b) 'Myth today' in *Mythologies*, London, Cape.

BARTHES, R. (1975) *The Pleasure of the Text*, New York, Hall and Wang.

BARTHES, R. (1977) *Image–Music–Text*, Glasgow, Fontana.

BRYSON, N. (1990) *Looking at the Overlooked: four essays on still life painting*, London, Reaktion Books.

COUSINS, M. and HUSSAIN, A. (1984) *Michel Foucault*, Basingstoke, Macmillan.

CULLER, J. (1976) *Saussure*, London, Fontana.

DERRIDA, J. (1981) *Positions*, Chicago, IL, University of Chicago Press.

DREYFUS, H. and RABINOW, P. (eds) (1982) *Beyond Stucturalism and Hermeneutics,* Brighton, Harvester.

DU GAY, P. (ed.) (1997) *Production of Culture/Cultures of Production*, London, Sage/The Open University (Book 4 in this series).

DU GAY, P., HALL, S., JANES, L., MACKAY, H. and NEGUS, K. (1997) *Doing Cultural Studies: the story of the Sony Walkman*, London, Sage/The Open University (Book 1 in this series).

FOUCAULT, M. (1970) *The Order of Things*, London, Tavistock.

FOUCAULT, M. (1972) *The Archaeology of Knowledge*, London, Tavistock.

FOUCAULT, M. (1973) *The Birth of the Clinic*, London, Tavistock.

FOUCAULT, M. (1978) *The History of Sexuality*, Harmondsworth, Allen Lane/ Penguin Books.

FOUCAULT, M. (1977a) *Discipline and Punish*, London, Tavistock.

FOUCAULT, M. (1977b) 'Nietzsche, genealogy, history', in *Language, Counter-Memory, Practice*, Oxford, Blackwell.

FOUCAULT, M. (1980) *Power/Knowledge,* Brighton, Harvester.

FOUCAULT, M. (1982) 'The subject and power' in Dreyfus and Rabinow (eds).

FREUD, S. and BREUER, J. (1974) *Studies on Hysteria*, Harmondsworth, Pelican. First published 1895.

GAY, P. (1988) *Freud: a life for our time*, London, Macmillan.

HALL, S. (1980) 'Encoding and decoding' in Hall, S. et al. (eds) *Culture, Media, Language*, London, Hutchinson.

HALL, S.(1992) 'The West and the Rest', in Hall, S. and Gieben, B. (eds) *Formations of Modernity*, Cambridge, Polity Press/The Open University.

HOEG, P. (1994) *Miss Smilla's Feeling For Snow*, London, Flamingo.

LACLAU, E. and MOUFFE, C. (1990) 'Post-Marxism without apologies' in Laclau, E., *New Reflections on the Revolution of our Time*, London, Verso.

MCNAY, L. (1994) *Foucault: a critical introduction*, Cambridge, Polity Press.

MACKAY, H. (ed.) (1997) *Consumption and Everyday Life*, London, Sage/The Open University (Book 5 in this series).

SAUSSURE, F. DE (1960) *Course in General Linguistics*, London, Peter Owen.

SHOWALTER, E. (1987) *The Female Malady*, London, Virago.

WEEKS, J. (1981) *Sex, Politics and Society*, London, Longman.

WEEKS, J. (1985) *Sexuality and its Discontents*, London, Routledge.

READING A:
Norman Bryson, 'Language, reflection and still life'

With Cotán, too, the images have as their immediate function the separation of the viewer from the previous mode of seeing […]: they decondition the habitual and abolish the endless eclipsing and fatigue of worldly vision, replacing these with brilliance. The enemy is a mode of seeing which thinks it knows in advance what is worth looking at and what is not: against that, the image presents the constant surprise of things seen for the first time. Sight is taken back to a [primal] stage before it learned how to scotomise [break up/ divide] the visual field, how to screen out the unimportant and not *see*, but scan. In place of the abbreviated forms for which the world scans, Cotán supplies forms that are articulated at immense length, forms so copious or prolix that one cannot see where or how to begin to simplify them. They offer no inroads for reduction because they omit nothing. Just at the point where the eye thinks it knows the form and can afford to skip, the image proves that in fact the eye had not understood at all what it was about to discard.

The relation proposed in Cotán between the viewer and the foodstuffs so meticulously displayed seems to involve, paradoxically, no reference to appetite or to the function of sustenance which becomes coincidental; it might be described as anorexic, taking this word in its literal and Greek sense as meaning 'without desire'. All Cotán's still lifes are rooted in the outlook of monasticism, specifically the monasticism of the Carthusians [monks], whose order Cotán jointed as a lay brother in Toledo in 1603. What distinguishes the Carthusian rule is its stress on solitude over communal life: the monks live in individual cells, where they pray, study – and eat – alone, meeting only for the night office, morning mass and afternoon vespers. There is total abstention from meat, and on Fridays and other fast days the diet is bread and water. Absent from Cotán's work is any conception of nourishment as involving the conviviality of the meal – the sharing of hospitality[…]. The unvarying stage of his paintings is never the kitchen but always the *cantarero*, a cooling-space where for preservation the foods are often hung on strings (piled together,

or in contact with a surface, they would decay more quickly). Placed in a kitchen, next to plates and knives, bowls and pitchers, the objects would inevitably point towards their consumption at table, but the *cantarero* maintains the idea of the objects as separable from, dissociated from, their function as food. In *Quince, Cabbage, Melon and Cucumber* [Figure 1.3] no-one can touch the suspended quince or cabbage without disturbing them and setting them rocking in space: their motionlessness is the mark of human absence, distance from the hand that reaches to eat; and it renders them immaculate. Hanging on strings, the quince and the cabbage lack the weight known to the hand. Their weightlessness disowns such intimate knowledge. Having none of the familiarity that comes from touch, and divorced from the idea of consumption, the objects take on a value that is nothing to do with their role as nourishment.

What replaces their interest as sustenance is their interest as mathematical form. Like many painters of his period in Spain, Cotán has a highly developed sense of geometrical order; but whereas the ideas of sphere, ellipse and cone are used for example in El Greco to assist in organising pictorial composition, here they are explored almost for their own sake. One can think of *Quince, Cabbage, Melon and Cucumber* as an experiment in the kind of transformations that are explored in the branch of mathematics know as topology. We begin on the left with the quince, a pure sphere revolving on its axis. Moving to the right, the sphere seems to peel off its boundary and disintegrate into a ball of concentric shells revolving around the same vertical axis. Moving to the melon the sphere becomes an ellipse, from which a segment has been cut; a part of the segment is independently shown. At the right the segmented shapes recover their continuous boundary in the corrugated form of the cucumber. The curve described by all these objects taken together is not at all informal but precisely logarithmic; it follows a series of harmonic or musical proportions with the vertical co-ordinates of the curve exactly marked by the strings. And it is a complex curve, not just the arc of a graph on a two-dimensional surface . In relation to the quince, the cabbage appears to come forward slightly; the melon is further forward than the quince, the melon slice projects out beyond the ledge, and the cucumber overhangs it still further. The arc is therefore not on the same plane as its co-ordinates, it curves in three dimensions: it is a true hyperbola [...]

The mathematical engagement of these forms shows every sign of exact calculation, as though the scene were being viewed with scientific, but not with creaturely, interest. Geometric space replaces creatural space, the space around the body that is known by touch and is created by familiar movements of the hands and arms. Cotán's play with geometric and volumetric ideas replaces this cocoon-like space, defined by habitual gestures, with an abstracted and homogeneous space which has broken with the matrix of the body. This is the point: to suppress the body as a source of space. That bodily or tactile space is profoundly unvisual: the things we find there are things we reach for – a knife, a plate, a bit of food – instinctively and almost without looking. It is this space, the true home of blurred and hazy vision, that Cotán's rigours aim to abolish. And the tendency to geometrise fulfils another aim, no less severe: to disavow the painter's work as the source of the composition and to re-assign responsibility for its forms elsewhere – to mathematics, not creativity. In much of still life, the painter first arrays the objects into a satisfactory configuration, and then uses that arrangement as the basis for the composition. But to organise the world pictorially in this fashion is to impose upon it an order that is infinitely inferior to the order already revealed to the soul through the contemplation of geometric form: Cotán's renunciation of composition is a further, private act of self-negation. He approaches painting in terms of a discipline, or ritual: always the same *cantarero*, which one must assume has been painted in first, as a blank template; always the same recurring elements, the light raking at forty-five degrees, the same alternation of bright greens and yellows against the grey ground, the same scale, the same size of frame. To alter any of these would be to allow too much room for personal self-assertion, and the pride of creativity; down to its last details the painting must be presented as the result of discovery, not invention, a picture of the work of God that completely effaces the hand of man (in Cotán visible brushwork would be like blasphemy).

Source: Bryson, 1990, pp. 65–70.

READING B:
Roland Barthes, 'The world of wrestling'

[T]he function of the wrestler is not to win; it is to go exactly through the motions which are expected of him. It is said that judo contains a hidden symbolic aspect; even in the midst of efficiency, its gestures are measured, precise but restricted, drawn accurately but by a stroke without volume. Wrestling, on the contrary, offers excessive gestures, exploited to the limit of their meaning. In judo, a man who is down is hardly down at all, he rolls over, he draws back, he eludes defeat, or, if the latter is obvious, he immediately disappears; in wrestling, a man who is down is exaggeratedly so, and completely fills the eyes of the spectators with the intolerable spectacle of his powerlessness.

This function of grandiloquence is indeed the same as that of ancient theatre, whose principle, language and props (masks and buskins) concurred in the exaggeratedly visible [...]. The gesture of the vanquished wrestler [signifies] to the world a defeat which, far from disguising, he emphasizes and holds like a pause in music [...]. [This is] meant to signify the tragic mode of the spectacle. In wrestling, as on the stage in antiquity, one is not ashamed of one's suffering, one knows how to cry, one has a liking for tears.

Each sign in wrestling is therefore endowed with an absolute clarity, since one must always understand everything on the spot. As soon as the adversaries are in the ring, the public is overwhelmed with the obviousness of the roles. As in the theatre, each physical type expresses to excess the part which has been assigned to the contestant. Thauvin, a fifty-year-old with an obese and sagging body, whose type of asexual hideousness always inspires feminine nicknames, displays in his flesh the characters of baseness ... [H]is part is to represent what, in the classical concept of the *salaud*, the 'bastard' (the key-concept of any wrestling-match), appears as organically repugnant. The nausea voluntarily provoked by Thauvin shows therefore a very extended use of signs: not only is ugliness used here in order to signify baseness, but in addition ugliness is wholly gathered into a particularly repulsive quality of matter: the pallid collapse of dead flesh (the public calls Thauvin *la barbaque*, 'stinking meat'), so that the passionate condemnation of the crowd no longer stems from its judgement, but instead from the very depth of its humours. It will thereafter let itself be frenetically embroiled in an idea of Thauvin which will conform entirely with this physical origin: his actions will perfectly correspond to the essential viscosity of his personage.

It is therefore in the body of the wrestler that we find the first key to the contest. I know from the start that all of Thauvin's actions, his treacheries, cruelties and acts of cowardice, will not fail to measure up to the first image of ignobility he gave me; I can trust him to carry out intelligently and to the last detail all the gestures of a kind of amorphous baseness, and thus fill to the brim the image of the most repugnant bastard there is: the bastard-octopus. Wrestlers therefore have a physique as peremptory as those of the characters of the *Commedia dell'Arte*, who display in advance, in their costumes and attitudes, the future contents of their parts: just as Pantaloon can never be anything but a ridiculous cuckold, Harlequin an astute servant and the Doctor a stupid pedant, in the same way Thauvin will never be anything but an ignoble traitor, Reinières (a tall blond fellow with a limp body and unkempt hair) the moving image of passivity, Mazaud (short and arrogant like a cock) that of grotesque conceit, and Orsano (an effeminate teddy-boy first seen in a blue-and-pink dressing-gown) that, doubly humorous, of a vindictive *salope*, or bitch (for I do not think that the public of the Elysée-Montmartre, like Littré, believes the word *salope* to be a masculine).

The physique of the wrestlers therefore constitutes a basic sign, which like a seed contains the whole fight. But this seed proliferates, for it is at every turn during the fight, in each new situation, that the body of the wrestler casts to the public the magical entertainment of a temperament which finds its natural expression in a gesture. The different strata of meaning throw light on each other, and form the most intelligible of spectacles. Wrestling is like a diacritic writing: above the fundamental meaning of his body, the wrestler arranges comments which are episodic but always opportune, and constantly help the reading of the fight by means of gestures, attitudes and mimicry which make the intention utterly obvious.

Sometimes the wrestler triumphs with a repulsive sneer while kneeling on the good sportsman; sometimes he gives the crowd a conceited smile which forebodes an early revenge; sometimes, pinned to the ground, he hits the floor ostentatiously to make evident to all the intolerable nature of his situation; and sometimes he erects a complicated set of signs meant to make the public understand that he legitimately personifies the ever-entertaining image of the grumbler, endlessly confabulating about his displeasure.

We are therefore dealing with a real Human Comedy, where the most socially-inspired nuances of passion (conceit, rightfulness, refined cruelty, a sense of 'paying one's debts') always felicitously find the clearest sign which can receive them, express them and triumphantly carry them to the confines of the hall. It is obvious that at such a pitch, it no longer matters whether the passion is genuine or not. What the public wants is the image of passion, not passion itself. There is no more a problem of truth in wrestling than in the theatre. In both, what is expected is the intelligible representation of moral situations which are usually private. This emptying out of interiority to the benefit of its exterior signs, this exhaustion of the content by the form, is the very principle of triumphant classical art. [...]

Source: Barthes, 1972a, pp. 16–18.

READING C:
Roland Barthes, 'Myth today'

In myth, we find again the tri-dimensional pattern which I have just described: the signifier, the signified and the sign. But myth is a peculiar system, in that it is constructed from a semiological chain which existed before it: it *is a second-order semiological system*. That which is a sign (namely the associative total of a concept and an image) in the first system, becomes a mere signifier in the second. We must here recall that the materials of mythical speech (the language itself, photography, painting, posters, rituals, objects, etc.), however different at the start, are reduced to a pure signifying function as soon as they are caught by myth. Myth sees in them only the same raw material; their unity is that they all come down to the status of a mere language. Whether it deals with alphabetical or pictorial writing, myth wants to see in them only a sum of signs, a global sign, the final term of a first semiological chain. And it is precisely this final term which will become the first term of the greater system which it builds and of which it is only a part. Everything happens as if myth shifted the formal system of the first significations sideways. As this lateral shift is essential for the analysis of myth, I shall represent it in the following way, it being understood, of course, that the spatialization of the pattern is here only a metaphor:

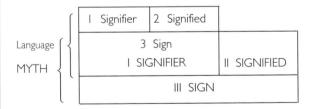

It can be seen that in myth there are two semiological systems, one of which is staggered in relation to the other: a linguistic system, the language (or the modes of representation which are assimilated to it), which I shall call the *language-object*, because it is the language which myth gets hold of in order to build its own system; and myth itself, which I shall call *metalanguage*, because it is a second language, *in which* one speaks about the first. When he reflects on a metalanguage, the semiologist no longer needs to ask himself questions about the composition of the language-object, he no longer has to take into account the details of the linguistic schema; he will only need to know its total term, or global sign, and only inasmuch as this term lends itself to myth. This is why the semiologist is entitled to treat in the same way writing and pictures: what he retains from them is the fact that they are both *signs*, that they both reach the threshold of myth endowed with the same signifying function, that they constitute one just as much as the other, a language-object.

Source: Barthes, 1972b, pp. 114-5.

READING D:
Roland Barthes, 'Rhetoric of the image'

Here we have a Panzani advertisement: some packets of pasta, a tin, a sachet, some tomatoes, onions, peppers, a mushroom, all emerging from a half-open string bag, in yellows and greens on a red background. Let us try to 'skim off' the different messages it contains.

The image immediately yields a first message whose substance is linguistic; its supports are the caption, which is marginal, and the labels, these being inserted into the natural disposition of the scene […]. The code from which this message has been taken is none other than that of the French language; the only knowledge required to decipher it is a knowledge of writing and French. In fact, this message can itself be further broken down, for the sign *Panzani* gives not simply the name of the firm but also, by its assonance, an additional signified, that of 'Italianicity'. The linguistic message is thus twofold (at least in this particular image): denotational and connotational. Since, however, we have here only a single typical sign, namely that of articulated (written) language, it will be counted as one message.

Putting aside the linguistic message, we are left with the pure image (even if the labels are part of it, anecdotally). This image straightaway provides a series of discontinuous signs. First (the order is unimportant as these signs are not linear), the idea that what we have in the scene represented is a return from the market. A signified which itself implies two euphoric values: that of the freshness of the products and that of the essentially domestic preparation for which they are destined. Its signifier is the half-open bag which lets the provisions spill out over the table, 'unpacked'. To read this first sign requires only a knowledge which is in some sort implanted as part of the habits of a very widespread culture where 'shopping around for oneself' is opposed to the hasty stocking up (preserves, refrigerators) of a more 'mechanical' civilization. A second sign is more or less equally evident; its signifier is the bringing together of the tomato, the pepper and the tricoloured hues (yellow, green, red) of the poster; its signified is Italy or rather *Italianicity*. This sign stands in a relation of redundancy with the connoted sign of the linguistic message (the Italian assonance of the name *Panzani*) and the knowledge it draws upon is already more particular; it is a specifically 'French' knowledge (an Italian would barely perceive the connotation of the name, no more probably than he would the Italianicity of tomato and pepper), based on a familiarity with certain tourist stereotypes. Continuing to explore the image (which is not to say that it is not entirely clear at the first glance), there is no difficulty in discovering at least two other signs: in the first, the serried collection of different objects transmits the idea of a total culinary service, on the one hand as though Panzani furnished everything necessary for a carefully balanced dish and on the other as though the concentrate in the tin were equivalent to the natural produce surrounding it; in the other sign, the composition of the image, evoking the memory of innumerable alimentary paintings, sends us to an aesthetic signified: the '*nature morte*' or, as it is better expressed in other languages, the 'still life'; the knowledge on which this sign depends is heavily cultural. […]

Source: Barthes, 1977, pp. 33–5.

READING E:
Ernesto Laclau and Chantal Mouffe, 'New reflections on the revolution of our time'

Discourse

[...] Let us suppose that I am building a wall with another bricklayer. At a certain moment I ask my workmate to pass me a brick and then I add it to the wall. The first act – asking for the brick – is linguistic; the second – adding the brick to the wall –is extralinguistic. Do I exhaust the reality of both acts by drawing the distinction between them in terms of the linguistic/extralinguistic opposition? Evidently not, because, despite their differentiation in those terms, the two actions share something that allows them to be compared, namely the fact that they are both part of a total operation which is the building of the wall. So, then, how could we characterize this totality of which asking for a brick and positioning it are, both, partial moments? Obviously, if this totality includes both linguistic and non-linguistic elements, it cannot itself be either linguistic or extralinguistic; it has to be prior to this distinction. This totality which includes within itself the linguistic and the non-linguistic, is what we call discourse. In a moment we will justify this denomination; but what must be clear from the start is that by discourse we do not mean a combination of speech and writing, but rather that speech and writing are themselves but internal components of discursive totalities.

Now, turning to the term discourse itself, we use it to emphasize the fact that every social configuration is *meaningful*. If I kick a spherical object in the street or if I kick a ball in a football match, the *physical* fact is the same, but *its meaning* is different. The object is a football only to the extent that it establishes a system of relations with other objects, and these relations are not given by the mere referential materiality of the objects, but are, rather, socially constructed. This systematic set of relations is what we call discourse. The reader will no doubt see that, as we showed in our book, the discursive character of an object does not, by any means, imply putting its *existence* into question. The fact that a football is only a football as long as it is integrated within a system of socially constructed rules does not mean that it thereby ceases to be a physical object. A stone exists independently of any system of social relations, but it is, for instance, either a projectile or an object of aesthetic contemplation only within a specific discursive configuration. A diamond in the market or at the bottom of a mine is the same physical object; but, again, it is only a commodity within a determinate system of social relations. For that same reason it is the discourse which constitutes the subject position of the social agent, and not, therefore, the social agent which is the origin of discourse – the same system of rules that makes that spherical object into a football, makes me a player. The existence of objects is independent of their discursive articulation [...].

[...] This, however, leaves two problems unsolved. The first is this: is it not necessary to establish here a distinction between meaning and action? Even if we accept that the meaning of an action depends on a discursive configuration, is not the action itself something different from that meaning? Let us consider the problem from two angles. Firstly, from the angle of meaning. Here the classical distinction is between semantics – dealing with the meaning of words; syntactics – dealing with word order and its consequences for meaning; and pragmatics – dealing with the way a word is actually used in certain speech contexts. The key point is to what extent a rigid separation can be established between semantics and pragmatics – that is, between meaning and use. From Wittgenstein onwards it is precisely this separation which has grown ever more blurred. It has become increasingly accepted that the meaning of a word is entirely context-dependent. As Hanna Fenichel Pitkin points out:

> Wittgenstein argues that meaning and use are intimately, inextricably related, because use helps to determine meaning. Meaning is learned from, and shaped in, instances of use; so both its learning and its configuration depend on pragmatics. ... Semantic meaning is compounded out of cases of a word's use, including all the many and varied language games that are played with it; so meaning is very much the product of pragmatics.
>
> (Pitkin, 1972)

[…] That is to say, in our terminology, every identity or discursive object is constituted in the context of an action. […]

The other problem to be considered is the following: even if we assume that there is a strict equation between the social and the discursive, what can we say about the natural world, about the facts of physics, biology or astronomy that are not apparently integrated in meaningful totalities constructed by men? The answer is that natural facts are also discursive facts. And they are so for the simple reason that the idea of nature is not something that is already there, to be read from the appearances of things, but is itself the result of a slow and complex historical and social construction. To call something a natural object is a way of conceiving it that depends upon a classificatory system. Again, this does not put into question the fact that this entity which we call a stone exists, in the sense of being present here and now, independently of my will; nevertheless the fact of its being a stone depends on a way of classifying objects that is historical and contingent. If there were no human beings on earth, those objects that we call stones would be there nonetheless; but they would not be 'stones', because there would be neither mineralogy nor a language capable of classifying them and distinguishing them from other objects. We need not stop for long on this point. The entire development of contemporary epistemology has established that there is no fact that allows its meaning to be read transparently.

Reference

Pitkin, H.F. (1972) *Wittgenstein and Justice*, Berkeley, CA, University of Californa Press.

Source: Laclau and Mouffe, 1990, pp. 100–103.

READING F:
Elaine Showalter, 'The performance of hysteria'

The first of the great European theorists of hysteria was Jean-Martin Charcot (1825–1893), who carried out his work in the Paris clinic at the Salpêtrière. Charcot had begun his work on hysteria in 1870. While he believed that hysterics suffered from a hereditary taint that weakened their nervous system, he also developed a theory that hysteria had psychological origins. Experimenting with hypnosis, Charcot demonstrated that hysterical symptoms such as paralysis could be produced and relieved by hypnotic suggestion. Through careful observation, physical examination, and the use of hypnosis, Charcot was able to prove that hysterical symptoms, while produced by emotions rather than by physical injury, were genuine, and not under the conscious control of the patient. Freud, who studied at the Salpêtrière from October 1885 to February 1886, gave Charcot the credit for establishing the legitimacy of hysteria as a disorder. According to Freud, 'Charcot's work restored dignity to the subject; gradually the sneering attitude which the hysteric could reckon meeting with when she told her story, was given up; she was no longer a malingerer, since Charcot had thrown the whole weight of his authority on the side of the reality and objectivity of hysterical phenomena.' Furthermore, Charcot demonstrated that hysterical symptoms also occurred in men, and were not simply related to the vagaries of the female reproductive system. At the Salpêtrière there was even a special wing for male hysterics, who were frequently the victims of trauma from railway accidents. In restoring the credibility of the hysteric, Freud believed, Charcot had joined other psychiatric saviors of women and had 'repeated on a small scale the act of liberation commemorated in the picture of Pinel which adorned the lecture hall of the Salpêtrière' (Freud, 1948, p. 18).

Yet for Charcot, too, hysteria remained symbolically, if not medically, a female malady. By far the majority of his hysterical patients were women, and several, such as Blanche Wittmann, known as the 'Queen of the Hysterics,' became celebrities who were regularly featured in his books, the main attractions at the Salpêtrière's Bal des Folles, and hypnotized and exhibited at his popular public lectures. Axel Munthe, a doctor practicing in Paris, wrote a vivid description of Charcot's Tuesday lectures at the Salpêtrière: 'The huge amphitheatre was filled to the last place with a multicoloured audience drawn from tout Paris, authors, journalists, leading actors and actresses, fashionable demimondaines.' The hypnotized women patients put on a spectacular show before this crowd of curiosity seekers.

> Some of them smelt with delight a bottle of ammonia when told it was rose water, others would eat a piece of charcoal when presented to them as chocolate. Another would crawl on all fours on the floor, barking furiously when told she was a dog, flap her arms as if trying to fly when turned into a pigeon, lift her skirts with a shriek of terror when a glove was thrown at her feet with a suggestion of being a snake. Another would walk with a top hat in her arms rocking it to and fro and kissing it tenderly when she was told it was her baby.
>
> (Munthe, 1930, pp. 296, 302–3)

The grand finale would be the performance of a full hysterical seizure.

Furthermore, the representation of female hysteria was a central aspect of Charcot's work. His hysterical women patients were surrounded by images of female hysteria. In the lecture hall, as Freud noted, was Robert-Fleury's painting of Pinel freeing the madwomen. On the opposite wall was a famous lithograph of Charcot, holding and lecturing about a swooning and half-undressed young woman before a room of sober and attentive men, yet another representation that seemed to be instructing the hysterical woman in her act [Figure 1.8].

Finally, Charcot's use of photography was the most extensive in nineteenth-century psychiatric practice. As one of his admirers remarked, 'The camera was as crucial to the study of hysteria as the microscope was to histology' (quoted in Goldstein, 1982, p. 215). In 1875 one of his assistants, Paul Régnard, had assembled an album of photographs of female nervous patients. The pictures of women exhibiting various phases of hysterical attacks were deemed so interesting that a photographic workshop or atelier was installed within the hospital. By the 1880s a professional photographer,

Albert Londe, had been brought in to take charge of a full-fledged photographic service. Its methods included not only the most advanced technology and apparatus, such as laboratories, a studio with platforms, a bed, screens, black, dark-gray, and light-gray background curtains, headrests, and an iron support for feeble patients, but also elaborate adminstrative techniques of observation, selection of models, and record-keeping. The photographs of women were published in three volumes called *Iconographie photographique de la Salpêtrière.* Thus Charcot's hospital became an environment in which female hysteria was perpetually presented, represented, and reproduced.

Such techniques appealed to Charcot because his approach to psychiatric analysis was strongly visual and imagistic. As Freud has explained, Charcot 'had an artistically gifted temperament – as he said himself, he was a '*visuel*', a seer. ... He was accustomed to look again and again at things that were incomprehensible to him, to deepen his impression of them day by day until suddenly understanding of them dawned upon him' (Freud, 1948, pp. 10–11). Charcot's public lectures were among the first to use visual aids – pictures, graphs, statues, models, and illustrations that he drew on the blackboard in colored chalk – as well as the presence of the patients as models.

The specialty of the house at the Salpêtrière was *grande hystérie*, or 'hystero-epilepsy,' a prolonged and elaborate convulsive seizure that occurred in women. A complete seizure involved three phases: the epileptoid phase, in which the woman lost consciousness and foamed at the mouth; the phase of clownism, involving eccentric physical contortions; and the phase of *attitudes passionnelles*, a miming of incidents and emotions from the patient's life. In the *iconographies,* photographs of this last phase were given subtitles that suggested Charcot's interpretation of hysterical gestures as linked to female sexuality, despite his disclaimers: 'amorous supplication', 'ecstasy', eroticism' [Figure 1.10]. This interpretation of hysterical gestures as sexual was reinforced by Charcot's efforts to pinpoint areas of the body that might induce convulsions when pressed. The ovarian region, he concluded, was a particularly sensitive hysterogenic zone.

Because the behavior of Charcot's hysterical stars was so theatrical, and because it was rarely

FIGURE 1.10 Two portraits of Augustine: (top) Amorous supplication, (bottom) Ecstasy.

observed outside of the Parisian clinical setting, many of his contemporaries, as well as subsequent medical historians, have suspected that the women's performances were the result of suggestion, imitation, or even fraud. In Charcot's own lifetime, one of his assistants admitted that some of the women had been coached in order to produce attacks that would please the *maître* (discussed in Drinker, 1984, pp. 144–8). Furthermore, there was a dramatic increase in the incidence of hysteria during Charcot's tenure at the Salpêtrière. From only 1 percent in 1845, it rose to 17.3 percent of all diagnoses in 1883, at the height of his experimentation with hysterical patients (see Goldstein, 1982, pp. 209–10).

When challenged about the legitimacy of hystero-epilepsy, however, Charcot vigorously defended the objectivity of his vision. 'It seems that hystero-epilepsy only exists in France,' he declared in a lecture of 1887, 'and I could even say, as it has sometimes been said, that it only exists at the Salpêtrière, as if I had created it by the force of my will. It would be truly marvellous if I were thus able to create illnesses at the pleasure of my whim and my caprice. But as for the truth, I am absolutely only the photographer; I register what I see' (quoted in Didi-Huberman, 1982, p. 32). Like Hugh Diamond at the Surrey Asylum, Charcot and his followers had absolute faith in the scientific neutrality of the photographic image; Londe boasted: 'La plaque photographique est la vraie rétine du savant' ('The photographic plate is the true retina of the scientist') (ibid., p. 35).

But Charcot's photographs were even more elaborately framed and staged than Diamond's Victorian asylum pictures. Women were not simply photographed once, but again and again, so that they became used to the camera and to the special status they received as photogenic subjects. Some made a sort of career out of modeling for the *iconographies*. Among the most frequently photographed was a fifteen-year-old girl named Augustine, who had entered the hospital in 1875. Her hysterical attacks had begun at the age of thirteen when, according to her testimony, she had been raped by her employer, a man who was also her mother's lover. Intelligent, coquettish, and eager to please, Augustine was an apt pupil of the atelier. All of her poses suggest the exaggerated gestures of the French classical acting style, or stills from silent movies. Some photographs of Augustine with flowing locks and white hospital gown also seem to imitate poses in nineteenth-century paintings, as Stephen Heath points out: 'a young girl composed on her bed, something of the Pre-Raphaelite Millais's painting *Ophelia*' (Heath, 1982, pp. 36–7). Among her gifts was her ability to time and divide her hysterical performances into scenes, acts, tableaux, and intermissions, to perform on cue and on schedule with the click of the camera.

But Augustine's cheerful willingness to assume whatever poses her audience desired took its toll on her psyche. During the period when she was being repeatedly photographed, she developed a curious hysterical symptom: she began to see everything in black and white. In 1880, she began to rebel against the hospital regime; she had periods of violence in which she tore her clothes and broke windows. During these angry outbreaks she was anaesthetized with ether or chloroform. In June of that year, the doctors gave up their efforts with her case, and she was put in a locked cell. But Augustine was able to use in her own behalf the histrionic abilities that for a time had made her a star of the asylum. Disguising herself as a man, she managed to escape from the Salpêtrière. Nothing further was ever discovered about her whereabouts.

References

DIDI–HUBERMAN, G. (1982) *Invention de l'Hystérie: Charcot et l'Iconographie Photographique de La Salpêtrière*, Paris, Macula.

DRINKER, G. F. (1984) *The Birth of Neurosis: myth, malady and the Victorians*, New York, Simon and Schuster.

FREUD, S. (1948) 'Charcot' in Jones, E. (ed.) *Collected Papers, Vol. 1*, London, Hogarth Press.

GOLDSTEIN, J. (1982) 'The hysteria diagnosis and the politics of anticlericalism in late nineteenth-century France', *Journal of Modern History*, No. 54.

HEATH, S. (1982) *The Sexual Fix*, London, Macmillan.

MUNTHE, A. (1930) *The Story of San Michele*, London, John Murray.

Source: Showalter, 1987, pp. 147–54.

REPRESENTING THE SOCIAL: FRANCE AND FRENCHNESS IN POST-WAR HUMANIST PHOTOGRAPHY

Peter Hamilton

CHAPTER TWO

Contents

1   Introduction: the paradigm of French humanist photography

You will recall the discussion in Chapter 1 of this volume of Roland Barthes's analysis of the semiotics of a *Paris-Match* cover picture of the 1950s, and how the presentation and the encoding of visual elements within that image produced a certain conception of France and French society. This chapter is more widely concerned with photographic representations of society. But rather than taking a single image as its subject, it explores in detail the representational role of a body of images which deal with French society in the era of post-war reconstruction, defined as running from the Liberation of Paris in 1944 until the end of the 1950s. The role of such representations in offering a redefinition of 'Frenchness' to a people which had suffered the agonies and divisions of war, invasion, occupation and collaboration, are explored here, through an examination of the form and content of what we term the **dominant representational paradigm** of illustrative reportage photography in that era.

dominant
representational
paradigm

The concept of dominant representational paradigm indicates that this photographic approach offers a certain vision of the people and events that it documents, a construction which rests on how they were represented by the choices of both photographers and the press. Like all forms of photographic representation it is not simply a 'record' of a given moment, for it cannot be innocent of the values and ethics of those who worked within it. As the previous chapter made clear, we are concerned here with a *constructionist* approach to representation.

It will be important to note that, when we talk about photographers and photography here, we are concerned primarily with professionals producing images for sale to the publishing industry (for newspapers, magazines, books, etc.), and for related commercial purposes (e.g. advertising). Because such uses were widely diffused, the styles of imagery associated with illustrative reportage photography also influenced amateur practice: but we are not concerned with this secondary aspect of representation, fascinating though it may be.

The representational paradigm discussed in this chapter is referred to as 'humanist photography' because its main focus was on the everyday life of ordinary people who – for almost the first time – formed the staple subject-matter of the illustrated press. Along with the radio and cinema newsreels, the illustrated press formed the main source of information and entertainment for the French public in the period from 1945 to the late 1950s: although TV began to be available in this period, the number of television sets in French households did not exceed the significant threshold of one million until 1960.

The argument developed here is that illustrative documentary photography within the paradigm we are concerned with was one amongst a number of important elements contributing to the reconstruction of 'Frenchness' as an inclusive representational category after the 1939–45 war, during a period of considerable tension and instability which included economic penury, colonial wars, political disarray, social strife, rapid industrial development, and major demographic changes.

Through an examination of the development of key representational themes in the work of the main 'humanist' photographers of the time, the chapter explores how their work and its subsequent presentation in the French illustrated press contributed to the creation of a more 'inclusive' image of France, of French society and of French culture during this period.

This is not to argue that humanistic photographers were obsessed above all else with representing France and the French as an inclusive whole, from which division or strife were excluded – for that is manifestly not the case. Neither can their photography (a term used here and throughout the chapter to refer to their professional practices as well as their choice of subject and aesthetic) simply be reduced to a form of propaganda for an 'ideal' Frenchness associated with a particular form of state organization.

Though many of the photographers dealt with in this chapter were, for longer or shorter periods, members of the French communist party in this era, and most if not all would have placed themselves in a broad sense firmly on the left, it would be implausible to argue that a shared political agenda is evident in the form and content of their photography. Although a shared 'social' perspective could more plausibly be identified as providing a unifying thread for this work (in the sense of a common tendency to concentrate upon the urban working class and petty bourgeoisie, and the marginal underclass), a careful reading of this body of photographic work shows that its social aspects were hardly if ever presented in a strident or assertive way. This is probably because these photographers were more interested in representing what, for want of a better term, we must identify as the cultural aspects of Frenchness. To the extent that we can identify strong social and political dimensions in the French humanists' work, these appear as if magnified by their cultural framework, so that, within the most widely characteristic of its images, key aspects of social structure and social interaction, of political order and dissent, appear coloured or coded by the expression of a distinctive Frenchness. Whilst many seemingly universalistic images of childhood, love, or popular entertainment seem to be abundantly available within this body of work, few indeed could really be said to elude the bounds of time and place. This is a photography of the cultural, a body of images which created a system of representations of what made France *French* in a particular era. Its attractions to later generations than those for whom it was originally made – as shown by the widespread appeal of such imagery in the latter part of the 1980s and early 1990s – simply underscores the point.

The approach I take here is underpinned by sociological and historical perspectives on the evolution of a cultural moment. Though this may seem disconcerting, it must be said that we have no way of knowing whether the French humanists provided a fair or typical set of representations of French culture in their imagery: a point I will return to later when referring to the 'truth-value' of documentary photography in section 2. They could not photograph everything: they had to select subjects, and they had to decide how to go about photographing them. Their personal motives thus entered into the choice of subject and into the way in which certain meanings and values were encoded in the content of the image. These things were central to the *paradigm* of French humanist photography, and before we get further into the analysis it will be helpful to outline why and how the concept of *paradigm* is used in this chapter.

1.1 Dominant paradigms in photography

The concept of paradigm first emerged in the history of science, and is associated with the work of Thomas S. Kuhn (1962). He employed it to describe the process by which certain theories about nature come to exert a dominant role in sciences, such as Einsteinian relativity theory in the case of physics. Rather than being a smooth evolutionary process by which knowledge advances incrementally, Kuhn showed that science is characterized by revolutionary upheavals and changes, breakthroughs in which the supporters of new theoretical systems overthrow what they consider to be the outmoded views and practices of their predecessors. He argued that scientific theories, experimental practices, training methods and forms of professional organization and publication 'cluster' together in characteristic ways. These clusters are what he terms a **paradigm** for they offer a complete system whose elements define the very structure and content of the knowledge considered 'scientific'.

paradigm

One important element of the paradigm is that it contains a 'world-view', a set of statements which define its subject-matter, lay out what constitutes the role of the scientist, and at the same time offer scientists working within the paradigm interesting puzzles about the natural world to be solved. Generally speaking, paradigms 'die' when they run out of interesting puzzles to solve, when they come up against anomalies which cannot adequately be dealt with from their theoretical base, and when new groups of scientific 'young Turks' appear with the elements of a new paradigm. Then a 'paradigm-shift' occurs, which allows familiar things to be seen in revolutionary ways. It is only when the community of scientists accepts a new conceptual structure that matters settle down. In between the periods of crises leading up to scientific revolutions, 'normal science' takes place – by which Kuhn means puzzle-solving informed by the conceptual and instrumental framework of the paradigm.

In one sense Kuhn is arguing that scientists like to agree on and then follow the 'scientific' rules of the game, but that every once in a while – and principally when the pay-off from following them has become less rewarding – these rules get radically redefined. So the concept of paradigm covers, amongst other things, this idea that a consensus is formed among scientists over 'the rules of the game'. These tend to be fixed in the form of the scientific community's recognized textbooks, lectures and laboratory exercises. It is not difficult to see that this way of looking at how change occurs in scientific thought might be applied to other bodies of knowledge and aesthetic values, and particularly those – like photography – which seem less aptly handled, for instance, by Michel Foucault's discursive theory of knowledge and power. None the less, Kuhn's theory is in some respects closely similar to that of Foucault (developed around the same time despite the lack of cross-influences), although they are formulated within what Kuhn would term 'different paradigms' and Foucault 'different discursive formations'! In particular, both concentrate on the radical breaks and discontinuities in conceptual systems between one period and another. Although Foucault's ideas about the relationship between knowledge and power have been usefully employed in certain analyses of photography, these have tended to concentrate – not surprisingly – on the exercise of *power* through photographic technologies and apparatuses, particularly that of surveillance (Tagg, 1988). But photography's role in the knowledge produced by the social and human sciences, Foucault's primary area of interest, is not the major theme of this chapter. Here the focus is upon understanding how photography as a set of visual practices is situated in a historical and cultural context. By contrast with those Foucauldian approaches which have looked at the exercise of *power* through photographic technologies and apparatuses, the main concern in this chapter is to understand the life-history and defining principles of a specific approach to photographic representation.

What the concept of paradigm offers us is a way into understanding how groups of photographers shared a common perspective on representation, how they clustered together in a way that ensured the dominance of the humanistic paradigm as a form of representation, developed a common agenda of central themes which expressed their 'world-view', and offered alternative images of French society which debunked and contested other forms of representation. By examining the *representational paradigm* in more detail we can focus more closely on the condition of photographic production, the social context in which the work was created.

Kuhn's concept of paradigm has been successfully applied to the arts, including both painting and photography (see Davis, 1995, pp. 106–7). The idea of paradigm is helpful because it suggests that photographic approaches – as with 'schools' in fields such as painting or philosophy – follow cyclical processes of paradigm-shift not dissimilar to those in science. But instead of denoting a new form of scientific imagery, a paradigm-shift in photography generally denotes the appearance of a new visual aesthetic, so that a novel conception of representation becomes dominant. However, just as in a scientific paradigm-shift, familiar things are seen – or re-seen – in revolutionary ways. This is usually because one or more photographers has developed a new 'theory' about representation: a decision for instance to concentrate on a certain type of subject-matter, perhaps to make images of it which are framed or coloured in a certain way. The novel or revolutionary new image attracts attention from other photographers: it may be associated with innovative forms of publication or display, and it may be located within a social group who cluster together and derive solidarity from the fact that they are in opposition to the status quo. Usually they have rejected as uninteresting the visual puzzles posed by 'normal photography', in the same way as dissident groups of scientists whose work will lead to a new paradigm tend to reject the puzzles posed by 'normal science'. They have a new set of visual puzzles to explore, and this may in due course influence the community of photographers to adopt the new visual paradigm. This occurs through a complex process similar to that which happens in sciences, whereby the paradigm becomes institutionalized through training practices, the creation of standard reference works such as 'textbooks' (although in fields like photography these are more likely to be books of images or even exhibitions, rather than instructional texts), and the emergence of standardized work techniques.

Where aesthetic domains like painting, literature or photography differ from sciences is in their essentially multi-paradigmatic as opposed to uni-paradigmatic nature. In sciences, by and large, dominant paradigms such as Newtonian mechanics or Darwinian evolution rule entire fields like physics or biology. In the arts (and perhaps also the social sciences), dominant paradigms may conquer significant groupings (e.g. Impressionism in western painting of the late nineteenth and early twentieth century) yet not characterize the majority of output in a given field, which may see several competing paradigms struggling for dominance at any one moment.

Understanding photography as a body of practices and aesthetic values which follows a paradigmatic structure is helpful in understanding its representational role, for it focuses our attention on the interactions between the conceptions of photographers in constructing their images and the uses to which their photographs are put. To follow the Kuhnian scientific analogy, it is in the publication and diffusion of the output of those working within the paradigm that its influence is most clearly felt. Since we are primarily interested in the photographs of those working in the field of illustrative reportage photography, it is within this domain that we are concerned with exploring the paradigmatic nature of French humanism. Once those working within this approach have reached a point where their imagery is widely diffused in the illustrated press, we can begin to say that their photographic paradigm is *dominant*, in the sense that other practitioners are obliged to construct their own images within this set of visual rules in order to get their work published.

2   Documentary expression and photography

Before we go deeper into the French humanist paradigm it will be helpful to consider a further aspect of the representational issues which photography raises. We need to resolve certain questions about the 'truth-value' of the 'documentary' images produced by those working within the paradigm.

There is a central ambiguity within photography: 'depending on whether the mind or the eye is struck by its capacities to record or express, it is regarded now as a tool of documentation, now as an instrument of creation' (Lemagny in Lemagny and Rouillé, 1987, p.12). This problem derives from the invention of the photographic medium which was conceived as was so much else in the nineteenth century as a process which would reconcile art and industry. It will be helpful to consider certain of the meanings and uses of the 'documentary' aspects of photography, the senses in which a photographic image can be seen as either representing some important fact or as a means of recording an event, place, person or object in ways which have an 'objective' quality.

It is important to distinguish between at least two definitions of the term *documentary* which are pertinent to the dominant paradigm of photography we are concerned with in this chapter: *documentary as objective representation* vs. *documentary as subjective interpretation*.

2.1   Documentary as objective representation

Let us take first the idea of documentary as simply relating to *documents* of some sort (in this case *photographic* images). In this context, the image is normally referred to as a sort of impersonal 'legal proof', an objective record, similar in nature to an official form, a letter, a will, etc. It has purely informational value.

objective
representation

In so far as the image is merely a simple record (i.e. a photographic reproduction of a letter, a painting, an object, a building, a scene, a passport portrait of a person, etc.), its factual or objective basis seems at first glance quite unexceptional. Like a letter or an object itself, the photograph is held to be an **objective representation** of something factual, the image a way of presenting 'facts' about its subject in a purely informational way. But complications begin to seep in to this apparently clear-cut notion of the photographic 'document', and they concern exactly how and on what authority the record is held to divulge its objectivity. Like all documentary records, photographic documents may of course be altered in order to offer a false or different interpretation from that which they would disclose if they had not been tampered with. But this is not at issue. What we are concerned with is the general belief that photography is an *inherently* objective medium of representation. This belief has grown up with the medium and it is still routinely in play whenever we open a book or magazine or newspaper. The historian Beaumont Newhall put it most succinctly when he argued that 'the photograph has special value as evidence or proof'. We believe it because we believe our eyes.

As John Berger has pointed out, photography emerged (during the 1830s) at a time when the philosophy of positivism was also moving into its heyday, and the two developed alongside each other. In essence (and simplifying enormously), positivism held that science and technology advanced our capacity to understand the physical and social world through the acquisition of factual knowledge (Berger, 1982, p. 99). Photography, as a modern technology – the combination, as David Hockney once memorably put it, of a renaissance drawing instrument and nineteenth-century chemistry – provided a tool whose seemingly objective mechanism for trapping factual representations fitted precisely within this positivist philosophy. Yet this understanding of photography was not in fact 'given' with the emergence of the medium.

When photography appeared in the 1830s, it was initially seen not as a primarily scientific tool but as an essentially creative medium, as summed up in Edouard Manet's remark on seeing the first photographs: 'from today, painting is dead'. Early uses of photography concentrated on landscape and portraiture, both modes of representation until then considered typical of painting and drawing, neither of which were considered as inherently 'objective' modes of representation in the scientific connotations of the term.

The great advantage of photography for its inventors – aptly summed up in Fox Talbot's term 'photogenic drawing' – was that it provided a technological solution to the manual problems posed by the 'quest for resemblance' which dominated western art. Treatises on art from antiquity until the eve of the twentieth century gave an important role to the concept of *imitation*. However, this was not to be a merely slavish reproduction of nature:

> An artistic work should introduce the soul into a world governed by supreme truth and ideal beauty. Often the artists could accomplish this only at the cost of exactitude: one example out of many is provided by the extra vertebrae given to Ingrès's *Odalisque,* painted in 1814. The transcription of reality was not an objective undertaking but a means, available to man alone, of using the work which he produced or contemplated to establish a correlation with a world of infinity. Essentially, an image was the product of a mental effort: whether figurative or abstract, it constituted the substance of the only iconographical system that existed before 1839, the system generically known as 'the arts of drawing'.
>
> (Lemagny in Lemagny and Rouillé, 1987, p. 13)

As photography gradually supplanted the earlier iconographical system founded on the arts of drawing, a whole series of transactions occurred which placed its modes of representation within new iconographic frameworks. Technological and aesthetic developments saw the uses of the medium extend into many domains. As a result, a series of 'paradigms' of photographic representation emerged, each of which offered a particular vision of the world which photography could take within its remit. These included various artistic-aesthetic movements in which the expressive power of the photographic image was held to be of central value. However, this was in opposition to the emergence of a dominant paradigm, underpinned by a *reflective* approach to representation, which asserted that the photograph offered a 'true image' of the world. The 'camera eye' was considered to be like a 'mirror held up to Nature'. The emergence and eventual dominance of such a paradigm in the nineteenth century helped the new medium become an integral part of the processes of industrialization, of scientific development and of social control/surveillance (Tagg, 1988, pp. 5–8). In this new paradigm of visual representation, the photographic image acquired truth-value. A photograph was seen as *inherently* objective (because of its combination of physical and chemical technology). The camera produced *visual facts* or *documents.* Thus, the very practice of photography could be said to offer a d*ocumentary objectivity* to the images which it created.

2.2   Documentary as subjective interpretation

The second definition of documentary is in many ways richer but less apparently clear-cut, and deals with the more social and personal aspects of the term – as when we speak of something being a 'human document'. Examples might include a journal or diary, someone's written account of their experiences, a 'documentary' film about a person's life, a picture story in a magazine. In this context, the document's informational value is mediated through the perspective of the person making it, and it is presented as a mixture of emotion *and* information. Indeed, it is in creating images which have the power to move the viewer, to retain their attention through the presentation of a telling image, that this form of *documentary* works. Edward Steichen described the work of a group of photographers who recorded the rural and urban changes which America underwent from 1935 to 1943 as a body of images which struck the viewer by their dramatic verisimilitude: 'it leaves you with a feeling of a living experience you won't forget' (quoted in Stott, 1973, p. 11). Roy Stryker, who led the group referred to by Steichen, argued that 'good documentary should tell not only what a place or a thing or person *looks* like, but it must also tell the audience what it would *feel* like to be an actual witness to the scene' (ibid., p. 29). One of the photographers in Stryker's team, Arthur Rothstein, underpinned these ideas when he formulated his belief that 'the lens of the camera is, in effect, the eye of the person looking at the print' (ibid., p. 29) – with the implication that the two are interchangeable, so that the viewer is in effect 'there' when the shutter clicked.

You may note in reading what follows that what I describe as **subjective interpretation** in this section sits rather awkwardly between Chapter 1's categories of *reflective* and *intentional* representation. However, it is difficult to disentangle such conceptual distinctions from the practices and statements of documentary photographers, as the discussion below makes clear, for the subjective mode of 'documentary' representation became *paradigmatic* during the 1930s and 1940s and has remained influential until the present day within illustrative reportage photography, or 'photo-journalism'. William Stott, in his classic study (1973) of the emergence of this mode of representation in 1930s' America, makes the point that during that period the idea was forged that the documentary nature of a work gained force from its association with the individual 'real' experience of its author. The authenticity which derives from the sense of 'being there' conveyed a special truth-value to works which could claim they were fashioned from experience.

subjective
interpretation

This form of 'documentary' gained currency in photography with the rise of the mass illustrated magazines in the 1930s, but it should be pointed out that its general form was also evident in other genres such as film and books, where the idea of documentary as objectively grounded but subjectively constructed interpretation was widely used – as in famous examples such as John Grierson's film *Night Mail* (1936) or James Agee's and Walker Evans's book *Let Us Now Praise Famous Men* (1965/1941), or even John Steinbeck's novel *The Grapes of Wrath* (1966/1938). Such ideas have come to infuse documentary photography. As Marianne Fulton has written:

> Photojournalism is intertwined with the major events of the twentieth century. Indeed, the public's judgements about historical and contemporary incidents are often based on the photographs available to show them. It is a powerful medium, capable of focusing attention on the significant issues of our time; its descriptive ability is no less than that of words. As critic A.D. Coleman wrote, 'We are becoming visually sophisticated enough as a culture to realize that photography is not a transcriptive process but a descriptive one'. Despite the increasing awareness that depiction does not embody truth itself, photography remains a principal medium for our understanding of the world. This trust and expectation give special significance to a two-dimensional medium, which in reality can only record the outward appearance of things. That it succeeds in seeming to go beyond the surface is a testament to our acceptance of its verisimilitude and the individual insight of the photographer. As a consequence, just as the Civil War became a shockingly real encounter through the work of Matthew Brady's studio, so photojournalism still provides important access to both feeling and facts.

> Photojournalists, in the photographic tradition of Brady, are more than spectators in an historical grandstand. Being there is important, being an eyewitness is significant, but the crux of the matter is bearing witness. To

bear witness is to make known, to confirm, to give testimony to others. The distribution and publication of the pictures make visible the unseen, the unknown and the forgotten.

... in Europe the coming of the smaller camera influenced photographers' style and manner of working, and this in turn had an impact on picture editors' approach to magazine layout. At the same time, the rise of Hitler forced many of the prominent photojournalists to relocate, sending them to France, England and subsequently the United States. The migration would have a profound effect on photojournalism. The European 35mm, candid style soon challenged the traditional large format work of American newspapers.

In the United States newly developed printing methods allowed for large, high-quality magazines based on European models. Especially important in the days before television, the magazines, such as *Life* and *Look,* became a sort of national newspaper showing labour strife, political figures, and world conflicts. In the 1930s, as in other eras, technology, the picture-making it facilitated, and the world-wide political situation combined to shape our ideas of photojournalism and the world it pictured. One writer was moved to say, 'All hell broke loose in the '30s and photography has never been the same since'. While referring to changes in camera design and specifically to the Leica, the quote aptly encapsulates the flux of events.

...

Because photojournalism is of the moment, it presents a sense of continual present, which in turn conditions our expectations of the medium and thereby defines the course of technological experimentation. For example, in the 1930s anticipation that photographs and stories could be published together resulted in the achievement of commercially transmitting photographs over telephone lines or radio waves, bringing the world into everyone's home.

(Fulton, 1988, pp. 106–7)

As Fulton makes clear, the 'documentary' nature of photographic journalism, whether for a newspaper, magazine or book, is essentially *interpretative.* The representations that the photographer produces are related to his or her personal interpretations of the events and subjects which he or she chooses to place in front of the camera lens. However, they are also assumed to have some 'truth-value' in the sense that they allow the viewer privileged insight into the events they depict.

There is thus a *double* process of construction at work here. First, the photographer is involved in a process of construction in choosing and framing his or her images so as 'to make known, to confirm, to give testimony to others'. Through the photographer's construction of their existence at a given moment of time and space, subjects (for instance 'ethnically cleansed' refugees in Bosnia) who have no opportunity to speak directly to people outside their immediate area are provided with the chance of 'giving testimony' to the readers of a newspaper or magazine. This occurs through the 'distribution and publication' of a photographer's pictures, which, as Fulton argues, makes 'visible the unseen, the unknown and the forgotten'. But this is, in other words, to pass through a *second* process of construction, where the photographs are then selected out from their original ordering and narrative context, to be placed alongside textual information and reports in a publication. Their selection, placing and framing, their connection with the content of the text, their captioning, all provide ample evidence that the meanings available to the viewer/reader on the basis of a documentary photograph are a complex representational *construction* in the sense discussed in the previous chapter.

The fact that the constructed nature of photographic social documentary relies upon more than mere visual fact-collection is also implied more directly in Fulton's contention that 'photojournalism still provides important access to both *feeling* and facts' (my emphasis). Thus, those photographers who define themselves as working within the dominant humanistic paradigm of documentary reportage would tend to associate themselves with an early exponent of the genre, the American Lewis Hine, when he said 'I wanted to show things that had to be corrected. I wanted to show the things that had to be appreciated' (quoted in Stott, 1973, p. 21). It is significant that Hine had been a sociologist before adopting photography, because he believed that the camera would be a mightier weapon than the pen against poverty: 'if I could tell the story in words, I wouldn't need to lug a camera' (ibid., p. 30).

The socially ameliorative strain running through photographic social documentary (evident today, for instance, in the work of the Brazilian photographer Sebastiao Salgado, who undertakes lengthy and widely published projects on global social issues such as famine, manual labour and migration) reminds us again of the essentially constructionist form of representation on which it draws. Yet part of the power of such work – its ability to influence the perceptions of the viewer – derives from the ambiguity of the photographic representation itself, the notion that the images so produced are not the product of a human brain but of an impersonal 'camera eye'. Lewis Hine felt that the camera was 'a powerful tool for research' because it mechanically re-creates reality as crafts such as writing or painting never can (quoted in Stott, 1973, p. 31). Another American photographer working on social documentary in the 1930s, Margaret Bourke-White, argued that 'with a camera the shutter opens and closes and the only rays that come in to be registered come directly from the object in front'. By contrast, writing was clearly less objective to her: 'whatever facts a person writes have to be coloured by his prejudice and bias' (ibid., pp. 31–2). Though such a binary opposition (photography = objectivity: writing = bias) is completely unsustainable, Bourke-White's statement none the less underlines the point that the representations available through photography are qualitatively different from those available through writing. Photography deals with the images of real people, whereas writing is made of words: the photograph seems closer to lived experience than words ever can be. This tends to privilege the photographic image over the written word for many viewers, and therefore underpins its claim to documentary objectivity. Although few of us now believe that 'the camera never lies', the apparent objectivity of the camera-produced image may help to fix the meaning of a given text, by providing it with a *representational legitimacy*. Thus, the association of the photographer's interpretative grasp of his or her subject with the ostensibly objective photographic image secures a status for the work of documentary which places it beyond mere opinion.

If such ambiguities are indeed in play when we look at a work of social documentary photography, they derive from two aspects of the process of representation. First, they are inherent in the practice of social documentary photographers who in 'witnessing' events on our behalf are by their own accounts typically also concerned with showing us, in Hine's words, 'the things that ha[ve] to be corrected [and] the things that ha[ve] to be appreciated'. It is worth pointing out that the idea of the 'committed photographer' – a classic contemporary example being Sebastiao Salgado – is enshrined as a role-model amongst documentary photographers. Secondly, the ambiguities also derive from the mode of presentation of such images – either in the form of pictures used to illustrate magazine or newspaper articles, or as the material of books. In both cases, there may be more or less textual support for the images – from a detailed essay to simple captions. But the general and implicitly objective nature of the images made by the mechanical process of the 'camera eye' confers a truth-value on the documentary idiom. The very act of publishing images which have a self-consciously documentary purpose – *You Have Seen Their Faces*, *An American Exodus*, *A Night in London*, *Vietnam Inc.*, *Forbidden Land*, *La Banlieue de Paris*, *Workers: An Archaeology of the Industrial Age*: the titles of some notable books in this genre – invites the reader to enter the process by which the representation of their subjects is constructed (Calder and Bourke-White, 1937; Lange and Schuster Taylor, 1939; Brandt, 1938; Jones-Griffiths, 1971; Godwin, 1990; Cendrars and Doisneau, 1949; Salgado, 1993). The reader engages with the work as a body of images which aim to disclose a deeper truth – about, to take the works cited above, the Depression in American, about street life in 1930s' London or 1940s' Paris, about the Vietnam war, about access to the English countryside, about the nature of labour-intensive industry. Far from being a mere recitation of visual facts, social documentary turns out to be a mode of representation deeply coloured by ambiguities, and generally representative of the paradigm in which it has been constructed.

3   The historical context

In order to better comprehend the relationship between French humanist photography and its historical context, it will be necessary to take a brief and rather simplistic look at key trends in the history of France from the Front Populaire era (the mid-1930s) to the advent of the Fifth Republic (i.e. about 1960). At the end of this chapter we also glance at France and its contemporary problems, to examine divisions within French society in the late 1980s and early 1990s, a discussion which will provide some insight into the reasons for the widespread nostalgia in more recent times for representations of Frenchness in the 1940s and 1950s.

France in the 1930s was in many ways a deeply conservative society, still shaken by the after-effects of a terrible war (1914–18) and of the rapid economic change which followed it, leading to the crisis of the period from 1932 onwards. Alongside the social malaise of a *société bloquée,* where many groups and institutions turned in upon themselves to close off external threats or pressures, one also finds numerous attempts to change and to innovate, a classic struggle between tradition and modernity. The introversion of the Third Republic, founded in 1871, is symbolized by its Maginot Line, a great white elephant of a defensive system running along the borders of eastern France, which was to prove irrelevant to modern warfare when put to the test in 1940. The pacifism which characterized the left had the same effect as the nationalism of the right: a refusal to see the dangers mounting outside France.

The Third Republic was dominated by two great social groups, the peasantry and the 'independent' middle classes (artisans, shopkeepers, property-owners, professionals). In 1936, the agricultural population still made up 36 per cent of the workforce, and although its share of the cake was slowly reducing in size, by contrast the *monde ouvrier* of industry and manufacture remained comparatively small and was widely regarded as a necessary evil rather than as a respectable source of wealth or a key factor in modernization. Successful industrialists were disdained by polite society, whilst the regime within factories was characterized by an oppressive discipline designed to keep the worker firmly in his place. The working class was effectively excluded from the 'republican synthesis' resting on the village and the bourgeoisie. Leon Blum, the leader of the Popular Front government which came to power in 1936, summed up his social policies most aptly as his desire to 'bring into the city those who camp at its gates' – the *classe ouvrière* or working class. Many of those who made up the industrial workforce were immigrants, another factor reinforcing their exclusion: on the eve of war, fully half of all those who worked in the mining industry came from outside France (mostly from eastern and southern Europe). At the census of 1931, about 7 per cent of the population were registered as foreign. Xenophobia was rampant, fed by a strong nationalist movement. This helped Daladier's government of 1938–9 to turn back the clock after the brief advances of worker interests during the Popular Front (paid holidays, limited social security). A common fear of the bourgeoisie was that, once they were given paid holidays, the unwashed hordes of the working classes would invade the beaches of 'their' resorts.

Although it contained advanced industries and modern technology, France was a society built on the peasant farm, the small workshop, the family firm. Savings were put aside rather than invested in the business, food was consumed on the farm rather than produced for sale, and many industrial organizations only survived because their access to a captive market in the French colonies meant they were insulated from market forces in the outside world. To make matters worse, France also suffered from a declining birthrate which meant that its population was reducing in size: 'the Frenchman is getting rarer', as one commentator put it in 1939.

The Vichy regime, which was set up to rule France after the defeat of 1940, sought both to accommodate the occupier and to return the country to an earlier condition. 'La France', argued its president Marshal Pétain, 'est un pays essentiellement agricole' (France is essentially an agricultural nation). Vichy also reinforced and exploited the xenophobia of the French, its anti-Semitic laws enacted in October 1940 owing less to Nazism than to the fear of the foreigner which since the 1930s had afflicted much of French society. By contrast, in the emergent Resistance (and particularly after the German invasion of Russia in 1941), the role of former unionists and the working class generally became determinant. The strike of May–June 1941 in the Nord-Pas-de-Calais region made the miners into mythical patriotic heroes. Socialists and communists were key players in the Resistance movement, and prepared the ground for a fundamental change in the social topography of post-war France.

By the Liberation in 1944, France had lost 1,450,000 of its population, of which 600,000 were military and civilian deaths, whilst the remainder were the result of the outflow of foreigners and the decline in births. The population, at 40 million, was now slightly smaller than in 1901. Three-quarters of the country had been damaged by the war, and finding housing was virtually impossible. Feeding the towns was made difficult by the total disorganization of the transport system. Industrial production was at 38 per cent of its level in 1938. Few products were available, whilst the money in circulation had increased during the war: classic conditions for runaway inflation. As prices were controlled, the black markets which had appeared during the occupation simply got larger. Everyday life, difficult enough between 1940 and 1944, became even harder. By the winter of 1945–6, the food ration was lower even than it had been in the height of the occupation. To make matters worse, the *épuration* (purges) which followed the Liberation made it harder initially to heal the wounds of political and social division which the occupation had opened up in French society. The peasantry was sometimes accused of having profited from the food shortages of the period 1940–4; whilst those who ran shops and businesses frequently found themselves blamed for having amassed fortunes from the shortage of consumer goods. Perhaps not accidentally, the two social groups which provided the backbone of the Third Republic were those most often accused of having derived advantage from the war.

Profiting from a post-war consensus about the need for radical social change, the Fourth Republic, created in 1946, turned its back on the traditional groups of French society. Reconstruction could no longer depend on the pre-war ruling élites or the resources of a backward rural world. The state itself – in the form of a national plan – was involved in actively directing the modernization process. From 1944 to 1946, a series of important decisions were taken by a government which brought together Gaullists, republicans, communists and socialists: nationalizations to extend the public services (trains, mines, banks, insurance companies, gas, electricity, Renault); the creation of the national plan; social security and family benefits; councils giving workers a say in the running of companies.

Of course, the bourgeoisie and its ruling élites had not been magically erased in 1945. Its gradual reappearance in the post-war world indicated that traditional France coexisted alongside the forces of social renewal. But a new social force now took an important place on the socio-political stage and in the public imagination: the *classe ouvrière* or working class. Its appearance had been prepared during a long struggle since the beginning of the century which had both defined its identity and its characteristic modes of expression. The strikes of 1936 and 1938, the struggles of the resistance, and the major strikes in the autumn of 1947 and 1948 'gave the group a common history and nationalized labour conflicts, so making the state henceforth the essential interlocutor of the working class' (tr. from Borne, 1992, p. 24). The *classe ouvrière*, concentrated in its 'great industrial bastions' (coal mines in the north, iron and steelworks and textiles in the east, automobile works in the suburbs of Paris, the great docks at le Havre, Cherbourg, Marseilles, etc.), became more homogeneous and stable. As Philippe Ariès found when studying the industrial suburbs (*banlieue*) of Paris in the late 1940s, workers were by this stage less inclined than they had been earlier in the century to seek ways out of their class (into shopkeeping or public service for instance) because they were conscious that their position now gave them a security and certain privileges which had not existed before.

The post-war consensus began to dissolve after 1947, with strikes and violent confrontations between workers and the forces of order, which continued into 1948. The trade unions divided into those associated with the socialist party and those with the communist party. The developing cold war outside France played a part in this, and henceforth put the state and the CGT (Confédération Générale du Travail – the trade union most closely associated with the French communist party, the PCF) into direct opposition.

Conditions for workers remained very hard until at least the mid-1950s. Inflation continued to be a problem until the end of the decade, constantly depressing wages, and housing was a nightmare, resulting in the growth of shanty towns (*bidonvilles*) around the great cities. The countryside began to decant its inhabitants towards the towns as industrialization progressed, and about 1 million male workers left the land between 1946 and 1954, with another 700,000 following them from 1955 to 1962. The pressure on the towns was intensified by the post-war 'baby-boom' whereby the French abandoned wholesale the 'Malthusianism' which had hitherto characterized their demography. At the Liberation, de Gaulle had called upon the French to produce '12 million beautiful babies in the next decade' as an act of patriotism, and they responded with gusto.

If the period 1945–55 witnessed the rising importance of the *classe ouvrière* within French society, it also saw the emergence of a key struggle within the middle class over the future direction of society and the economy. On the one hand were those who came to be known as 'Poujadistes', after Pierre Poujade, the founder of an important movement of shopkeepers, artisans, and those who ran small independent businesses. Poujadism symbolized the defence of all the 'little people' threatened by the beginnings of modernization and development in the French economy. Poujade was the spokesman for the old provincial middle classes, who turned towards the past and wanted to restore 'the real France': their discourse evoked memories of the 1930s – xenophobia, radicalism, defence of empire. Opposed to them was those who wanted to modernize France, linked most closely to the ideas of Pierre Mendès-France, who described his party as the 'new left'. The Mendèsistes belonged to the new middle classes of salaried employees, students, the 'enlightened' neo-bourgeoisie of managers and technicians. They wanted a republic of technocrats and intellectuals, not one of shopkeepers and farmers, and were ready to give up empire in favour of modern industry:

> Thus, in the middle of the 1950s, the major social conflict, because it was decisive for the future of French society, was less an opposition between the working class and the bourgeoisie, than at the heart of society, between the middle classes themselves. In the end, and this is the direction of the 1960s, the troops of Pierre Poujade were defeated; the new middle classes triumphed because they carried within them both economic modernity and a style of life which was contemporaneous with this modernity.
>
> (tr. from Borne, 1992, p. 33)

Behind these changes loomed larger problems for France which came from its colonial empire: defeat in Indo-China, and a bloody independence struggle in Algeria. The crisis which brought de Gaulle back to power in 1958, and created the Fifth Republic, was compounded by internal and external problems. Simplifying greatly, it was the forces of the new France which won out, as the quotation from Borne above underlines. France withdrew from its empire; economic modernization was reinforced.

4   The paradigm in practice: key themes of post-war humanism, 1945–60

To reiterate for a moment: at the end of the 1939–45 war, the French people were obliged to confront the consequences of a period which had thrown into question what it meant to be French. Since 1939, France had experienced war, humiliating defeat, occupation, collaboration, resistance, insurrection, and liberation by the invading armies of its erstwhile allies. These events had combined to divide French people amongst themselves, and, before any reconstruction could begin, it seemed as if a ritual 'cleansing' of society (*épuration*) would be necessary.

The purges and reprisals against those known or suspected of collaboration or fraternization were often savage, and continued for some while after the end of the war. There was considerable disorder in the regions, including cases of banditry by gangs of collaborationist thugs who had taken to the hills. The mixed sentiments and violent events of this period explain some of the turmoil surrounding the transition which France underwent in 1944–5 from occupied state to free republic.

This was the context in which, from 1944–5 onwards, the humanist photographers worked to produce images for publication. After the *épuration*, it may seem hardly surprising that French people rapidly sought ways of creating a new sense of unity, to reconstruct a sense of what it was to be French. The role of the photographer in providing illustrative images to the press may not have been of critical importance, but it certainly played a part in the evolution of new representations of Frenchness which can be seen as having a primarily solidaristic role. These images tended to cluster around certain themes which will be examined more closely below, but the majority contain a central core of symbols which have to do with community and solidarity, and with the sense of happiness or contentment which derives from human association.

According to a number of commentators on popular culture, the immediate post-war period was characterized by the French public's passion for illustrated magazines. Many new titles emerged (often to disappear as swiftly), but this was the period when magazines such as *Paris-Match* regularly achieved print runs in the region of 1 million copies per issue. French people's fascination with such media seems to have been in large part a response to the agonies and deprivations of the war years, when France was cut off from the rest of the world and from images about it. Reviewing the type of material contained in these publications indicated that one feature of this *folle soif d'images* (crazy thirst for pictures), as it has been called, was the prevalence of images of what could be regarded as 'quintessential Frenchness'. Such images may be seen as providing a means of representing France and the French in an inclusionary way, representations which may have played a part in healing the wounds of a society divided by war, defeat, occupation, collaboration and resistance. The visual approach and social perspective of humanistic reportage produced the images which such a market demanded.

Moreover, this concentration on the inclusionary, on solidarity and communality, is neither accidental nor epiphenomenal: as we have seen, such values were related closely to widely felt needs in post-war France, as witnessed by General de Gaulle's speech as head of state in September 1944:

> [France] needs to ensure that special interests are always obliged to give way to the common good, that the great sources of common wealth may be exploited and managed not for the profit of a few but to the advantage of all, that the coalitions of interest which have weighed so heavily on the conditions of men and even on the policies of the state itself might be abolished once and for all, and that finally each of her sons and daughters might be able to live, to work, to bring up their children in security and dignity.
>
> (tr. from quotation in Borne, 1992, p. 21)

Such sentiments of equality, of communality, are also evident in the widespread nationalizations and comprehensive social legislation enacted in France during the period of post-war consensus which lasted from 1945–7. Women gained the vote for the first time in 1945. There was a comprehensive recentring of social discourse in progress. As the historian Dominique Borne has argued:

> Without doubt for the first time in the history of France, [the word 'worker'] is foregrounded without any reticence ... Exaltation then of the worker, essential producer of wealth; on the morrow of the war political parties and unions of all persuasions called for production to be intensified. By contrast the *bourgeoisie* is devalued by much of public opinion. The bosses are 'beyond the pale'. In his book which appeared just after the war, Leon Blum [prime minister of France in the Popular Front government from 1936–8] accuses the *bourgeoisie* of being responsible for the defeat of 1940 and thereby denounces the bankruptcy of the ruling élites.
>
> (tr. from Borne, 1992, p. 21)

Although the post-war consensus about such values was to hold both left and right in France in a fragile alliance only until 1947, it is easy to see in the social and political discourse of the era that 'humanism' is strongly foregrounded. Yet, as many commentators have emphasized, outside perhaps of the communist party, the consensus was founded more on a sentimental than an ideological terrain:

> *Combat*, the journal of Aron, Bourdet and Camus, carried the sub-title 'From resistance to revolution', but what revolution? and for which society? A general humanism, the desire for a society more just and

fraternal, consensus on the role of the state, but absence of a more precise vision of the society to be reconstructed. The social future defined itself negatively, against the overcautious bourgeoisie of the Third Republic, against the ruralist society of Pétain.

(tr. from Borne, 1992, p. 22)

A consensus founded more on a sentimental than an ideological terrain, a 'general humanism, the desire for a society more just and fraternal, consensus on the role of the state, but absence of a more precise vision of the society to be reconstructed': such could be the general definition of what constitutes the social vision of the photographers whose work we consider here. Their humanism is most evident in the 'universal' character of many of their themes: family, community, comradeship, love, childhood, popular pleasures. However, the foregrounding of the *classe ouvrière* in the post-war consensus meant that the humanist photographers tended to focus their cameras on this group or rather included workers within a slightly less clear-cut social order, the *classe populaire*, which encompassed social categories normally placed outside the *classe ouvrière*, such as small shopkeepers and self-employed artisans.

The term *class populaire* requires a little explanation, as when literally translated into English as 'popular class' it completely loses the meaning it has within a French context. Dictionaries often simply translate it as 'working class' which is too limiting, for in French the term evokes the idea of the popular masses, who might include a wide range of economic or occupational groups in addition to manual workers – office workers, teachers, nurses, retired people, even agricultural workers and peasant smallholders, etc. The term has political connotations, too, for there is constantly present the idea that the *classe populaire* is a potentially revolutionary social grouping. We might in English describe the sorts of people it includes as 'the common people', but this is both vaguer and less indicative of the values or culture of the *classe populaire*, which for French society of the mid-twentieth century was a term quite clearly redolent of a whole range of associations: a revolutionary history (whose most recent outburst had been the Popular Front in 1936 and the Liberation of Paris in 1944); and particular forms of leisure and entertainment which revolved around the *bistrot* or *guinguette*, the *bal musette*, music hall and the lyrical ballads of an Edith Piaf or Maurice Chevalier.

The emphasis on universal humanity, in this context, means the representation of major issues and concerns through their impact on specific individuals who are shown as the agents of their own destinies. It is a reaction against those totalitarian ideologies and impersonal economic forces which tend to treat people as a monolithic and de-individualized mass. Although this approach is most characteristically and dynamically displayed in the magazines and books of the period 1945–60, its roots are clearly visible in the new wave of reportage photography for the mass-market illustrated magazines which had appeared earlier, in the 1930s. This was the period in which the role of professional editorial photographer was created, and in which the modern image of the photo-journalist pacing the streets, Leica in hand, in search of the 'decisive moment', was defined.

The new magazines of the post-war era could not compare in quality with their pre-war counterparts, but in the scope and multiplicity of the subjects which they treated they were far ahead. They also allowed a freer rein to the expression of political values (and particularly a commitment to the *classe populaire*) on the part of the photographer.

Many of the photographers within the humanistic reportage group shared a left-wing perspective on the social changes underway in post-war France, and some of their photographic projects attest to a more subversive and questioning approach to the 'new France'. At the same time, those images of joy, pleasure, happiness, romance, which appear so frequently among the work of the group, also support the notion that they shared an essentially optimistic and positive perspective on human nature, and a belief in its ability to surmount hardship and handicap. A more considered view would argue that the approach of the photographers is one in which both an optimism about social reconstruction and a pessimism about its effects seem to be balanced.

All of this was occurring at a time when magazines and other periodicals were experiencing a post-war surge (in Paris alone, some 34 daily papers were being published in the harsh conditions of 1945 as compared to 32 in 1939), and the demand for illustrative photography of the type practised by Doisneau, Ronis and their colleagues was extensive and growing. Yet the magazines were not exclusively concerned with France; indeed there was a fascination with what was going on abroad, particularly in America. Raymond Grosset, director from 1946 of the photographic agency Rapho, recalled:

> In the first two or three years after the war the press was avid for reportages coming from the United States showing American life. There was no interest in views of ruins and of privation – moreover, to do a reportage in France represented an additional cost. Only *Regards* (a magazine funded by the PCF) was able to send Robert Doisneau to photograph a coal mine in the Nord!
>
> (tr. from unpublished interview, 1990)

Despite many problems with paper and other materials, new magazines continued to appear: many of course soon disappeared or merged with other titles, but this activity supplied a constant flow of work – although it was, recalled Grosset, extremely poorly paid. Indeed, it was this major boost in demand for illustrative photography of human interest which provided the impetus for the development of humanistic photo-journalism: in such conditions, specialized organizations could emerge and flower, whilst the social role of the photo-journalist became recognized and his or her status elevated. However, this did not necessarily mean that such photographers – as in Doisneau's or Ronis's case – could survive simply on low-paid reportage work, and their typical range of activities would also include advertising, portraiture, industrial photography, public relations work and what we would now term 'travel' photography. The strict specialization and role-differentiation which were being ushered in by post-war change had not yet begun to bite amongst those who practised photography for a living. Like the typical peasant who farms a scattering of plots with a range of produce, the typical 'freelance' reportage photographer working within the humanist paradigm of the 1940s would have hoped to have a variety of clients in different domains, for in that lay security, the spreading of risk over several distinct sources of income.

4.1 Elements of the paradigm

Turning now to look more closely at the photographs made by the French humanists, we shall examine first an image originating in the period we are concerned with, but which was extremely popular during the period from around 1985 until at least the time when this chapter was being written (1995). There's a strong likelihood that many readers will have seen it, and that some may have a copy somewhere, as a poster, postcard or as a picture torn from a newspaper or magazine (see Figure 2.1(a)).

FIGURE 2.1(a)
Robert Doisneau,
*Le baiser de
l'Hôtel de Ville*
(kiss outside the
Town Hall), 1950.

The photograph, which is now known as *Le baiser de l'Hôtel de Ville* (kiss outside the Town Hall), was made in April 1950 as part of a reportage for *Life* magazine by the French photographer, Robert Doisneau (1912–94). As you will see from the spread from the magazine reproduced as Figure 2.1(b), it was initially given a supporting role. At the time, each issue of the magazine was read by perhaps 24 million people (the print-run in 1950 was about 8 million copies per week, and the calculation was that about three people on average looked at each copy); moreover *Life* was distributed throughout the world. As Irving Penn, a young American photographer, pointed out:

> The modern photographer stands in awe of the fact that an issue of *Life* magazine will be seen by 24,000,000 people. It is obvious to him that never before in the history of mankind has anyone working in a visual medium been able to communicate so widely. He knows that in our time it is the privilege of the photographer to make the most vital visual record of man's existence. The modern photographer, having … the urge to communicate widely is inevitably drawn to the medium which offers him the fullest opportunity for this communication. He then works for

FIGURE 2.1(b)   Pages from *Life* magazine, 12 June 1950, showing the original use of Robert Doisneau's photograph now known as *Le baiser de l'Hôtel de Ville*, but then captioned *Kiss rapide* by *Life*. As can be seen by its placement within the context of the photo-story (two pictures are not shown here), the photograph was not considered a key image when it was first published.

publication, he has become in fact a journalist ... The modern photographer does not think of photography as an art form or of his photograph as an art object. But every so often in this medium, as in any creative medium, some of the practitioners are artists. In modern photography that which is art, is so as the by-product of a serious and useful job, soundly and lovingly done.

(quoted in Davis, 1995, p. 218)

The photographic agency for which Doisneau worked at the time, Raymond Grosset's Rapho, was continually seeking such assignments, which would pay their photographers well during a period when the French magazines could pay very little, even for a cover shot. Many of those made by Doisneau himself for French magazines were lucky if they earned 300 francs at 1990 prices (i.e. about £30/$45) – whilst a story sold to *Life* could multiply that figure by twenty or thirty times! The idea behind this particular assignment was extremely banal, built on what now seems to be the rather outworn cliché of romance in springtime Paris. At the time, however, such a 'picture-story' would have seemed an amusing and uplifting contrast to certain weightier issues (such as the Cold War; McCarthyism; the developing war in Korea) which would have appeared elsewhere in the magazine. America, like France, Britain and other countries recovering from the war, was going through a post-war marriage and baby-boom, so the story can also be seen as a classic 'post-war reconstruction' story.

The assignment was given to Robert Doisneau, because he had already begun to develop a series of images of *les amoureux* (people in love). As with a number of the magazine photographs he was making at the time, Doisneau knew that for reasons of common decency he could not risk using images of real couples kissing, and that the only way to carry out such an assignment was to use *figurants* (models) and to place them in interesting situations using very 'Parisian' settings as backdrops. The models were all young actors, who were paid to play the role of young lovers (some indeed could readily play their parts without acting!). Doisneau took them to various locations in Paris, photographing them in the rue de Rivoli, near the Hôtel de Ville, by the place de la Concorde, on the Metro steps at the Opéra, in a *bistrot*, at the gare St Lazare, by the Elysée Palace, on Pont Neuf, by a street market in the quartier Latin, on a three-wheeled delivery cycle, on the *quais* of the Seine, by the Square du Vert Galant, etc. Though the names of many of these locations might not mean a great deal to a non-French reader, they would all have had a certain cultural significance to the many French readers of illustrated magazines, as places which even a person who did not live in Paris might recognize as typically Parisian. As an experienced photographer of the Parisian scene, Doisneau was using his intimate knowledge of city backdrops to make images which had a wider remit, and which were designed to illustrate certain cultural stereotypes about the French: 'in Paris young lovers kiss wherever they want to and nobody seems to care' as *Life* sub-titled the article. The text continued: 'In other cities bashful couples usually seek out parks or deserted streets for their romancing. But in Paris vigorous young couples, determined to uphold the municipal honour, can be observed in unabashed courting in even the most crowded parts of the city.' The photographs and the text express very clearly a strong representation of one aspect of Frenchness: that French people are very romantic, and are not afraid to demonstrate this aspect of their culture in public (although at the time such behaviour would perhaps have been frowned upon by ordinary French people).

The resulting article and picture series in *Life* was extremely popular, attracting a good deal of correspondence. But rather more significantly perhaps for our concerns, it was also published a little later in a slightly modified form in the French paper *Ce Soir* as 'ce reportage qui a fait ravir les Américains' ('the article which delighted the American public'). The images were presented as being 'unposed pictures' by *Life*, a rubric which rather awkwardly leaves open their documentary nature, but which was entirely in keeping with the typical form of representation of such 'human interest' stories at the time. Given its origins, it is remarkable that the apparently documentary form of the story has caused such controversy in the case of one image, *Le baiser de l'Hôtel de Ville*, which became the focus of a court case in the 1990s based on a claim that the couple featured had not consented to appearing in the photograph. Whilst this is an *image à la sauvette* as another prominent French photographer of Doisneau's generation – Henri Cartier-Bresson (b. 1908) – would have called it, the record of a 'decisive moment' as his phrase has come to be rendered in English, it has acquired a notoriety which has gone far beyond its merits as an image.

What is significant for our purposes about *Le baiser de l'Hôtel de Ville* is that it exemplifies certain key themes in the representational paradigm of French humanist photography. First and foremost however – and a fact easily forgotten – is that, like many of the rest of the images of the humanists, this is a black-and-white photograph. At the outset it has reduced the complexity of the original scene to shades of grey, a convention which we nevertheless readily accept, for this transposition has become the most readily understood representation of this time and place, to the extent that if we were to see a colour image of the same type of scene it would strike us as odd. Yet the 1950s were not black-and-white: people lived them in colour.

Ostensibly this is an image about *everyday life*. We can try to 'read' the image as it would have appeared to contemporary viewers. Forget for a moment the fact that Doisneau used models. His reasons for doing so are not that he wanted to fake something, but that he did not want to embarrass people who might be kissing somebody other than their current partner! If he had not had such scruples, Doisneau could have used many of his *instantanés* (snapshots) of anonymous couples, taken during his walks around Paris, to create the series. But this might have caused problems. So, on the basis of his unposed photographs, he 're-constructed' a new series of photographs of lovers kissing, asking his models to embrace in locations which would evoke Paris, and thus creating a set of representations of this idea of 'young love in Paris' which corresponded with what he had already observed. In this sense, the photograph is closer to a fashion picture than what is simple-mindedly assumed to be a documentary photograph. But as we have seen, the whole idea of documentary is shot through with ambiguities. This did not, as indicated above, prevent Doisneau being sued shortly before his death in 1994 by a couple who maintained that *Le baiser de l'Hôtel de Ville* was indeed a documentary image of themselves, taken anonymously in 1950.

The *amoureux* are photographed doing what other Parisians were doing everyday on the streets of the city – as they walk along, they kiss. The backdrop of the photograph is the Hôtel de Ville, a recognizably Parisian landmark: an area where there are many shops patronized by ordinary members of the *classe populaire*.

If we look at the couple kissing, what do we see? Firstly they are in their early twenties, and are dressed quite informally for the time: he has a scarf round his neck, his shirt is open and he does not wear a tie. He has what seems to be a cigarette-end in his free hand, his hair is wind-blown. She has an open cardigan, a blouse and skirt. Neither wears a hat. Certainly they are not well or expensively dressed. (As everybody else seems to be more warmly dressed, they might also be oblivious to the weather.) The fact that they are walking in a busy public place whilst kissing suggests that their passion is a normally acceptable behaviour for such a situation. (Remember that *Life* captioned the whole story with the rubric 'in Paris young lovers kiss wherever they want to and nobody seems to care' – which implies that in the USA at that time, such behaviour would have been scandalous or at least remarked upon.) None of the several passers-by seems concerned by it. The couple are evidently of modest means, like the people around them: two men in berets, a classic signifier either of the *classe populaire* or of the peasantry. This tells us we are not in a chic, upper-class or expensive area; but neither are we in a poor one. Although we have no way of deciding the occupation or class background of the subjects, they seem to be 'ordinary people' and thus we might easily assume that they too are from the *classe populaire* – he might be a skilled craftsman, she a shop-assistant.

Observe also the position from which the photograph is made: we are evidently viewing this scene from the pavement seats of a café. At our left side is a customer: again a person who seems quite 'ordinary' in dress and attitude. He is not particularly aware of the couple either. The angle of the shot – looking slightly upwards – means that we, as viewers, are hardly in a position to dominate its subjects as voyeurs. Indeed, this angle and the turning of the man's body towards us seem to give us a privileged view of what is going on, as if it were a play being performed for the benefit of the camera. The subjects seem content to display their intimacy to us, thus depriving the photograph of any hint of voyeurism. They are in that sense displaying a sense of complicity with the viewer, who might be assumed therefore to share their social position and outlook on life. (We now know that there was in fact more complicity between photographer and subject than the image offers, but that simply foregrounds the aspect of *construction* implicit in this as in all modes of representation.)

Within this image, then, are a number of representational elements which place it within the humanistic paradigm, and then register the specificity of time and place. First, the photo is about young love: a universal human emotion. In 1950 in France, young lovers frequently married and had children; so a second and third order of universal human behaviour are implied in the image. Secondly, the setting in which the image is made locates it quite precisely as the first *arrondissement* of Paris, and tells us that it represents the everyday life of the streets. Thirdly, styles of clothing and the models of cars in the image fix its date fairly well (some time between 1945 and 1955). Fourthly, the cues as to the social groups which the participants belong to also fix the image as concerned with the *classe populaire*. Fifthly, the image is not exploitative or voyeuristic: the subjects, by their apparent ignorance of passers-by and photographer, indicate that they are complicit with their representation in this way. The photographer has merely grasped a 'decisive moment' from what any passer-by would see, a slice of everyday life from the free spectacle of the street. But the passer-by would typically be a member of the *classe populaire* him/herself. And finally, the image is a monochrome (black-and-white) representation of the original scene.

These six elements help us to devise a useful categorization of the central features of the humanistic paradigm:

1 *Universality*: The centrality of 'universalistic' human emotions as subject-matter.

2 *Historicity*: A place–time specificity in the framing (e.g. backgrounding, contextualization) of the image.

3 *Quotidienality*: A concentration on everyday life, the ordinary existence of the *classe populaire*.

4 *Empathy*: A sense of empathy or complicity with the subject of representation.

5 *Commonality*: The viewpoint of the photographer mirrors that of the *classe populaire*.

6 *Monochromaticity*: The image is rendered in monochrome.

Each of these elements is discernible in the output of the humanists for the illustrated press, as well as in their personal work (much of which was used for publication, either at the time of production, or later). It will be evident from the discussion so far that the general perspective of humanism represents an inclusive and generally solidaristic representation of Frenchness, anchored in the *classe populaire* – which, as we have seen, provided the central group in the public imagination in post-war France. We shall now turn to look in greater detail at the themes and subject-matter of humanistic reportage, to explore how each of its themes served to round out the picture of the *classe populaire* and underpin its centrality to images of France and Frenchness in the post-war era.

4.2 The themes and subject-matter of humanistic reportage

The choices of subject-matter by the humanists – and thus the images they made available to the picture agencies and magazines for which they worked, as well as those which formed their personal archives – reflect a number of influences: aesthetic considerations; socio-political interests; cultural linkages to other art forms; and, of course, market forces – the demand for images with particular themes.

If we examine the themes commonly appearing in the work of the humanists, we find a considerable number of images which tend to cluster around ten major areas relating to the wider concerns of French society at this time, and also to the photographers' own personal interests.

These are:

1   *La rue* – the street
2   Children and play
3   The family
4   Love and lovers
5   Paris and its sights
6   *Clochards* – homeless and marginal characters
7   *Fêtes populaires* – fairs and celebrations
8   *Bistrots*
9   *Habitations* – housing and housing conditions
10 Work and craft.

Although far from constituting an exhaustive list, these ten themes are of central importance. They constitute a sort of multi-layered grid on which images of this era made by photographers working within the humanist paradigm can readily be placed. You will recall Kuhn argued that in the 'normal' phase of a scientific paradigm's life-history there are certain recognized puzzles that all adherents of the paradigm have to 'solve'. If we liken Kuhn's puzzles in science to the thematic issues handled by photographers, we can see that the prevalence of these themes within the work of the French humanists functions in much the same way. To work as a humanist was to privilege certain subjects, certain themes, over others. They become the 'puzzles' of normal photography in the humanist paradigm, a series of issues which link directly to the context of the time and place where they were made.

The privileging of specific subjects and themes is also directly connected in a broader sense to the world-view or perspective embraced by the photographers. Though he was speaking about the Popular Front period when he said that 'For a short time the French really believed that they could love another. One felt oneself borne along on a wave of warm-heartedness' (quoted in Galassi, 1987, p. 75), Henri Cartier-Bresson's words could as easily be applied to the immediate post-war period. In 1951, Cartier-Bresson told a journalist that the most important subject for him and his colleagues 'is mankind; man and his life, so brief, so frail, so threatened'. The world-view of the humanists placed great emphasis on the unifying perspective of solidarity, the idea that it is through association and comradeship that French society will be made better, that the *bonheur* (happiness) which each photographer sought to express in his imagery will be found in striving for the general good rather than for individual advantage. More recently, a key member of the humanist group, Willy Ronis, alluded to the concern with solidarity which appears in his work, influencing his approach and his choice of subjects in the immediate post-war period:

> This atmosphere of what I would call feeling, which is strongly imprinted in my photographic choices of the time, it was not simply due to my character and my sensitivity, it was equally present in the ambience of the moment, since we had rediscovered liberty, and we felt very united. There was no longer the fear that existed during the occupation, of not knowing what your neighbour was thinking, for sometimes it was dangerous to speak to your neighbour, because every so often there were denunciations … and then all of a sudden [after the liberation] there was a free press, the occupation forces were gone, it was over and we were all together again. Naturally other problems came up, but they were not problems resulting from war and occupation. That changed everything.
>
> (tr. from a television interview, 1995)

One image which perhaps illustrates this general perspective on *solidarity* very aptly is a photograph by Robert Doisneau, made near his home in Montrouge, on the outskirts of Paris, in 1949 (see Figure 2.2). This deals with solidarity in an intriguing way, and it demonstrates that photographs rarely operate as representations simply on one level.

ACTIVITY 1

Look at Figure 2.2 and try to answer the following questions:

1   How does this photograph fit within the paradigm of French humanism as set out above? In other words, how does it deal with the six elements of the paradigm?

Universality: The centrality of 'universalistic' human emotions as subject-matter.

Historicity: A place–time specificity in the framing (e.g. backgrounding, contextualization) of the image.

Quotidienality: A concentration on everyday life, the ordinary existence of the *classe populaire*.

Empathy: A sense of empathy or complicity with the subject of representation.

Commonality: The viewpoint of the photographer mirrors that of the *classe populaire*.

Monochromaticity: The image is rendered in monochrome.

2   How does Robert Doisneau deal with the concept of *solidarity* in this photograph?

FIGURE 2.2   Robert Doisneau, *La rue du Fort, manifestation pour la paix* (peace demonstration, rue du Fort), Montrouge, 1949.

In the work considered in this chapter, we often find a picture where many themes cross-cut within a single image, and produce a layering of important themes whose representational value increases as each symbolic element is introduced. Such a process is quite evident in Doisneau's photograph, *La rue du Fort, manifestation pour la paix* (peace demonstration, rue du Fort), Montrouge, 1949.

This photograph was made as part of a reportage assignment Doisneau carried out for the French communist party-financed magazine *Regards*. He was assigned to photograph a demonstration organized by the CGT (Confédération Générale du Travail, the union closely linked to the French communist party), which took place at the stade Buffalo (Buffalo Stadium). This sports stadium was not far from the place Jules Ferry where Doisneau was living, whose trees can be seen traversing the image at the top centre of the photograph. Doisneau had gone to the top of a building near the stade Buffalo so that he could photograph the interior of the stadium, filled with demonstrators and their banners, from a high viewpoint, and also have an interesting angle on the procession as it came up the street towards the stadium.

So this is a photograph which is about political events, and also about the area where Doisneau lived, the *banlieue* (industrial suburbs) of Paris, a subject on which he was also then working to produce a book with a noted populist writer, Blaise Cendrars. Now, at the same time as it is an image about Doisneau's interests and work, it is also an image which has certain things to say about the visual approaches of humanist photography, for in its composition it bears all the landmarks of photographic modernism. This is best seen in the tilted angle of view that Doisneau would have seen in his viewfinder frame. But this composition has not been constructed just to make the image more visually interesting. It has a role to play in suggesting the meaning of the photograph. For the strong diagonal tilt has the effect of emphasizing the solitary worker digging his vegetable plot. Thus, the *chacun pour soi* (everyone for himself) individualism which Doisneau had observed amongst some of his neighbours in the *banlieue*, the cultivation of his own little garden, is effectively counterposed to the sense of *solidarity* communicated by the mass of demonstrators with their banners who stream up the rue du Fort. The photograph was used in the book Doisneau published with Blaise Cendrars later in 1949, *La Banlieue de Paris* (Cendrars and Doisneau, 1949). It was Cendrars who chose the images for this book: he also organized the sequence in which they appeared, and wrote captions for them, although his selection and layout followed principles laid down by Doisneau over a decade or more of work on a personal project about the *banlieue* and its people (Hamilton, 1995b, pp. 147–78). You can see that Cendrars was fully aware of the political construction of this image, which he captioned 'They annoy us with their politics ...', for he is careful to point out in his caption that the *décentrement* (tilting) of the image was used to that end.

How does the photograph fit within the grid of the paradigm of French humanist photography? Let us examine each of the constituent elements in turn. First, let's consider *universality*. By using a visual juxtaposition between the group and the individual, Doisneau makes the image turn on the tension between a pair of universals: individual needs and the common good. If we all decide to dig our gardens rather than demonstrating together (acting solidaristically), isn't it unlikely that world peace will be achieved? If we (the French) had acted more solidaristically a few years ago, perhaps we would not have lost a war and suffered occupation? On the other hand, is it not natural that people fear being caught up in the irrationality of the crowd? The presence of the child between the procession and the gardener introduces a further note of ambiguity into the image. World peace is something we dream of for our children's sake, so perhaps the child represents childhood, and stands for the universality of this dilemma, the tension between individualism and solidarity.

Secondly, how does the image invoke *historicity*? To begin with, this is an image which is about the *banlieue* of Paris, a setting which is quite precisely conveyed by the buildings and in particular by their heterogeneous nature and the fact that we can see some allotments in the foreground. Although we can't see the people in detail, we can see they are dressed quite uniformly, and this, with the few vehicles which are also in the frame, provides some clues as to its dating: we are quite clearly in the *banlieue rouge* (left-wing suburbs) of the post-war period.

The photograph deals with *quotidienality* in interesting ways. Doisneau's careful tilt of the frame to emphasize the man digging his garden in effect forces a dynamic juxtaposition, contrasting the ordinary everyday-ness of this activity among the *classe populaire* with the fact that, occurring alongside it, there is indeed an 'event' – a special day on which there is a peace rally at the stade Buffalo in Montrouge. In this way, he creates a framework of *quotidienality* in which the event takes place, and anchors this political event within the everyday life of the *classe populaire*.

The extent to which Doisneau's *empathy* is engaged with the subjects of representation seems at first glance to be quite severely mitigated by his choice of a distant and panoramic viewpoint. This could be taken as distancing him from the scene, almost as an impartial observer. But the frame-tilting works against this, for it pushes our attention towards the solitary digger, and suggests that his individualism is aberrant in this context. Moreover, along the wall which separates allotments from street we see a group who are watching the demonstration, who have laid down their spades to participate in it, if only as complicit observers. By framing the picture in this way, Doisneau suggests that he shares the solidaristic values of those who are actively demonstrating and of those who are passive but sympathetic observers.

Does this photography suggest *commonality* – that the viewpoint of the photographer mirrors that of the *classe populaire*? I think it does this by offering an inclusive view of a fairly mundane side of the event. The peace rally has not yet assembled in the stadium to hear the addresses of the invited speakers. So we are seeing what goes on as the event is being prepared. We, as observers via Doisneau's lens, are offered a 'backstage' view. We are shown a slice of the landscape of the *banlieue*, a sort of cross-section of what goes on there, a scene familiar to any denizen of a small apartment building off the main thoroughfares of the town. Thus, the inclusive viewpoint translates immediately into that of the *classe populaire.* It is exactly what any member of that group could have seen of the event, would have witnessed as it was prepared.

Lastly, the image is provided to us in black-and-white: *monochromaticity* supports the other elements to offer us a photograph which is unmistakably rooted in the typical concerns of the French humanist paradigm. Although it is not impossible to envisage a colour rendering of this scene, such a representation would have been highly anomalous at the time, for two reasons. First, the majority of magazines for which Doisneau and his colleagues worked were only printed in black-and-white (occasionally with a second colour, and sometimes using four colours for the front cover) because the cost of colour printing was beyond their means. Secondly, although colour photography was reasonable advanced by 1949 and its principles were well-known to Doisneau, its use for such a subject in the *banlieue* would have been in marked contrast to its typical uses at the time – highly coloured scenes of major occasions such as a state visit or the wedding of a film-star, postcard views of 'noble' settings (e.g. the great buildings of Paris), or 'charm' photographs for magazine covers (a pretty girl with bright flowers, for instance). Colour photography represented luxury and decoration rather than humanist photo-journalism.

As we have seen by examining *La rue du Fort, manifestation pour la paix*, Montrouge, 1949, each of the elements characteristic of the paradigm of French humanistic photography also has an important relation to the historical moment. Now we can take the analysis a stage further by examining the central themes explored in the work of the French humanists: as the discussion of key trends in the social development of France from the 1930s to the late 1950s in section 3 has demonstrated, these themes translate directly into the preoccupations of the French during this era, and reflect the social changes which France was experiencing.

4.3 *La rue* – the street

If any one locale could be said to characterize French humanism it is *la rue.* This is due in part to the characteristic mode of working of these photographers, the fact that they preferred to make their photographs *sur le vif* (on the spur of the moment) in the street rather than in the studio. This implies a naturalism in their approach, a stress on the use of available rather than artificial light, the attempt to reproduce the ambience of the scene in the photograph. We should not ignore the fact that the overwhelming majority of their images were made in black-and-white, thus reducing the complexity of the street scene to a more manageable palette of shades of grey.

Yet *la rue* is not simply a visually interesting place. For the humanists it is the quintessential site *par excellence* where the public life of ordinary people occurs. The street is the site of market life, of the *spectacle gratuit* (free entertainment). It offered what the writer Pierre Mac Orlan (1882–1970) called the 'fantastique social de la rue' (social fantastic of the street). His formulation indicates that *la rue* was itself a space which was the object of much literary and artistic activity, a site whose nature was a sort of construction of debates which go back in France to mid-nineteenth-century writers such as Baudelaire. Such debates are intimately connected to ideas about modernity itself – a modernity first expressed by Charles Baudelaire (1821–67) as a world of the contingent, the transitory, the fleeting, whose quintessential expression is the modern city. And no city is more 'modern' than Paris. In the work of photographers such as Cartier-Bresson, Doisneau, Ronis and several others working within the humanist paradigm, we see a common tendency to produce pictures which represent the city with all the ambivalence characteristic of modernism, as both a well-oiled machine, and a strange, even magical, place. Even the form of photography in which they engaged – which involved a good deal of wandering about on the streets – could be said to represent the viewpoint of Baudelaire's modernist *flâneur* (strolling onlooker). For Baudelaire, the natural milieu of the *flâneur* is the ebb and flow of the urban crowd. It is significant that nearly a century later such a viewpoint continued to underpin the approach of the humanists: for instance, when describing his approach to photographing in the street, Robert Doisneau would often cite an old adage that 'Paris est un théâtre où on paie sa place avec du temps perdu' (Paris is a theatre where you pay for your seat by wasting time) (see Hamilton, 1995b, p. 249).

Thus, for photographers working in the French humanist paradigm, the street was a terrain which had already been circumscribed by the artistic debates around modernity and modernism. They grew up and learned their photography during a period marked by extensive change in both society and the visual arts. Much of this change turned around the modern city as a site of new approaches to society and culture, as the locus of the new forms of industry and commerce which would transform the world. By the late 1920s, when the modernist 'new vision' photography pioneered in Germany and Eastern Europe was beginning to attract attention in France, its influence was subject to modification by other artistic movements challenging the 'machine-age utopia' which such work seemed to celebrate. The surrealist movement found in photography a means of exploring the fundamental irrationalism which its members defined as underpinning the apparent order of modern life. Salvador Dali proposed that even the most humble photographic document was a 'pure creation of the mind', whilst André Breton used photographic views of Parisian streets without any special visual merit to illustrate his novel *Nadja* of 1928. Surrealists believed in the power of the image to reveal the unconscious. As Louis Aragon put it in his novel *Paysan de Paris* of 1925, '[For] each man there awaits ... a particular image capable of annihilating the entire universe'. The belief that photographs could be prised loose of their usual context and employed to challenge accepted conventions explains the surrealists' fascination with the apparently purely 'documentary' photographs of Eugéne Atget (1858–1927). In his pictures of the city streets and their inhabitants, often blurred or ghostlike because of the long exposures his methods and equipment demanded, surrealists could find support for the idea that Paris was a 'dream capital', an 'urban labyrinth of memory and desire':

> Even for photographers working at several removes from organized groups like Breton's, surrealist themes and ideas proved inescapable. Especially for those beginning to explore the world outside the studio with unobtrusive handheld cameras, the surrealist model of an urban *flâneur*, a wanderer open to chance encounters, was crucial. ... [Aragon] believed that if one were attuned to the fleeting gestures, enigmatic objects, and veiled eroticism glimpsed in the street, an unsuspected pattern of affinities – a new kind of poetic knowledge – might be revealed. In the late twenties and early thirties the belief that the camera could snare and fix these moments of instantaneous, lyrical perception had many important adherents, among them Germaine Krull, Eli Lotar, and especially André Kertész and Henri Cartier-Bresson.
>
> (Hambourg and Phillips, 1994, p. 101)

If the surrealists identified the street as a key site for a fantastic world which lay just below the surface of mundane reality, they were not alone: other literary and artistic movements also focused on this space because it was the arena of popular life and culture. One important source of such ideas was the writer Pierre Mac Orlan, who shared with the surrealists an interest in the work of Eugéne Atget. Though he only began to write about such work at about the same time as Atget died, Mac Orlan provided a rationale for the primacy of the street in the emergent French humanist paradigm when he put forward the idea that such a photography was especially effective at transmitting 'le fantastique social de la rue':

> Known primarily for his stories of outsiders in atmospheric locales (of which *Quai des brumes* remains the best known), Mac Orlan was no surrealist ... He was, however, perhaps the most perceptive French photographic critic during this period, and he developed what amounted to a modern poetics of the medium. Taking his cue from Léger, who had noted the 'shock of contrast' provided by a modern billboard set in the countryside, Mac Orlan reflected at length on the collision between technological civilization and the remnants of a popular culture rooted in the past. His notion of the 'social fantastic' referred to the frequently bizarre juxtapositions of the archaic and the modern, the human and the inanimate, glancingly encountered each day in the streets of the modern city – as, for example, in Kertész's split-second perception of the uncanny correspondence between anonymous passers-by and the cut-out figures of an advertising display [see Figure 2.3]. This mysterious new dimension of social reality could, according to Mac Orlan, be best

explored by photographers, the most 'lyrical, meticulous witnesses' of the present.

Mac Orlan recognized Eugéne Atget as the precursor of this new photographic sensibility, but his Atget bore little resemblance to the Atget claimed by the surrealists. No primitive but 'a man who loved his métier and practised it with mastery', Mac Orlan's Atget could translate a place or a moment into an image saturated with evocative power – an image that launched its viewer on an 'adventure of interpretation'.

Mac Orlan identified Atget's contemporary heirs as the photographic reporters. For these 'visionaries of the objective', photography was not an art of deliberate meditation but of instinct and immediacy.

(Hambourg and Phillips, 1994, pp. 101–2)

Later in the 1930s, writing about Kertész's photographs of Paris, Mac Orlan declared that 'photography is the great expressionist art of our time' (1934). The ideal activity for both photographer and writer as visualized by Mac Orlan was thus to be a *flâneur*, a casual spectator who observes the 'fantastique social' of the street by taking part in it.

Although Mac Orlan was not a surrealist, his vision of the city has certain links to their point of view. But whilst Breton, Aragon, Man Ray and others saw the city as a metaphor for the essential irrationality of modern life, Mac Orlan's perspective was more concerned with the senses in which the city street is a stage on which all sorts of amazing stories are enacted. The street offered a continuous spectacle, an unending series of tableaux, immortalized in popular song and in the oral narrative tradition of ordinary Parisians. Mac Orlan believed that the street photography of those working in the French humanist paradigm was particularly effective at capturing moments in this flowing stream of daily life, at producing, as he termed them, 'poems of the street'. It is thus highly significant that Mac Orlan should later (in an unpublished letter to Willy Ronis in 1948) spontaneously describe some of Ronis's photographs of the popular quarter of Belleville-Ménilmontant as 'poems of the street', and be keen to associate himself with a book of photographs which Ronis and he published in 1954 (Ronis and Mac Orlan, 1954; see also Hamilton, 1995a, p. 31).

ACTIVITY 2

Now look at the three photographs of *la rue* shown in Figures 2.3, 2.4 and 2.5. Whilst looking at these images, consider how they fit within the French humanist paradigm, and what they tell us about how the photographers represented the daily life of the *classe populaire*.

FIGURE 2.3   André Kertész, *Dubo, Dubon, Dubonnet*, Paris 1934.

FIGURE 2.4   Willy Ronis, *Avenue Simon Bolivar, Belleville-Ménilmontant*, Paris, 1950.

FIGURE 2.5   Robert Doisneau, *L'accordéoniste de la rue Mouffetard* (the accordionist of rue Mouffetard),
Paris, 1951.

These three photographs span three decades. The earliest is by André Kertész, a Hungarian photographer who, although strictly speaking not a central member of the French humanist group in the period which concerns us (for he had left Paris for New York by 1936), none the less created a body of work which was highly influential. This photograph also demonstrates how his work encapsulated Mac Orlan's ideas about the 'social fantastic'. As the above extract from Hambourg and Phillips points out, this idea:

> … referred to the frequently bizarre juxtapositions of the archaic and the modern, the human and the inanimate, glancingly encountered each day in the streets of the modern city – as, for example, in Kertész's split-second perception of the uncanny correspondence between anonymous passers-by and the cut-out figures of an advertising display. This mysterious new dimension of social reality could, according to Mac Orlan, be best explored by photographers, the most 'lyrical, meticulous witnesses' of the present.
>
> (Hambourg and Phillips, 1994, p. 102)

Kertész's work was widely published in the magazines which the young humanist photographers most admired in the early 1930s: *Vu, Art et Medicine, Minotaure.* Although the content of this image is more in line with Mac Orlan's 'social fantastic' than it is with humanism, nevertheless the approach which Kertész takes to his subject-matter appears to have greatly influenced his younger French colleagues. But, as the images of Doisneau and Ronis demonstrate, their fascination with 'the frequently bizarre juxtapositions of the archaic and the modern, the human and the inanimate, glancingly encountered each day in the streets of the modern city' is more *humanized* than that of Kertész, for whom the formal juxtaposition dominates the imagery. The people and the advertising images are as one: that is the point of the photograph. We don't really see them as members of a social group at all, so this is not a picture which informs our understanding of the *classe populaire.*

In Ronis's *Avenue Simon Bolivar, Belleville-Ménilmontant,* Paris, 1950, the sense of juxtaposition between each of the elements – archaic and modern, human and inanimate, to adopt the phraseology of Hambourg and Phillips – is quite clear-cut. However, in this case what we see in the image are people who seem less like cardboard cut-outs than they do in Kertész's photograph. A woman with her child carefully negotiates the steps. A man drives his horse and cart along the street, a shoe-mender converses with his customer, a couple push their child in a pram, a worker mends the traffic-light, a woman walks along with her small child in a push-chair. Even though we see none of these figures in close-up, they all seem to be real human beings, going about their normal activities. They represent the normal life of the street, and they humanize it as a space by their presence. The relationship between the figures hints at an order which is more inclusive; in other words, it suggests that we are viewing a community. The relative uniformity of the individuals who are pictured also suggests that their social condition is relatively similar. We have no trouble in identifying them as members of the *classe populaire*. We are in a working-class quarter of Paris, and the photograph represents an organic community.

In Robert Doisneau's photograph of *L'accordéoniste de la rue Mouffetard*, Paris, 1951, we are in slightly more enigmatic territory. We see three individuals quite clearly in this photograph: a woman on the right; a young man (art-student?) who is probably sketching just off-centre; and a blind accordionist in the left foreground. The remainder of the dramatis personae have their backs to us, and are obviously absorbed in something obscure. Perhaps to reinforce its obscurity, a no-entry sign looms above their heads. We are definitely in the territory of the social fantastic of the street, of which Mac Orlan was so fond. However, if we explore a little deeper we see this is a photograph which goes beyond bizarre juxtaposition, to tell us something about solidarity and the *classe populaire*. Apart from the art-student, whose dress and demeanour suggest he is an observer from the outside, all of the figures in this photograph are simply, even modestly, dressed. We are on the corner of a shopping street in Paris's Latin Quarter: in fact in an area then (1951) quite run-down, where many homeless people or *clochards* lived. So clearly we are in the habitat of the *classe populaire*.

The crowd has turned its back on the blind accordionist, more interested in the amusement of the street corner. The woman is gazing out of frame, she has little interest in the accordionist either. He is an object of the gaze of the photographer and of the art-student alone, a man isolated by his disability (blindness) from involvement in the spectacle of the street, yet part of it as a producer of street entertainment. Let's assume for an instant that he is a *mutilé de guerre* (someone wounded in the war). By framing his image in this way, is Doisneau suggesting to us (the viewer in 1951) that we have begun to forget about those who made a sacrifice for France? That we are beginning to be all too concerned with our own welfare to the detriment of others? The only person seemingly taking notice of the accordionist wants to appropriate him for his own purposes, as a subject in his drawing.

4.4 Children and play

The centrality of imagery about childhood and play in the post-war era seems readily explicable in the context of post-war reconstruction in France. The fact that 'old France' was so closely associated with 'Malthusianism' – essentially birth control practices which limited the population – placed even greater emphasis on the need to rebuild the society and the nation. The move from being a country in which the population was declining pre-war to one which would need to make up its numbers by reproducing at as rapid a rate as possible involved a transformation in attitudes. From 1945 it was a socially responsible thing to have children: the *famille nombreuse* (large family) became an object of veneration rather than moral disapproval. De Gaulle himself had called upon the French to produce '12 million beautiful babies'. Under the Third Republic the large family had increasingly come to be seen as either a signifier of bourgeois domesticity and wealth or of immigrant penury; now it was respectable amongst the *classe populaire*, a duty even. Mothers who had borne more than five children were entitled to receive a medal from the prefect of their *département*.

The 'baby boom' of the post-war era (the birth-rate was at its highest between 1946 and 1950, before a slightly higher peak between 1961 and 1965) was the result of a number of factors: the return of a large proportion of the younger male population either from imprisonment in Germany or from internal exile in the southern half of the country; the lifting of the threat of imprisonment, deportation or worse; the natural sense of optimism which occurs within populations from whom the threat of war has been lifted. In this context, which saw the birth-rate rise from about 630,000 a year before the war to over 800,000 a year from 1945 onwards, and an equivalent decline in infant mortality as well, it would be surprising if the humanist photographers had not widely represented childhood in their work. But another factor is also relevant. Most of the photographers themselves became parents during this period, for, as we have seen earlier, one important aspect of their work was that it drew upon the same sources which nourished their own lives. Often, the photographs which represent childhood are of their own children: as in Willy Ronis's famous image of his son Vincent launching a model aeroplane in 1952.

FIGURE 2.6 Henri Cartier-Bresson, *Michel Gabriel, rue Mouffetard*, Paris, 1952.

ACTIVITY 3

Now look at the three photographs on childhood and play shown in
Figures 2.6, 2.7 and 2.8. How do these images represent childhood within
the context of the *classe populaire*?

FIGURE 2.7   Robert Doisneau, *La voiture des enfants* (the children's car), Porte d'Orléans, Paris, 1944.

FIGURE 2.8
Willy Ronis, *École maternelle, rue de Ménilmontant* (nursery school in the rue de Ménilmontant), Paris, 1954.

Henri Cartier-Bresson's photograph of the young Michel Gabriel proudly carrying home his two bottles of wine manages to convey the idea of a new and exuberant generation of French children and the sense of a *classe populaire* confident of its position in society. Michel is evidently proud that he's been given the responsibility of bringing back the *vin de table*, then a staple part of the diet of the *classe populaire*. He is proud perhaps of being photographed. (Was he aware? Cartier-Bresson always tried to make pictures without alerting his subjects.) He is showing off to the girls we can see in the background: for this is not merely an errand, but a game. The street which forms its background is the natural site of such play, the locus for the entertainment of the *classe populaire*.

In Robert Doisneau's *La voiture des enfants,* Porte d'Orléans, Paris, 1944, we have another image, this time one in which representations of childhood and play offer a solidaristic viewpoint. Different age groups – from a boy aged perhaps 14–15 to a pair of infants – happily coexist in their wrecked car, photographed on the wasteland of the zone on the outskirts of the city, not far from Doisneau's home in Montrouge. This photograph was taken in the late summer of 1944 (probably soon after the Liberation of Paris), but from 1942 onwards the French birth-rate had been steadily growing so the evidence of a latent 'baby boom' was mounting even before post-war reconstruction had begun. The signs of waste and destruction in the image are visual ploys which put emphasis on the vulnerability and attractiveness of the children by the effect of juxtaposition; but are they there for a purpose which has to do with the imminent end of the war? The framing and selection of the image invokes a universal value – the sanctity of a happy childhood – but this is counterposed and reinforced by the wrecked car and rubble, symbolic of war and conflict. Play is symbolic of freedom, so the photograph has something to say not simply about childhood but also about liberation from an occupying power. (It is fascinating to note that when Doisneau photographed the insurrection which led to the Liberation of Paris in August 1944, some of his photographs concentrated on how Parisian children were reacting to the events by, for instance, camouflaging toy prams to imitate the camouflaged tanks and lorries of the retreating German army.)

In the later photograph (1954) *École maternelle, rue de Ménilmontant*, Willy Ronis offers an image which must have been very familiar to parents of the era: a line of children, holding hands two by two, are led by their teacher across a school yard. By Ronis's framing of the image we are immediately drawn into the context, for we observe from a window of the school itself. So this is a privileged image of the nursery school, one usually available only to teachers or pupils. This framing also offers another interpretation of the scene: the idea that these children are being carefully protected and nurtured, because they are the future of France. (It is interesting to note that this photograph was also used for a poster campaign at the time to encourage parents to ensure they had their children immunized: this campaign, though not explicitly mentioning it, evidently traded on the same idea.)

4.5   The family

For reasons which will be obvious, the emphasis on familial themes has clear linkages to others, particularly those of childhood and play, housing and housing conditions, and love and lovers. But, as we have noted, the immediate post-war period in France was also one in which there were severe strains on the family as a social institution. The return of the 1.7 million prisoners and deportees from Germany from early 1945 onwards created many difficulties, leading to a high rate of divorce and separation. Poor housing conditions must have played a role in this, as did the penury of the period 1945–7. Despite de Gaulle's exhortations to the French to create 'beautiful babies', social surveys indicated that fully one-third of all pregnancies were unwanted. Compared with other developed countries, birth control remained primitive, and abortion continued on a massive scale (perhaps half a million a year) with probably 20,000 women dying per year as a result of the back-street or self-induced nature of most of these terminations. The first French family planning clinic was not set up until as late as 1961 (Larkin, 1988, p. 180).

The introduction of social welfare reforms by governments of the liberation era (which were added to those instituted just before the war, and by the Vichy regime during it) served to bolster the family, and by 1958 the proportion of working-class family income accounted for by welfare payments (family allowances etc.) amounted to as much as 20–25 per cent as opposed to less than 3 per cent pre-war (Larkin, 1988, p. 206). Although the family as an institution was under some threat in post-war France, the long-run increase in the birth-rate and social welfare measures placed great emphasis, both in public policy and in the popular consciousness, on the *centrality* of the family as a pillar of reconstruction, as a means of rebuilding France. The tax regime favoured larger families and penalized the single and households without children. Over the period 1943–62, average family size was at its highest in 1950 (when it reached 2.45 persons). Speaking of the post-war change in attitudes to the family, Dominique Borne writes 'the measures were taken at a moment when a change in climate began to be seen, a rehabilitation of the family: from the constricting social unit which the literature and the theatre of the 1930s had commented upon ironically, it became the household in which the child took a central place and was the source of happiness' (tr. from Borne, 1992, p. 81).

Although the constitution of 1946 had confirmed that women shared equal rights with men, the older Code Napoléon which regulated marriage and the family was in force until 1965. This ensured that husbands retained formal authority in a marriage:

> … until 1970, the man had legal control of the children. Authority was the property of the father, tenderness of the mother. Of course the model was often contradicted by the facts – in the case of divorce children were almost always given to the mother – but, since the birth-rate was so important, the bourgeois family model remained dominant, and the mother's place was in the household. Moreover, few middle and upper class women worked, and even working-class women were less likely to work than before the war.
>
> (tr. from Borne, 1992, p. 82)

> From the war until the 1960s, the family changes: larger than in the 1930s, vigorously encouraged by the state, founded on a couple which relies far more than before on their feelings of affection as the criterion for the choice of partner. However, traditions remain: the foundation of the union is the institution of marriage, the family is virtually the only place of reproduction, family relations are highly hierarchical. Sexuality is still a taboo subject, single mothers (called girl-mothers at the time) are pointed out in the streets.
>
> (tr. from Borne, 1992, p. 82)

What we see therefore in the representations of the family produced by the humanists is a large number of images which deal with these themes, and in large measure reproduce the moral framework emphasized by Borne.

ACTIVITY 4

Now look at the four photographs on the family shown in Figures 2.9 to 2.12.

Rather than being given a commentary on the content of these images as in the earlier examples, you should now feel confident enough with this mode of analysis to start providing your own notes on how these images fit with the general thesis that the themes that most concerned the French humanists played a role in offering more inclusive representations of France and Frenchness.

How do these images represent the family in post-war France?

FIGURE 2.9
Robert Doisneau, *La ruban de la mariée* (marriage ceremony in Poitou), Haut Vienne, 1952.

FIGURE 2.10
Robert Doisneau,
La paix du soir (a peaceful
evening), Montrouge, 1955.

FIGURE 2.11
Willy Ronis, *Le départ du morutier*
(a cod-fisherman takes his leave),
Fécamp, 1949.

FIGURE 2.12   Henri Cartier-Bresson, *Family being photographed outside their shack in the zone*, Paris, 1953.

4.6 Love and lovers

As Dominique Borne has emphasized, in the 1940s and 1950s, 'the family changes: larger than in the 1930s, vigorously encouraged by the state, *founded on a couple which relies far more than before on their feelings of affection as the criterion for the choice of partner. …* Sexuality is still a taboo subject, single mothers (called girl-mothers at the time) are pointed out in the streets' (ibid., p. 82; my emphasis). The centrality of love and affection as the basis of marriage and the family in post-war France is translated into a rich vein of imagery by the humanists.

As you will recall from the detailed analysis of Robert Doisneau's *Le baiser de l'Hôtel de Ville* in section 4.1, the theme of love and lovers is a central element in the humanists' imagery of post-war France: not merely for internal consumption, but for export abroad as well. The 'poetic realism' which seems to characterize their approach is, as Marie de Thézy points out,

closely linked to their 'love of humanity' (de Thézy, 1992, p. 15). Thus, the young lovers – whose representational role in the context of post-war reconstruction bridges issues about the family and about fraternity generally – have a central part to play in representations of France itself. Within the work of all of the humanist photographers there are many images which deal with a theme which has more than simply romantic associations.

In Henri Cartier-Bresson's photograph of a couple embracing in front of a motorcycle (*Paris,* 1952; see Figure 2.13) and Willy Ronis's slightly later image (*Les amoureux de la Bastille* (lovers at the Bastille), 1957; see Figure 2.14), the representation of the lovers confines sexuality to, at best, a kiss or close physical proximity. More overt forms of sexuality were generally speaking simply not represented because of a shared

FIGURE 2.13 Henri Cartier-Bresson, *Paris*, 1952.

FIGURE 2.14   Willy Ronis, *Les amoureux de la Bastille* (lovers at the Bastille), 1957.

sense of *pudicité* (modesty, discretion) on the part of the photographers. They might however be alluded to, for instance in images of the 'world of the night' (night-clubs, bars, dance-halls, etc.). In Robert Doisneau's photographs of the tattooed people he found in squalid *bistrots* on the Left Bank or near the Les Halles produce market, for instance, there are examples of erotic imagery as part of the tattoos; but in most cases he ensured that the pictures were cropped so as to exclude them.

4.7   Paris and its sights

The predominance of Paris and its sights in the imagery of the humanists also has its social and economic overtones. For if Paris and its architecture, its streets and public places, represents France, it was also a place to which large numbers of French people flocked after the war. France experienced a massive exodus from the countryside as those hitherto employed on the land came to the Paris region to work on building sites, in factories and in offices. Between 1946 and 1954, one million male workers left agriculture for the cities, followed by a further 700,000 between 1954 and 1962.

But the role of Paris in the new France contains certain ambiguities, especially in the representations of the humanists. Whilst the capital represented modernism, it also stood for older ideas about the city as a collection of smaller communities, each with its own distinctive character. As de Thézy points out, the humanists were also overwhelmingly attracted to the less salubrious aspects of the city:

They roamed in a Paris still resembling a village, a Paris of people who over the years and the centuries had left their imprint. The friend and walking companion of Brassaï, the American writer Henry Miller, expressed himself in these terms: '… when I come back in the evening, the rue Tombe Issoire, ugly, morbid, particularly in those parts where it is falling into ruins, is a street from a fairy-story. I hope it will always be like that, that no house is repainted, no window repaired; it is perfect as it is in its obsolescence. It is a small history of French thought, of French feeling, of French taste. From the little two-place urinal (*pissotiére*) on the crossroads, up to the wash-house, a little higher, it is a pure masterpiece. It has been mended and patched, piecemeal, but it has not changed' …

(tr. from de Thézy, 1992, p. 15)

A classic of this genre is Willy Ronis's study of Belleville-Ménilmontant in north-east Paris (Ronis and Mac Orlan, 1954). As Ronis has said: 'I can't remember if I thought that the *quartier* would disappear as soon as it did, but so much of Paris was changing in this period (1947–50) that I wanted to record this way of life before it went forever' (tr. from unpublished interview).

This hilly *quartier*, with its winding roads, old buildings and frequent dead-ends, had the reputation of being slightly dangerous, on the edge between the civilization of the city and the savagery of the 'zone' – the wasteland between Paris and the countryside. In popular mythology it was the home of the Communards of 1870, and of the *titi Parisien* such as Maurice Chevalier and *la môme* Piaf who were both born there. It was a place where ordinary people went to drink and socialize in the many tiny b*uvettes* (drinking stalls), *cafés* and *bals populaires* (small dance halls). It was a vibrant, colourful community, with a solid social base, where many artisans and craftsmen lived, and in which small factories and workshops proliferated.

Ronis could not immediately find a publisher for his work, despite an offer by the writer Pierre Mac Orlan, who wrote to him saying that he must:

> … write a study for your great collection on the life of Ménilmontant. I already have the cardinal elements of it in front of me: they are part of what I have always called the social fantastic (*fantastique social*) which for want of a better term designates a contemporary romanticism. I find this presence of the poetic and mysterious force of everyday life in your poems of the street. You take images of life in a way which is already familiar to me. One detail, of a violent discretion, gives to a spectacle its literary value. Photography is far more a part of literary art than it is of the plastic arts. But that would be the theme of my preface.

(quoted in Hamilton, 1995a, p. 31)

FIGURE 2.15
Willy Ronis, *Place Vendôme*, 1947.

The idea that the photographs of Ronis and other humanists are concerned with a 'poetic realism' is aptly expressed by Mac Orlan. But it is also closely connected to the existing demand within the publishing trade for books about Paris and its sights. There was a strong market in France for album books – well-reproduced collections of photographs on a given theme, supplemented with a text usually presented in the form of a preface written by a prominent author. In the late 1940s and early 1950s, several of Ronis's confrères had produced such works: Robert Doisneau with Blaise Cendrars in *La Banlieue de Paris* (1949) and *Instantanés de Paris* (1955); Henri Cartier-Bresson with Tériade in *Images à la Sauvette* (1952); Izis with Jean Cocteau in *Paris des Rêves* (1950); Izis with Jacques Prévert in *Grand Bal du Printemps* (1951) and *Charmes de Londres* (1952); and Izis with Colette in *Paradis Terrestre* (1953). There were also several compilations where many of the humanists were represented, such as François Cali's *Sortilèges de Paris* (1952). All of these publications encapsulated one or other aspect of the poetic realism of humanist photography. Interestingly, they could contain more oblique references to Parisian monuments, as in Willy Ronis's *Place Vendôme,* 1947 (see Figure 2.15) and Robert Doisneau's *Place de la Bastille*, 1947 (see Figure 2.16). The symbolic role of Paris as the representation of a new France in which past and present intermingle thus combined with a demand for touristic images consumed as much if not more in France than abroad (many of the photographic albums of Paris published in this era with images by the humanists have only French texts).

FIGURE 2.16
Robert Doisneau,
Place de la Bastille,
1947.

4.8 *Clochards* – homeless and marginal characters

The emphasis on *clochards*, and on the exotic world of the marginal people
of the night which occurs throughout the iconography of the humanists, is
explained by the role which such figures play in the construction of an
inclusive Frenchness in such imagery.

For the humanists, as Marie de Thézy argues: 'The symbol of [a] rediscovered
internal freedom then was the *clochard* [homeless person or vagrant], an
omnipresent theme in literature and image. Free of all attachments, of all
conventions, he is humanity in its purest state' (de Thézy, 1992, p. 15). Rather
than marginalizing the *clochard*, he or she is included within the framework
of humanism. However, whilst the *clochard* certainly figures as a romantic
and mysterious figure in the literature of writers like Mac Orlan, Jacques
Prévert, Jean Paulhan, and Raymond Queneau, and is celebrated in the
artistic theories of avant-garde painters such as Jean Dubuffet, it is evident
that such people also played a well-established role in the economy and

FIGURE 2.17
Robert Doisneau, *l'Amiral, roi des clochards, Germaine, sa reine et leur buffon, l'ancien clown Spinelli* (the Admiral, king of the tramps, his queen Germaine and their jester, the former clown Spinelli), Paris, 1952.

society of post-war Paris. *Clochards* both define the limits of normality and are represented as an integral element of the city's populace. But even more remarkably, they are represented as a microcosmic *community*.

In the immediate post-war period there was a population of perhaps 5,000 or more *clochards* in the Maubert and Mouffetard districts of the Left Bank alone (out of the total of perhaps 10,000 or so in Paris), living amongst the derelict *hôtels particuliers* (private mansions) and ancient apartment buildings of the *quartier*. There, and across the Seine around Les Halles (the central market until 1968), there existed a whole network of restaurants, *bistrots* and even small hotels which catered for the *clochards*. They formed a shifting and precarious society and economy – but most interestingly of all, a subculture – which functioned at the heart of the great city. As a noted writer on this world (and a collaborator with several of the humanist photographers), Robert Giraud, puts it: 'the *clochard* does not work, he carries out obligations. Everyone has his fiddle, or his "defence" (his way of getting by), that he will not give up to anyone else, and of which he jealously guards the secret. The *clochard* gets by during the night and often sleeps during the day wherever he is taken by fatigue, on a bench, a ventilation

FIGURE 2.18
Robert Doisneau,
*Monsieur et
Madame Garofino,*
1951.

grille, even on the pavement or on the paths along the Seine' (quoted in
Hamilton, 1995b, p. 190).

These were the people who begged outside the churches of the Latin Quarter,
who collected cigarette-ends in the streets and *bistrots* to sell at the 'dog-end'
market (*marché des mégots*) in the place Maubert, who were engaged as
casual help in the markets, and who foraged in the detritus of the 'stomach of
Paris' at Les Halles. Others worked as *biffins* during the night, ensuring that
the rubbish bins were placed out in the street to be collected by the dustmen
as they passed through the city, and sifting through the rubbish for anything
worth selling which could be carried away in an old pram. They slept rough
on the *quais* of the Seine and under the bridges of Paris, and plied a
miserable trade as freaks in cafés and bars, showing their tattoos and
deformities to the clientele for a few *sous*. They were a reserve army of labour
for the market traders of Les Halles, unloading the produce delivered each
night to the stalls, and clearing up the old cabbages and butchers' scraps
which could not be sold. It was taken for granted that those who worked the
markets stole some of what they handled, an amount traditionally allowed
for by the traders who called it *la redresse*.

4.9 *Fêtes populaires* – fairs and celebrations

In the huge body of work produced by the humanists, there are many images which depict the celebration of solidaristic community, and this – apart from the extremely photogenic nature of such events – goes a long way to explain the prevalence of *fêtes populaires* (fairs and celebrations) in the corpus. Certain moments were privileged: the common practice of holding street parties for the 14 July celebrations can be seen as expressive of both local *and* national solidarities. Bastille Day of course must be considered as being an important celebration of the French state as well as an occasion for simple enjoyment. In the aftermath of war, such festivities had a representational value of great significance. But they were also celebrations of a more traditional and communitarian style of life. In the contact sheet of twelve images taken from Robert Doisneau's photographs of the 14 July celebrations in the Latin Quarter, 1949 (reproduced in Figure 2.19), we get a glimpse of how the humanists approached such themes. It seems clear that Doisneau wanted to record the communal aspects of the street party: for the images deal with various aspects of the idea that popular entertainment involved everybody, young and old, and that the celebrations spill over from public into private space. Perhaps it is significant that the band is set up in front of the 'Maison de la Famille' – it is certainly no accident that Doisneau ensured that his photograph contained this juxtaposition of building and people.

It is also probable that humanist photographers fastened on the *fêtes populaires* because they were the symbol of a more traditional and solidaristic society, one which was tied to a particular place and time, integrated within the pattern of work (the *fêtes populaires* generally being celebrations of key moments in the agricultural cycle) and within a restricted framework of everyday life. In the immediate post-war period, the rural connections of the *fêtes* were in process of being severed, and the local events, such as that shown by Robert Doisneau in his *Course de valise* (suitcase race) at Athis-Mons (see Figure 2.20), made in the outer suburbs of Paris in 1945, offer an image of urbanized festival. The ritualistic aspects of the festival are already in process of being redefined: for, as the 1940s and 1950s progressed, they began to give way to the development of leisure, in itself a largely urban construction. Leisure is the opposite of work; it is less integrated within the framework of everyday life, being rather a symbol of *another* life. As life for ordinary French people became more privatized, the tendency for people to go out into the street to celebrate at *fêtes populaires* became less marked. The wider diffusion of the four great symbols of privatized life – the car, the television, the refrigerator and the washing machine – began to occur on a major scale towards the end of the 1950s. Until that time, few households had access to the goods which helped to create a 'civilization of leisure', as one famous book of the early 1960s put it (Dumazedier, 1962).

Thus, the emphasis on popular celebrations in the work of the humanists attests to a desire on their part to represent the life of the *classe populaire* as

FIGURE 2.19 Robert Doisneau, Contact sheet showing twelve photographs of the 14 July celebrations, Latin Quarter, 1949.

FIGURE 2.20
Robert Doisneau,
Course de valise
(suitcase race, at
Athis-Mons, near
Paris), 1945.

solidaristic, and this also partly explains their great fascination with side-shows and fairgrounds. But the fact that high culture was contemptuous of popular entertainment was also a motivating force. Humanism contained subversive notions and its imagery often included pictures which cocked a snook at authority. As the *forains* (side-show people) represented a marginal and alternative popular subculture, many humanists were drawn to photograph them out of a desire to record this aspect of life. Until the late 1950s, touring fairs would regularly visit most of the *quartiers populaires* of Paris, whilst *banquistes* (itinerant street performers) were a common everyday sight – as in Henri Cartier-Bresson's *Fire-eater,* place de la Bastille, 1952 (see Figure 2.21). Whilst such material is evidently highly photogenic, it also strongly evokes the solidaristic aspects of popular entertainment, an element also found in the concentration of imagery around the *bistrot*.

FIGURE 2.21   Henri Cartier-Bresson, *Fire-eater,* place de la Bastille, 1952.

4.10 *Bistrots*

In the post-war era, the *bistrot* (a sort of cross between café, bar and pub) was a critical locus of community life, a public space in which many solidaristic activities could take place. Within an urban context, the *bistrot* formed a central element in the functioning of local communities. It was the place where political groups could meet, as well as the headquarters of a local sports club such as a football team, or the regular venue for a card-school, as in Willy Ronis's *Café-guinguette, rue des Cascades*, Belleville, 1949 (see Figure 2.22). Its omnipresence in the photographs of the humanists thus attests to its centrality in the life of the popular community. Indeed, there was an entire literature focused on *la vie du bistrot* (*bistrot* life), which was held to be almost a cultural form in its own right – the place where the oral narrative tradition had its securest moorings, the space where people met as friends, as lovers, for business, or to exercise their profession (writers like Sartre, de Beauvoir, Queneau, for instance, worked daily at a café table).

Marie de Thézy argues that the centrality of the *bistrot* in the humanist paradigm derives from its universality: 'Accessible to everyone, the *bistrots* were the meeting place of the people of the street. Even the most scruffy wanderer could always experience "the inexpressibly simple pleasure of entering a familiar café … of shaking hands … of talking about his life"' (de Thézy, 1992, p. 16). Robert Doisneau's *Un café d'été* (a summer café), Arcueil, 1945 (see Figure 2.23) perfectly expresses this common thread in the humanist corpus.

FIGURE 2.22 Willy Ronis, *Café-guinguette, rue des Cascades*, Belleville, 1949.

FIGURE 2.23
Robert Doisneau,
Un café d'été (a
summer café),
Arcueil, 1945.

FIGURE 2.24
Robert Doisneau,
*Restaurant
tiquetonne, les
Halles,* Paris,1952.

The *bistrot* was also a space where itinerant entertainers – from accordionists to those who exhibited their tattoos and deformities – could ply their trade. This might be a simple eating-place, as shown in Robert Doisneau's 1952 image *Restaurant tiquetonne*, in the Les Halles produce market area, where the diners are entertained by Pierrette d'Orient and Madame Berthe (see Figure 2.24). As a site of popular entertainment, the *bistrot* offered a place where its enjoyment was communal rather than privatized. It is thus a symbolic locus of sociability – the tendency to associate and communicate with others which cements society together.

4.11   *Habitations* – housing and housing conditions

Post-war France had to rebuild itself: all of its new families had to be housed, industry had to be renovated, the needs of an expanding society had to be met. The *crise du logement* (housing crisis) which afflicted almost everyone in France was exacerbated by the rural exodus and by the need to renovate the industrial base. After energy, transport, and steelmaking, housing was only fourth in the list of priorities of the liberation governments. Shanty towns (*bidonvilles*) grew up around the great cities as the pace of rebuilding could not keep up with the demand for housing, particularly for the rural people and the immigrants pulled in by France's great need for industrial and service workers. Such themes are clearly evident in Jean-Philippe Charbonnier's *Les mal logés* (bad housing conditions), La Corneuve, 1952 (see Figure 2.25); and in Willy Ronis's *Bidonville* (shanty town), Nanterre, 1958 (see Figure 2.26). It was not until 1953, eight years after the end of hostilities, that the construction industry managed to achieve 100,000 new homes per annum. During the decade which followed the war, the housing deficit amounted to 1.5 million homes – in other words, about 4.5 million people at any one time lacked a roof over their head (Sorlin, 1971, p. 65).

The solution to this problem in many cities, and particularly in and around Paris, was the creation of *grands ensembles* – vast apartment blocks of social housing built on greenfield sites – well illustrated by Willy Ronis's *HLM* (social housing), Porte de Vanves, Paris, 1957 (see Figure 2.27). Although this helped solve the housing problem in the medium term, in the longer term it has created major problems in that these old estates are now the locales for many contemporary social problems.

In the context of the housing problems of the reconstruction era, the emphasis on *habitations* in the photography of the humanists demonstrates how much their work mirrors the social issues of the time. Perhaps not surprisingly in a body of work which sought to represent the main features of everyday life, the use of domestic space is a theme to which these photographers often returned. As in all their work, the reasons for this depend not simply on the nature of the assignments which they received but also on their own preferences.

FIGURE 2.25
Jean-Philippe
Charbonnier,
Les mal logés
(bad housing
conditions), La
Corneuve, 1952.

FIGURE 2.26   Willy Ronis, *Bidonville* (shanty town), Nanterre, 1958.

FIGURE 2.27
Willy Ronis, *HLM*
(social housing),
Porte de Vanves,
Paris, 1957.

4.12 Work and craft

The period 1945–55 witnessed the rising importance of the working class or
classe ouvrière within French society. As we have seen, the crisis of
reconstruction put great strains on a productive apparatus which relied upon
the labour of the workers, and it is therefore not accidental that miners,
industrial workers and all those who laboured with their hands should be
represented in a generally positive light, and the Frenchness of their labour
accentuated, by the humanists. The photographers identified closely with the
classe populaire, and in their work their identification is often focused quite
explicitly on the worker – as seen particularly well in Jean-Philippe
Charbonnier's *Miner being washed by his wife*, Lens, 1954 (see Figure 2.28).

As you will recall from section 3, in post-war France a new social force had
effectively taken on an important place on the socio-political stage and in the
public imagination: the *classe ouvrière*. Its appearance had been prepared
during a long struggle since the beginning of the century which had both
defined its identity and its characteristic modes of expression. The strikes of

FIGURE 2.28
Jean-Philippe
Charbonnier,
*Miner being
washed by his wife,*
Lens, 1954.

1936 and 1938, the struggles of the resistance, and the major strikes in the autumn of 1947 and 1948 'gave the group a common history and nationalized labour conflicts, so making the state henceforth the essential interlocutor of the working class' (tr. from Borne, 1992, p. 24). The *classe ouvrière*, concentrated in its 'great industrial bastions' – coal mines in the north, iron and steelworks and textiles in the east, automobile works in the suburbs of Paris, the great docks at le Havre, Cherbourg, Marseilles, etc. – became more homogeneous and stable.

Photographers such as Robert Doisneau and Willy Ronis, who worked regularly for the communist press, naturally produced a considerable body of work on 'social' themes – work conditions, strikes, welfare issues. This is well illustrated in two photographs by Ronis: *Artisan, Belleville-Ménilmontant*, 1948 (see Figure 2.29); and the more overtly 'political' *Délégué syndical* (shop-steward), strike at Charpentiers de Paris, Paris, 1950 (see Figure 2.30). References to the heroism of physical labour are common in the corpus, of which Henri Cartier-Bresson's *Un fort des Halles* (porter of Les Halles market), 1952 (see Figure 2.31), is a good example. These representations of workers dealt with key issues about the working class during the post-war era in France.

FIGURE 2.29
Willy Ronis,
*Artisan, Belleville-
Ménilmontant,*
1948.

FIGURE 2.30
Willy Ronis,
Délégué syndical
(shop-steward),
strike at
Charpentiers de
Paris, Paris, 1950.

FIGURE 2.31   Henri Cartier-Bresson, *Un fort des Halles* (porter of Les Halles market), Paris, 1952.

5   The end of humanism

The photography which we have examined here ceased to play so important a role in the reintegration of French society from the early 1950s onwards. The apogee of such work really occurred in about 1955, for by the end of the decade new interests and other internal divisions within France (and external threats from the loss of empire) had begun to rend the fragile consensus of the immediate post-war era. In addition, the increasing privatization of French society which followed modernization and economic development progressively eroded the solidaristic base of urban communities, so that everyday life itself was increasingly conducted not in public space but behind closed doors. We have to add to these social changes factors which reflect aesthetic shifts, particularly in the use of the photographic image on the printed page.

There was an increasing belief (amongst editors, graphic artists and photographers), evident from at least the early 1950s, that the visual images created by photography constituted a new and distinctive language. A prominent book editor, François Cali, argued that 'A hundred good photographs explain immediately, infinitely better than a hundred pages of text, certain aspects of the world, certain current problems' (quoted in de Thézy, 1992, p. 52). In the leading photographic circles of the time, it was increasingly thought that the image itself could be freed from the burden of documentary representation linked to a text or at least a caption, and thus take on any number of forms. The idea that the picture should speak for itself – become in effect a universal language – was very persuasive, particularly to photographers who thus saw their profession elevated by its autonomy from the printed word.

In France, the diffusion of ideas about photography as a universal language was encouraged by a number of events during the 1950s, including a major exhibition at the Grand Palais in Paris in 1954, the *Biennale Photo-Cinéma*, launched by the magazine *Photo-Monde*, and organized by Maximilien Vox. To accompany this exhibition, the magazine published an album entitled *Cent photos sans paroles* (One hundred photos without words). Later, a similar publication to mark the tenth anniversary of the United Nations was produced with 84 photographs of people from 36 countries, presented completely un-captioned. A major conference on the role of the image in contemporary culture was held at UNESCO, and several initiatives to further the universalizing tendency of photography were undertaken. They fell on largely fallow ground, yet the conceptions of photography which had given rise to them became established principles by the early 1960s. It is important to note that many of the photographs made by Ronis, Doisneau and their confrères had a contemporary resonance as universal expressions of humanistic themes.

These ideas about photography as a universal language were not confined to France, for on the other side of the Atlantic similar propositions were taking form. The creation of the humanist-inspired Magnum Photos agency in Paris and New York in 1947 (its founders included Henri Cartier-Bresson) may be seen as an integral part of this process, for the ambitious projects which its founders hatched – which had names such as 'People are people the world over', 'Generation X', etc. – led to the hugely popular exhibition *The Family of Man* which was mounted in The Museum of Modern Art (MOMA) in New York in 1955. Magnum's approach was founded on the idea that its members could work on integrated story ideas which bespoke a universal humanity, and that their images could be sold to a mass magazine audience which, if not yet global, was at least very numerous (in its heyday in the late 1940s, each issue of *Life* was seen by 24 million people). Edward Steichen, director of the department of photography at MOMA, had long been fascinated by the idea of photography as a universal language and a tool of mass communication (Davis, 1995, p. 221). This democratic and inclusive notion of photography also informed the aesthetic of Willy Ronis, who had begun to attract attention from America as early as 1947, when Louis Stettner of the left-wing *Photo League* in New York came to see him with the view of mounting an exhibition of French photography. It is likely that his initiative may have influenced Steichen's decision to mount a major show in The Museum of Modern Art in late 1951/early 1952, called *Five French Photographers*, in which Willy Ronis exhibited 25 of his prints in a 180-print exhibition which also featured the work of Brassaï, Doisneau, Cartier-Bresson and Izis. In his introductory text panel, Steichen emphasized the humanistic universality of the images on show:

> There is a deep undercurrent of unity in their photography with its forthright emphasis on the human aspect of things, moments and places portrayed. Here is tender simplicity, sly humour, warm earthiness, the 'everydayness' of the familiar and the convincing aliveness found only in the best of the world's folk arts.
>
> It offers a new sphere of influence and inspiration in photography, particularly to amateur photographers. It supplies a threshold leading to the first universal folk art which could be created by the millions of amateurs practising photography throughout the world.
>
> (Archives of the Photography Department,
> Museum of Modern Art, New York)

In his later show, *The Family of Man* (seen by 9 million people throughout the world from 1955 onwards), Steichen developed a form of presentation of the photographic image in which it was completely de-contextualized. Editorial photographs whose role had been to supply an image to support a written account were presented in a form which effectively denied this.

As the 1950s drew to an end and magazine photography became more specialized, a younger generation of photographers with a new and more aggressive perspective began to make their presence felt in the editorial field,

and the humanist aesthetic itself lost impetus, in France as in the rest of the world. William Klein's close-up photographs of street scenes in New York are only one example of the way in which the humanist paradigm was contested by new forms of representation (see Figure 2.32).

Television began to compete more directly with illustrated magazines for the attention of the reader. The celebration of daily life and of Frenchness for its own sake now seemed increasingly outmoded, and were no longer inclusive categories within which the spectator could find him or herself securely located. Traditional celebrations of the life of the urban community began to disappear: the 14 July as a popular street celebration submitting to the increasing practice of the French to divide themselves into those who took the whole of July as a holiday and those who took the whole of August. The day was still celebrated, but elsewhere – in seaside resorts.

FIGURE 2.32
William Klein, *Gun*, New York, 1954–5.

Robert Doisneau's files contain photographs of a 14 July street party somewhere in Paris for nearly every year from 1945 until 1958. After that, the practice became more and more difficult to find, and perhaps less and less interesting to photograph.

6   Conclusion

In this chapter, we have continued the discussion of representation generally, by taking a close look at how documentary photography operates in relation to images of society. We have examined a particular set of photographic representations of society: those concerned with France in the era of post-war reconstruction from the Liberation of Paris in 1944 until the end of the 1950s. The argument advanced here has been that these representations played a particular role. They helped to offer an image of French society and a redefinition of 'Frenchness', of what it meant to have a French identity, to a people which had suffered the agonies and divisions of war, invasion, occupation and collaboration. These experiences had fractured or even dishonoured prevailing conceptions of French identity, by calling into question certain consensual and central notions which had underpinned the Third Republic. As we have seen, in the typical representations of Frenchness which appear in the work of humanist photographers, a new consensus about French society and about what it means to have a French identity is in the process of being forged. It is built around certain key themes or 'sites' – *la rue* (the street); children and play; the family; love and lovers; Paris and its sights; *clochards* (homeless and marginal characters); *fêtes populaires* (fairs and celebrations); *bistrots*; *habitations* (housing and housing conditions); work and craft. Representations of these themes served to reconstruct Frenchness as a unifying identity in a period of major social, political, economic and cultural change.

We have examined how humanism constituted the *dominant representational paradigm* of illustrative reportage photography in France during the era we have explored. The concept of *dominant representational paradigm* is taken from the work of T.S. Kuhn, and is employed as an alternative to the discursive theory of knowledge and power advanced by Michel Foucault because it allows us to better explain the links between the ideas and images of the photographers working within the humanist paradigm and the social and cultural contexts in which they worked.

We have also addressed questions about the 'truth-value' of the 'documentary' images produced by those working within the paradigm, for the idea that groups of photographic works can be understood in this way also implies that they offer a certain vision of the world. We considered two models of the truth-claims of documentary photography: documentary as objective representation and documentary as subjective interpretation. In the first, which developed during the nineteenth century, photography was readily perceived as an inherently 'objective' mode of representation, for as one view puts it 'the photograph has special value as evidence or proof'. We believe it because we believe our eyes. This model was shown to be underpinned by a *reflective* approach to representation, which asserted that the photograph offered a 'true image' of the world. The 'camera eye' was considered to be like a 'mirror held up to Nature'.

Contrasted with this approach to documentary as *objective representation* – in which the documentary nature of the image as a true reflection of reality is assured by the very mechanical–physical–chemical processes which define the medium of photography – is that of the idea of documentary as *subjective interpretation*. It is this notion on which the 'documentary' claims of photographic journalism depend. In essence, and whether produced for a newspaper, magazine or book, such work derives its claim to be 'truthful' by being fundamentally *interpretative*. The representations that the photographer produces are related to his or her personal interpretations of the events and subjects which he or she chooses to place in front of the camera lens. They are validated by the fact that the photographer experienced or 'witnessed' the events or sentiments which they portray, and thus lay claim to a wider truth. They are not merely records, for the apparent objectivity of the camera-produced image may help to fix the meaning of a given text, by providing it with a *representational legitimacy*. Thus, the association of the photographer's interpretative grasp of his or her subject with the ostensibly objective photographic image secures a status for the work of documentary which places it beyond mere opinion. It is in this sense that we can begin to see how the paradigm of French humanist photography may be understood within the constructionist model of representation.

It is important to consider how the paradigm of French humanist photography contributed to the construction of 'Frenchness' as an inclusive identity during the period of post-war reconstruction. In this context we cannot, however, neatly separate the construction of national identity from how it was represented. If the humanists fastened on to certain themes to construct their images of Frenchness, this was – as has been argued – because they had certain ideas about what being French meant, and also because those ideas had some symmetry with political and ethical ideals, and with visually observable behaviour. Other 'models' of Frenchness might have been possible. What we get from the corpus of humanist representations is a particular composite image of national identity, and, as I have argued, this was provided with *representational legitimacy* by the apparent objectivity of the camera-produced imaged. Humanism offers a composite representation of essential Frenchness in the 1940s and 1950s, but it is neither true nor exclusive in any fundamental sense – a point recognized by Robert Doisneau who once described himself as a *faux temoin* (false witness).

The fact that subjective interpretation is so tightly woven into the work helps to explain some of its appeal today. For we cannot ignore the fact that such representations have, since the mid-1980s, proven to be extremely popular with a new audience. If we take one photographer as an example, we know that Robert Doisneau's photograph *Le baiser de l'Hôtel de Ville* (considered earlier) has sold over half a million copies as a poster in its official form since 1985. Illegally copied versions – which have been widely sold throughout the world – take this figure into the millions. A 1992 survey found that 31 per cent of the French public knew about Robert Doisneau. But Doisneau is only the tip of the iceberg: all of his humanist contemporaries experienced a similar phenomenon of 'rediscovery' during the late 1980s and early 1990s. It seems as if the French (and the rest of the world) found in such images something exciting and attractive. What?

Obviously I cannot provide an exhaustive explanation of the nostalgia for French humanist representations of Frenchness of the era 1945–1960 in the conclusion to this chapter, but it is possible to suggest a number of factors which might go some way towards explaining their appeal. First, the fact that French society began to experience mounting problems of urban decay and social disorder in the 1980s, linked to areas where there was a high concentration of people of North African origin, helped to increase support for nationalist parties. Jean-Marie Le Pen's *Front Nationale* acquired a voter base of perhaps 15–20 per cent of the electorate (in opinion polls) although its success in elections was less pronounced. In such a context, ideas about French 'identity' became contested and volatile. In the black-and-white images of French life in the 1940s and 1950s, such issues seem unproblematic, easily resolved.

Secondly, the decline in the 1970s and early 1980s of manual labour and the disappearance of the industrial heartlands – a traumatic experience for miners, shipbuilders, steelworkers, etc. – swept away a defining feature of national life in the post-war era. It broke the consensus that French society was founded on the labour of the *classe ouvrière*. It may not be coincidental that much of Le Pen's support came from workers who had hitherto supported the French communist party. Here again, the images of French humanism tend to present the *classe ouvrière* as heroic and solidaristic. Nostalgia for such photographs may express hopes for a return to a time when work and economic conditions were more secure.

Thirdly, the facts of urbanization and privatization, and the omnipresence of the car have led to a situation where the street has become increasingly represented as a place of danger – for children and adults alike. In the imagery of the humanists, life takes place in the public spaces of the city. It is not privatized, and the car hardly appears as a threat.

We could easily multiply the examples in which the imagery of the humanists provides an apparent contrast with contemporary life. What is most evident in the contrasts, however, is that life 'then' appears to be a 'golden age': hard, but rewarding, not bereft of conflicts and disputes, but warm and communal – a sense in which everybody shared the hardships of the era, in which social, cultural and ethnic differences were levelled. The humanist paradigm appears, then, to offer an 'ideal' image of French identity, from which all contemporary problems have been miraculously erased: as in L.P. Hartley's famous view that 'The past is another country, they do things differently there'.

From this point it is but a small step to the conclusion that, far from being a mere recitation of visual facts, social documentary photography turns out to be a mode of representation deeply coloured by ambiguities, and generally representative of the paradigm in which it has been constructed. Our consideration of the post-war history of France, and in particular of the atmosphere of the country in the period immediately following the liberation, shows quite clearly how the paradigm of French humanist photography developed and diffused a certain view of France and of French identity in the period 1945–60 – a view which has subsequently re-emerged to play another role in the 1980s and 1990s.

References

AGEE, J. and EVANS, W. (1965) *Let Us Now Praise Famous Men*, London, Peter Owen (first published 1941).

BERGER, J. (1982) 'Appearances' in Berger, J. and Mohr, J. *Another Way of Telling*, London, Writers and Readers.

BORNE, D. (1992) *Histoire de la Société Française depuis 1945*, Paris, Armand Colin.

BRANDT, B. (1938) *A Night in London*, London, Country Life.

CALDER, E. and BOURKE-WHITE, M. (1937) *You Have Seen their Faces,* New York, Viking Press.

CALI, F. (1952) *Sortilèges de Paris*, Paris, Arthaud.

CARTIER-BRESSON, H. (1952) *Images à la Sauvette,* Paris, Tériade.

CENDRARS, B. and DOISNEAU, R. (1949) *La Banlieue de Paris*, Paris, Editions Pierre Seghers.

COLETTE and IZIS (BIDERMANAS) (1953) *Paradis Terrestre*, Lausanne, La Guilde du Livre.

DAVIS, K.F. (1995) *An American Century of Photography: from dry plate to digital, The Hallmark Photographic Collection*, New York, Harry N. Abrams Inc.

DE THÉZY, M. with NORI, C. (1992) *La Photographie Humaniste 1930–1960: histoire d'un mouvement en France*, Paris, Editions Contrejour.

DOISNEAU, R. (1955) *Instantanés de Paris*, Lausanne, Editions Claire-Fontaine.

DUMAZEDIER, J. (1962) V*ers une Civilisation des Loisirs,* Paris, Editions du Seuil.

FULTON, M. (ed.) (1988) *Eyes of Time*: photojournalism in America, Boston, MA, Little, Brown and Co.

GALASSI, P. (1987) *Henri Cartier-Bresson: the early work*, New York, The Museum of Modern Art.

GODWIN, F. (1990) *Forbidden Land*, London, Jonathan Cape.

HAMBOURG, M.M. and PHILLIPS, C. (1994) *The New Vision: photography between the World Wars*, New York, Metropolitan Museum of Art and Harry N. Abrams Inc.

HAMILTON, P. (1995a) *Willy Ronis: photographs 1926–1995,* Oxford, Museum of Modern Art.

HAMILTON, P. (1995b) *Robert Doisneau: a photographer's life,* New York, Abbeville Press.

IZIS (BIDERMANAS), COCTEAU, J. et al. (1950) *Paris des Rêves,* Lausanne, La Guilde du Livre.

JONES-GRIFFITHS, P. (1971) V*ietnam, Inc.*, New York, Collier Books.

KUHN, T.S. (1962) *The Structure of Scientific Revolutions,* Chicago, IL, University of Chicago Press.

LANGE, D. and SCHUSTER TAYLOR, P. (1939) *An American Exodus: a record of human erosion in the thirties,* New York, Reynal and Hitchcock.

LARKIN, M. (1988) *France Since the Popular Front: government and people 1936–1986,* Oxford, The Clarendon Press.

LEMAGNY, J-C. and ROUILLÉ, A. (1987) *A History of Photography: social and cultural perspectives,* Cambridge, Cambridge University Press.

MAC ORLAN, P. (1934) *Paris Vu par André Kertész*, Paris, Société des Editions d'Histoire et d'Art.

PRÉVERT, J. and IZIS (BIDERMANAS) (1951) *Grand Bal du Printemps*, Lausanne, La Guilde du Livre.

PRÉVERT, J. and IZIS (BIDERMANAS) (1952) *Charmes de Londres,* Lausanne, La Guilde du Livre.

RONIS, W. and MAC ORLAN, P. (1954) *Belleville-Ménilmontant*, Paris, Arthaud.

SALGADO, S. (1993) *Workers: an archaeology of the industrial age*, London, Phaidon.

SORLIN, P. (1971) *La Société Française,* Vol. II, 1914–1968, Paris, Arthaud.

STEINBECK, J. (1966) *The Grapes of Wrath*, London, Heinemann (first published 1938).

STOTT, W. (1973) *Documentary Expression and Thirties America*, London, Oxford University Press.

TAGG, J. (1988) *The Burden of Representation*, London, Macmillan.

CHAPTER THREE

THE POETICS AND THE POLITICS OF EXHIBITING OTHER CULTURES

Henrietta Lidchi

Contents

1 Introduction

As the title suggests this chapter develops the central theme of the book, representation. It is about objects, or more specifically *systems of representation* that produce meaning through the display of objects. Like the two previous chapters it is concerned with the process of representation – the manner in which meaning is constructed and conveyed through language and objects. It will consider *representation* in the singular – the activity or process – as well as *representations* – the resultant entities or products. Where this chapter differs is in its focus: it examines not so much language, as how meaning is created through classification and display. Moreover it contemplates this process in the particular context of objects said to be 'ethnographic'. So the chapter is concerned with ethnographic museums, in other words institutions whose representational strategies feature the ethnographic objects or artefacts of 'other cultures'. It will not, however, seek to answer fully the question of how these representational systems are received. The question of consumption is too large to be tackled in any great detail here (though see the brief discussion in section 5.5 below); for a fuller discussion, see **du Gay**, ed., 1997.

Why investigate ethnographic exhibitions and displays? Because ethnographic museums have had to address themselves in a concerted fashion to the problems of representation. Museum curators are no longer automatically perceived as the unassailable keepers of knowledge about their collections; museums are no longer simply revered as spaces promoting knowledge and enlightenment, the automatic resting place for historic and culturally important ethnographic objects. How the West classifies, categorizes and represents other cultures is emerging as a topic of some debate.

Two significant critiques of museums have recently been advanced. Both take a *constructionist* view of representation. The first uses the insights from *semiotics* and the manner in which language constructs and conveys meaning to analyse the diversity of ways in which exhibitions create representations of other cultures. By considering how meanings are constructed and produced, this critique concerns itself primarily with the semiotics or *poetics* of exhibiting. The second critique forefronts questions of discourse and power to interrogate the historical nature of museums and collecting. It argues that there is a link between the rise of ethnographic museums and the expansion of Western nations. By exploring the link between knowledge of other cultures and the imperial nations, this critique considers representation in the light of the *politics* of exhibiting.

This chapter therefore considers both the *poetics* and the *politics* of exhibiting. In doing so, it builds on the twofold structure delineated in Chapter 1, contrasting the approach which concentrates on *language* and *signification*, with another which prioritizes *discourse* and *discursive practices*. The differences at the heart of these critiques will be brought out by the case studies deployed. In these, the insights gained will be used in specific contexts to discuss how objects, exhibitions and museums function to represent other cultures.

The chapter is divided into four main sections. Section 2 presents some preliminary working definitions. First it will review what is meant by a 'museum' and 'ethnography'. Then it will reflect on how objects acquire meaning as a prelude to considering how meaning is produced within the context of an exhibition or museum.

Section 3 attends to one of the principal ways in which museums represent other cultures – the exhibition. Using a case study, it will highlight the manner in which ethnographic displays are vehicles of meaning, how objects, texts and photographs work to create a representation of a particular people, at a precise historical moment. The focus of this section will be an exhibition which opened at the Museum of Mankind – the Ethnography Department of the British Museum – in 1993 entitled *Paradise: Change and Continuity in the New Guinea Highlands*. The theme of section 3 is the *poetics* of exhibiting.

Section 4 explores the critiques that go beyond the issue of construction and the exhibition context to question the politics of the museum. The main thrust of this critique concerns the relationship between knowledge and power. The focus here is on the institution whose activities of collecting and curating cease to be neutral or innocent activities but emerge as an instrumental means of knowing and possessing the 'culture' of others. This section will consider in detail the collection and interpretation of the artefacts known as The Benin Bronzes.

Finally, section 5 will provide a brief coda to the chapter, examining how curatorial activities have become a contested site and how the salience of the critiques tackled in this chapter has had tangible effects on the policies of collection, storage and display.

2   Establishing definitions, negotiating meanings, discerning objects

2.1   Introduction

Section 2 begins by considering the key terms: 'museum', 'ethnography', 'object', 'text' and 'context'. Reflecting on the meaning and function of a museum through analysing alternative definitions will provide a basis on which to question contemporary usage and assumptions underlying these terms in later sections. Section 2 argues that a museum is a historically constituted space, and uses this to highlight contemporary definitions of an ethnographic museum. It then moves on to consider the status of 'objects' in order to investigate the manner in which their meaning is constructed. Using the unusual case of a horse called Comanche, it shows how even the most mundane object can be endowed with value and thus be transformed into a vehicle of contested meaning.

2.2 What is a museum?

If you look up the definition of 'museum' in a dictionary. It is likely that you will find a definition *approximating* to the functional one I have chosen here: 'Museums exist in order to acquire, safeguard, conserve, and display objects, artefacts and works of arts of various kinds' (Vergo, 1993, p. 41). But we must also ask: is this definition essential or historical? Does its interpretation vary over time?

To answer this, let us seek an older, alternative definition of the museum. If we explore the classical etymology of the word museum (*musaeum*) we find that it could encompass two meanings. On one hand it signified 'a mythological setting inhabited by the nine goddesses of poetry, music, and the liberal arts', namely 'places where the Muses dwell' (Findlen, 1989, p. 60). Nature as the 'primary haunt of the Muses' was a museum in its most literal sense. On the other hand, the term also referred to the library at Alexandria, to a public site devoted to scholarship and research. So this early classical etymology allows for the museum's potential for expansiveness. It does not specify spatial parameters: the open spaces of gardens and the closed confines of the study were equally appropriate spaces for museums. Museums could therefore reconcile curiosity and scholarship, private and public domains, the whimsical and the ordered (Findlen, 1989, pp. 60–2).

In the sixteenth and seventeenth centuries an alternative and varied terminology was accorded to contemporary 'museums', depending partly on the social and geographical location of the collectors. The *Wunderkammer* and *Kunstkammer* (the cabinets of 'wonder' and 'arts') of European aristocrats and princes were contemporaneous with the personal 'theatres of nature', 'cabinets of curiosities' and *studiolo* of the erudite and scholarly collector. British collecting occurred 'lower down' the social scale: the British scholar collected 'the curiosities of art and nature', establishing cabinets with less ordered and hierarchical collections than their continental counterparts (MacGregor, 1985, p. 147). Let us examine the constitution of a British 'cabinet of curiosities' or 'closet of rarities' (the name given to diverse assemblages of rare and striking artefacts), to pry deeper into its systems of classification and the representation of the world that it generated and disclosed.

John Tradescant the elder, a botanist and gardener, built a 'collection of rarities' from his early visits to the European mainland and the Barbary coast, where he collected plants and natural specimens. Later, partly owing to the enthusiasm of his patron, the powerful (subsequently assassinated) Duke of

Buckingham, others were commissioned to undertake collecting to augment the Tradescant 'cabinet', though this was always an adjunct to Tradescant's botanical interests.   In 1628, upon settling in Lambeth, Tradescant transformed his cabinet of curiosities into an ever-expanding *musaeum*. After his appointment in 1630 as Keeper of His Majesty's Gardens, the collection was bequeathed in its entirety to his son, John Tradescant the younger.

What did it contain?

The collection was composed of an extraordinary rich amalgam of miscellaneous objects, harvested 'with less than critical discrimination' according to MacGregor (1985, p. 152). In his catalogue of 1656, '*Musaeum Tradescantianum* or A Collection of Rarities Preserved At *South Lambeth, neer London*', Tradescant the younger described the content of the museum in some detail .

READING A

Reading A at the end of this chapter contains four extracts from the 1656 catalogue '*Musaeum Tradescantianum* or A Collection of Rarities Preserved At *South Lambeth,* neer *London*', prepared by Tradescant the younger. Read them in the light of the following questions.

1   Extracts 1 and 2 detail the categories used by Tradescant the younger. What are they?

2   Consider Extracts 3 and 4 to discern what type of material is included in these categories.

3   How does such a classification differ from one you might expect to find today?

In Extracts 1 and 2 Tradescant the younger divides his 'materialls' into two types – Natural and Artificial – and within these types, he further subdivides into categories. He also classifies the materials into two separate spaces – the closed internal space of the *Musaeum Trandescantianum* and the open external space of his garden.

The difference between Natural and Artificial 'materialls' – or *naturalia* and *artificialia* – is ostensibly between that which is naturally occurring and that which is derived from nature but transformed by human endeavour. The 'materialls' included under both categories are, however, exceedingly diverse.

In Extracts 3 and 4 we find that the category of *naturalia* includes naturally occurring specimens ('Egges' of 'Estridges', 'Pellican'); mythical creatures ('Phoenix', 'Griffin'); or objects which qualify by virtue of provenance ('Kings-fisher from the *West India's*'), an unusual association ('… Cassaway or Emeu that dyed at *S. James's, Westminster*') or the 'curious' and colourful nature of the specimen ('two feathers of the Phoenix tayle'). The categories are tolerant of a variety of materials and provenances. Natural specimens from Continental Europe are juxtaposed with those of the West Indies or

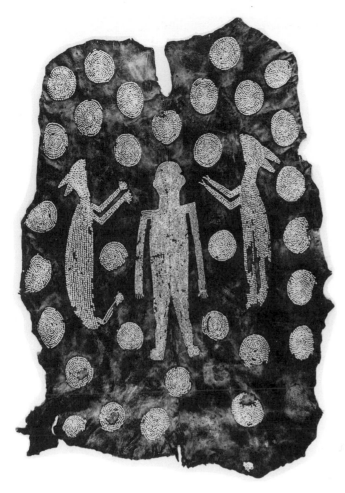

FIGURE 3.1
Powhatan's Mantle, from Tradescant's collection of rarities, now housed at the Ashmolean Museum, Oxford. Originally described as '*Pohatan*, King of *Virginia's* habit …'.

Brazil, parts of natural specimens are classified with wholes, the identified is listed with the unidentifiable, common birds are classed with the Mauritian 'Dodar'. The manner in which Tradescant and his collaborators divided and subdivided the natural world seems by today's standards fairly idiosyncratic: birds (which they dismember), four-footed beasts, fishes, shell-creatures, insects, minerals, outlandish fruit (see Extract 2).

The divisions implemented in the more qualitative category of *artificialia* seem even more eccentric. This medley of curious items produces an equivalence between 'ethnographic' objects ('*Pohatan,* King of *Virginia's* habit …', see Figure 3.1); artefacts with mythological references ('Stone of *Sarrigs*-Castle where *Hellen* of *Greece* was born'); objects that are the product of feats of human ingenuity ('Divers sorts of Ivory-balls'); fantastical objects ('blood that rained in the *Isle of Wight*') or merely fanciful ones ('*Edward the Confessors* knit-gloves'). The category of 'rarities' appears particularly discretionary, since most of the objects in the collection could be classified as 'rare, or supposedly rare, objects' (Pomian, 1990, p. 46) – '*Anne of Bullens* Night-vayle embroidered with silver', for instance.

The information or *interpretation* contained in the catalogue indicates certain priorities. The descriptions of the Natural 'materialls' are quite often objective and economic except in those circumstances where the curiosity of the item or the particularity of its association is being recorded (outlandish fruit). This kaleidoscopic view of nature predates the introduction of the hierarchical Linnaean system of classification (named after the Swedish botanist, Linne), so typical of contemporary natural history collections (and the one adapted for ethnographical collections in the Pitt Rivers Museum – see section 4). The description of the Artificial 'materialls' is often fuller, though this depends on their categorization. Those objects featured for their technical virtuosity are described in this light, whereas other items are recorded in terms of their surprising nature ('Match-coat from *Greenland* of the Intrails of Fishes'). Some *artificialia* are remarkable for their association with well-known historical characters or their exotic origins, or both, in the case of '*Pohatan*, King of *Virginia's* habit', for instance.

The descriptions are, nevertheless, very different from those one might find today. There is little of what one might call 'hard information', or 'objective description'. Garments are not described in terms of their shape, their dimensions, their colour, their age, their maker or their owner, unless the latter was a renowned personage. The constituting materials are noted if they are remarkable, in the same way that the properties of *naturalia* are only noted if they are extraordinary. There are no references to how these 'materialls' were collected, when, or by whom. These 'facts' or insights, inconsequential to the Tradescants, would nowadays be considered indispensable elements to the proper cataloguing of materials.

What does Tradescant's museum represent?

What is being *represented* here is the puzzling quality of the natural and artificial world. In the early sixteenth century a conspicuously extraordinary object with puzzling and exotic associations was worthy of inclusion in a cabinet by virtue of its 'curiosity' – its unusualness as perceived by the collector. To the contemporary observer, the internal arrangement appears arbitrary, and the terminology – 'closet of rarities' or 'cabinet of curiosities' – further corroborates the view that these cabinets were the specious products of personal preference, non-scientific and whimsical. To dismiss these cabinets on the basis of their exuberance, the plethora and diversity of items included, and the singularity of the classificatory system would, however, be a mistake. It would deny the methods – those 'rational' principles – that underpinned these stunning constructions:

> These were collections with encyclopaedic ambition, intended as a miniature version of the universe, containing specimens of every category of things and helping to render visible the totality of the universe, which otherwise would remain hidden from human eyes.
>
> (Pomian, 1990, p. 69)

To collect curiosities or rarities indicated a particular kind of inquisitiveness: 'curiosity' emerged, momentarily, as a legitimate intellectual pursuit, signifying an open, searching mind. The collector's interest in spectacular and curious objects was born of an attitude which saw Nature, of which man was part, not as 'repetitive, or shackled to a coherent set of laws' but as a phenomenon which 'was subject to unlimited variability and novelty' (Shelton, 1994, p. 184). For the curious, collecting was quest. Its purpose? To go beyond the obvious and the ordinary, to uncover the hidden knowledge which would permit him (for it was always him) a more complete grasp of the workings of the world in all its dimensions (Pomian, 1990, p. 57). This alternative definition of science tolerated diversity and miscellany because they were 'essential elements in a programme whose aim was nothing less than universality' (Impey and MacGregor, 1985, p. 1). So Tradescant's 'closet of rarities', unique though it undoubtedly was, was also part of a larger socio-cultural movement adhering to a broadly unified perception of the world and the purpose of collecting which reached its apogee in the sixteenth and seventeenth centuries.

The Tradescants' collection was exceptional for another reason. The collection was personal, expansive and varied, but not exclusive. Interesting specimens were placed at the disposal of serious scholars *and* the general public:

> More significant ... than these distinguished visitors were the ordinary people who flocked to see the collection for a fee – seemingly sixpence – for the Tradescants differed ... from every collector then known of in England – in the general accessibility of their collections. Most of these visitors no doubt saw the rarities in much the same light as had the founder of the collection – 'the Biggest that Can be Gotten ... Any thing that Is strang'.
>
> (MacGregor, 1985, p. 150)

This aspect was to come into its own once the collection had been acquired by deed of gift by Elias Ashmole, who in turn gave it to the University of Oxford, thereby ensuring its transformation into the twentieth-century public museum that bears his name – the Ashmolean.

This exploration of the *Musaeum Tradescantianum* brings several important points to light about the nature of museums.

1 *Representation.* Collecting and uniting these extraordinary and varied articles – be they naturally or artificially produced – into one cabinet served to create a staggering encapsulation of the world's curiosities. This account was, in turn, an attempt at a complete *representation* of the diversity of existence in miniature – a 'microcosm'.

2 *Classification.* In describing the world, the *Musaeum Tradescantianum* worked within a classificatory system which made a distinction between two types of objects: *artificialia* and *naturalia*. Other contemporary cabinets included the categories of *antiqua* (mementoes from the past) and *scientifica* (implements, etc.). The Tradescant classificatory system did not articulate the divisions we might use today between the real and the mystical, the antique and the contemporary, the New World and the Old. The representation of the world generated by the museum applied rules of classification and collection which were, for the original collectors and cataloguers, logical and consistent with a historically specific form of knowledge and scholarship, however inappropriate they' may seem to us today.

3 *Motivation.* The *Musaeum* is a *motivated* representation of the world in the sense that it sought to encapsulate the world in order to teach others about it and to convert others to the salience of this approach. Moreover, quite exceptionally for its time, this representation was aimed at a larger audience than scholars.

4 *Interpretation.* If we reflect back to the definition which began this section, namely that 'museums exist to acquire, safeguard, conserve and

display objects, artefacts or works of arts of various kinds', we find that the *Musaeum Tradescantianum* fits this description as easily as a contemporary museum might. Yet the manner and spirit in which the *Musaeum Tradescantianum* undertook these activities was clearly quite different. This is particularly evident in its mode of classification. The way in which the *Musaeum Tradescantianum* acquired, safeguarded, conserved, and displayed was in accordance with a distinct world-view which saw sense in what might be termed a hodge-podge of marvellous objects, a logical vision which had abandoned theological principles of classification, but had yet to adopt scientific ones (Pomian, 1990, p. 64).

So, unexpectedly perhaps, we find that our preliminary definition still holds; but, more importantly, we have established that a museum does not deal solely with *objects* but, more importantly, with what we could call, for the moment, *ideas* – notions of what the world is, or should be. Museums do not simply issue objective descriptions or form logical assemblages; they generate representations and attribute value and meaning in line with certain perspectives or classificatory schemas which are historically specific. They do not so much reflect the world through objects as use them to mobilize representations of the world past and present.

If this is true of all museums, what kind of classificatory schema might an 'ethnographic' museum employ and what kinds of representations might it mobilize?

2.3   What is an ethnographic museum?

To answer this we must know what the word 'ethnography' means.

Ethnography comes from *ethnos* meaning 'people/race/nation', and *graphein*   ethnography
meaning 'writing/description'. So a common definition might state that ethnography seeks 'to describe nations of people with their customs, habits and points of difference'. We are confronted by the knowledge that a definition of ethnography seeks to include notions of science and difference. In fact ethnography is a word which has acquired a range of meanings. Contemporary usage frequently invokes 'ethnography' to describe in-depth empirical research and a variety of data collection techniques which rely on prolonged and intensive interaction between the researcher and her/his subjects of research, which usually results in the production of an 'ethnographic text'. But, historically, the definition has been far more specific. In the British context, 'ethnography' refers to the research methods and texts that were linked most particularly with the human sciences of *anthropology* (the science of man or mankind, in the widest sense) and *ethnology* (the science which considers races and people and their relationship to one another, their distinctive physical and other characteristics). So when one refers to ethnographic museums today, one is placing them within a discrete discipline and theoretical framework –

anthropology – which is itself allied to a research technique – ethnographic fieldwork and the specific ethnographic texts which report on these studies.

Until the nineteenth century most of what we would now label as 'ethnographic' objects were collected in a spasmodic and fortuitous way, acquisitions whose value lay in their novelty or 'curiosity'. For these objects to be labelled as ethnographic and to be lodged within an 'ethnographic' museum or department, necessitated the development of a human science which would identify them as such, and therefore set in train a different system of classification and generate other motives for collecting them. In the context of museums, ethnographic and ethnological collections predated the establishment of anthropology, which emerged as a human science in the late nineteenth century but more properly in the early twentieth century. But the rise of anthropology as an academic discipline was significantly linked to the rise of ethnographic departments in museums (section 4). What this new human science (anthropology), but also the older sciences of cultures (ethnography and ethnology), sought to study was the way of life, primarily but not exclusively, of non-European peoples or nations. The classificatory system devised in ethnographic museums is, therefore, predominantly a geographical or social one. The objects which ethnographic museums hold in their collections were mostly made or used by those who at one time or another were believed to be 'exotic', 'pre-literate', 'primitive', 'simple', 'savage' or 'vanishing races', and who are now described as, amongst other things, 'aboriginal', 'indigenous', 'first nations', or 'autochthonous': those peoples or nations whose cultural forms were historically contrasted with the complex civilizations of other non-European societies like China or Islam or Egypt and who, at various moments in their history, encountered explorers, traders, missionaries, colonizers and most latterly, but inevitably, western anthropologists.

So in referring to 'ethnographic museums' or 'ethnographic exhibitions', one is identifying institutions or exhibitions which feature objects as the 'material culture' of peoples who have been considered, since the mid-nineteenth century, to have been the appropriate target for anthropological research. Ethnographic museums produce certain kinds of representations and mobilize distinct classificatory systems which are framed by anthropological theory and ethnographic research. As such what needs to be noted about ethnographic museums is that they do not simply reflect *natural* distinctions but serve to create *cultural* ones, which acquire their cogency when viewed through the filtering lens of a particular discipline. The geographical and social distinctions deployed are constructed, but equally they are located historically: in the struggle for power between what has been called 'the West and the Rest' (Hall, 1992). Contrary to popular assumptions, we can assert that the science of anthropology, like all sciences 'hard' or otherwise, is not primarily a *science of discovery*, but a *science of invention*. In other words it is not *reflective* of the essential nature of cultural difference, but classifies and *constitutes* this difference systematically and coherently, in accordance with a particular view of the world that emerges in a specific place, at a distinct historical moment and within a specific body of knowledge. So, at any historical juncture, the specific definitions of 'museum' and 'ethnography' function as floating signifiers, naming devices which attach themselves and serve to signify certain kinds of cultural practice. They are contingent, not essential.

2.4 Objects and meanings

Do the artefacts which form the core of a museum's collections provide it with stability, amidst all this flux and contingency? Not necessarily. Any such stability would rest on the conflation between two notable characteristics of museum objects (and objects in general) – their **physical presence** and their **meaning**. In the next section, we shall consider the dialectic between the two, and look at how their meanings fare as classification systems change.

physical presence

meaning

Collected objects (and written records – themselves objects) are sometimes identified as the most persistent and indissoluble connection museums have between the past and present. 'Other peoples' artefacts are amongst the most 'objective' data we can expect from them, and provide an intelligible baseline from which to begin the more difficult task of interpreting cultural meanings' (Durrans, 1992, p. 146).

So objects are frequently described as documents or evidence from the past, and are regarded as pristine material embodiments of cultural essences which transcend the vicissitudes of time, place and historical contingency. Their *physicality* delivers a promise of stability and objectivity; it suggests a stable, unambiguous world.

But this is a simplification and we can see this once we turn to the question of *meaning*. To treat these physical manifestations of the social world as permanent objective evidence is to fail to make a distinction between their undisputed *physical presence* and their ever-changing *meaning*:

> All the problems that we have with metaphors raise their head in a new guise when we identify objects. We do not escape from the predicaments that language prepares for us by turning away from the semiotics of words to the semiotics of objects. It would be illusory to hope that objects present us with a more solid, unambiguous world.
>
> (Douglas, 1992, pp. 6–7)

The fixity of an object's physical presence cannot deliver guarantees at the level of meaning. In the museum context, a conflation may be encouraged between the stability of presence and that of meaning. The status of the object as invariant in presence and meaning is underpinned by the popular representation of museums as grand institutions safeguarding, collecting, exhibiting and engaging in a scholarly fashion with the nation's material wealth. The popular perception of curatorial practice as a descriptive rather than an interpretative activity lends further support to this elision. But it is clear that artefacts do not 'spirit' themselves into museum collections: they are collected, interpreted and exhibited – all purposeful and motivated activities (as we shall see in sections 3 and 4). If, unlike other historical events, artefacts can survive relatively intact as authentic primary material from the past, this *does not* mean that they have kept their primary or 'original' meaning intact, since the specifics of these can rarely be recaptured or replayed. The distinction between physical presence and meaning must, therefore, be maintained.

It may be useful to illustrate this point by an example. Through the following reading we will consider how a fairly mundane object might change its meaning over time.

READING B

Read and make notes on the edited extracts of 'His very silence speaks: the horse who survived Custer's Last Stand' by Elizabeth A. Lawrence – Reading B at the end of this chapter – paying particular attention to the reasons behind the horse's value as an object. How might the semiotic tools you were introduced to in Chapter 1 equip you to understand the changing meaning of the horse as object?

Lawrence's article features the life of an unusual horse – Comanche (Figure 3.2) – and its extraordinary afterlife as an artefact, in order to catalogue its changing meaning. The article is useful since common expectation would be that a stuffed horse would, in all probability, have a relatively unambiguous meaning.

FIGURE 3.2
Comanche, 'the horse who survived Custer's Last Stand'.

Lawrence shows that the value bestowed on Comanche as an object was not due to his intrinsic worth: as a natural specimen of the equine species, he was only as good as any other. His distinction was his intimate connection with a significant historical encounter, the Battle of the Little Big Horn which came to be known as 'Custer's Last Stand'. This is signalled by Comanche's changing fate as a museum exhibit. Initially displayed as an oddity amongst zoological specimens at the World's Columbian Exposition in Chicago in 1893, Comanche was subsequently transformed into a valued exhibit at the University of Kansas. In this second incarnation, Comanche became the site of struggle, initially revolving around his proper niche, but subsequently around his symbolic meaning.

In her article, Lawrence draws out the distinctions between Comanche's physical presence as live and stuffed horse, in addition to giving an account of his shifting meaning. Here I propose to extend her analysis by disaggregating the different levels of meaning, using the semiological tools provided by Roland Barthes in *Writing Degree Zero* (1967), *Elements of Semiology* (1967) and *Image–Music–Text* (1977) (previously introduced in Chapter 1).

As a lone exhibit and a stuffed horse, very little recommends Comanche, apart from his function as a *sign*. As you may recall from Chapter 1, the *sign* is defined by its components, the *signifier* and the *signified*. The difference between these two components as defined by Barthes is as follows: the 'substance of the *signifier* is always material (sounds, objects, images)', whereas the *signified* 'is not "a thing" but a *mental representation of "the thing"*' (1967, pp. 112, 108) (my emphasis). So Comanche, both as a living horse, but more importantly as stuffed object, is the *signifier;* what is repeatedly *signified* is 'Custer's Last Stand', or more precisely, *the mental representation* of a defeat and a military tragedy. However, such a brief semiotic 'reading' does not provide a comprehensive explanation of Comanche's endurance as a powerful and changeable sign in the century since his death. It might be productive to investigate the different levels at which *signification* takes place.

As you know, for Barthes, signs operate within systems, but these systems function to create different orders of meaning. In the following analysis I shall use Barthes's concepts of **connotation** and **denotation** to explore the articulation of signification around Comanche. In his usage of these terms Barthes courted some controversy, but here I shall bypass this debate and use these terms to invoke two levels of meaning creation. Here, *denotation* will refer to the first level, or order, of meaning which derives from a *descriptive* relationship, between signifier and signified, corresponding to the most obvious and consensual level at which objects mean something. In this case, Comanche most obviously and consistently denotes a horse, and on this most people would agree. *Connotation* refers to a second level, or order, of meaning which guides one to look at the way in which *the image (object) is understood*, at a broader, more associative, level of meaning. It therefore makes reference to more changeable and ephemeral structures, such as the

connotation
denotation

rules of social life, of history, of social practices, ideologies and usage. At this level, as we shall see, Comanche's meaning undergoes great variation. For obvious reasons: its connotations cannot weather, intact, the changes in society's perception of itself.

Let us apply the concepts of *denotation* and *connotation* – to see how they can further extend our understanding of Comanche's enduring popularity. Comanche, initially as a living animal and subsequently as an object or sign *denotes* immediately, repeatedly and mechanically *a horse*, and the historic event and traumatic defeat of which he, as a horse, was a silent witness – namely, 'Custer's Last Stand'. As a horse, he also denotes the valued bond between a man and his mount. At these two levels his meaning never changes.

Comanche's *connotations*, however, change over time. Initially he is the link between the living and the dead, connoting the 'anger of defeat', the 'sorrow for the dead cavalrymen' and the 'vengeance towards the Indians'. Later, as an incongruous feature in the Columbian Exposition in Chicago in 1893, he connotes conquest and the victory of the civilized over the murderous savage. In the twentieth century, he ceases to have an objective value, connoting alternatively late nineteenth-century sentimentalism, good professional taxidermy, or a lucky charm. For some communities, his significance increases. For the Native American students at the University of Kansas he forcibly signifies the extreme partiality of white historical narratives and a denial of the Native American experience. These connotations deny Comanche his role as an objective witness. They transform him into a subjective and temporarily invalid symbol of white oppression. At the time of Lawrence's essay (1991), Comanche's legitimacy had been re-established by means of a text which navigates the reader towards a newer and, from today's perspective, more balanced and comprehensive interpretation of the events of 'Custer's Last Stand'.

Thus, Comanche's popularity derives from the shifting relationship between his connotations and denotations. His descriptive power maintains a greater stability (denotation) than his relevance and meaning which are both questioned and re-negotiated (connotation). It is after all the perception of 'Custer's Last Stand' that changes – not Comanche's link with it. Over time, this allows his meaning to be 'read' in different ways. Comanche continues to denote the historic battle, but what the battle *means* for Americans, native or non-native, has irrevocably altered – as has Comanche's function as he metamorphoses from oddity, to lucky symbol, to educational tool.

So, to summarize, Lawrence's article argues that the value of objects resides in the meaning that they are given – the way they are *encoded*. By charting the trajectory of a once living and banal object – a stuffed horse – and demonstrating how even steadfast categories like 'horse' can acquire extraordinary and controversial meanings, Lawrence demonstrates how the physical presence of an object cannot stabilize its meaning. Comanche's relevance derives from the fact that, as a symbol, he remains powerful, in part because his presence is differently interpreted in different periods and in different contexts.

But Lawrence's article offers other valuable insights; the first relating to *text*, the second concerning the *context*. Let us survey each of these briefly as they build on some of the work of Chapter 1.

2.5   The uses of text

If we consider the object of Lawrence's article we find no difficulty in identifying it. It is, after all, a horse. With ethnographic objects, taken from distant and unfamiliar cultures, such convenient points of reference may be difficult to establish, because they are not so immediately recognizable. For these objects, the function of any accompanying text is crucial. As we have seen, the defining feature of ethnographic objects is that they are products of the practice of ethnography. To read and understand them, therefore, we need *texts* that can interpret and translate their meaning for us. 'Texts' here refers not only to the written word, but fabrics of knowledge that can be used as reference, including oral texts, social texts and academic texts. These perform the same function – they facilitate interpretation. In the ethnographic context the primary, though not exclusive, source of this background knowledge is the ethnographic text.

As Chapter 1 argued, language is not an empty transparent 'window on the world', it produces meaning and understanding. The purpose of ethnographic texts is ostensibly that of **decoding** – to render comprehensible that which is initially unfamiliar, to establish a 'reading' of an event or an object. In ethnographic texts, such a 'reading' is frequently accomplished by a translation, the transposition of alien concepts or ways of viewing the world, from one language to another or from one conceptual universe to another. This is a far from simple process. Ethnographic texts adopt an objective and descriptive mode, but their production necessitates a substantial degree of translation, transposition and construction. Ethnographic texts can only successfully *decode* – unravel the meaning of that which is unfamiliar, distant, incomprehensible – if they simultaneously *encode* – translate, de-exoticize, and transform that which is alien into that which is comprehensible.

decoding

All texts involve an economy of meaning: foregrounding certain interpretations and excluding others, seeking to plot a relatively unambiguous route through meaning. Ethnographic texts, more consciously than others perhaps, direct the reader towards a *preferred reading* since they must navigate the reader on a directed route through potentially complex and unfamiliar terrain. This preferred reading involves the dual process of unravelling certain meanings – *decoding* – but equally of selection and creativity which allows certain meanings to surface – **encoding**. A basket, for instance, might be decoded in many ways (the work of a particular artist; a fine exemplar; an ancient, unique specimen; etc.) but the accompanying text

encoding

will encode it towards one or other of these, thereby guiding its interpretation and circumscribing its meaning. It will render intelligible the nature, history and cultural particularity of ethnographic objects. In so doing it will provide a compelling and convincing reading – it will 'quicken' and solidify the meaning. Recalling Lawrence's article, we may remember that it was the label – the *text* – which fixed Comanche's meaning in the most direct way and it was the text, therefore, which became the focus of dispute and subsequent reinterpretation.

2.6 Questions of context

On reading Lawrence's article one of the points that emerges most forcefully is the manner in which new layers of meaning are appended to Comanche over time, but in such a way that no new layer completely eclipses the previous one. Whatever Comanche's re-contextualization, he never completely loses his original meaning; it is re-articulated or added to. The palimpsest provides a useful metaphor for this process, where new layers of meaning are superimposed over older ones, or re-articulated, once the object is placed in a different context. This process, illustrated by Comanche's trajectory, is true for all objects. It is a particularly relevant way of perceiving the overlapping meanings of ethnographic collections, since they are most frequently the result of cultural, spatial and temporal displacement. 'Almost nothing displayed in museums was made to be seen in them. Museums provide an experience of most of the world's art and artefacts that does not bear even the remotest resemblance to what their makers intended' (Vogel, 1991, p. 191).

Ethnographic objects in historically important collections accumulate a palimpsest of meanings. So we can think of objects as elements which participate in a 'continuous history' (Ames, 1992, p. 141), where the makers, collectors and curators are simply points of origination, congregation and dispersal (Douglas, 1992, p.15): a history that extends 'from origin to current destination, including the changing meanings as the object is continually redefined along the way' (Ames, 1992, p. 141).

Viewing objects as palimpsests of meaning allows one to incorporate a rich and complex social history into the contemporary analysis of the object. Contemporary curatorial practice does attempt to chart the flow by attempting to establish when objects were collected, by whom, from where, for what purpose, what the originating culture was, who the maker was, what the maker intended, how and when it was used (was it strictly functional or did it have other purposes?) and what other objects were used in conjunction with it. However, as we shall see in section 3, this does not sufficiently problematize the manner in which objects acquire meanings. Those who critique museums from the standpoint of the *politics* of collecting argue that such an analysis fails to address the fact that ethnographic objects have entered into western collections purely as the result of unequal relationships of power. The questions of context and collecting can become far more vexed than the above framework suggests.

2.7 Summary

> Museums not only collect and store fragments of culture: they themselves
> are part of culture …; a special zone where living culture dies and dead
> culture springs to life.
>
> (Durrans, 1993, p. 125)

This section started by arguing that at different points in history museums
have had distinct ways of viewing objects and conferring meaning, value and
validity. Using the example of the *Museaum Tradescantianum*, we saw that
museums endow objects with importance because they are seen as
representing some form of cultural value, perhaps an unusual association, a
geographical location, or a distinct type of society. This initial example
allowed us to argue that the meaning of objects is neither natural nor fixed: it
is culturally constructed and changes from one historical context to another,
depending on what system of classification is used. This theme was
elaborated in relation to 'ethnographic' objects. It was argued that the
category of 'ethnography' emerged as a particular academic discipline. It
followed that objects were not intrinsically 'ethnographic', but that they had
to be collected and described in terms that rendered them so. This analysis
was taken further when we considered the ways in which objects acquire
meaning. It was argued that to understand the levels at which objects acquire
meaning, we have to investigate the texts that are used to interpret them in
addition to the nature of their historical trajectory. It was argued that an
object offers no guarantees at the level of signification; the stability which
derives from its *physical presence* must be conceptually divorced from the
shifting nature of its *meaning*.

In the next section we will consider how objects may acquire meaning in the
distinct context of an exhibition.

3 Fashioning cultures: the poetics of exhibiting

3.1 Introduction

In this section we move from discussion of the object to the practices of
exhibiting. It is the exhibition context which seems to provide us with the
best forum for an examination of the creation of meaning. Exhibitions are
discrete events which articulate objects, texts, visual representations,
reconstructions and sounds to create an intricate and bounded
representational system. It is therefore an exceedingly appropriate context
for exploring the **poetics of exhibiting**: the practice of producing meaning   poetics of exhibiting
through the internal ordering and conjugation of the separate but related
components of an exhibition.

In order to provide a 'reading' of some depth I have chosen a case study format. The exhibition chosen – *Paradise: Change and Continuity in the New Guinea Highlands* – was an unusual exhibition in many ways, most particularly because of the manner in which it sought to examine the contemporary moment amongst the Wahgi people of the Highlands of Papua New Guinea, but equally because it incorporated a record of its own creation. It was the subject of two extended commentaries: one by Michael O'Hanlon, the anthropologist/curator of the exhibition (*Paradise: portraying the New Guinea Highlands*, 1993), the other by James Clifford (*Paradise,* 1995), an anthropologist and cultural critic. The following section will not, however, dwell on its uniqueness, but more on what it can teach us about the general principles of meaning construction in the exhibition context. In this sense, therefore, the 'reading' presented here articulates a particular view of the exhibition. It is not, nor can it be, a comprehensive assessment of the diversity of issues involved; it is necessarily selective. Those who want other 'readings' should refer to the texts cited above in their original, full state, rather than the extracts included here.

3.2 Introducing *Paradise*

The exhibition *Paradise: Change and Continuity in the New Guinea Highlands* opened at the Museum of Mankind, the Ethnographic Department of the British Museum, on the 16 July 1993 and closed on 2 July 1995. During the two years of its life *Paradise: Change and Continuity in the New Guinea Highlands* could be found on the second floor of the Museum of Mankind. As part of a programme of rolling temporary exhibitions, its ostensible purpose was to bring the culture and history of the Wahgi people of the Highlands of Papua New Guinea to the attention of the public in Britain. A wheelchair ramp, a narrow corridor and two glass doors separated *Paradise* from the rest of the museum. Walking through them one entered the introductory space, with a large full-colour picture (Plate 3.I in the colour plate section) of:

> ... a genial-looking man stand[ing] casually in front of a corrugated iron wall and frame window; he wears a striped apron of some commercial material, exotic accoutrements and gigantic headdress of red and black feathers. His face is painted black and red; a bright white substance is smeared across his chest. He looks straight at you, with a kind of smile.
>
> (Clifford, 1995, p. 93)

The introductory panel, 'Paradise', on the left of the photograph, disclosed the aim of the exhibition: to show 'something of the history and culture of the Wahgi people of the New Guinea Highlands'. It then introduced the structuring themes of the exhibition – change and continuity.

ACTIVITY I

Read as much as you can of the panel text from Plate 3.I and consider how the exhibition is being introduced – what does the text tell you about the significance of the term 'Paradise'?

How might this establish a *preferred reading* of the exhibition?

This introductory text tells us a number of things: primarily, that 'Paradise' symbolizes both *change* – the transforming effect of coffee wealth – and *continuity* – the capacity for cultural forms to adapt to transforming circumstances. This tension is symbolized by the elements of the photograph: the birds of paradise feathers versus the corrugated iron for example, both integral to the picture, and by implication, Wahgi life. But this introduction also foregrounds the issues of *representation*: Paradise, the exhibition – the reconstruction of reality – is a subversion of Paradise, the 'myth' – the stereotype of the South Pacific. In contrast to a false image, it implies, this exhibition proposes a corrective, more authentic description of a particular South Pacific community. Closer to the truth but not all-inclusive – we are only shown 'something' of the history and culture of the Wahgi. So the introduction alerts us to the veracity of the reconstruction or representation. Although it makes claims of objectivity and representativeness, it disavows claims to comprehensiveness.

So even at the moment of entry we are drawn into the practice of signification and construction. The introductory panel contains within itself the structure of the whole exhibition, providing us with a mental map. We learn of the rationale of the exhibition and are alerted to its possible future content. So this initial panel sets the parameters of the representation and establishes a distinct narrative and sequencing.

What is the exhibition about? Wahgi history and culture.

What does this mean? It means recent contact, change and continuity reflected through material culture, including adornment, as transformed and preserved through the income from cash-cropping coffee.

The introductory narrative helps to guide the unfamiliar visitor through difficult and potentially dazzling terrain – the complexities of Wahgi culture could not, pragmatically, be fully explicated in this restricted exhibition space. To generate a meaningful path through the exhibition, the curator, the designers and technicians must choose which objects to display and which display methods might achieve the greatest impact, as well as what kinds of information might be included in the panels, label text or captions. These choices are in part 'repressive', in the sense that they direct the visitor towards certain interpretations and understandings, opening certain doors to meaning but inevitably closing off others.

But let us consider the importance and use of the photographic image (Plate 3.I). We might first remark that the persuasiveness of the text is significantly enhanced by the photograph that accompanies it. Photographs

PLATES 3.1-3.XV: Views of the *Paradise* exhibition, Museum of Mankind, London

PLATE 3.1
The introductory section of the exhibition

PLATE 3.II Foreground: (right) the bridewealth banners and First Contact display; (left) the compensation payment poles. Background: wall cases and free-standing glass cases containing Wahgi wigs and other items of adornment.

PLATE 3.III Sequential parts of the exhibition: (left to right) coffee production, the trade-store and shield displays.

PLATE 3.IV Wall case containing Wahgi items of adornment, old and new. Note the headband made of flame-coloured Big Boy bubble gum wrappers.

PLATE 3.V *Bolyim* house (right). Note the simulated pig jaws strung around the middle, and upturned beer bottles around the base.

PLATE 3.VI *Bolyim* house, showing accompanying panel text and photographs.

PLATE 3.VII Coffee production display. Note the artificial coffee bush, the coffee beans drying on the plastic sheeting, the hand-powered coffee pulper, and weighing scales.

PLATE 3.VIII Coffee production display, panel text and photographs. Note the similarity between the display and the photographs featured on the panel.

PLATE 3.IX First Contact display, showing First Contact panel with black-and-white photographs displayed against enlargement of black-and-white photograph taken by Mick Leahy.

PLATE 3.X First Contact display, showing *kula jimben* spears against scene painting (reflecting photograph in Plate 3.1X).

PLATE 3.XI First Contact display, showing bridewealth banners, and the '... and after' panel text and photographs. Note the similarity between the blow-up of the middle photograph and the reconstructed bridewealth banner.

PLATE 3.XII Trade-store display. Note the warning on the door (and weighing scales from neighbouring coffee production display).

PLATE 3.XIII Interior of trade-store display, showing the variety of products on sale.

PLATE 3.XIV The side of the trade-store display, showing how a connection was created with the neighbouring shield display.

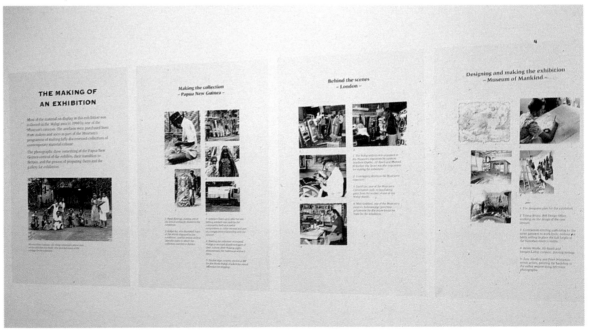

PLATE 3.XV Panels on 'The Making of the Exhibition', showing the process of collecting in the field with the assistance of the Wahgi, and the process of exhibiting in London.

can ease the work of representation within the exhibition context by virtue of their verisimilitude. As we shall see later, photographs in this exhibition were also used more actively in the practice of *signification*.

The personal image which initiates the exhibition declares that this is not the South Pacific as we all know it from the Rogers and Hammerstein film – a stereotype – this is an *authentic* Waghi. The image *denotes* Wahgi reality; it is one of a collection of photographs which objectively records an event – the opening of the store. It purports to be an adequate and truthful reflection of the event. But this denotation of Wahgi 'reality' has meaningful effects.

First, it 'naturalizes' the text: by this I mean that the photograph makes it appear less as a *construction* of Wahgi reality than a *reflection* of it, since both the 'reality' and the effects of the processes being described in the exhibition (those of change and continuity) are represented in the photograph. The concept of 'naturalization' is an important one which will be taken up through this analysis and later on in this section in the discussion of 'myth'.

But the photograph relays a complex message. It includes *connotations* of the hybrid nature of adornment (the bamboo frame is covered with imported fabric, the paints are commercially produced); the ambivalence of coffee wealth and its effect on taste (the adoption of black plumes for adornment); the nature of a typical Papua New Guinea trade-store (reconstructed in the main gallery). These only become clear once the visitor has completed the full circuit of the exhibition: on passing this photograph on the way out s/he may 'read' it more fully, being less startled by its exuberance and more aware of its encapsulation of the exhibition themes.

Second, it tends to legitimate the photographer/curator voice since the image denotes and guarantees O'Hanlon's having been there in the Highlands. It connotes *authentic* anthropological knowledge which means being appropriately familiar with the Wahgi. By association it authenticates the objects: they were collected while *he-was-there*.

But this brilliant photograph has an additional 'ethnographic' purpose. It connotes difference in all its exotic resplendence (a connotation incorporated into the exhibition poster) while simultaneously domesticating and transcending it. As one's eyes move from photograph to text, what is at first stunning and vibrant but indecipherable – except for the smile – is subsequently *translated*. This is recognizably a wealthy man in the midst of a celebration. He quickly becomes *known* and *familiar* to us. He is not simply 'a Wahgi', he is Kauwiye (Andrew) Aipe, a genial entrepreneur. Moreover he is welcoming us to the exhibition space, to the Wahgi way of life and the context in which Wahgi artefacts acquire meaning. Once the exotic is translated and proves hospitable, we can proceed into the remainder of the exhibition space.

This brief introduction alerts us to the type of construction and representation attempted in ethnographic exhibitions. Ethnographic exhibitions most usually adopt the format of contextualizing and reconstructing. Curators/ designers work with objects and contextualize them so that these assume a purposive role; objects are commonly selected as representative, rather than unique, examples. As both cultural expressions and physical proof, these provide insights into cultural phenomena of which they are taken to be the physical manifestation ('representation'). The visitor is, therefore, drawn into a new and different world in which unfamiliar objects might be made intelligible, where the design encourages the distance between the visitor and the 'originating culture' (the culture from which the objects were appropriated) to be reduced. Since the primary purpose of such exhibitions is the translation of difference – to acquaint the viewer with unfamiliar concepts, values and ideas – their key motive is communication through understanding and interpretation. Ethnographic exhibitions are typically syncretic (pulling together things from different sources). Nevertheless, though their ostensible form is that of *mimesis*, the imitation of 'reality', their effectiveness depends on a high degree of selectivity and construction. It is this – the *poetics* of exhibiting – that the rest of this section will address.

3.3 *Paradise* regained

> [T]he next, larger, space [of the exhibition] draws you in. It contains striking things: a reconstructed highland trade-store, rows of oddly decorated shields, wicked-looking ... spears, and bamboo poles covered with leaves which, on closer inspection, turn out to be paper money.
>
> (Clifford, 1995, p. 93)

The themes of the next large space are those of contact and coffee, war, shields and peacemaking. It is here that we notice the full effect of the design of the exhibition, the cacophony of colour and objects promised by the initial photograph of Kauwiye Aipe.

ACTIVITY 2

Look at a selection of photographs of the exhibition spaces following the introductory space (Plates 3.II–3.V). These will give you a flavour of the exhibition. When looking at these, consider how the objects are exhibited. How might different methods of display affect your perception of the objects?

In the exhibition we discover that there are several methods of display. I have disaggregated them as follows:

- on open display – shields (Plate 3.III)
- table cases – shells, items of adornment (Plate 3.II)
- wall cases – items of adornment (Plate 3.IV)
- reconstructions – bridewealth banners, trade-store, *bolyim* house (Plates 3.II, 3.III, 3.V)
- simulacra – compensation payment poles (Plate 3.II).

We could think of these methods of display as different but equivalent techniques, but this interpretation is not wholly adequate. In the *Paradise* example, the selection of these different contexts was influenced by lack of funds which meant that the curator was obliged to use a display structure inherited from the previous exhibition (O'Hanlon, 1993, pp. 82–5).

Here we are concerned with the *effects* of these different display techniques. *Paradise* utilized a diversity of display techniques, so its richness allows us to address the different levels in which methods of display create contexts for the production of meaning.

All these forms of display incorporate Wahgi material culture, but the different techniques affect our perception and reaction to the objects. Let us illustrate this by taking a simple example. A simple reconstruction such as the coffee production display (Plates 3.VII, 3.VIII) includes artefacts known as Wahgi because of their context of use. They are included because of their role in Wahgi life. These are not ostentatious objects but mechanical and mundane items which appear to need very little interpretation. They exemplify the literal reality of Wahgi life in which they feature quite heavily. The combination of the artefacts is not ambiguous, it is 'obvious' they belong together: the accompanying photographs show just such a combination of artefacts being used by the Wahgi. So the visitor is encouraged to trust – by virtue of the presence and combination of artefacts – that this is a 'reflection' of Wahgi reality. Such representations work to *denote* 'Wahgi reality' and *connote* the 'naturalness' of the display technique.

The glass cases, in contrast, establish distance by placing the object in a more sterile and ordered environment (Plates 3.II, 3.IV). This more conventional museum approach connotes the artificiality of display technique. Ethnographic objects are rarely made for glass cases, nor are they habitually selected and disaggregated from other associated objects while in use. Putting material artefacts in glass cases therefore underlines the dislocation and re-contextualization that is at the root of collecting and exhibiting. So whereas reconstruction may establish a context which evokes and recreates the 'actual' environment of production or use of an object, glass cases render the objects more distant; they do not merge into their context in the same way as they might if they were placed in a reconstructed site (Plates 3.II, 3.III).

These distinctions are amplified by the use of text. In the reconstructions, numerous objects are displayed in combination and assigned communal labels; but in the glass cases the objects are given individual identities. Each object, then, is accorded a particular value, interpreted and explained. So in open displays the presence of the object and its context or *presentation* eclipses the fact that it is being *represented*. The fact of representation is obscured. We perceive here the process of *naturalization*, as the objects appear *naturally* suited to this context, seeming to speak for or represent themselves. In glass cases, however, the work involved in representation is made more overt by virtue of the artificial separation and presentation of the object.

But there is one last type of display that remains unmentioned – the simulacra. The differences between reconstructions and simulacra are subtle. The reconstructions are partially 'authentic' artefacts – made by the museum technicians according to Wahgi design and incorporating Wahgi materials, be it shells, fibre or trade goods. The simulacra are *imitations* of real Wahgi objects such as the compensation payment poles (Plate 3.II). These are neither genuine Wahgi objects, nor do they incorporate them, but as objects they draw from Wahgi 'reality' in their design. We can designate them, after Barthes, as 'trick effects': since their purpose is to make what is heavily *connoted* pass as *denoted* (Barthes, 1977, pp. 21–2). Their presence is initially unquestioned – they appear to denote 'Wahgi reality' – until we see the 'real thing' in the photographs on the curving adjacent wall (Plate 3.II). At first these banners appear authentic, it is the accompanying text and photographs that intentionally alert us to their subterfuge:

> The … banners made of banknotes only really make sense when one sees the nearby color photograph of men holding them aloft in a procession. The 'Ah ha' response comes when looking at the picture, not the object. The banners are strange and beautiful in their way, but clearly simulacra … They become secondary, not 'the real thing' seen so clearly in the image.
>
> (Clifford, 1995, p. 99)

But their presence is nevertheless important, since these tangibly simulated objects smooth the representational work: if the text interprets and directs the reading of the object, then the object draws the reader to the text. The 'trick' is to validate the text. The presence of these simulacra in conjunction with the 'real thing' in the form of the photograph anchors the representation of Wahgi peace-making and compensation written about in the accompanying text.

3.4 Structuring *Paradise*

This part of section 3 will examine how images and texts can be used to create meaning in the exhibition context, by analysing a specific display in *Paradise*.

Clearly texts and images can have a number of functions. In order to disaggregate these I shall use the terms 'presentation', 'representation' and 'presence'. I will use the terms **presentation** to refer to the overall arrangement and the techniques employed; **presence** to imply the type of object and the power it exerts; and **representation** to consider the manner in which the objects work in conjunction with contexts and texts to produce meaning (Dubé, 1995, p. 4).

presentation
presence
representation

ACTIVITY 3

Looking at the photographs of the First Contact display carefully
(Plates 3.IX, 3.X, 3.XI), examine how the texts and the images are used in
the context of this discrete space. You do not need to dwell at length on
this. Simply reflect on the different types of texts used in this display.
What might their roles be? What roles are the photographs given: do they
illustrate, amplify, authenticate the text? How might these photographs
denote a changing historical period?

Let us consider the 'texts' and what narrative techniques are used, before
moving on to consider the function and significance of photographs in
Paradise. As in most exhibitions *Paradise* used several types of *texts*:

1   *Panels*. These contain thematic information or delineate a particular
    arena of human activity.

2   *Labels*. These are assigned to particular objects, offering explanations of
    how the object is articulated in its social contexts.

3   Photographic *captions*. These exemplify or subvert certain concepts or
    descriptions contained in other texts.

The difference between these texts is quite subtle. Panel texts connote
authority but are, conversely, more interpretative. Labels and captions, on
the other hand, are more 'literal'; they claim to describe what is there. This is
partly determined by space. Nevertheless these texts work together and
separately, each *encoding* through the semblance of *decoding*. The difference
between these texts, but also their contribution to signification, can be
exemplified at the level of translation.

Ethnographic exhibitions frequently make use of indigenous terms within the
substance of their texts. This is done for many reasons, partly to
acknowledge the insufficiency of translation, but equally because in an
ethnographic exhibition it accords 'a voice' to the people featured. Such
concessions to indigenous language have, furthermore, proved popular and
acceptable to the audiences who visit ethnographic exhibitions. But utilizing
indigenous languages has certain effects. On labels, they are often entered as
descriptions to signify the object – the *bolyim* house, a *mond* post – and a
connection is created between object and description which appears
transparent, definitive and transcendent. This is a *bolyim house* – no need
for translation (Plate 3.VI). Panels frequently have sayings, asides or
proverbs, in unfamiliar languages encouraging the reader to enter,
momentarily at least, into the conceptual universe – the way of seeing – of the
people concerned. In the First Contact panel, for instance, Kekanem Goi's
remark recounting his first reaction to the patrol's arrival ('*Alamb kipe gonzip
alamb ende wom mo?*') is translated ('Is it ghosts, the dead who have come?')
to denote the shock of the encounter between the Whites and the Wahgi (Plate
3.IX). But equally the process of inclusion is a complex one, involving
selection, translation and interpretation. Meaning must be altered so that an
allegory or metaphor deriving from one culture is made comprehensible in the
language of another.

So here we see that, though texts impart information, they are also economies of meaning, selecting what they would ideally like the visitor to know – what is important. They also reinforce certain aspects of design. In the First Contact display the spears are not given labels, but one can easily 'read' them since their arrangement (Plate 3.X) overtly reflects the content of one of the large photographs (Plate 3.IX). No overt guidance (text) is needed since they can be interpreted against the photograph.

This is one of the functions of the photographs in the First Contact display. At one level the type of reconstruction attempted seeks simply to mimic the content of the photographs. The scene painting reflects the image of Mick Leahy's encampment (Plate 3.X), the reconstructed fence and the group of *kula jimben* spears – some collected in the 1930s, others in the 1990s – recreate the situation in the black-and-white photograph of the Leahy patrol camp (Plate 3.IX). The bridewealth banner reflects the colour picture, itself a blow-up of one of the pictures in the panel (Plate 3.XI). This is not all. The images, in addition to authenticating the (re)construction and the objects, serve to connote the passage of time. This is related by the quality of the reproduction (grainy/clear) and its type (colour/black and white) – a message easily understood. The 'faded' colour of the bridewealth banner picture (taken in the 1950s) contrasts with the 'true' colour of the other, more recent, pictures (taken in the 1980s) and the black-and-white grainy reproductions of those taken in the 1930s (Clifford, 1995, pp. 99–100). The interplay and proximity of these images of changing quality and type reinforces the theme of the text and locates the objects to create a very rich representation of change and continuity.

But some photographs have a function which go beyond that of *presentation* and *representation*. In the *Paradise* exhibition they are equally a substitute for *presence*. In the case of the bridewealth banners, most particularly, the large blow-up photograph *substitutes* for the object (Plates 3.II and 3.XI). Moreover, the photograph – the representation of the real banner – overshadows the adjacent reconstruction – the partially authentic artefact which incorporates *real* Wahgi shells and fibre – by being far more splendid:

> It is no longer a question of a photo providing 'context' for an object. We confront an object that cannot be present physically, a 1950s bridewealth banner – long disassembled, as is its proper fate. This banner has been 'collected' in the photographs. Given its prominence, the color image seems somehow more real, in a sense more 'authentic' than ... the less impressive older banner propped beside it ...

> (Clifford, 1995, p. 100)

Clifford comments that, for him, this is preferable. Collecting would artificially remove the object and make it immortal, whereas collecting the object-as-photograph provides a legitimate alternative: recording the existence of the object without interrupting its proper cultural disposal. So photographs, in the exhibition context, can accord a *presence* to ephemeral artefacts – artefacts that would be destroyed in their proper social context: the bridewealth banners and *bolyim* house for instance – and those that cannot be exported legally – such as the Bird of Paradise feathers (Plate 3.I) – or practically – the Wahgi themselves (Plate 3.XV).

In the *Paradise* exhibition, therefore, photographs have three effects: they enhance the *presentation* of the exhibition; they substitute for the physical *presence* of ethnographic 'objects' or 'subjects'; and they ease the work of *representation* by providing a 'real' context which either contextualizes the object or allows a blueprint for the display design.

3.5 *Paradise*: the exhibit as artefact

In the preceding sections we have considered how objects, texts and contexts have worked in conjunction to produce meaning. Let us bring these to bear on the trade-store exhibit to examine how the context of display, and by extension the exhibition, can be considered as a fiction and an artefact. The word fiction is not used here in a derogatory way, but rather in its *neutral* sense: the Latin verb *fingere* from which fiction derives means that something has been fashioned and made through human endeavour. O'Hanlon himself boldly acknowledges his role in this process of authorship (1993, Introduction, Chapter 3). As an articulated but bounded representational system, the trade-store will be used here as a metaphor for the *Paradise* exhibition as a whole (Plate 3.III).

The trade-store clearly operates on the level of *presentation*. It mimics a 'real' Highland store with a corrugated iron roof. The reconstruction is 'authentic' even down to its incorporation of the usual notice on its door – *No ken askim long dinau* (Don't ask for credit) – and the floor – sandy and littered with beer bottle tops (Plates 3.XII, 3.XIV). The hodge-podge of goods, all imported, purposefully attempts to 'capture something of the raw colours of such enterprises' (O'Hanlon, 1993, p. 89) (Plate 3.XIII). And is their function purely presentation? No. The presence of these goods clearly heightens our power of imagination; the combination is fascinating; each item draws our attention. One stops to read the different brand names – Cambridge cigarettes, *LikLik Wopa* ('little whopper' biscuits), Paradise *Kokonas* (coconut biscuits), Big Sister pudding, the ubiquitous Coca Cola – and to take in the exuberance of the display.

On the level of *presence*, the items denote 'the expanding range of goods on sale' (O'Hanlon, 1993, p. 89), most particularly what can be bought with coffee wealth. The store was intended as 'a reconstruction, stocked with the goods which would be on sale during the Wahgi coffee season' (panel text). So these objects are genuine and representative samples of the totality of artefacts that could be found in a store (they were brought over from Papua New Guinea). The store *enlivens* the representation of Wahgi life. Its presence – as an artefact in its own right – *anchors* the narrative in the panel text, which conversely interprets the meaning of the whole and the miscellany of goods which it contains.

Considering the context of display – the trade-store – the arrangements of these objects seems appropriate, 'natural' even. Imagine these trade goods ordered in a glass case: the isolation would affect our perception, drawing us to the object rather than the combination. It is the contrived miscellany of objects in the trade-store that makes it compelling and produces meaning; the whole is bigger than the sum of its parts. The trade-store is itself a system of representation, externally and internally narrated. Each object is interpreted through its label, which cross-refers to others, the advertising slogans and to the panel text. Furthermore the store goods are interpreted in two different languages – *tok pisin* (the local *lingua franca)*, and English. These trade labels reaffirm difference but also transcend it.

The trade-store is an enabling context which 'quickens' our understanding of the ambivalent impact of coffee wealth, transforming exchange relations, encouraging warfare. But this representation is articulated with the adjacent displays (Plate 3.III), coffee production – the source of money – and the shields, which connote in their design and form 'South Pacific' beer cans (Plate 3.III, 3.XIV). Indeed the trade-store, though denotative of a 'typical' Highlands store, has another level of artifice – two 'trick effects'. O'Hanlon tells us that he has had to cut away the front to permit visibility and surreptitiously included 'South Pacific' empties along the far wall, not because this is representative of reality, but because a reference to beer must be included in a depiction of New Guinea life (1993, pp. 89–90). Their inclusion here enables us to make an effortless move to the next display (Plate 3.III and 3.XIV).

The display takes us back to the initial image and functions covertly as a focal point for our other senses. It is the first time one can remark the change in the scene painting and it is from the trade-store that we become aware that the sounds can be heard. What effects might these have?

Let us first take the case of the scene painting. In the introductory space, scene painting is restricted to the depiction of two mountain ranges and the sky. In the main exhibition space it is varied to denote the physical and social environment of the Highlands of New Guinea, alternatively dense Highlands vegetation (behind the trade-store and the hand-coffee mill) and an enclosed camp identical to the one in the photographs of the Leahy expedition or a Wahgi village (behind the *bolyim* house and *mond* post). The scene painting works with the photographs and the reconstructions to innocently denote the Wahgi world, to reflect the physical environment of the Highlands of New Guinea 'as-it-really-is'. This denotation of Wahgi reality is affirmed aurally, by the continuous looped three-minute tape featuring New Guinea early morning sounds, cicadas, singing, jew's harp, but also bingo calls, issuing from the trade-store. These sounds locate the visitor in the Highlands. Providing a contrast with the busy London streets, but equally with the quiet reverence of the other galleries, these aural representations deepen the impression of entering the Wahgi physical and social world because they work on an affective, emotional level. Amplifying the themes of the exhibition, these sounds 'collected in the field' denote the Highlands but connote tradition (through sounds of jew's harp, singing) and change (through the recognizable sound of bingo). So what at first seemed different, is with repetition made familiar and the visitor is encouraged to imagine they are in the New Guinea Highlands. But this representation of 'how-it-really-is' necessarily supports a distinct thematic narrative about the way in which change and continuity shape contemporary Wahgi life.

Thus we can think of *Paradise,* the exhibition, as a complex representational system featuring objects (made and used by the Wahgi), reconstructions (of Wahgi material, of Wahgi design, but made by Museum staff) and simulacra whose cogency derives from the articulation of these different elements into a narrative with texts, images and sounds. At one level the *Paradise* exhibition is 'typically' ethnographic: its focus is the socio-cultural whole that is Wahgi life, and it uses objects as exemplars, each a sample of a representative type whose presence guarantees the veracity of the representation. It is equally typical in the sense that it is necessarily selective: what we are presented with is a representation of Wahgi life, authored and partial.

3.6 The myths of *Paradise*

In the preceding analysis two things were learned:

1   the extent to which exhibitions are constructions,

2   that the end of this construction is to persuade, to render 'natural' or 'innocent' what is profoundly 'constructed' and 'motivated'.

The first point has been extensively investigated, the second point is that which concerns us now. The point of departure – the argument to follow – is simply that *all* cultural producers – advertisers, designers, curators, authors (including this one) – are involved in the creation of 'myths' in the manner in which Barthes defines this. As a consequence, these producers are inevitably the holders of symbolic power.

We shall look at 'myth' by critically assessing the contrasting accounts of both Clifford (1995) and O'Hanlon (1993) concerning the production of exhibitions. The *Paradise* exhibition, unusually, included panels and text which highlighted the conditions of production of the exhibition, the role of the author and curator and his relationship with the community he chose to represent. Such a candid account is placed at the end of the exhibition, and so in a sense one 'reads' the exhibition as a partial truth, retrospectively. It is worth noting that it is precisely because the *Paradise* exhibition was not a standard unreflective exhibit, but a resourceful and complex exhibition that addressed the problematic aspects of its own production and political accountability, that it has provoked such valuable and reflexive comment, of a kind that can push the student and cultural critic alike beyond simply stereotyping the process of exhibiting.

Let us consider certain extracts from O'Hanlon's (1993) book and Clifford's (1995) commentary, Readings C and D at the end of this chapter.

These two texts have alternative purposes and voices. O'Hanlon writes as a curator/anthropologist. He recounts the process of collecting and exhibiting as he sees it, to strip it of its aura of 'magic'. Clifford's text offers a different perspective, from the point of view of the cultural critic and the visitor; someone who is enthusiastic about *Paradise*, but who uses it to push the analysis on to questions of power. *These are both partial views – texts about texts – and must be read as such.* They constitute part of an ongoing dialogue.

You should take notes on these two extracts, particularly the differing views on *collecting* and *exhibiting*. How does each seek to qualify their point of view? How do their interpretations contrast?

Let us first consider O'Hanlon's perspective.

O'Hanlon's account of collecting adopts a reflexive tone which acknowledges the contingencies of collecting as well as the potential inapplicability of an anthropologist's categories. He represents collecting as a valuable educational experience. He argues that collecting does not involve a 'rupture' of artefacts from their local context, but requires complex negotiations between the Wahgi and himself, dictated by existing – Wahgi – categories of social relations and local political agendas. He is directed by and drawn into a complex series of relationships in which he is attributed the status of an agent by his Wahgi friends. His departure places him at one remove from these expectations of a continuing relationship of indebtedness.

Collecting Wahgi material culture, and prompting its production, pushes O'Hanlon to recognize the limits of knowledge. It alerts him to cultural complexities and the convoluted meanings of certain artefacts. It creates an artificial social situation, bringing the subtleties of Wahgi classification and definitions, which he might otherwise have missed, to his attention. For instance, although the Wahgi are prepared to make certain ritually significant items for O'Hanlon (*geru* boards), they are not prepared to make others (*bolyim* house).

So collecting emerges from O'Hanlon's account as a complex, negotiated process, where the anthropologist does *not* have the power one might otherwise expect. It necessitates, instead, local knowledge, resources and resourcefulness.

In relationship to exhibiting, O'Hanlon stresses that the exhibition is an authored text and assemblage – an *artefact*. He avows his desire that the Wahgi should have a degree of *presence* in the exhibition and writes that he would like to honour the Wahgi's request for stones and posts to be put in the first antechamber of the exhibition (an antechamber that was subsequently changed by the designers). He notes, furthermore, that his exhibition should accord the Wahgi a 'voice' by using Wahgi or *tok pisin* text. Secondly, he overtly signals the constructed nature of the exhibition within the exhibition itself: the last panels foreground the different stages of its production (Plate 3.XV).

Clifford (1995) on the other hand reviews the exhibition, in part because it does tackle issues and provide information which in most exhibitions is backgrounded. While acknowledging this, however, he subjects the materials provided to further scrutiny. For Clifford, like O'Hanlon, *Paradise* is an artefact fashioned by the interplay between curators, designers and the museum institution, but not necessarily the Wahgi. He critically questions the extent to which the Wahgi could be considered as partners or co-authors and cites the following evidence. First, the lack of a significant Wahgi 'voice'. Second, his view that the self-reflexivity incorporated into the exhibition (Plate 3.XV) is less provocative than it might be. Lastly he questions the exact nature of the 'continuing relationship of indebtedness' between O'Hanlon and the Wahgi. Using the example of the 'taboo stones' he argues that the Wahgi had little effective power. Finally, he asks to what extent specific interpersonal relationships struck up between the anthropologist and his colleagues or friends within the community ('in the field') can be mapped onto the institutional setting.

ACTIVITY 4

We now have two different views of the process of collecting and exhibiting. What do you think of these views? Which strikes you as the more compelling, and why?

We can add to these two commentaries on the practices of collecting and exhibiting another critical dimension, using Barthes's theory of 'myth', or mythical speech, which was discussed in Chapter 1. Two aspects of his exposition may be useful here, to push the dialogue, and the analysis of exhibiting above, further.

First, Barthes calls 'myths' a second order semiological language. This means that, in contrast to ordinary language, it does not work on the basis of an arbitrary, unmotivated relationship between the signifier and signified. With 'myth' there is always some form of 'motivation', namely some purpose, intent or rationale underlying its use. Furthermore the persuasiveness of 'myths' derive from their 'natural justification' of their purpose:

> What the world supplies to myth is an historical reality, defined, even if this goes back quite a while, by the way in which men have produced or used it; what myth gives back in return is a *natural* image of this reality.

> (Barthes, 1989, p. 155)

So myth 'naturalizes' speech, transmuting what is essentially *cultural* (historical, constructed and motivated) into something which it materializes as *natural* (transhistorical, innocent and factual). Myth's duplicity is therefore located in its ability to 'naturalize' and make 'innocent' what is profoundly motivated.

The second point follows from this and concerns the ability of myth to 'de-politicize' speech:

> Myth does not deny things, on the contrary, its function is to talk about them; simply, it *purifies* them, it makes them *innocent*, it gives them a *natural* and *eternal* justification, it gives them a clarity which is not that of an explanation but that of a statement of fact.

> (Barthes, 1989, p. 156, my emphasis)

So by asserting that 'myth' de-politicizes speech, Barthes argues that myth does not hide or conceal its motivation. Instead, by giving it a universal, transhistorical basis and by stressing objectivity, and its origins in nature, myth **purifies** its motivation.

purification by myth

How might these insights provide an additional 'reading' of the texts to the ones we have just explored?

In this section we have treated the *Paradise* exhibition as a fashioned event and a complex system of signification. Both these aspects can be addressed by Barthes's analysis of 'myth'.

Let us first consider 'motivation'. *Paradise*, like all exhibitions or any other cultural products, was clearly the result of a series of deliberate actions: the collection was purchased, the exhibition planned, written and constructed. The objects were removed from Wahgi cultural life and re-presented in cases, restored in the quasi-'natural' setting of a reconstruction or represented in scene paintings and photographs. *Paradise* was not a rambling narrative with a number of disconnected objects thrown together; it was a highly structured event, in which *even* the apparent miscellanies were designed to seem 'real'.

Moreover the overwhelming purpose of the exhibition was that of representing Wahgi *reality*: the artefacts, once part of the Wahgi social universe, visibly correspond to Wahgi 'reality' as captured in the photographs, or mimicked in the reconstructions. So the phenomenon of Wahgi cultural life is domesticated and transformed – it is 'naturalized'. The exhibition adopts a factual, easy tone where selected representative objects are described in objective terms and where sounds, scene painting reconstructions, photographs, quotations, all accord a *presence* to the Wahgi.

So the *Paradise* exhibition, like all exhibitions, is a descriptive and motivated event. But doesn't O'Hanlon go some way to recognizing this?

O'Hanlon does not deny his agency as an anthropologist; he incorporates it into his narratives (the exhibition and the book). Aware as he is of the complexities of collecting and exhibiting, he sets out to explore the contingencies and conditions of possibility of both. O'Hanlon's motivations are clearly 'natural' and acceptable, given his professional status, as is his desire to show a recent collection. Being the first major display of Papua New Guinea Highlands material culture in Britain, the exhibition was considered to be both appropriate and timely. Collecting, furthermore, affords him the opportunity of speculating on the blurred category of Wahgi material culture that he has to work within. He argues that, in the New Guinea context, collecting is not necessarily rupture but exchange (his methods have differed quite considerably from the directly exploitative collecting trips of others), conceived and effected in synchrony with the Wahgi view of the world. O'Hanlon therefore questions whether the Wahgi would necessarily view collecting as *appropriation*, belonging, as they do, to an elaborate culture of exchange.

Clearly O'Hanlon explores his motivations as a collector/curator. But for Barthes, this might be perceived as an act of *purification*. The intense attention to the intricacies of the various practices leading up to the exhibition encourages a reading of collecting and exhibiting as exchanges in which the collector and the Wahgi are partners. The panel at the end of the exhibition particularly hints at the **symbolic power** of the exhibition, namely the way in which it constructs and persuades through delineating a path through meaning. The presentation of the Waghi as knowing agents and cultural producers, and of O'Hanlon as author and curator, *purifies* the *symbolic power* of the exhibition and the curator.

symbolic power

Clifford, on the other hand, implicitly draws a distinction between the *symbolic power* of the exhibition and the **institutional power** of the British Museum. He agrees that O'Hanlon has acknowledged his relatively powerful role as author and circumscriber of meaning through his last panel, and through his book. But Clifford remains unconvinced that the relationship between the Wahgi and the institution – the British Museum – is sufficiently examined. Clifford argues that the two – *symbolic power* and *institutional power* – are symbiotic, and that while O'Hanlon fully acknowledges his symbolic power, he does not tackle the institutional relationship.

institutional power

What might the implications be of prioritizing a reading of exhibition as *mythical structure* rather than simply as *artefact*? There are implications concerning authorship and power. If the exhibition is a form of mythical speech, then the anthropologist is a kind of mythologist: out of the oddments of the present and the debris of the past s/he puts together new constructions and meanings that are persuasive and necessarily disguised because they are interpretations which are received as facts and truths. But it must be remarked that if one opts to perceive an exhibition as a mythical structure, then the *symbolic power* of the anthropologist is not a choice but an *inevitability*. Collecting and authorship necessitate the production of 'partial truths' and 'persuasive fictions'.

Clifford, however, in his analysis, hints at an important distinction. We can differentiate between *symbolic power* – which is inevitable and located around the author (and therefore under individual control: for example, the relationship between O'Hanlon and the Wahgi) – and *institutional power* – which is more exclusionary and situated round the institution (the direct relationship between the British Museum and the Wahgi, and the latter's relative power of sanction). As we shall see (section 4) the question of *institutional power* is an influential critique when exercised in relation to museums since it reaches beyond the internal articulation of meaning to the broader issue of the role of the museum in society at large and its relationship to knowledge.

> ### ACTIVITY 5
>
> So, to the two different views of the process of collecting and exhibiting, we have added another dimension. Has this discussion of 'myth' altered your view of exhibiting? Why?

3.7 Summary

This section subjected ethnographic displays to a particular type of analysis. Drawing on semiotic theory – the work of Barthes – in relation to a case study – the *Paradise* exhibition – we showed how exhibitions trace a particular path through meaning and motivation. Initially treating the exhibition as an artefact, the analysis explored the various ways in which objects, contexts, texts and visual representations were deployed to construct meaning. It explored the internal ordering of the various elements and their articulation, but disaggregated the display into several levels: presence, presentation and representation, allowing us to examine the *poetics* of exhibiting. Treating an ethnographic display as an artefact provided a means of detecting the complex web of signification and how it was produced. We then considered the different views that the commentaries on *Paradise* offered on the practices of collecting and exhibiting. We found that these commentaries gave distinct interpretations, and we added to this a theoretical alternative which pushed us towards a more 'political' interpretation of exhibiting, by proposing that an exhibition is a mythical structure. This, in turn, permitted us to question exhibitions and museums in line with two different analyses of power: *symbolic* and *institutional*.

4 Captivating cultures: the politics of exhibiting

4.1 Introduction

The last section considered exhibiting in terms of its *poetics* – the internal articulation and production of meaning. This section will invoke a theoretical model and texts to explore the *politics* of exhibiting – the role of exhibitions/museums in the production of social *knowledge*. Whereas section 3 used the work of Roland Barthes, this section will appeal to the work of Michel Foucault whose writings were also discussed in Chapter 1. So the model of representation used in this section will focus on broader issues of knowledge and power. Examining the **politics of exhibiting** will cause the question of *institutional power*, raised in section 3, to be specifically addressed. As we noted in previous sections, museum collections do not simply 'happen': artefacts have to be made to be collected, and collected to be exhibited. They are historical, social and political events. This section will present yet another 'reading' of the practices of exhibiting: a critique which argues that the practices of collecting and exhibiting are powerful activities, and that an analysis of the relationship between power and knowledge should be incorporated into any investigation into exhibiting/museums. Examples from a specific historical, political moment – the late nineteenth century – will be used in this section for reasons that will become apparent.

politics of exhibiting

4.2 Knowledge and power

The aspects of Michel Foucault's work which we shall investigate here concern the specific definition he gives to *discourse* and the axis he defines between *power/knowledge*. In establishing these definitions, we are adopting a new interpretation of anthropological knowledge.

discourse

Discourse, as you may recall from Chapter 1, section 4, is a group of statements which provides a language for talking about a particular topic, one that constructs that topic in a particular way. It is a way of formulating a topic and a field of inquiry which answers specific 'governing statements' (questions) and produces 'strategic knowledge': *savoir*. For Foucault, in contrast to Barthes, knowledge cannot be reduced to the realm of pure 'meaning' or 'language' because all knowledge operates as a historically situated social practice: all knowledge is **power/knowledge**. So 'strategic knowledge' is knowledge inseparable from relationships of power (Foucault, 1980, p. 145). Discourses, according to this definition, do not simply reflect 'reality' or innocently designate objects. Rather, they *constitute them in specific contexts according to particular relations of power*. So if the subject of anthropological enquiry is discursively constituted, this implies that this knowledge does not simply operate at the level of 'meaning' or 'ideas', nor does it innocently reflect 'reality'. On the contrary:

power/knowledge

> [anthropology] itself is possible only on the basis of a certain situation, of an absolutely singular event ...: [anthropology] has its roots, in fact, in a possibility that properly belongs to the history of our culture ... [Anthropology] can assume its proper dimensions only within the historical sovereignty – always restrained, but always present – of European thought and the relation that can bring it face to face with all other cultures as well as with itself.

(Foucault, 1989, pp. 376–7)

So if we take the emergent social science of anthropology or ethnology in the latter part of the nineteenth century, we could characterize it as a rather diffuse body of knowledge constituted by scholars, which acquired a hesitant disciplinary status by virtue of its placement in small institutional bases, most particularly the museum. Alternatively, one can see it as more complicit, a discipline which, despite its aspiration to general human relevance and enlightenment, was primarily a discourse about the culturally or racially despised, developed by the members of a dominant culture in the imperial context (Stocking, 1985, p. 112). Stocking, for example, argues that it is a discipline which codified knowledge in such a manner that it could be called upon as 'a moral as well as a scientific justification for the often bloody process' of imperial expansion (1987, p. 273). By providing a classificatory schema for the 'races' of humankind, it can be argued, it encouraged and aided their regulation.

Foucault's meditation on the subject of discourse reflected his more general preoccupation with the genesis of the human sciences. For Foucault, studying the genesis of the human sciences revealed that these are not 'enlightened' sciences – progressive views of the human condition – but particular forms of knowledge which emerged at a distinct historical moment. While they frequently constituted themselves as enlightened, they were more properly united in their desire to regulate human subjects. For Foucault, the new human 'sciences', of which anthropology is one, sought to codify and regulate certain sections of society: women, 'natives', the insane, the infirm and the criminal classes, which, as sciences, they discursively constituted as real subjects of knowledge on the basis of material evidence (see Chapter 1). These sciences were allied to techniques of regulation (the prison, the mental asylum, the hospital, the university) and the rise of the nation-state. Discourses systematically 'form the objects [subjects] of which they speak' (Barrett, 1991, p. 130), but in accordance with newly emerging relationships of power which sought not to control violently but to discipline in institutional settings, most usually through the emphasis on the body.

Using a Foucauldian perspective suggests that anthropology emerged as a distinctive type of knowledge at a defined historical moment (the middle of the nineteenth century) and was inscribed with particular relationships of power (Empire and colonial expansion) and therefore largely depended in some measure on the unequal encounter of what has elsewhere been called 'the West and the Rest' (Hall, 1992).

One may ask to what extent does this new critical dimension contribute to an analysis of ethnographic display?

Employing a Foucauldian framework necessitates recasting the field of anthropology as a discursive formation: one constituted through the operation of several discourses; equally one which does not simply reflect 'real' distinctions between peoples, but creates them. Moreover, as a science which mobilizes a classificatory system, it manufactures these distinctions on the basis of a certain *representation* of this difference, and subsequently uses this typology to determine whom it seeks to study and what the best research methods to employ might be. Correspondingly, as anthropological discourses change, so do representations and the kinds of evidence needed to support these types of knowledge. These factors clearly have implications in terms of material culture and methods of display.

Let us now see how using a Foucauldian argument about the relationship between discourse and representation might present a different perspective on the museum context to that of section 3.

4.3 Displaying others

Ethnographic artefacts were constituent items of the oldest collections, but in many cases the delineation of artefacts as specifically 'ethnographic', whether by virtue of circumscribed displays, specific departments, or museums, only took on a scientific status late in the nineteenth century. Indeed anthropology was to find its first institutional home in museums, rather than universities. 'In a period when not only anthropology, but science generally was much more "object" – or specimen – orientated than today' (Stocking, 1987, p. 263), the existence of collections propelled anthropology towards institutionalization, as curators started to define themselves professionally as anthropologists. One of the most notable museums to emerge in the nineteenth century was the Pitt Rivers Museum in Oxford.

We will examine the relationship between discourse and exhibiting in the context of the Pitt Rivers Museum. Older displays seem to furnish us with particularly good examples of the processes at work, perhaps because we recognize their artifice more readily (Lavine and Karp, 1991, p. 1).

Augustus Henry Lane Fox (later Pitt Rivers, after inheriting a substantial fortune), the founder and patron of the Pitt Rivers Museum, developed a particular interest in collecting objects after visiting the Great Exhibition at Crystal Palace in 1851. Initially a collector of arms, he soon broadened his interest to encompass archaeological and ethnographic items (Chapman, 1985, p. 16). He was interested in theories of evolution and human antiquity as well as 'racial' theories. By the comparison of artefacts from different periods and places, in particular the 'commoner class of objects', he sought to establish historical sequences which visibly mapped technological development and small alterations in form over time. He believed that only through the 'persistence of forms' could one 'show that disparate peoples possessed common traits, and thus re-established their past connection' (Chapman, 1985, p. 23). By arranging sequences of artefacts one could reflect on 'the sequence of ideas by which mankind has advanced from the condition of lower animals' (Lane Fox quoted in Chapman, 1985, p. 33) because the technological sophistication of objects stood for or represented the intangible aspects of culture. For Lane Fox, continuities in the form of artefacts provided decisive evidence for ethnological and evolutionary connections (Figure 3.3).

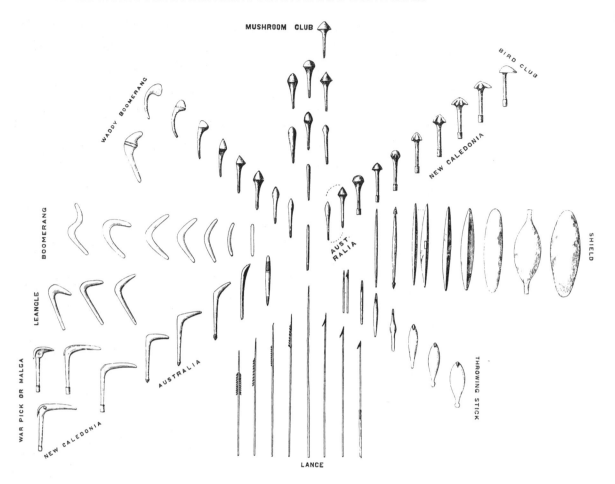

FIGURE 3.3

'Clubs, Boomerangs, Shields and Lances': an illustration from Henry Lane Fox's *The Evolution of Culture* (Oxford, Pitt Rivers Museum, 1875).

Lane Fox was dedicated to the idea of displaying these connections in a museum. In the early 1860s he sought a wider audience for his collection and eventually, in 1883, offered the whole collection to Oxford on condition that it was exhibited in the manner he determined.

The Pitt Rivers collection thus distinguished itself by virtue of its arrangement. Its systematic approach owed more to a Linnean natural historical classification (of groups, genera and species) than the more common geographical classification typical of other contemporary ethnographic displays (Figure 3.4) (Chapman, 1985, pp. 25–6; Coombes 1994a, pp. 117–9; Lane Fox, 1874). Pitt Rivers arranged his artefacts primarily in a *typological* manner, namely one which privileged form and function but was cross-cut by geographical principles of regional groupings. Artefacts were arranged sequentially to permit comparative analysis. Archaeological artefacts from ancient peoples and contemporary ethnographical materials – from 'survivals' – were arranged side by side to form a complex representation whose purpose was the illustration of human evolution and history. In this manner the Pitt Rivers collection and museum provided a predominant and compelling *typological* representation, which spoke volumes about the determination of its founder to promote a particular

FIGURE 3.4
An ethnographic gallery of the British Museum, c. 1900.

FIGURE 3.5
The main exhibition hall of the Pitt Rivers Museum, Oxford, c. 1970.

strand of anthropological inquiry, and therefore of knowledge and discourse (Figure 3.5). The representation of other cultures that it gave rise to was determined by Pitt Rivers' preferred view of functional *evolutionary discourse*. In presenting this focused view, the Pitt Rivers Museum did not reflect the 'complex and comprehensive' debates taking place in the emerging discipline of anthropology or among the Museums Association concerning the classification of ethnographic material, but accorded with more popular views of the relationship between the 'races' which it legitimated by virtue of its position as a scientific discourse (Coombes, 1994a, p. 117).

What issues are raised by examining the Pitt Rivers display and in what manner is this form of representation different to that of the *Musaeum Tradescantianum*?

First, one has to consider how the inclusion of the artefacts was determined by the type of knowledge that was brought to bear on them and how these legitimated certain discourses. As 'curiosities', ethnographic artefacts occupied an equivalent place to other decontextualized objects – artefacts to prompt the imagination and philosophical reflection. The Tradescant display now appears whimsical and disorderly in its arrangement, reflective of a particular world view which applied classificatory criteria (Artificial versus Natural curiosities) but also a hierarchy of value (in terms of curiosities and rareties) very different from the evolutionary ones. Collecting was seemingly an idiosyncratic process, even though undeniably already the product of exploration, conquest and colonization.

Ethnographic artefacts in the Pitt Rivers collection, by contrast, were subjected to the seemingly more rigorous discourse of science. Utilized as 'evidence' and 'proof', they were the material embodiment of the socio-cultural complexities of other cultures. These ethnographic artefacts were systematically collected, selected and arranged according to a classificatory schema whose function was to illustrate the progress of human history by according different cultures different places on the evolutionary ladder (Coombes, 1994a, p. 118). Pitt Rivers himself was keen to contrast the science and comprehensive reach of his approach with the incompleteness of earlier cabinets of curiosities. '[T]hese ethnological *curiosities*, as they have been termed, have been chosen without any regard to their history or psychology ... they have not been obtained in sufficient number or variety to render classification possible' (Lane Fox, 1874, p. 294).

What distinguishes Pitt Rivers' approach is the fact that the classificatory and evaluatory schema that it invokes is seen as 'scientific', where this refers to a positivistic framework of knowledge, and where the representation (the method of display) reinforces and derives from the evolutionary discourse that frames it.

Second, the Pitt Rivers Museum as a nineteenth-century museum had a more instrumental vision of its role in public education and the specific benefits for its audience. Its typically congested display was less a collection for the edification of the contemplative scholar or the interested visitor, than a detached, objective, positivist tool promoting the 'diffusion of instruction' and 'rational amusement' of the mass of the British population, whom he judged as improperly ignorant of the nature of human development and 'history' (Coombes, 1994a, p. 121, 123). So the Pitt Rivers Museum mobilized an evaluative discourse concerning the civilizing effect of culture on the mass of the population. The museum was expected to bring social benefit by shaping the intellect and transforming social behaviour (Bennett, 1994, p. 26).

In the late nineteenth century, bids for anthropology to be recognized as a science of humanity coincided with the rapid expansion of the 'museum idea'. The 'museum idea', simply put, was the belief that museums were an ideal vehicle for public instruction: by contemplating cultural artefacts on display, the common man/woman could become receptive to 'their improving influence' (Bennett, 1994, p. 23). The belief in the 'multiplication of culture's utility' was not restricted to museums but extended to art galleries and libraries (ibid.). The rise of anthropology as a discipline coincided with and was supported by the ferment in exhibiting activity, either in the shape of the great exhibitions or in the shape of museums which arose in great numbers all over Britain between 1890–1920 (Greenhalgh, 1993, p. 88). So one can argue that the Pitt Rivers Museum was implicated in other discourses of 'self' and 'other' which produced a division between geographically distanced cultures, but also between the cultures of the different classes of British society.

To conclude, it has been shown that both the Tradescant and the Pitt Rivers collections/museums are historical products. But it has equally been stated that what distinguishes the Pitt Rivers collection is the particular articulation between the evolutionary discourse and the method of display which it implemented. The Pitt Rivers Museum, it can be argued, at this historical juncture (the late nineteenth century) promoted and legitimized the reduction of cultures to objects, so that they could be judged and ranked in a hierarchical relationship with each other. This anthropological – or more properly, ethnographic – discourse did not reflect the 'real' state of the cultures it exhibited so much as the power relationship between those *subjected* to such classification and those *promoting* it.

4.4   Museums and the construction of culture

As we have shown in the previous section, a Foucauldian interpretation of exhibiting would state that ethnographic objects are defined and classified according to the frameworks of knowledge that allow them to be understood. We have considered the representations that museums produced and how these are linked to discourse. But, as was hinted in the last section and as you saw in Chapter 1, Foucault also argues that discourses do not operate in isolation, they occur in formations – **discursive formations**. The term *discursive formation*, refers to the systematic operation of *several* discourses or statements constituting a 'body of knowledge', which work together to construct a specific object/topic of analysis in a particular way, and to limit the other ways in which that object/topic may be constituted. In the case of museum displays, such a formation might include anthropological, aesthetic,

discursive
formations

and educational discourses. The internal cohesion of a *discursive formation*, for Foucault, does not depend on putative 'agreement' between statements. There may seem to be fierce internal debates, and different statements within the field of knowledge may appear antagonistic or even irreconcilable. But this does not undermine the cohesion or the creation of a 'body of knowledge' or a 'body of truth' around a particular object in a systematic and ordered fashion (Hall, 1992, p. 291).

In the following activity, we will consider how several competing discourses served to construct particular objects as desirable and valuable ethnographic artefacts. The case under consideration is that of the Benin Bronzes.

READING E

The extracts in Reading E are drawn from the work of Annie E. Coombes (1994a). Although these extracts may seem a little fragmented, it is important to understand the argument that Coombes makes concerning the articulation of discourses around the West African artefacts known as the Benin Bronzes (Figure 3.6 (a) and (b)). Some background context may be of use here. These artefacts were the subject of controversy both because of the manner in which they were appropriated (in a punitive expedition that was mounted in 1897 as a reprisal for the killing of a British party by Benin forces), and because of the objects' technical expertise and aesthetic qualities. So Coombes has selected her case well to explore these issues: the appropriation and exhibiting of the Benin Bronzes is particularly well documented. Coombes can, therefore, examine how these objects were discursively produced through the articulation of a number of discourses, but equally how power/knowledge worked in the institutional context.

Read the Coombes' extracts (Reading E) and make notes in the light of the following questions:

1   How were the Bronzes discussed? How did commentators rationalize their origins? How were these objects discursively produced?

2   How were they displayed?

3   What institutional factors determined the Bronzes' prestige among curators?

Coombes argues the Benin Bronzes are an important case for two reasons.

First, they are counter-suggestive. She argues that the artistry of the Benin Bronzes should have challenged prevailing scientific and aesthetic discourses which held that African cultures were incapable of complex artistic achievement. The Benin Bronzes were first discursively produced as survivals of the impact of the foreign forces – the Portuguese – but most particularly of 'recognized' civilizations such as Egypt, since, it was argued, the people of Benin were not capable of such artistic expression. Those scholarly publications which questioned these assumptions were initially

FIGURE 3.6 (a)   An Oni of Ife (dead king),
Benin bronze, sixteenth/seventeenth century.

FIGURE 3.6 (b)   Bronze figure from Benin,
sixteenth/seventeenth century.

ignored, whereas those which integrated these atypical artefacts into pre-existing discourses, most particularly the discourse on 'degeneration', gained ground. Coombes recounts how the Benin Bronzes were incorporated into a discourse in which degeneration and artistic ability were proved to be compatible. So the Bronzes' uniqueness did not challenge prevailing discourse; rather the discourse domesticated the problem of the Bronzes. Coombes employs a Foucauldian framework to understand how the Benin artefacts were discursively constructed, making reference to the various 'scientific' – notably anthropological – and aesthetic discourses that competed to incorporate the Benin artefacts. She alludes to a discursive formation that is particularly rigid.

Coombes, moreover, asserts that these scientific discourses derived a significant measure of their persuasiveness from their agreement with other popular discourses on 'race'. She explores, in this connection, the images of Benin produced by the popular press. She shows that these *acknowledged* the artistic quality of the artefacts but always in the context of reports illustrating *the degeneracy* of Benin civilization and amidst frequent mentions of the massacre of the English prior to the punitive raid.

Secondly, Coombes delineates the relationship between the Benin Bronzes, anthropological discourses and museums, in ways which allow museums to be seen as the seats of institutional power. She investigates the relationship between power/knowledge in three separate museum contexts: the Horniman Museum, the British Museum and the Pitt Rivers. Coombes shows the distinctions in their discursive constructions of the Benin Bronzes but connects these differences to struggles for power within and between these institutions. At the Horniman, Quirk alters his opinion of the Benin Bronzes, once these are displayed at the British Museum, to gain prestige. For Read and Dalton, at the British Museum, the transformation in their discursive construction of the Benin artefacts is linked to bids for power and recognition within the British Museum (and to their being thwarted in their desires to purchase the totality of the Bronzes). The Pitt Rivers, predictably perhaps, manages to incorporate the Benin Bronzes into a typological display of casting technology and therefore a display on ironwork, paying particular attention to the *cire perdue* method.

Coombes articulates a further argument which considers the link between the Benin Bronzes and colonial power. She argues that these Benin artefacts did not come to occupy the status of artefacts by accident, but by virtue of colonial **appropriation** (Figure 3.7). She deepens this connection between colonialism and collecting by observing that the artefacts were sold to pay for the Protectorate.

appropriation

So in summary, by considering the historical articulation of several sets of discourses, Coombes shows how a body of knowledge can be created not only around a particular region of the world, but also around the material culture that it produces. She demonstrates how there is consistency despite disagreement. Discourses, she argues, work in formations which frame the manner in which one can think and talk of these objects and the subjects that produce them. She incorporates a discussion of power, concluding that collecting and exhibiting are the by-products of colonial power. So in relationship to a particular category of objects – the Benin Bronzes – she argues that knowledge is indissolubly yoked to power, and in this case *institutional power* since it is the museum and its internal struggles that shape how the Bronzes are ultimately perceived.

Let us push this analysis further by considering the link between exhibiting and looking.

FIGURE 3.7
British officers of the Benin punitive expedition with bronzes and ivories taken from the royal compound, Benin City, 1897.

4.5 Colonial spectacles

The interconnection between power and exhibiting outlined by Coombes (1994a, 1994b) seems most persuasive when one explores the issue of 'living exhibits': the peoples that were brought over to feature in the colonial, national and international exhibitions staged in Europe and America in the nineteenth and twentieth centuries (see the discussion of 'the Hottentot Venus' in Chapter 4, section 4.4). Let us review the work of Foucault to discern how **power and visibility** or spectacle are joined.

power and visibility

Foucault's analysis of power/knowledge incorporates a theory of *visibility*. Foucault can be thought of as a 'visual historian' because he examined the manner in which objects and subjects were 'shown'. He argued the phenomenon of 'being seen' was neither an automatic nor a natural process, but linked to what power/knowledge guides one to see – it relied on one's being 'given to be seen' (Rajchman, 1988). Furthermore, in the human sciences, what is seen and counts as 'evidence' is most usually linked to corrective action. The human sciences therefore differ from the hard sciences: perceiving electrons does not elicit questions of what to *do* with them, but 'seeing' the poor, the infirm, the mad or 'savages', unleashes precisely these questions (Rajchman, 1988, p. 102). So being made visible is an ambiguous pleasure, connected to the operation of power. Applying this to the instance of ethnographic objects: in the Pitt Rivers Museum the subtlety and significance of differences in material culture can only be properly 'seen' if one is implicated in a discourse that applies an evolutionary schema in which these objects can be used as 'proof' of the discourse and thus differentiated, ordered and classified in that way.

The link between visibility and power is rendered most compelling when one considers human subjects and in particular the great spectacles of the colonial period – the national and international exhibitions that were mounted in Great Britain between 1850 and 1925. These exhibitions were notable for a great many things: their promotion of exploration, trade, business interests, commerce; their dependence on adequate rail links, colonial trading networks, and advertising; their launching of now familiar products: Colman's mustard, Goodyear India rubber and ice cream; their notable effect on the institutionalization of collecting and internalization of commerce (Beckenbridge, 1989). Among these other notable distractions, they provided another type of spectacle: the display of peoples. In this section we will look, very briefly, at ethnographic displays which showed people, not objects.

The Exposition Universelle (Paris) in 1867 was the first to include colonial subjects as service workers, while the first exhibition to inaugurate displays of people simply *as spectacle* – as objects of the gaze – was the Exposition Universelle (Paris) of 1889. These 'authentic' manifestations of 'primitive culture' became a popular feature of most exhibitions into the early decades of this century. The last exhibition to feature dependent peoples in this manner in Britain took place at the British Empire Exhibition (1924–5) at Wembley (though some might argue it continues today in other forms) (Benedict et al., 1983, p. 52). As displays, dependent peoples were brought over to provide viewers with the experience of being in other worlds; situated in 'authentic' villages, they were asked to re-enact, for the viewing public, their everyday lives. These peoples were classified in terms of the geography of the exhibition, but equally, sometimes, according to putative notions of their 'relationship' to each other in evolutionary terms. At the St Louis Louisiana Purchase Exposition of 1904, where people from the Philippines were accorded a significant place in the Hall of Anthropology, the various villages and their tribes were helpfully ordered in a fashion which 'faithfully' portrayed the evolution of human development, from the lowest to the highest level (Greenhalgh, 1988, p. 101).

In the era where the primary data used for the comparison of cultures was often provided by colonial administrators and not anthropologists, such displays provided remarkable opportunities. The 'armchair anthropologists' of the period were initially keen to derive benefit from the presence of these authentic living 'specimens' or scientifically significant objects. These human exhibits provided valuable evidence for an emerging discipline. They were real, authentic exemplars of 'primitive' people, 'survivals' of other histories, 'vanishing races' or genuine 'degenerates' (depending on the particular anthropological discourse one held). On their bodies were written the traces of earlier cultures. This physical evidence provided 'proof' that could not otherwise be obtained but which could tangibly substantiate contemporary physical anthropological discourses. In 1900, W.H. Rivers, who was to become an influential figure in British anthropology, suggested that 'the Anthropological Institute should seek special permission from the exhibition proprietors in order to "inspect" these people prior to the exhibits opening to the general public' so that evidence could be collected (Coombes, 1994a, p. 88).

They could be and were measured, classified and photographed. Photographic representations in the shape of photographs of anthropometric measurements or colour postcards fuelled scientific speculation and popular belief. The popularity of these exhibitions – many millions of visitors from all walks of life trooped past native villages – helped to support the dominant popular discourse that other cultures were 'survivals' or 'savages'. This was particularly so when 'primitive' or 'savage' customs came into view: the Igorots at the St Louis Fair purchasing, roasting and eating dog meat (Figure 3.8) or the Ainu at the Japan British Exhibition of 1910 photographed with a bear skull.

So one can argue that the blurring of 'scientific' and 'popular' anthropological discourses served in more or less subtle ways to legitimize and substantiate a discourse of European imperial superiority (Greenhalgh, 1988, p. 109). To understand these displays the visitor had to bring certain kinds of knowledge with him/her, reinforced by other representations – photographs, postcards, museum displays, paintings – and had to be implicated within a particular

FIGURE 3.8
Igorots eating dog
meat in the
Philippine exhibit
at the St Louis
Louisiana
Purchase
Exposition, 1904.

geography of power. The display of people was a display of a power
asymmetry, which these displays, in a circular fashion, served to legitimize
(Benedict et al., 1983, p. 45; Coombes, 1994a and 1994b, p. 88). The
exhibitions and displays can equally be thought of as 'symbolic wishful
thinking' which sought to construct a spurious unity (a 'one world' framed in
evolutionary terms) in which colonizer and colonized could be reunited and
where those of 'vastly different cultural tradition and aspirations are made to
appear one' (Benedict et al., 1983, p. 52).

Thus, a Foucauldian model allows one to argue that being able to 'see' these
native villages and their constituent populations was clearly neither a
'natural' process, nor an accidental one, but a socio-historical one, which was
associated with and reinforced standard museological representations of
peoples through ethnographic artefacts. The argument which connects
museological representations with spectacular ones is supported when it
becomes clear that certain of the ethnographic collections featured in the
colonial, national or international exhibitions, or the photographs of these
visitor peoples, were often incorporated into the ethnographical collections
or archives of established museums.

So here the relationship between scientific knowledge (anthropology),
popular culture, the geography of power (colonialism) and visibility
(photograph, display) is rendered particularly overt. But a note of caution
must also be inserted. The Foucauldian model is a totalizing one. By this I
mean that a Foucauldian model produces a vision of museums and exhibiting
which is primarily based on a belief in social control. If Coombes' (1994a)
analysis is taken to its logical end point, that even the Benin Bronzes fail to
pierce the solid structure of pre-existing ethnographic disclosure, then one is
left with questions of how intellectual paradigms change. How have we come

to the point where such artefacts as the Benin Bronzes can be 'seen' as art
when previously they could not? And how are we to understand this new
state of knowledge? Although Coombes' longer text (1994a) provides a much
more comprehensive account of the tensions in the process of exhibiting,than
the extract presented here, it is nevertheless the case that a Foucauldian-
based analysis argues convincingly that collections are not extracted
willingly from originating cultures, they are always excisions, removed, often
painfully from the body of other, less powerful, cultures. These collections,
it further argues, assume the rationale of education to be to lend future
purpose but also to justify the original act. Collecting is constructed as a
pursuit inevitably dogged by its own history, always betrayed by hidden
intent. Collecting is, in short, a discredited and ignoble activity. This
Foucauldian critique links collecting and exhibiting to such an extent that it
puts into question whether the ends can ever justify the means. Provocative
and thought-provoking though this critique undoubtedly is, it fails to
produce either a convincing evocation of the paradoxical relationship
between ethnography and the museum, or an acknowledgement of the
bureaucratic and pragmatic decisions at the heart of the process of exhibiting.

4.6 Summary

This section has specifically addressed the *politics of exhibiting*. It has
advanced a significantly different view to the one proposed by Mary Douglas
(see section 2.4 above), namely that objects circulate in continuous history
where makers, collectors and curators are simply points of origination,
congregation and dispersal, in a circular system (1992, p. 15). In this view,
the activities of collecting and exhibiting are not neutral, but powerful.
Indeed it has been argued, through using a Foucauldian model, that it is
impossible to dissociate the supposedly neutral and enlightened world of
scholarship on one hand from the world of politics and power on the other.
So this section does not focus on the production of meaning, but the linkages
between representation and museums as seats of institutional power. The
examples used substantiate the proposition that significant linkages existed
in the nineteenth century between desires for institutional power, the rise of
anthropology as an academic discipline, and the popularity of colonial
discourses.

Thus, an argument that considers the *politics of exhibiting* advances the view
that museums *appropriate* and *display* objects for certain ends. Objects are
incorporated and constructed by the articulation of pre-existing discourses.
The museum becomes an arbiter of meaning since its institutional position
allows it to articulate and reinforce the scientific credibility of frameworks of
knowledge or *discursive formations* through its methods of display.

Moreover we have found that an argument about power/knowledge can be
articulated around exhibiting and displays, particularly in terms of *visibility*.
The *politics of exhibiting* means museums make certain cultures *visible*, in
other words they allow them to be subjected to the scrutiny of power. This

derives from a historically unequal relationship between western powers and other peoples.

We have seen that, at one moment, what allowed a *human subject* to be transformed into an *ethnographic object* was a particular relationship of knowledge to power in association with wider social changes whereby, in the exhibition context, the colonizer/seer/knower was made separate and distinct from the colonized/seen/known. In this section, therefore, it has been argued that, just as power reduced cultures to objects (in the Pitt Rivers collection), it also allowed the objectification of human subjects (in displays). In this manner the ability to display ethnographic objects or subjects required certain types of knowledge (for interpretation and narrative) allied with a particular relationship of power.

5   The futures of exhibiting

5.1   Introduction

> The very nature of exhibiting ... makes it a contested terrain.
>
> (Lavine and Karp, 1991, p. 1)

The purpose of the last three sections has been to contextualize and analyse the practices of exhibiting, using theoretical models which forefront the *poetics* and *politics of representation*. So now if we re-evaluate our original definition of the museum, namely that it is an institution which exists 'in order to acquire, safeguard, conserve, and display objects, artefacts and works of arts of various kinds' (Vergo, 1993, p. 41), we find that these terms have acquired far from objective or neutral meanings.

While those types of analyses that we have attempted in the previous sections have become more commonplace, they cannot account for the complexity of the exhibiting process or the position of present-day museums. An analysis that forefronts the *poetics of exhibiting,* by examining the product – the exhibit – rather than the process of exhibiting, runs the risk of wishing to fix meaning to the exclusion of the 'hidden history' of production. Similarly an analysis that seeks to investigate the *politics of exhibiting* may produce an over-deterministic account revolving around social control, which may be best illustrated by taking nineteenth-century examples. In this brief coda to the chapter, I shall provide four reasons why these two models of representation might have become popular, and how the adoption of such perspectives has altered the practices of exhibiting. In so doing I shall argue that we have reached a turning point in the history of ethnographic museums in particular, but equally of museums in general. As you may notice, I link the changes in ethnographic museums to changes within the discipline of anthropology but also to wider changes in society and therefore to the consumers of exhibits in western nations.

5.2 Disturbance of anthropological assumptions by decolonization

If anthropology thrived in the colonial era, then it follows that it has had to reassess its hold in the light of decolonization. Anthropologists have had to question how a discipline which has a growing awareness of its own complicity with colonial forces, whose primary research method – fieldwork – was dependent on colonial support, can ring the changes in the wake of decolonization, globalization and cultural revivalism among indigenous people. Today anthropologists are asked and ask themselves *why* they seek to study those 'other' than themselves. They must justify their thirst for and entitlement to knowledge. These questions of politics and ethics have impacted on the field of exhibiting, since cultural producers are asked to be accountable to the cultures whom they represent.

5.3 Partiality of anthropological knowledge

In recent years the assertion that anthropological knowledge is by its very nature 'partial' (like all forms of knowledge, scientific and otherwise) has taken hold. By 'partial' one should understand two things: (1) that what it aims to construct and produce through ethnographic texts can only ever comprise part of the whole; and (2) 'partial' in the sense of subjective.

5.4 Anthropological knowledge as representation

When in section 2.3 we described anthropology as a science of invention not discovery, we highlighted moves that have taken hold of the discipline. During the last twenty years some of the critical debates that have transformed the discipline of anthropology have revolved around the nature of the ethnographic text as a form of representation. Asserting that ethnographic texts are not accurate descriptions made of one culture by another but by the *writing of one culture by another* would, today, be a starting point in an analysis of ethnographic work, rather than a radical statement. At the early stages of the discipline, the production of ethnographic texts seemed difficult in a technical sense: how could the values, beliefs and structures of other societies be accurately translated into terms that were understandable to other anthropologists? Today, the term 'writing' foregrounds something quite different: the fact that an active process of representation is involved in constructing one culture for another. What is being produced therefore is not a reflection of the 'truth' of other cultures but a representation of them. Inevitably, therefore, the task of writing ethnographies has become 'morally, politically, even epistemologically delicate' (Geertz, 1988, p. 130). Claims about the inevitable indeterminacy of anthropological knowledge have been accompanied by associated claims about its power. So anthropological knowledge is now considered to have a powerful but ambiguous role.

How might these changes in anthropology have affected ethnographic exhibitions? The changing shape of ethnographic displays cannot, and does not, reflect directly the wealth of transformative debates within anthropology, but it *is* indirectly affected by the grosser shifts. This is partly because museums now employ anthropologists with fieldwork experience, rather than train professional curators to deal specifically with material culture. Classical anthropological enquiry sought to define the essence of 'traditional societies' by ignoring the powerful structures that surrounded and facilitated the anthropological endeavour. Correspondingly, ethnographic displays admitted largely 'authentic', 'traditional' objects as evidence. The present turn towards anti-essentialism has prompted ethnographic exhibitions which, in contrast, increasingly feature incongruous cultural products, denoting the perpetuation and re-creation of tradition through the appropriation of new forms or consumer products.

Amongst other things, the *Paradise* exhibition reflects such a shift. The presence of the later panels and the chapters on exhibiting and collecting in the accompanying book acknowledges the partiality of anthropological knowledge and the ambiguous role of the anthropologist. The theme of this exhibition – change and continuity – specifically allows for the inclusion of hybrid Wahgi artefacts: headbands sewn from Big Boy bubble gum wrappers (Plate 3.IV) reflect the colour of older headbands, for instance, or the shields used for warfare but appropriating new derivative ornamentation. The contexts of display are not classical: reconstructions include modern consumer items (Coca Cola in the trade-store, South Pacific beer surrounding the *bolyim* house), simulacra mimicking the hybrid nature of the peace-making banners (incorporating money). The objects, the reconstructions, the simulacra and the photographs frustrate the categories of 'authenticity' and 'tradition'. The category of Wahgi material culture includes artefacts which are both hybrid and syncretic. O'Hanlon indicates through this strategy that he recognizes that objects are not *innately* 'ethnographic' but that they must be *designated* as such.

We have seen that changes in the academic discipline, itself affected by larger cultural movement (such as post-modernism), have created new boundaries for exhibiting: to name but three, the inclusion of self-reflexivity, or dialogue or polyvocality (many voices, interpretations of objects); the move towards incorporating hybrid and syncretic objects; and a right for those represented to have a say in exhibition construction (Coombes, 1994b). The latter point directs us to another sphere of influence. In locating the causes of changes in the practices of exhibiting, and therefore representing, we must also look at the wider social context. Museums as public institutions seek and survive on the basis of a constituency. Ethnographic displays may be affected by the changes in anthropological discourse, but it is their relevance and popularity with visitors that determines their survival. Now, therefore, we must briefly address the issue of consumption.

5.5   The question of audience

For some, the equation is simple: if museums have to appeal to the public, their messages have in some way to concord with the collective view of this audience, since their survival depends on making the collection, the exhibition and the museum meaningful to this pre-defined group (Ames, 1992). The public nature of the ethnographic museum has two implications. First, that museums as educational institutions can serve to deepen knowledge but they are usually not directly confrontational; their representations must be held to be appropriate and to concord broadly with the view of social reality the visitor holds (Ames, 1992, p. 21). The public attending museums expect their representations of the world to be confirmed, if a little extended, by the museum. Second, as museums seek to widen their natural constituency to reach more varied audiences, so the visiting public will become increasingly more diverse and may have more varied, or even competing, demands. In particular, if this new audience includes those communities which the museum *represents*, or their descendants, then the museum's representations may have to concord with the sense of self this new constituency holds in addition to that of the wider public. So museums in the 1990s have to address a plurality of views. As 'multicultural and intercultural issues' emerge ever more on the public's agenda, so 'the inherent contestability of museum exhibitions is bound to open the choices made in those exhibitions to heated debate' (Lavine and Karp, 1991, p. 1). As museums become more concerned about their public image and are increasingly asked to transform themselves into commercially viable institutions, the degree of control which the public can exert on them through attendance, protest or, the most powerful of all, publicity, grows. Public access therefore 'entail[s] … a degree of public control over the museum enterprise' (Ames, 1992, p. 21).

To illustrate this, I shall use a Canadian example. Below I shall delineate very briefly how a reaction towards an exhibition might present a new challenge to the politics of representation.

On 14 January 1988 the exhibition *The Spirit Sings: Artistic Traditions of Canada's First Peoples* opened at the Glenbow Museum, in Calgary, Alberta, as part of a cultural festival which was planned to coincide with the Winter Olympics. The exhibition brought together hundreds of artefacts from foreign museums with some of the earliest aboriginal materials in the Glenbow collection. It had several aims which were largely achieved: to highlight the 'richness, diversity and complexity' of Canada's native cultures at the moment of contact; to emphasize the 'distinctive view' of these cultures by examining the 'common threads' between them; and, finally, to emphasize the 'adaptability and resilience' of these cultures in the face of European domination (Harrison, 1988a, p. 12).

In April 1986 Shell Oil announced that it would provide sponsorship enabling the project to go ahead. Shortly after this the Lubicon Lake Indian Band of

Cree of Northern Alberta called for a boycott of the 1988 Winter Olympics, to draw attention to their unsolved, but outstanding, claim for the return of their traditional lands. Although the Lubicon Lake Indian Band of Cree initially sought primarily to target wealthy and powerful interests, later their attention was drawn to the politics of exhibiting. They focused on the exhibition for one outstanding reason: Shell Oil was drilling on land claimed as part of their traditional lands (Ames, 1991, p. 9). 'The irony of using a display of North American Indian artefacts to attract people to the Winter Olympics being organized by interests who are still actively seeking to destroy Indian people seems painfully obvious' (Chief Bernard Ominayak, 1988, quoted in Harrison, 1988b, p. 7)

The protests challenged the cultural authority of experts and institutions, and their 'entitlements' to native material culture, and gained much media attention, popular and international support. The exhibition did open, but the controversy surrounding it catapulted relations between museums and native peoples of Canada into a new era.

The most direct result was the creation of a Task Force whose mission was 'to develop an ethical framework and strategies for Aboriginal nations to represent their history and cultures in concert with cultural institutions' (quoted in Herle, 1994, pp. 40–41). The published report, *Turning the Page: Forging New Partnerships Between Museums and First Peoples* (1992), contained several recommendations. The essence of these was increased 'dialogue' between curators and native peoples and 'partnership' – a sharing of responsibility for the management of cultural property. Museums were asked to accord a role and a voice to native peoples without denying the work, experience or expertise of non-native museum staff (Herle, 1994, pp. 41–3). The response from Canadian institutions has been to work out relations on an individual basis: each museum entering different sets of negotiation with the elders, spiritual leaders or native cultural organizations. Certain museums loan sacred objects on a long-term basis to native-run cultural centres; others return sacred or ceremonial items regularly to communities for short periods. The 'institutional' and scientific imperative of conservation is temporarily waived in favour of 'moral' imperatives and 'spiritual' care (Herle, 1994, p. 47; Ames et al., 1988, p. 49). These collaborations have wider ramifications: acknowledging the sacred nature of material and the importance of native values means re-assessing the imperatives underlying conservation (is it acceptable to treat sacred or other material according to scientific views of impermanence?), storage (where and how should sacred material be stored?) and display (should certain items be seen? and, if so, in what context?).

As we saw in sections 3 and 4, one cannot read directly from culture to politics or vice versa. Dialogue and polyvocality (many voices) in the exhibition or the museum context do not map easily onto the state of national politics. The Lubicon Lake Cree land claim was not propelled to a solution by virtue of the protest or the ensuing reconciliation between the museums and the native communities. But national politics did provide the context in which these issues were negotiated. The controversy surrounding *The Spirit Sings* must be read against the specific history of conquest, local indigenous politics, contemporary popular opinion and Canada's particular national interpretation of what it means to be a multicultural country.

6   Conclusion

> Selective memories cannot be avoided, but they can be counteracted.
>
> (Davies, 1995, p. 11)

In section 5, we considered the implications of the two previous sections by considering how practices of exhibiting/representing must be affected by critiques which forefront both the 'poetical' and 'political' nature of exhibiting. We considered briefly the practical effects of such critiques. We showed that the movement towards hybrid forms and syncretism could be read as a result of changing perceptions of anthropology of itself and its subject matter. The incorporation of other values at more structural levels indicates an acceptance on the part of museums that collecting and exhibiting are 'political' activities: ethnographic objects are increasingly defined and represented by the originated peoples or their descendants in an 'auto-ethnographic' process.

The beginning of this chapter set up a relatively uncontroversial definition of museums which has been progressively re-assessed. The result has been that museums have emerged as highly contestable entities, with distinct histories and purposes. It has been argued that in order to enquire into the types of representation produced by a museum one might use one of several strategies. One could consider the historical location of the museum, to examine the 'world view' it sought to put across. Alternatively one could highlight the manner in which the museums make objects meaningful and exhibitions create a complex web of signification – the *poetics of exhibiting*. Lastly, one could try to look at museums in terms of the link between power and knowledge in order to look at the discourses articulated throughout their displays – the *politics of exhibiting*.

Each of these views has been considered. Section 2 sought to look at the history and method of a museum in a critical light through the use of two case studies. In section 3, museum collections were described as inevitably selective and exhibitions as a further selection. The task was to show how this selective process might facilitate the path of meaning creation. To do this, it selected a case study – the *Paradise* exhibition – which was then analysed in terms of its *poetics*. The elements of exhibitions – objects, texts, contexts of display, visual representation – were investigated separately and together in order to ascertain how their articulation might produce meaning, how they might be used to represent and re-present other cultures. It was argued that exhibitions could be viewed as mythical structures invested with symbolic power. In section 4, selectivity was given a more ambivalent gloss by contending that it was a product of power and its relationship to knowledge. Focusing on the museum as an institution allowed an examination of the *politics of exhibiting* and an exploration of the manner in which anthropological knowledge had legitimized certain ways of seeing and means of controlling other cultures. Section 5 considered, briefly, what the effects of these highly cogent critiques might be in the context of contemporary exhibits.

What conclusion can one reach? We can assert that museums *are* systems of representation. They are also contested entities, which establish systems that confer certain kinds of meaning and validity upon objects in line with specific or articulated discourses. A museum will endow objects with importance and meaning because these come to represent certain kinds of cultural value. Museums are arbiters of meaning and the processes of making collecting plans, acquiring objects, mounting displays require both symbolic and institutional power. But equally we can argue that the result of the potent critiques delineated in this chapter has been to challenge the authority of ethnographic exhibitions and museums. This has, in turn, resulted in a new movement which recognizes that selectivity is inevitable and endeavours to broaden the base of who works in and who visits museums, and thereby actively seeks to integrate other perspectives and new voices.

References

AMES, M. M., HARRISON, J. D. and NICKS, T. (1988) 'Proposed museum policies for ethnological collections and the peoples they represent', *Muse*, Vol. 6, No. 3, pp. 47–52.

AMES, M. M. (1991) 'Biculturalism in exhibitions', *Museum Anthropology*, Vol. 15, No. 2, pp. 7–15.

AMES, M. M. (1992) *Cannibal Tours and Glass Boxes: the anthropology of museums*, Vancouver, University of British Columbia Press.

BARRETT, M. (1991) *The Politics of Truth: from Marx to Foucault*, Cambridge, Polity Press.

BARTHES, R. (1967a) *Writing Degree Zero* (tr. A. Lavers and C. Smith), London, Jonathan Cape.

BARTHES, R. (1967b) *Elements of Semiology* (tr. A. Lavers and C. Smith), London, Jonathan Cape.

BARTHES, R. (1977) *Image–Music–Text* (tr. S. Heath), New York, Hill and Wang.

BARTHES, R. (1989) *Mythologies* (tr. A. Lavers), London, Paladin.

BENEDICT, B. et al. (1983) *The Anthropology of World Fairs: San Francisco's Panama Pacific International Exposition of 1915*, London, Lowie Museum/Scolar Press.

BECKENBRIDGE, C. A. (1989) 'The aesthetics and politics of colonial collecting: India at World Fairs', *Comparative Studies in Society and History*, Vol. 31, No. 2, pp. 195–216.

BENNETT, T. (1994) *The Multiplication of Culture's Utility: the art gallery versus the alehouse*, Inaugural lecture, Brisbane, Griffith University.

CHAPMAN, W. R. (1985) 'Arranging ethnology: A.H.L.F. Pitt Rivers and the typological tradition' in Stocking, G. W. Jr (ed.) *Objects and Others*, London, University of Wisconsin Press.

CLIFFORD, J. (1995) 'Paradise', *Visual Anthropology Review*, Vol. 11, No. 1, pp. 92–117.

COOMBES, A. E. (1994a) *Reinventing Africa: museums, material culture and popular imagination in late Victorian and Edwardian England*, London, Yale University Press.

COOMBES, A. E. (1994b) 'The recalcitrant object: culture contact and question of hybridity' in Barker, F. et al. (eds) *Colonial discourse/postcolonial theory*, Manchester, Manchester University Press.

DAVIES, N. (1995) 'The misunderstood victory in Europe', *The New York Review of Books*, 25 May, p. 11.

DOUGLAS, M. (1992) *Objects and Objections*, Toronto Semiotic Circle, Monograph Series of TSC No. 9, Toronto, University of Toronto.

DUBÉ, P. (1995) 'Exhibiting to see, exhibiting to know', *Museum International*, Vol. 47, No. 1, pp. 4–5.

DURRANS, B. (1992) 'The future of the other' in Lumley, R. (ed.), *The Museum Time Machine*, London, Comedia.

DURRANS, B. (1993) 'The future of ethnographic exhibitions', *Zeitschrift für Ethnology*, No. 118, pp. 125–39.

FINDLEN, P. (1989) 'The museum: its Classical etymology and Renaissance genealogy', *Journal of the History of Collections*, Vol. 1, No. 1, pp. 59–78.

FOUCAULT, M. (ed.) (1980) *Power/Knowledge* (tr. C. Gordon, L. Marshall, J. Mepham and K. Soper), Hemel Hempstead, Harvester Wheatsheaf.

FOUCAULT, M. (1989) *The Order of Things*, London, Tavistock/Routledge.

GEERTZ, C. (1988) *Works and Lives: the anthropologist as author*, Cambridge, Polity Press.

GREENHALGH, P. (1988) *Ephemeral Vistas: the* Expositions Universelles, *Great Exhibitions and World Fairs, 1851–1939*, Manchester, Manchester University Press.

GREENHALGH, P. (1993) 'Education, entertainment and politics: lessons from the Great International Exhibitions' in Vergo, P. (ed.) *The New Museology*, London, Reaktion Books.

HALL, S. (1992) 'The West and the Rest: discourse and power' in Hall, S. and Gieben, B. (eds) *Formations of Modernity*, Cambridge, Open University Press/ Polity Press.

HARRISON, J. D. (1988a) 'Museums and politics: *The Spirit Sings* and the Lubicon Boycott: Co-ordinating Curator's statement', *Muse*, Vol. 6, No. 3, p. 12.

HARRISON, J. D. (1988b) '*The Spirit Sings* and the future of anthropology', *Anthropology Today*, Vol. 4, No. 6, pp. 6–9.

HERLE, A. (1994) 'Museums and First Peoples in Canada', *Journal of Museum Ethnography*, Vol. 6, pp. 39–66.

IMPEY, O. and MACGREGOR, A. (eds) (1985) *The Origins of Museums: the cabinet of curiosities in sixteenth- and seventeenth-century Europe*, Oxford, Clarendon Press.

IMPEY, O. and MACGREGOR, A. (1985a) 'Introduction' in Impey and MacGregor (eds) (1985).

KARP, I. and LAVINE, S. D. (eds) (1991) *Exhibiting Cultures: the poetics and politics of museum display*, Washington, Smithsonian Institution Press.

LANE FOX, A. H. (1874) '*On* Principles *of* Classification *adopted in the* Arrangement *of his* Anthropological Collection, now exhibiting in the Bethnal Green Museum', *Journal of the Royal Anthropological Institute*, Vol. 4, pp. 293–308.

LAVINE, S. D. and KARP, I. (1991) 'Introduction: museums and multiculturalism' in Karp, I. and Lavine S. D. (eds).

LAWRENCE, E. A. (1991) 'His very silence speaks: the horse who survived Custer's Last Stand', in Browne, R. B. and Browne, P. (eds), *Digging into Popular Culture: theories and methodologies in archaeology, anthropology and other fields*, Ohio, Bowling Green State University Popular Press.

MACGREGOR, A. (1985) 'The cabinet of curiosities in seventeenth-century Britain' in Impey, O. and MacGregor, A. (eds).

O'HANLON, M. (1993) *Paradise: portraying the New Guinea Highlands*, London, British Museum Press.

POMIAN, K. (1990) *Collectors and Curiosities: Paris and Venice, 1500–1800*, (tr. Wills-Portier, E.), Cambridge, Polity Press.

RAJCHMAN, J. (1988) 'Foucault's Art of Seeing', *October*, Vol. 44 (Spring), pp. 89–117.

SHELTON, A. A. (1994) 'Cabinets of transgression: Renaissance collections and the incorporation of the New World' in Elsner, J. and Cardinal, R. (eds) *The Cultures of Collecting*, London, Reaktion Books.

STOCKING, G. W. Jr (ed.) (1985) *Objects and Others*, Madison, WI, University of Wisconsin Press.

STOCKING, G. W. Jr. (1987) *Victorian Anthropology*, London, Collier Macmillan.

TRADESCANT, J. (1656) Museum Tradescantianum *or A collection of Rarities preserved at* South Lambeth *neer* London, London, John Grismond.

VERGO, P. (1993) 'The reticent object' in Vergo, P. (ed.) *The New Museology*, London, Reaktion Books.

VOGEL, S. (1991) 'Always true to the object, in our fashion' in Karp, I. and Lavine, S. D. (eds).

Acknowledgement

The author would like to thank Michael O'Hanlon in particular for his invaluable assistance and critical readings of the chapter. Brian Durrans and Jonathan King provided consistently incisive comments. Alison Deeprose and Saul Peckham ensured that the excellent photographs were taken promptly.

READING A:
Tradescant the younger, 'Extracts from the *Musaeum Tradescantianum*'

The following are four extracts all from the 1656 catalogue 'Musaeum Tradescantianum or A Collection of Rarities Preserved At *South Lambeth neer London*', prepared by John Tradescant the younger.

Extract 1

The first extract is contained in the preface addressed *To The Ingenious Reader*.

[…] Now for the materialls themselves I reduce them unto two sorts; one *Naturall,* of which some are more familiarly known & named amongst us, as divers sorts of Birds, fourefooted Beasts and Fishes to whom I have given usual *English* names. Other are lesse familiar … as the shell Creatures, Insects, Mineralls, Outlandish-Fruits and the like, which are part of the *Materia Medica;* … The other sort is *Artificialls* such as Utensills, Householdstuffe, Habits, Instruments of Warre used by severall Nations, rare curiosities of Art &c. These are also expressed in *English* (saving the Coynes, which would vary but little if Translated) for the ready satisfying whomsoever may desire a view thereof. The *Catalogue* of my *Garden* I have also added in the Conclusion (and given the names of the *Plants* both in *Latine* and *English)* that nothing may be wanting which at present comes within view, and might be expected from

> Your ready friend
>
> John Tradescant.

Extract 2: The index

A view of the whole

1. Birds with their eggs, beaks, feathers, clawes, spurres. (page 1)
2. Fourfooted beasts with some of their hides, hornes, and hoofs. (5)
3. Divers sorts of strange fishes. (8)
4. Shell-creatures, whereof some are called *Mollia*, some *Crustacea*, others *Testacea*, of these are both *univalvia*, and *bivalvia*. (10)
5. Severall sorts of Insects, terrestrial – *anelytra, coleoptera, aptera, apoda*. (14)
6. Mineralls, and those of neare nature with them, as Earths, Coralls, Salts, Bitumens, Petrified things, choicer Stones, Gemmes. (17)
7. Outlandish Fruits from both the *Indies*, with Seeds, Gummes, Roots, Woods, and divers Ingredients Medicinall, and for the Art sof Dying. (26)
8. Mechanicks, choice pieces in Carvings, Turnings, Paintings. (36)
9. Other variety of Rarities. (42)
10. Warlike Instruments, European, Indian, &c. (44)
11. Garments, Habits, Vests, Ornaments. (47)
12. Utensils, and Householdstuffe. (52)
13. *Numismata,* Coynes ancient and modern, both gold, silver, and copper, Hebrew, Greeke, Roman both Imperial and Consular. (55)
14. Medalls, gold, silver, copper and lead. (66)

Hortus Tradescantianus

15. An enumeration of his Plants, Shrubs, and Trees both in English and Latine. (73)
16. A *Catalogue* of his Benefactors. (179)

Extract 3

The third and fourth extracts contain some examples of the entries featured in the catalogue into two of the sections listed above.

Under the subdivided section: 'I. Some kindes of *Birds* their Egges, Beaks, Feathers, Clawes, and Spurres' the following items are featured:

1. *EGGES*
   […]
   Crocodiles,
   Estridges,
   […]
   Divers sorts of Egges from *Turkie:* one given for a Dragons egge.
   Easter Egges of the Patriarchs of *Jerusalem*

2. *BEAKS, or HEADS*
   Cassawary, or Emeu,
   Griffin,
   […]
   Aracari of *Brasil,* his beak four inches long, almost two thick, like a Turkes sword.
   […]

Guarya of *Marahoon Brasil:* his beak like a
Poland sword.
Jabira,Brasil, [...]

3. *FEATHERS*
Divers curious and beautifully coloured feathers
of Birds from the West India's.
The breast of a Peacock from the West India's.
[...]
Two feathers of the Phoenix tayle.
[...]

4. *CLAWES*
The claw of the bird Rock; who, as Authors
report, is able to trusse an Elephant.
Eagles clawes.
Cock spurs three inches long.
A legge and claw of the Cassawary or Emeu that
dyed at *S. James's, Westminster.*
Twenty several sorts of clawes of other strange
birds, not found described by Authors.

5. *Whole BIRDS*
Kings-fisher from the *West India's.*
[...]
A black bird with red shoulders and pinions,
from *Virginia.*
Matuitui, the bigness of a Thrush, short neck
and legges.
[...]
Penguin, which never flies for want of wings.
[...]
Pellican. [...]
Dodar, from the Island *Mauritius;* it is not able to
flie being so big. [...]
The Bustard as big as a Turky, usually taken by
Greyhounds on *Newmarket-heath.*
Divers sorts of Birds-nests of various forms.

Extract 4

Under the sections 'VII Mechanick artficiall Works
in Carvings, Turnings, Sowings and Paintings',
'VIII. Variety of Rarities ' and 'X. Garments,
Vestures, Habits, Ornaments', the following items
are featured:

VII. Mechanick artificiall Works in Carvings,
   Turnings, Sowings and Paintings
   Several curious painting in little forms, very
   ancient.
   [...]
   The Indian lip-stone which they wear the in lip.
   [...]
   Halfe a Hasle-nut with 70 pieces of

householdstuffe in it.
A Cherry-stone holding 10 dozen of Tortois-shell
combs, made by *Edward Gibbons.*
[...]
Divers sorts of Ivory-balls turned one within
another, some 6, some 12 folds; very excellent
work.
[...]

VIII. Variety of Rarities
Indian morris-bells of shells and fruits.
[...]
Indian Conjurers rattle, wherewith he calls up
Spirits.
[...]
A Circumcision Knife of stone, and the
instrument to take up the *praeputium* of silver.
[...]
A piece of the Stone of *Sarrigs*-Castle where
Hellen of *Greece* was born.
A piece of the Stone of the Oracle of *Apollo.*
[...]
Ancient Iron-Money in crosse-plates, like
Anchors, preserved in *Pontefract*-Castle, *Yorke-
shire.*
[...]
A Brazen-ball to warm the Nunnes hands.
[...]
Blood that rained in the *Isle of Wight,* attested by
Sir *Jo: Oglander.* [...]

X. Garments, Vestures, Habits, Ornaments.
An Arabian vest.
[...]
A Portugall habit.
[...]
A Greinland-habit. [...]
Match-coat from *Greenland* of the Intrails of
Fishes.
Pohatan, King of *Virginia's* habit all
embroidered with shells, or Roanoke.
[...]
Nunnes penitentiall Girdles of Haire.
[...]
Handkerchiffs of severall sorts of excellent
needle-work.
Edward the Confessors knit-gloves.
Anne of Bullens Night-vayle embroidered with
silver.
[...]
Henry 8. hawking glove, hawks-hood, dogs-
coller.
[...]

READING B:
Elizabeth A. Lawrence, 'His very silence speaks: the horse who survived Custer's Last Stand'

No man of the immediate command of Lieutenant Colonel (Brevet Major General) George A. Custer survived to describe the dramatic clash between Seventh U.S. Cavalrymen and Sioux and Cheyenne warriors which became known as 'Custer's Last Stand'. Fought on a Montana hillside on June 25, 1876, the conflict in which approximately 210 cavalrymen lost their lives has evoked extraordinary interest […] Although the Custer Battle was part of a larger two-day military engagement, the Battle of the Little Big Horn, it is the 'Last Stand' that has exerted such a profound influence on people's imagination. The image of Custer's men, outnumbered and surrounded, fighting to the death against overwhelming odds is a perennially fascinating image. […]

Much of the appeal of Custer's Last Stand is rooted in the mystery that surrounds the event […]. [The sole being] who became famous as a survivor was mute […] [T]wo days following the battle a cavalry horse from Custer's command was found alive – Comanche, the mount [… of] Captain Myles W. Keogh of Troop I. Seldom in history have people wished so fervently that an animal could speak and illuminate the unknown elements of the battle, and the actions and motivations of its controversial leader. Although other Seventh Cavalry horses survived [… and] great numbers of victorious Indians lived through the battle, Comanche became widely known as the 'sole survivor' of Custer's Last Stand. This designation has been an inextricable part of his fame. […]

Following his discovery, the badly wounded horse was rescued from the battlefield, nursed back to health, and maintained as an honored member of the Seventh Cavalry. […]

From the cavalrymen he represented, Comanche took on the mantle of heroism. The horse […] became a link between the living and the dead. His endurance and invincibility were symbols for survival in the face of overwhelming odds. The wounded horse became the focus for various emotions – the bitter anger of defeat, sorrow for the dead cavalrymen and vengeance toward the Indian Nations.

Comanche lived for fifteen-and-a-half years following the Little Big Horn Battle […] As the 'lone survivor', he earned his own place in history through fortitude, and conferred fame upon his rider. The strong bond between Captain Keogh and his horse […] took on legendary proportions and was purported to be the reason for the animal's unlikely survival […] Comanche became known not only as a paragon of endurance, but of faithfulness as well […] a symbolic expression of humankind's ancient dream of unity with the animal world.

[…]

During his retirement, Comanche was not only an honored soldier referred to as the 'second commanding officer' of his regiment, but a pampered pet as well. […]

Throughout his life, Comanche stood for the honor of the defeated men who had died for their country and for the shame and anger the nation felt at the Indians' victory. As the years unfolded, the horse was also embued with broader meanings, for the United States was undergoing an era of dramatic change. Comanche's life as an Indian fighter came full circle, spanning the time from the great Indian victory at the Little Big Horn through the Indians' total defeat at Wounded Knee in 1890 (an engagement often referred to as 'the Seventh's revenge'). […]

When Comanche died at Fort Riley in 1891, […] his remains were preserved and mounted by Lewis L. Dyche of the Natural History Museum at the University of Kansas, where he is still displayed. One of [Dyche's] conditions […] was that he could exhibit the stuffed horse along with his other zoological specimens at the World's Columbian Exposition at Chicago in 1893. Thus Comanche's posthumous role began as an oddity – a domestic animal standing among wild species – an incongruous attraction for throngs of people who attended the fair. […] The purpose of the Exposition was to […] celebrate American progress. […] 1893 was a time to take pride in the accomplishments of expansion and the final conquest of a once wild continent, which many people construed as the victory of 'civilization over savagery'. […]

America was entering the machine age, and the end of the horse era [...] was fast approaching. Comanche was an extremely popular attraction at the Chicago Fair [...] In describing Dyche's display of wild fauna among which the horse stood, anthropomorphism and racism were often combined. For example, two wolverines were said to be 'meditating upon some kind of meanness' and so were referred to as 'Indian devils'. [...] Comanche, 'the old war horse', was designated as 'the only surviving horse of the Custer massacre' [...] Custer's Last Stand, became inextricably identified with the term 'massacre,' an inappropriate word since the battle involved armed fighting forces on both sides. [...]

Little information has come to light regarding Comanche's first few decades as a museum specimen, which [...] began in 1902 when he was placed in the newly constructed Dyche Hall at the University of Kansas. [...] From 1934 until 1941, the building which housed him was closed and Comanche was stored in the basement of a university auditorium. [...]

Comanche's significance [...] is reflected by the numerous requests to obtain him – either as a loan or permanent possession – that have been and still are received by the University of Kansas. [...]

Beginning in about 1938, and continuing sporadically [...] into the present, the greatest number of requests have involved relocating Comanche at the Custer Battlefield National Monument Museum. [...] In general, National Park officials and Custer Battlefield personnel have opposed transferring Comanche to the battle site. [...] One regional director, for example, considered the horse 'not essential to the proper interpretation of the battle,' stating that 'if we retrieved the horse, it would be entirely on sentimental grounds.' He added that though the horse would exert 'a potent spell' upon students [...] it would [...] make the visitor 'goggle and exclaim' rather than understand. One official even asserted that Comanche's main value was as 'an interesting example of the techniques of taxidermy in transition' [...]

[...] Whereas for those who want him at Fort Riley Comanche epitomizes the glory of cavalry life, and for those who would move him to Montana he is an inseparable part of the battle that made him immortal, for the University of Kansas he represents cherished tradition. [...]

To insure Comanche's retention [...] graduates wrote letters insisting that their alma mater 'hold that line' against any attempt to remove him, for they remembered 'battle-scarred old "Faithful"' who 'was "our silent partner" and in our hearts became a real part of the University.' Because of Comanche's courage and endurance, students would rub Comanche's nose or steal a strand of his tail hair to bring luck in exams (before he was encased in glass). [...]

And so Comanche has stayed, secure in his special humidified glass 'stall' at the University of Kansas. Prior to 1970, there was a brief label outlining the horse's history [...] The first sentence stated: 'Comanche was the sole survivor of the Custer massacre at the Battle of the Little Big Horn on June 25, 1876' [...] In 1970, the idea of Comanche as 'sole survivor' and the inaccuracy of 'massacre' for what was in reality a battle took on new significance. [...] American Indian students at the university took up the challenge that, for them, was embodied by the display and interpretation of the cavalry horse in the museum. As a result of this different kind of onslaught, Comanche's image would be transformed to accommodate new meanings. [...]

Calling the Comanche exhibit a 'racist symbol', a group of native American university students protested that the horse perpetuated the stereotype of Custer and his troops being 'massacred' by 'savage' Indians who were in the wrong. And since in reality large numbers of Indians lived through the battle, the students were distressed over the designation of the horse as the sole survivor of the Little Big Horn. [...]

A committee representing the native American students met with the museum director and asked that the Comanche exhibit be closed until a more accurate label was written. The director and other officials complied [...] Recalling those events, the museum director told me, 'Comanche was one of the greatest learning experiences of my life.' In November 1971, a celebration sponsored by both Indians and whites accompanied the reopening of the Comanche exhibit. There was now a long text that began by explaining that the horse stands 'as a symbol of the conflict between the United States Army and the Indian tribes of the Great Plains that resulted from the government's policy of confinement of Indians on reservations and extermination of those Indians who refused to be confined,' and detailed the Indians' struggle to retain their land and way of life. The Battle of the Little Big Horn was designated as an Indian victory, and the 1890 engagement was accurately termed 'the Massacre of Wounded Knee Creek'.

Although the Indians had first wanted the horse permanently removed from the museum, they compromised […] Comanche could be a 'learning tool' for both sides. Thus he was transformed from an object representing a federal defeat to a subject articulating the Indian peoples' way of life and struggle for existence.

[…]

Now, the horse was not just 'a symbol of the Indians' past victories, but 'what modern Indians can accomplish' ('Comanche Once Angered Indians', *Olathe Daily News*, January 10, 1978).

[…] Comanche, in his new role, led the way for further beneficial changes within the museum. […] Indian exhibits were disassociated from those dealing with 'primitive man'. Native American religious objects, previously appearing as 'curios', were labelled in a more respectful manner or removed. The whole idea of how best to exhibit cultural relics and artifacts was […] re-examined and addressed. […]

[…] Comanche has continued to be a highlight for the 120,000 annual visitors to the Dyche Museum […]

Although artifacts such as guns and arrows whose provenance can be traced to the Little Big Horn are highly valued […] Comanche still surpasses all battle relics. As a once-living creature whose posthumous existence is even more meaningful than his cavalry career, […] he has an image of courage and endurance with which people continue to identify, adapting it to their own ethos and times. Beyond [Comanche's] capacity to lend a sense of immediacy to Custer's Last Stand […and] more than a battle relic from a bygone era, 'his very silence speaks in terms more eloquent than words', articulating a timeless message protesting human kind's aggressive domination of nature, the oppression of the weak by the strong, and even the universal barbarity of war.

Source: Lawrence, 1991, pp. 84–94.

READING C:
Michael O'Hanlon, 'Paradise: portraying the New Guinea Highlands'

Collecting in context

[M]aking a collection itself proved to be more interesting than I had naively expected. It confronted me with my own taken-for-granted assumptions as to the nature of the transactions I was engaged in, the definition of 'material culture', and what actually constituted a 'Wahgi artefact'. […] I did not find myself a free agent […] My collecting was constrained by local processes and rules, with the upshot that the collection I made partly mirrored in its own structure local social organisation. And while many comments on collecting have focused upon the 'rupture' involved in removing artefacts from their local context to install them in the rather different one of a museum or gallery, this was not necessarily the way in which the Wahgi themselves chose to view the matter.

[…]

[W]hat I had in mind was the full repertoire of portable Wahgi goods, including personal adornment of all kinds, clothing, netbags, household goods, weaponry. Possibly I could also commission a *bolyim* house and *mond* post. The emphasis was to be on completeness, with contemporary material, such as the contents of a trade-store, represented equally with traditional items. […]

[T]he money which I had available to purchase artefacts and assistance still represented a substantial local asset. I worried that it might prove difficult to manage the tension between the demands of the immediate community, who would be likely to want me to buy exclusively from them, and my own wish to purchase a wider range of artefacts than they would be likely to possess […].

My concern was largely misplaced: Kinden proved to have quite clear ideas as to how to proceed. There should, he declared, be a specific order in which people should be entitled to offer artefacts for sale, particularly in the case of the most valuable category, netbags. […]

[...] While at one level [the collection] certainly reflected my own conception of what 'a collection of Wahgi material culture' should include, at another level the collection necessarily embodied local conditions and processes. The fact that it was constituted predominantly of Komblo artefacts reflected the *realpolitik* of field collection, and the order in which the artefacts were acquired partially reproduced local social structure, including its characteristic tensions [...] I suspect that most ethnographic collections contain much more of an indigenous ordering than their contemporary reputation – as having been assembled according to alien whim and 'torn' from a local context – often allows. A final arena of cultural negotiation related to what should be given in return for artefacts acquired [...].

[R]eluctance to specify a price stemmed from the fact that the transactions were rarely purchases in any simple sense. They had as much the character of local exchanges, in which precise amounts are not necessarily worked out in advance. [...]

As people became clearer as to what I wanted to collect (once they had internalised my stereotype of their material culture), they began to become interested in the collection's contents and representativeness. Some speculated that it would not be possible to obtain such discontinued items as aprons ornamented with pigs tails [...] Men began on their own initiative to make examples of abandoned categories of artefact [...]

Other artefacts, for example the *geru* boards believed to promote pig growth and to alleviate sickness, I knew I would have to commission. [...]

I also found that the practicalities entailed in making a collection of artefacts revealed complexities which I had not previously appreciated. Sometimes, these were minor social and technical details which I had observed before but never really seen [...] At other times, collecting highlighted variations among Wahgi themselves in their approach to artefacts. [...]

On occasion, collecting artefacts threw up points entirely new to me. While I did know that Wahgi men, like many other Highlanders, consider women to be polluting in certain respects, I had not realised that skirts were potentially defiling, or that washing rid them of their polluting qualities (worried women told me that my 'skin' would become 'ashy' if I handled unwashed skirts).

[...]

The way in which people react to the making of a collection tells us, in fact, something about their historical experience. In such areas as the Southern Highlands, which were subjected to colonial pressure that was even more sudden and overwhelming than was the case in the Western Highlands, making a collection may precipitate an emotional rediscovery of what was lost or suppressed in local culture. [...]

The Wahgi instance was rather different. Certain items, such as the *bolyim* house which I thought I might commission, most men were simply not prepared to make. Equally, after reflection, people abandoned their initial enthusiasm for staging a mock battle to mark my first departure from the field. Both *bolyim* houses and warfare remain sufficiently integral to on-going culture for it to be dangerous to invoke them without due cause. But the many cultural practices which *were* re-enacted in the context of making the collection did not seem to me to be done in any mood of emotional rediscovery. Rather, demonstrations of how stone axes used to be made, or of how highly pearl shells were formerly valued, tended to be carried out with a caricatured seriousness which collapsed into laughter. There was sometimes a sense that people felt they had been absurd to esteem shells in the way they had, to have laboured as long as they did to grind hard stones down to make axes. Now they knew better. Making items for the collection and demonstrating their use was, for the Wahgi, less a rediscovery of culture from which they had been estranged than a marker of how far they had come. Indeed, it was in the context of my collecting that some younger people encountered such items as wooden pandanus bowls and *geru* boards for the first time: such artefacts were becoming museum pieces in a double sense.

The notion that such older material cultural forms are becoming 'museumified' is supported by the recent establishment of the remarkable Onga Cultural Centre at Romonga, just to the west of the Wahgi culture area (Burton 1991). [...]

Its focus is entirely upon traditional material culture, narrowly conceived. [...]

As my period in the Highlands drew to a close, I felt a growing sense of interpenetration between Wahgi frames of reference and my collecting. [...]

[...] The crates which Michael Du had made for the collection had to be painted with the Museum of Mankind's address, and labelled as 'fragile'. It was important that this should be done legibly to minimise the risk of damage, or of the crates going astray. The only practised painter I knew was Kaipel, who had decorated many of the shields which the crates now contained, and he spent an afternoon meticulously labelling them. [...]

The extent to which my collecting activities had been partly assimilated to local frames of reference, emerged when the first of the collections I made in the Wahgi was being packed. On the one hand, the collection was a project which, in being exported, would be launched on a wider stage. It would 'be revealed', as Wahgi say of items like *geru* boards and ceremonial wigs. Before such objects are publicly revealed, those launching them solicit ghostly support through consuming a private sacrificial meal. As he outlined the arrangements for the meal he organised for the collection's departure, Kinden commented that he did not know who *my* ancestors were: the unspoken implication was that it would be *his* ancestors whose ghostly help would be sought.

On the other hand, the completion of the collection was also a leave-taking. If there is a single model for leave-taking in Wahgi society it is that of marriage, when a girl departs her natal kin to live among her husband's clanspeople. [...]

[Anamb] proposed that the collection should undergo the ceremony of beautification which is performed for a bride the evening before her departure. This was a suggestion with considerable political spin on it, a point I also noted when the same idiom of kinship was invoked in negotiating what was to be paid for artefacts. For if the collection was like a bride, then what I had paid for it was like bridewealth; and the point about bridewealth is that it is only the *first* of the payments which are owed to a bride's kin. [...] Anamb's comparison was his way of highlighting my continuing relationship of indebtedness to those who had helped me, as well as a specific attempt to constitute himself as the 'source person' of any benefit which might flow to me from the collection.

Exhibiting in practice

Exhibition outline

The gallery in which the exhibition is to take place lies at the end of a corridor. [...] the antechamber should include the only component of the exhibition specifically suggested by those Wahgi with whom I discussed the exhibition. Their main wish, as earlier noted, was that a contingent of performers should visit the museum to dance and to demonstrate traditional cultural practices. [...] In the absence of the sponsorship which might make such a visit possible, the only specific proposal they made was that the exhibition should have at its start the large stones, painted posts and cordyline plants which mark the entrance to an area that is in some way special or restricted (as Kinden had marked off my field-base). Kulka Nekinz even painted and presented me with two such posts. In part, I think it was felt that since Wahgi themselves traditionally mark special territory in this way, it was appropriate so to mark the entrance to a Wahgi exhibition. This was reinforced in Kinden's mind by a visit he and I had made a decade earlier to the ethnography exhibitions at the National Museum in the capital, Port Moresby. Kinden had observed near the museum entrance a row of posts or bollards which he had interpreted as similarly delimiting the exhibitions there.

[...]

Visitors to the earlier *Living Arctic* exhibition, which had also used such quotations from Native Americans, repeatedly recorded their approval at the provision of such an 'indigenous voice' – even though the selection of that voice is, of course, the curator's.

[...]

My argument in fact has been that the exhibition is itself a large artefact, whose manufacture merits a measure of the interest usually confined to the component objects included within it. [...]

[A]t the end of the exhibition, there is [...] vacant wall space [...] where an acknowledgement of the fabricated nature of the exhibition might be made.

This could best be done by including a miscellany of photographs to illustrate the artefacts' passage from field to museum display. The photographs

[...] would [...] acknowledge the exhibition's own 'sources' [and include] a picture of the crates leaving Mt. Hagen; an illustration of the artefacts being unpacked upon arrival in London; photographs of the gallery [...] showing its refitting for the present exhibition.

No photographic record remains, however, of the moment which for me illustrated an unavoidable contingency attached to collecting and preserving some artefacts but not others. In the museum's repository, the process of unpacking the crates in which the collection had travelled was complete. The crates' contents, now safely swaddled in tissue paper, awaited fumigation, conservation, registration and careful storage as Wahgi artefacts. Meanwhile, other Wahgi artefacts – the crates themselves, no less carefully made by Michael Du, painted by Zacharias and labelled by Kaipel the sign-writer – awaited disposal.

References

BURTON, J. (1991) 'The Romunga *Haus Tumbuna*, Western Highlands Province, PNG' in Eoe, S. M. and Swadling, P. (eds) *Museums and Cultural Centres in the Pacific*, Port Moresby, Papua New Guinea National Museum.

Source: O'Hanlon, 1993, pp. 55–93.

READING D:
James Clifford, 'Paradise'

The only consistently non-contemporaneous times signalled by the *Paradise* photographs are explorer Mick Leahy's black and white records of the 1933 'first contact' and the final 'Making of an Exhibition' panels. The former are appropriate [...] The latter seem more problematic. Why should a Wahgi man crafting objects for the exhibition be in small black and white, while other Wahgi performing at the pig festival ten years earlier are in full colour? Why should the work of the museum staff appear to be taking place in some different time from the complex, contemporary, real, historical times presented elsewhere in the show? Given the limited size of the exhibit, and its somewhat minimalist touch, 'The Making of an Exhibition' panels register the appropriate people and activities. But given the lack of color and size in the photos they risk appearing as an afterthought. Even at its current scale, the section might have included a large color image of the women who made many of the adjacent netbags, instead of a modest black and white. And I, at least, would have found a way to show Michael O'Hanlon in the highlands – an image missing from both exhibition *and* catalogue. How are modesty and authority complicit in this absence? [...]

O'Hanlon's original plan called for the prominent use of Wahgi quotations in the 'first contact' section. Arguing for this strategy, he noted that an earlier exhibit at the Museum of Mankind, *Living Arctic*, made extensive use of quotations from Native Americans, and that these had been much appreciated by visitors. In the current exhibit, Wahgi are very little 'heard'. Very brief quotations, often with allegorical resonances, are placed at the head of each long interpretive plaque, but these have no independent presence. Nor do we read, in the catalogue, any extended Wahgi interpetations of exhibit topics or process. Wahgi agency, stressed throughout, has no translated voice. As the *Living Arctic* experiment showed, this could be a powerful means of communication, albeit always under curatorial orchestration. Why was the tactic dropped? So as not to overcomplicate the message? So as not to privilege certain Wahgi? In order to avoid the awkwardness, even bad faith, that comes with 'giving voice' to others on terms not their own?

The staging of translated, edited 'voices' to produce a 'polyphonic' ethnographic authority has never been an unproblematic exercise. But represented voices can be powerful indices of a living people: more so than even photographs which, however realistic and contemporary, always evoke a certain irreducible past tense (Barthes 1981). And to the extent that quotations are attributed to discrete individuals, they can communicate a sense of indigenous *diversity*. One of the exhibit's scattered Wahgi statements chastises young women for their new, unrespectable, net bag styles. We immediately 'hear' a man of a certain generation. What if longer, more frequent, and sometimes conflicting personal statements had been included? My point is not to second-guess O'Hanlon and his collaborators at the Museum. There were trade-offs, and one cannot do everything in a small, or even in a large, exhibit. I wish, simply, to underline significant choices constituting both object and authority in *Paradise,* choices revealed but not analysed in the catalogue. [...]

[A] poignant scene ends the catalogue. Museum basements are revealing places, and here collecting is seen to be an act of both retrieval and disposal. The scene illustrates, for O'Hanlon, 'an unavoidable contingency attached to collecting and preserving some artefacts but not others.' But the phrase 'unavoidable contingency' may not quite do justice to the specific institutional constraints and (not-inevitable) choices at work. The custom-made crates could have made striking additions to a show differently conceived. Space considerations, conventions of proper collection and display, a concern not to overcomplicate the message – all these no doubt conspired to make their disposal seem inevitable. [...]

Paradise is directed at a certain London museum public and at a sophisticated (in places specialist) catalogue readership. That it is not addressed to the Wahgi is obvious and, given who is likely to see and read the productions, appropriate. This fact does not, however, close the personal and institutional question of responsibility to the Wahgi. It may be worth pushing the issue a bit farther than O'Hanlon does, for it is of general importance for contemporary practices of cross cultural collecting and display. What are the relational politics, poetics and pragmatics of representation here? In what senses do the *Paradise* exhibition and book reflect Wahgi perspectives and desires? Should they? [...]

O'Hanlon offers a sensitive account of all this, portraying himself yielding to, and working within, local protocols. He tends, overall, to present a potentially fraught process as a steady convergence of interests – a fable, if not of rapport, at least of complicity. He also gives glimpses of the relationship's more problematic aspects. As the collection is about to depart for London, it is ritually treated like a bride, departing to live with her husband's people (marriage being the primary model of leave-taking for the Wahgi). [...]

O'Hanlon closes his second chapter with Anamb's power play, an incident that reveals how dialogical relations of collecting both include and exclude people. Moreover, Anamb raises, Melanesian style, a far-reaching political question. What do O'Hanlon, the Museum of Mankind, and indeed the visitors and readers who 'consume' these artefacts owe the Wahgi who have sent them? Payment does not end the connection with 'source people'. Quite the opposite: in collecting relations money, objects, knowledge, and cultural value are exchanged and appropriated in continuing local/global circuits. How should the benefits of these relationships be shared? If collecting is conceived as exchanging, what ongoing constraints are imposed on exhibition practices? The catalogue chapter on 'Exhibiting in Practice' drops these political issues.

According to O'Hanlon, those who helped him in the Highlands made few specific requests about the nature of the exhibit. They did, however, want the personal and political relationships involved to proceed properly. Anamb's attempt to ensure a 'continuing relationship of endebtedness' doubtless had more to do with keeping the exchange going and sharing the wealth than with faithfully representing his viewpoint or giving him voice. Independent of exhibit content, the issue of reciprocity remains. Does the Museum officially recognize any ongoing exchange connection with Wahgi tribes or individuals? [...] What is the nature of the responsibility incurred in the making of this exhibit? Do Wahgi understand it primarily as a personal, kin-like relation with O'Hanlon? Or is there an institutional, even geo-political dimension? These questions, opened up by the catalogue, encourage more concreteness in our discussions of the politics of collecting and representation. […]

The most specific Wahgi request concerning the exhibition was, in fact, passed over. In the highlands, special or restricted places are marked off by small clusters of 'taboo stones' and painted posts. O'Hanlon's sponsor Kinden marked his highland collecting camp in this way, to keep the acquisitions safe. He and others asked that the exhibit be identified as a Wahgi area by placing similar stones and posts at the entry. Indeed, two posts were specially painted for the purpose and given to O'Hanlon. But no stones or posts appear at the entrance to *Paradise*. Apparently the museum design staff thought they might obstruct the flow of visitors (large school groups, for example) at a place where it was important that people move along. In this instance, practical concerns that were surely soluble (the stones are only a foot or two high) were here able to override a clearly expressed Wahgi desire for the exhibition.

London is distant from the New Guinea Highlands. There is no Wahgi community nearby that could constrain the exhibit organizers' freedom. It is worth noting this obvious fact because in many places, today, it is no longer obvious. An exhibition of First Nations artefacts in Canada will be under fairly direct scrutiny, often coupled with demands for consultation or curatorial participation (Clifford 1991). […] O'Hanlon's rather scrupulous reciprocity in collecting did not have to be reproduced in exhibiting. A general intent to do something that would not offend the (distant) Wahgi was enough. Thus if the Taboo Stones were 'impractical' they could go.

How far must an exhibition go in reflecting indigenous viewpoints? Some Wahgi urged O'Hanlon not to emphasize warfare in the exhibition. The exhibit does feature war (dramatic shields and spears) but compensates by following with peacemaking. Would this satisfy the Wahgi who asked that fighting be played down? And would we want to satisfy them on this score?

[A]ssuming requests come from individuals of wide local authority, should they be followed without question? Is the decision by a more powerful institution to override or supplement indigenous views always 'imperialist?' Yes *and* no. In a structural sense, large metropolitan museums stand in a relation of historical privilege and financial power with respect to the small populations whose works they acquire and recontextualize. This geo-political position is determining, at certain levels.

[…] O'Hanlon's pointed corrective, in its focus on collecting and exhibiting in practice, risks over-reacting, omitting more structural, or geo-political levels of differential power. Thus his lack of attention to the disappearance of Wahgi agency when discussing the work in London. […]

References

BARTHES, R. (1981) *Camera Lucida*, New York, Hill and Wang.

CLIFFORD, J. (1991) 'Four Northwest Coast museums: travel reflections' in Karp, I. and Lavine, S. D. (eds) *Exhibiting Cultures: the poetics and politics of museum display*, Washington, Smithsonian Institution Press.

Source: Clifford, 1995, pp. 92–117.

READING E:
Annie E. Coombes, 'Material culture at the crossroads of knowledge: the case of the Benin "bronzes"'

In 1897, a series of events took place in Benin City, in what was then the Niger Coast Protectorate, which ended in the wholesale looting of royal insignia from the court of Benin. These incidents, and the resulting loot, gained instant notoriety across a range of British journals and newspapers which serviced both a mass popular readership and a professional middle class. They also received coverage in the more specialist journals serving the emergent 'anthropological' professionals. Such a spread of coverage provides the basis for mapping the configurations of interests in Africa [...] and the possibility of understanding the interrelation of knowledges produced in what were often presented as discreet spheres [...]

If the valourisation of cultural production has any impact on a reassessment of the general culture and society of the producer, then the influx of sixteenth-century carved ivories and lost wax castings from Benin City onto the European art and antiquities market, together with the subsequent proliferation of popular and 'scientific' treatises which their 'discovery' generated, should have fundamentally shaken the bedrock of the derogatory Victorian assumptions about Africa, and more specifically, the African's place in history. Yet [...] this was certainly not the case.

[...]

Those museums whose collections were enriched as a result of the punitive raid on Benin received their share of public attention in both the 'scientific' press and in the local, national and illustrated press. The Benin collections acquired by Liverpool's Mayer Museum, the Pitt Rivers Museum in Oxford, and London's Horniman Free Museum and the British Museum, all featured prominently in the press over this period. [...]

The objects [from Benin] acquired by the Horniman Free Museum in London were among some of the earliest examples of artifacts from the expedition which claimed any attention in the general, as opposed to the scientific, press. Almost immediately after acquiring the Benin artifacts, Richard Quick, the curator of the Museum, began to expose them to a variety of publics, developing what was to become a very efficient publicity machine for the Horniman collection. Photographs of items in the Horniman collection appeared in the *Illustrated London News*, and other illustrated journals in both the local and national press. These were not the carved ivory tusks or bronze plaques which had already received so much acclaim, but consisted of a carved wooden 'mirror-frame' with two European figures in a boat, a hide and goat-skin fan, and two ivory armlets rather poorly reproduced. Described by the *Illustrated London News* reporter as 'relics of a less savage side of the native life', and noted for their 'fine carving' and 'antiquity', they were none the less accompanied by the inevitable descriptions of 'hideous sacrificial rites'. [...] Such sentiments, and the expression of regret concerning what was perceived at this early date as a dearth of relics from a lost 'civilisation which dates back far beyond the Portuguese colonisation of three centuries ago, and probably owes much to the Egyptian influence', are common in the early coverage of material culture from Benin. Quick's own publications on the collection favour the argument concerning Egyptian influence, which he goes to some lengths to substantiate. Significantly, at this early date of 1897, there is less astonishment or curiosity over the origin of the objects than emerges in later writings from the 'scientific' or museums establishment. [...]

One of the factors which transformed the terms of discussion of Benin material amongst emergent museum professionals, and which fired the interest in the origin of the bronzes, was the exhibition in September 1897, at the British Museum, of over three hundred bronze plaques from Benin City. By 1899, it is clear that the British Museum exhibition, together with the publications of Charles Hercules Read and O.M. Dalton (those curators at the Museum responsible for ethnographic material) and of H. Ling Roth, had extended the significance of the Benin artifacts beyond their original association with the bloody events leading up to their acquisition. Ironically, one of the results of this was to open up the possibility of an African origin for the bronzes.

To corroborate this, we have only to compare some of Quick's earlier statements with the radical changes of opinion and increased significance concerning the Benin material that appear in his writings published *after* the British Museum exhibition and publications. By 1899, he felt confidently able to describe the objects in the Horniman collection as 'valuable works of art' (Quick, 1899, p. 248) [...]

[...] Quick hoped that by demonstrating any similarities between some of the iconographic details of the objects in the Horniman collection, and those in the possession of the British Museum, he would register their importance and consequently increase the public profile of his own museum. This instance should signal the institutional allegiances and strategic negotiations that were partly responsible for the shift in terms used to describe and categorise Benin material, and, more specifically, its transformation from the status of 'relic' to 'work of art' in museum circles, with repercussions in other less specialised spheres.

[...]

In 1898, [...] H. Ling Roth, director of the Bankfield Museum in Halifax, and an individual who figured prominently in the history of interpretations of Benin culture, published his 'Notes on Benin Art' in the *Reliquary*. [...] Ling Roth's chief contention was that it was possible to define two phases or periods of Benin casting. [...] Ling Roth was not interested in setting up a hierarchy, since both phases were credited with equal workmanship and skill. [... He] makes clear his admiration for the work of both proposed periods, on the grounds of technical skill, elegant and thorough detailing, clarity and sharpness of design, and variety of illustration and ornamentation, together with what he perceived as an artistic sense of the balance between foreground relief and decoration, and background ornamentation. [...] Ling Roth also established a long history, from an early date, of iron smelting and gold casting amongst different African societies. Furthermore, while emphasising that there was a world of difference 'between the crude castings of the average native African and the beautiful results' from Benin, he emphasised that there was no evidence extant to suggest that there was any such 'high-class art' in the Iberian Peninsula at the end of the fifteenth century, and certainly not elsewhere in Europe. This, therefore, called into question the argument of a Portuguese origin for the bronzes.

[H]e advanced a hypothesis completely at odds with the ethnographic curators at the British Museum, Read and Dalton. [...] Ling Roth suggested that, because the Portuguese figures were later additions attached to the surface of many of the bronze plaques, this method of casting must have pre-dated the Portuguese colonisation of Benin (Ling Roth, 1898, p. 171). [...] The unsettled conclusion he arrived at, in 1898, was that this sophisticated art existed in Benin prior to the advent of the Portuguese, and was therefore entirely of African origin.

Lieutenant-General Pitt Rivers, whose substantial collection Ling Roth used to illustrate much of his article [...], supported Ling Roth's hypothesis in private. In a letter to the eminent Oxford anthropologist, Edward Burnett Tylor, in August 1898, Pitt Rivers suggested that, 'It does not follow that because European figures are represented that it all came from Europe. Most of the forms are indigenous, the features are nearly all negro, the weapons are negro' (Pitt Rivers Museum, 1898).

[...]

In September 1900, Charles Kingsley transferred Mary Kingsley's collection of objects from Benin and other parts of West Africa to the Pitt Rivers Museum. [...] The Benin material was highly prized by the Museum, the donation being praised as an example of 'the now extinct artistic bronze work of Benin, which has created so much stir of recent years, since the punitive expedition first brought these forgotten treasures to light' (Pitt Rivers Museum, 1900, p. 3). [...]

In 1903, this material was the subject of a special display in the lower gallery to demonstrate ironwork processes with particular reference to the *cire perdue* method associated with Benin, and illustrated in this instance with examples from both Benin and Ashanti. The display seems to have been a fairly permanent feature in the Museum [...] The entry in the annual reports for [1910] testifies to the consistent interest in Benin material from the point of view of the technological processes involved.

[...]

By 1898, Read and Dalton had already lectured at the Anthropological Institute exhibiting some [...] carved ivory tusks and also photographs of the brass plaques in the British Museum's collection.

[...]

[Read and Dalton (1898, p. 371) acknowledged] that these complex and detailed figures, cast with such skill and expertise, 'were produced by a people long acquainted with the art of casting metals'. The authors go so far as to compare their mastery of the *cire perdue* process to the best work of the Italian Renaissance, not only in relation to the plaques but because of the demonstrated facility for casting in the round. [...] Any question of the bronzes actually being contemporary, however, was immediately dismissed with reference to the inferior quality of contemporary casting. There was no danger here of transgressing the image of Benin as a degenerate culture.

Significantly, the point at which ethnologists decided to intervene in the debate over the origin of the Benin bronzes was precisely the moment when the paradox of technical sophistication versus social savagery threatened a break with the evolutionary paradigm, which up to that time had also supplied the classificatory principles under which most collections of material culture from the colonies were organised. Consequently, the concept of degeneration was summoned up as an aesthetic principle, to appease anxiety over these recalcitrant objects which refused to conform to comfortably familiar taxonomic solutions.

[...]

In 1899, Read and Dalton published a special presentation book entitled *Antiques from the City of Benin and other Parts of West Africa in the British Museum*. This contained several significant shifts from their earlier 1898 argument regarding the origin of the bronzes. [...] Read and Dalton [...] had initially rested their case on a Portuguese or Egyptian origin for the bronzes. However, by 1899, Read felt obliged to warn the reader that one of the dangers of this hypothesis was that, since Europeans were better acquainted with Egyptian material, there would inevitably be a tendency to compare other lesser known cultures with Egyptian civilisation. More importantly, Read and Dalton

were now both prepared to concede what Ling Roth had suggested in 1898, that although certain aspects of the ornamentation might still be attributable to the Egyptians, the Benin castings may well have preceded, or at any rate come into being independently of, Egyptian predecessors! [...] Why were the two spokespeople from the national collection prepared to concede such a thing, when by this date there was effectively very little additional empirical data available than the previous year?

I would argue that the degree to which the Benin aesthetic is assigned an African origin corresponds partly to the stepping up of pressure from ethnologists and anthropologists in the museum for government recognition and financial support. Furthermore, the course of Read and Dalton's argument for an African origin is inextricably linked to the fortunes of the Ethnographic Department within the British Museum itself. Unlike the already thriving department of Egyptology (the other tentative 'home' for the bronzes if an Egyptian origin were proven, and an autonomous department within the museum by 1886), ethnography was only granted the status of an autonomous department in 1941. The fact that so many commentaries could so confidently claim an Egyptian source for the Benin bronzes was not at all surprising, given the extent to which Ancient Egypt had made something of a comeback in the popular imagination of nineteenth-century Europe.

[...]

In September 1897, a series of some three hundred brass plaques from Benin were put on public exhibition in the British Museum. The provincial and national press almost unanimously described the exhibits as remarkable and extraordinary examples of skilled workmanship, often repeating the opinion that such work would not discredit European craftsmen [...] In the British Press, coverage of the exhibition positions the significance of the Benin bronzes as primarily relics of the punitive expedition [...] The same obsession with the origin of the exhibits and their alleged antiquity repeats itself here, although the most frequently posited solution is an Egyptian origin.

There is, however, another set of discourses running through both popular and scientific reports which suggest controversy of a different order [...] Initially, it was assumed that the vast hoard of brass plaques, temporarily on loan to the British Museum, would eventually become the property of the Museum through the Trustees' acquisition of the artifacts. The Foreign Office had agreed to the loan after official representation had been made to the government on behalf of the British Museum to secure some specimens. [...] In fact, over a third of the bronze plaques had already been sold off as revenue for the Protectorate. The ensuing public auction of items from Benin aroused much bitterness amongst those museum staff with an interest in the affairs of the Ethnographic department.

[...]

[T]he influx of Benin material culture into nineteenth-century Britain made an important impact in several ways. It generated debate amongst different communities of interest in Africa, which had the potential to shift certain popular pre-conceptions regarding the African's lack of competence to produce complex, technically sophisticated, art work. The attempts by those who saw themselves as part of the scientific community to provide an alternative context in which to interpret these finds, other than as 'curio' or 'relic' of past misdemeanours, drew public attention to a hidden history of long-established and affluent African societies. [...] Crucially, though, despite the promise of a revisionist history that such initiatives presented, whenever Benin material is discussed over the period 1897 to 1913, the writer invariably exhibits complete incredulity that such work could possibly be produced by Africans. While certain aspects of the anthropological knowledge on Benin suggested definitions and values which contradicted some of those stereotypes promulgated in the popular middle-class illustrated press, the fact that Benin was consistently treated as an anomaly of African culture by anthropologists ensured that the more racialised sense of the term 'degenerate', popularised by the press accounts, was always inherent in descriptions of Benin culture. This incredulity at the African's skill should also alert us to the fact that the degree to which the European credited a society with making 'works of art' (technically, conceptually and in terms of design) was not necessarily commensurate with any

reassessment of their position on the evolutionary ladder. Indeed, the value of the brasses and ivories was considerably enhanced by actually reinforcing their origins as African and by stressing their status as an anomaly in terms of other examples of African carving and casting. Through such a procedure their notoriety was assured. Their value as 'freak' productions in turn enhanced the status of the museum in which they were held.

[...] The ethnographic curators' decision to assign an African, as opposed to Egyptian, origin to the bronzes placed these contested and now highly desirable objects squarely in the domain of the Ethnographic department, rather than ambiguously positioned between Egyptology and European Antiquities. This highlighted the importance of ethnography as opposed to the already well-endowed Egyptology department in the Museum. How far such a hypothesis was a deliberate strategy for more recognition on the part of the ethnographers, remains a matter of conjecture. Yet one thing is certain: this history is instructive of the kinds of negotiative processes by which 'scientific' knowledge of the culture of the colonies was produced, and gives the lie to a simplistic empirical account which takes such narratives at face value, without acknowledging the institutional and other political factors at play.

References

LING ROTH, H. (1898) 'Notes on Benin art', *Reliquary*, Vol. V, p. 167.

PITT RIVERS MUSEUM (1898) E. B. Tylor Papers, Box 6 (1) and (2). Pitt Rivers to E. B. Tylor, 7 August 1898.

PITT RIVERS MUSEUM (1900) *Annual Report of the Pitt Rivers Museum 1900*, Oxford, Pitt Rivers Museum.

QUICK, R. (1899) 'Notes on Benin carvings', *Reliquary*, Vol. V, pp. 248–55.

READ, C. H. and DALTON, O. M. (1898) 'Works of art from Benin City', *Journal of the Anthropological Institute*, Vol. XXVII, pp. 362–82.

Source: Coombes, 1994a, pp. 7, 23, 26, 27, 44–8, 57–9, 61–2, 146–7.

THE SPECTACLE OF THE 'OTHER'

Stuart Hall

Contents

224

1   Introduction

How do we represent people and places which are significantly different from us? Why is 'difference' so compelling a theme, so contested an area of representation? What is the secret fascination of 'otherness', and why is popular representation so frequently drawn to it? What are the typical forms and representational practices which are used to represent 'difference' in popular culture today, and where did these popular figures and stereotypes come from? These are some of the questions about representation which we set out to address in this chapter. We will pay particular attention to those representational practices which we call 'stereotyping'. By the end we hope you will understand better how what we call 'the spectacle of the "Other"' works, and be able to apply the ideas discussed and the sorts of analysis undertaken here to the mass of related materials in contemporary popular culture – for example, advertising which uses black models, newspaper reports about immigration, racial attacks or urban crime, and films and magazines which deal with 'race' and ethnicity as significant themes.

The theme of 'representing difference' is picked up directly from the previous chapter, where Henrietta Lidchi looked at how 'other cultures' are given meaning by the discourses and practices of exhibition in ethnographic museums of 'the West'. Chapter 3 focused on the 'poetics' and the 'politics' of exhibiting – both how other cultures are made to signify through the discourses of exhibition (poetics) and how these practices are inscribed by relations of power (politics) – especially those which prevail between the people who are represented and the cultures and institutions doing the representing. Many of the same concerns arise again in this chapter. However, here, *racial and ethnic* difference is foregrounded. You should bear in mind, however, that what is said about racial difference could equally be applied in many instances to other dimensions of difference, such as gender, sexuality, class and disability.

Our focus here is the variety of images which are on display in popular culture and the mass media. Some are commercial advertising images and magazine illustrations which use racial stereotypes, dating from the period of slavery or from the popular imperialism of the late nineteenth century. However, Chapter 4 brings the story up to the present. Indeed, it begins with images from the competitive world of modern athletics. The question which this comparison across time poses is: have the repertoires of representation around 'difference' and 'otherness' changed or do earlier traces remain intact in contemporary society?

The chapter looks in depth at theories about the representational practice known as 'stereotyping'. However, the theoretical discussion is threaded through the examples, rather than being introduced for its own sake. The chapter ends by considering a number of different strategies designed to intervene in the field of representation, to contest 'negative' images and transform representational practices around 'race' in a more 'positive' direction. It poses the question of whether there can be an effective 'politics of representation'.

Once again, then, *visual* representation takes centre stage. The chapter sustains the overall theme by continuing our exploration of *representation* as a concept and a practice – the key first 'moment' in the cultural circuit. Our aim is to deepen our understanding of what representation is and how it works. Representation is a complex business and, especially when dealing with 'difference', it engages feelings, attitudes and emotions and it mobilizes fears and anxieties in the viewer, at deeper levels than we can explain in a simple, common-sense way. This is why we need theories – to deepen our analysis. The chapter, then, builds on what we have already learned about representation as a signifying practice, and continues to develop critical concepts to explain its operations.

1.1 Heroes or villains?

Look, first, at Figure 4.1. It is a picture of the men's 100 metres final at the 1988 Olympics which appeared on the cover of the Olympics Special of the *Sunday Times* colour magazine (9 October 1988). It shows the black Canadian sprinter, Ben Johnson, winning in record time from Carl Lewis and Linford Christie: five superb athletes in action, at the peak of their physical prowess. All of them men and – perhaps, now, you will notice consciously for the first time – all of them black!

ACTIVITY 1

How do you 'read' the picture – what is it saying? In Barthes' terms, what is its 'myth' – its underlying message?

One possible message relates to their racial identity. These athletes are all from a racially-defined group – one often discriminated against precisely on the grounds of their 'race' and colour, whom we are more accustomed to see depicted in the news as the victims or 'losers' in terms of achievement. Yet here they are, winning!

In terms of difference, then – a positive message: a triumphant moment, a cause for celebration. Why, then, does the caption say, 'Heroes and villains'? Who do you think is the hero, who the villain?

Even if you don't follow athletics, the answer isn't difficult to discover. Ostensibly about the Olympics, the photo is in fact a trailer for the magazine's lead story about the growing menace of drug-taking in international athletics – what inside is called 'The Chemical Olympics'. Ben Johnson, you may recall, was found to have taken drugs to enhance his performance. He was disqualified, the gold medal being awarded to Carl Lewis, and Johnson was expelled from world athletics in disgrace. The story suggests that *all* athletes – black or white – are potentially 'heroes' and 'villains'. But in this image, Ben Johnson personifies this split in a particular way. He is *both* 'hero' and

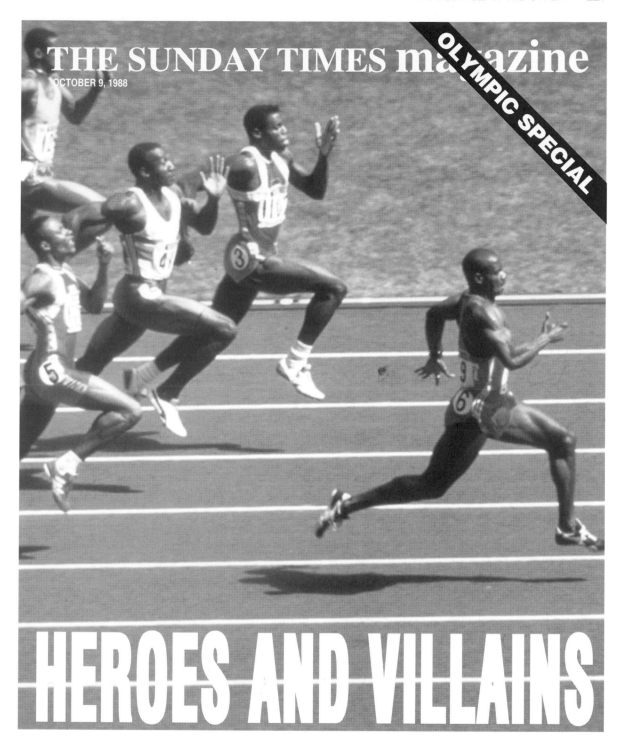

FIGURE 4.1 'Heroes and Villains', cover of *The Sunday Times Magazine*, 9 October 1988.

'villain'. He encapsulates the extreme alternatives of heroism and villainy in world athletics in one black body.

There are several points to make about the way the representation of 'race' and 'otherness' is working in this photo. First, if you think back to Chapters 1 and 3, you will remember the work of Barthes on the idea of 'myth'. This photo, too, functions at the level of 'myth'. There is a literal, denotative level of meaning – this *is* a picture of the 100 metres final and the figure in front *is* Ben Johnson. Then there is the more connotative or thematic meaning – the drug story. And within that, there is the sub-theme of 'race' and 'difference'. Already, this tells us something important about how 'myth' works. The image is a very powerful one, as visual images often are. But its *meaning* is highly ambiguous. It can carry more than one meaning. If you didn't know the context, you might be tempted to read this as a moment of unqualified triumph. And you wouldn't be 'wrong' since this, too, is a perfectly acceptable meaning to take from the image. But, as the caption suggests, it is *not* produced here as an image of 'unqualified triumph'. So, the same photo can carry several, quite different, sometimes diametrically opposite meanings. It can be a picture of disgrace or of triumph, or both. Many meanings, we might say, are potential within the photo. But there is no one, true meaning. Meaning 'floats'. It cannot be finally fixed. However, attempting to 'fix' it is the work of a representational practice, which intervenes in the many potential meanings of an image in an attempt to privilege one.

So, rather than a 'right' or 'wrong' meaning, what we need to ask is, 'Which of the many meanings in this image does the magazine mean to privilege?' Which is the **preferred meaning**? Ben Johnson is the key element here because he is both an amazing athlete, winner and record-breaker, *and* the athlete who was publicly disgraced because of drug-taking. So, as it turns out, the preferred meaning is *both* 'heroism' and 'villainy'. It wants to say something paradoxical like, 'In the moment of the hero's triumph, there is also villainy and moral defeat.' In part, we know this is the preferred meaning which the magazine wants the photo to convey because this is the meaning which is singled out in the caption: HEROES AND VILLAINS. Roland Barthes (1977) argues that, frequently, it is the caption which selects one out of the many possible meanings from the image, and *anchors* it with words. The 'meaning' of the photograph, then, does not lie exclusively in the image, but in the conjunction of image *and* text. Two discourses – the discourse of written language and the discourse of photography – are required to produce and 'fix' the meaning (see Hall, 1972).

preferred meaning

As we have suggested, this photo can also be 'read', connotatively, in terms of what it has to 'say' about 'race'. Here, the message could be – black people shown being good at something, winning *at last!* But in the light of the 'preferred meaning', hasn't the meaning with respect to 'race' and 'otherness' changed as well? Isn't it more something like, 'even when black people are shown at the summit of their achievement, they often fail to carry it off'? This

FIGURE 4.2 Linford Christie, holding a Union Jack, having won the men's 100 metres Olympic gold medal, Barcelona 1992.

having-it-both-ways is important because, as I hope to show you, people who are in any way significantly different from the majority – 'them' rather than 'us' – are frequently exposed to this *binary* form of representation. They seem to be represented through sharply opposed, polarized, binary extremes – good/bad, civilized/primitive, ugly/excessively attractive, repelling-because-different/compelling-because-strange-and-exotic. And they are often required to be *both things at the same time*! We will return to these split figures or 'tropes' of representation in a moment.

But first, let us look at another, similar news photo, this time from another record-breaking 100 metres final. Linford Christie, subsequently captain of the British Olympics squad, at the peak of his career, having just won the race of a lifetime. The picture captures his elation, at the moment of his lap of honour. He is holding the Union Jack. In the light of the earlier discussion, how do you 'read' *this* photograph (Figure 4.2)? What is it 'saying' about 'race' and cultural identity?

ACTIVITY 2

Which of the following statements, in your view, comes closest to expressing the 'message' of the image?

(a) 'This is the greatest moment of my life! A triumph for me, Linford Christie.'

(b) 'This is a moment of triumph for me and a celebration for black people everywhere!'

(c) 'This is a moment of triumph and celebration for the British Olympic team and the British people!'

(d) 'This is a moment of triumph and celebration for black people *and* the British Olympic team. It shows that you can be "Black" *and* "British"!'

There is, of course, no 'right' or 'wrong' answer to the question. The image carries many meanings, all equally plausible. What is important is the fact that this image both shows an event (denotation) and carries a 'message' or meaning (connotation) – Barthes would call it a 'meta-message' or *myth* – about 'race', colour and 'otherness'. We can't help reading images of this kind as 'saying something', not just about the people or the occasion, but about their 'otherness', their 'difference'. *'Difference' has been marked.* How it is then interpreted is a constant and recurring preoccupation in the representation of people who are racially and ethnically different from the majority population. Difference signifies. It 'speaks'.

In a later interview, discussing his forthcoming retirement from international sport, Christie commented on the question of his cultural identity – where he feels he 'belongs' (*The Sunday Independent*, 11 November 1995). He has very fond memories of Jamaica, he said, where he was born and lived until the age of 7. But 'I've lived here [in the UK] for 28 [years]. I can't be anything other than British' (p. 18). Of course, it isn't as simple as that. Christie is perfectly well aware that most definitions of 'Britishness' assume that the person who belongs is 'white'. It is much harder for black people, wherever they were born, to be accepted as 'British'. In 1995, the cricket magazine, *Wisden*, had to pay libel damages to black athletes for saying that they couldn't be expected to display the same loyalty and commitment to winning for England because they are black. So Christie knows that every image is *also* being 'read' in terms of this broader question of cultural belongingness and difference.

Indeed, he made his remarks in the context of the negative publicity to which he has been exposed in some sections of the British tabloid press, a good deal of which hinges on a vulgar, unstated but widely recognized 'joke' at his expense: namely that the tight-fitting Lycra shorts which he wears are said to reveal the size and shape of his genitals. This was the detail on which *The Sun* focused on the morning after he won an Olympic gold medal. Christie has been subject to continuous teasing in the tabloid press about the prominence and size of his 'lunchbox' – a euphemism which some have taken so literally that, he revealed, he has been approached by a firm wanting to market its lunchboxes around his image! Linford Christie has observed about these innuendoes: 'I felt humiliated … My first instinct was that it was racist. There we are, stereotyping a black man. I can take a good joke. But it happened the day after I won the greatest accolade an athlete can win … I don't want to go through life being known for what I've got in my shorts. I'm a serious person …' (p. 15).

ACTIVITY 3

What is going on here? Is this just a joke in bad taste, or does it have a deeper meaning? What do sexuality and gender have to do with images of black men and women? Why did the black French writer from Martinique, Frantz Fanon, say that white people seem to be obsessed with the sexuality of black people?

It is the subject of a widespread fantasy, Fanon says, which fixates the black man at the level of the genitals. 'One is no longer aware of the Negro, but only of a penis; the Negro is eclipsed. He is turned into a penis' (Fanon, 1986/1952, p. 170).

What, for example, did the French writer, Michael Cournot, whom Fanon quotes, mean when he wrote that 'Four Negroes with their penises exposed would fill a cathedral'? (Fanon, 1986/1952, p. 169). What *is* the relationship of these fantasies of sexuality to 'race' and ethnicity in the representation of 'otherness' and 'difference'?

We have now introduced another dimension into the representation of 'difference' – adding sexuality and gender to 'race', ethnicity and colour. Of course, it is well established that sport is one of the few areas where black people have had outstanding success. It seems natural that images of black people drawn from sport should emphasize the body, which is the instrument of athletic skill and achievement. It is difficult, however, to have images of bodies in action, at the peak of their physical perfection, without those images also, in some way, carrying 'messages' about *gender* and about *sexuality*. Where black athletes are concerned, what are these messages about?

ACTIVITY 4

Look, for example, at the picture from the *Sunday Times* 1988 Olympic Special, of the black American sprinter, Florence Griffith-Joyner, who won three gold medals at Seoul (Figure 4.3). Can you 'read' this photo without getting some 'messages' about 'race', gender and sexuality – even if *what* the meanings are remain ambiguous? Is there any doubt that the photo is 'signifying' along all three dimensions? In representation, one sort of difference seems to attract others – adding up to a 'spectacle' of

FIGURE 4.3   Florence Griffith-Joyner.

otherness. If you're not convinced, you might think of this in the context of the remark by 'Flo-Jo's' husband, Al Joyner, quoted in the text next to the photo: 'Someone Says My Wife Looked Like A Man'. Or consider the photo (which was reproduced on the following page of the article) of Al Joyner's sister, Jackie Joyner-Kersee, who also won a gold medal and broke world records at Seoul in the heptathlon, preparing to throw a javelin, accompanied by text quoting another observation by Al Joyner: 'Somebody Says My Sister Looked Like A Gorilla'(Figure 4.4).

FIGURE 4.4 Jackie Joyner-Kersee.

There is an additional point to be made about these photographs of black athletes in the press. They gain in meaning when they are read in context, against or in connection with one another. This is another way of saying that images do not carry meaning or 'signify' on their own. They accumulate meanings, or play off their meanings against one another, across a variety of texts and media. Each image carries its own, specific meaning. But at the broader level of how 'difference' and 'otherness' is being represented in a particular culture at any one moment, we can see similar representational practices and figures being repeated, with variations, from one text or site of representation to another. This accumulation of meanings across different texts, where one image refers to another, or has its meaning altered by being 'read' in the context of other images, is called **inter-textuality**. We may describe the whole repertoire of imagery and visual effects through which 'difference' is represented at any one historical moment as a *regime of representation*; this is very similar to what, in Chapter 2, Peter Hamilton referred to as a *representational paradigm*.

inter-textuality

An interesting example of *inter-textuality*, where the image depends for its meaning on being 'read' in relation to a number of other, similar images, can be found in Figure 4.5. This is Carl Lewis, one of the sprinters you saw in Figure 4.1, taken from a Pirelli advertisement. At first glance, the image summons up echoes of all the previous images we have been looking at – superbly-honed athletic bodies, tensed in action, super-men and super-women. But here the meaning is differently inflected. Pirelli is a tyre firm with a reputation for producing calendars with pictures of beautiful women, scantily clad, in provocative poses – the prototypical 'pin-up'. In which of these two contexts should we 'read' the Carl Lewis image? One clue lies in the fact that, though Lewis is male, in the ad he is wearing elegant, high-heeled red shoes!

FIGURE 4.5
Carl Lewis, photographed for a Pirelli advertisement.

ACTIVITY 5

What is *this* image saying? What is *its* message? How does it 'say' it?

This image works by the marking of 'difference'. The conventional identification of Lewis with black male athletes and with a sort of 'super-masculinity' is disturbed and undercut by the invocation of his 'femininity' – and what marks this is the signifier of the red shoes. The sexual and racial 'message' is rendered ambiguous. The super-male black athlete may not be all he seems. The ambiguity is amplified when we compare this image with all the other images – the stereotypes we are accustomed to see – of black athletes in the press. Its meaning is inter-textual – i.e. it requires to be read 'against the grain'.

ACTIVITY 6

Does this photo reinforce or subvert the stereotype? Some people say it's just an advertiser's joke. Some argue that Carl Lewis has allowed himself to be exploited by a big corporate advertiser. Others argue that he deliberately set out to challenge and contest the traditional image of black masculinity. What do you think?

In the light of these examples, we can rephrase our original questions more precisely. Why is 'otherness' so compelling an object of representation? What does the marking of racial difference tell us about representation as a practice? Through which representational practices are racial and ethnic difference and 'otherness' signified? What are the 'discursive formations', the repertoires or regimes of representation, on which the media are drawing when they represent 'difference'? Why is one dimension of difference – e.g. 'race' – crossed by other dimensions, such as sexuality, gender and class? And how is the representation of 'difference' linked with questions of power?

1.2 Why does 'difference' matter?

Before we analyse any more examples, let us examine some of the underlying issues posed by our first question. Why does 'difference' matter – how can we explain this fascination with 'otherness'? What theoretical arguments can we draw on to help us unpack this question?

Questions of 'difference' have come to the fore in cultural studies in recent decades and been addressed in different ways by different disciplines. In this section, we briefly consider *four* such theoretical accounts. As we discuss them, think back to the examples we have just analysed. In each, we start by showing how important 'difference' is – by considering what is said to be its positive aspect. But we follow this by some of the more negative aspects of 'difference'. Putting these two together suggests why 'difference' is both necessary and dangerous.

1 The first account comes from linguistics – from the sort of approach associated with Saussure and the use of language as a model of how culture works, which was discussed in Chapter 1. The main argument advanced here is that *'difference' matters because it is essential to meaning; without it, meaning could not exist.* You may remember from Chapter 1 the example of *white/black*. We know what *black* means, Saussure argued, not because there is some essence of 'blackness' but because we can contrast it with its opposite – *white*. Meaning, he argued, is relational. It is the *'difference'* between *white* and *black* which signifies, which carries meaning. Carl Lewis in that photo can represent 'femininity' or the 'feminine' side of masculinity because he can *mark his 'difference'* from the traditional stereotypes of black masculinity by using the *red shoes* as a signifier. This principle holds for broader concepts too. We know what it is to be 'British', not only because of certain national characteristics, but also because we can mark its 'difference'

from its 'others' – 'Britishness' is not-French, not-American, not-German, not-Pakistani, not-Jamaican and so on. This enables Linford Christie to signify his 'Britishness' (by the flag) while contesting (by his black skin) that 'Britishness' must always mean 'whiteness'. Again, 'difference' signifies. It carries a message.

So meaning depends on the difference between opposites. However, when we discussed this argument in Chapter 1, we recognized that, though binary oppositions – *white/black, day/night, masculine/feminine, British/alien* – have the great value of capturing the diversity of the world within their either/or extremes, they are also a rather crude and reductionist way of establishing meaning. For example, in so-called black-and-white photography, there is actually no pure 'black' or 'white', only varying shades of grey. 'Black' shades imperceptibly into 'white', just as men have *both* 'masculine' and 'feminine' sides to their nature; and Linford Christie certainly wants to affirm the possibility of being both 'black' *and* 'British' though the normal definition of 'Britishness' assumes that it is white.

Thus, while we do not seem able to do without them, binary oppositions are also open to the charge of being reductionist and over-simplified – swallowing up all distinctions in their rather rigid two-part structure. What is more, as the philosopher Jacques Derrida has argued, there are very few neutral binary oppositions. One pole of the binary, he argues, is usually the dominant one, the one which includes the other within its field of operations. There is always a relation of power between the poles of a binary opposition (Derrida, 1974). We should really write, **white**/*black*, **men**/*women*, **masculine**/*feminine*, **upper class**/*lower class*, **British**/*alien* to capture this power dimension in discourse.

2   The second explanation also comes from theories of language, but from a somewhat different school to that represented by Saussure. *The argument here is that we need 'difference' because we can only construct meaning through a dialogue with the 'Other'.* The great Russian linguist and critic, Mikhail Bakhtin, who fell foul of the Stalinist regime in the 1940s, studied language, not (as the Saussureans did) as an objective system, but in terms of how meaning is sustained in the *dialogue* between two or more speakers. Meaning, Bakhtin argued, does not belong to any one speaker. It arises in the give-and-take between different speakers. 'The word in language is half someone else's. It becomes 'one's own' only when … the speaker appropriates the word, adapting it to his own semantic expressive intention. Prior to this … the word does not exist in a neutral or impersonal language … rather it exists in other people's mouths, serving other people's intentions: it is from there that one must take the word and make it one's own' (Bakhtin, 1981 [1935], pp. 293–4). Bakhtin and his collaborator, Volosinov, believed that this enabled us to enter into a struggle over meaning, breaking one set of associations and giving words a new inflection. Meaning, Bakhtin argued, is established through dialogue – it is fundamentally *dialogic*. Everything we say and mean is modified by the interaction and interplay with another

person. Meaning arises through the 'difference' between the participants in any dialogue. *The 'Other', in short, is essential to meaning.*

This is the positive side of Bakhtin's theory. The negative side is, of course, that therefore meaning cannot be fixed and that one group can never be completely in charge of meaning. What it means to be 'British' or 'Russian' or 'Jamaican' cannot be entirely controlled by the British, Russians or Jamaicans, but is always up for grabs, always being negotiated, in the dialogue between these national cultures and their 'others'. Thus it has been argued that you cannot know what it meant to be 'British' in the nineteenth century until you know what the British thought of Jamaica, their prize colony in the Caribbean, or Ireland, and more disconcertingly, *what the Jamaicans or the Irish thought of them* ... (C. Hall, 1994).

3   The third kind of explanation is anthropological, and you have already met it in **du Gay, Hall et al.** (1997). *The argument here is that culture depends on giving things meaning by assigning them to different positions within a classificatory system. The marking of 'difference' is thus the basis of that symbolic order which we call culture.* Mary Douglas, following the classic work on symbolic systems by the French sociologist, Emile Durkheim, and the later studies of mythology by the French anthropologist, Claude Lévi-Strauss, argues that social groups impose meaning on their world by ordering and organizing things into classificatory systems (Douglas, 1966). Binary oppositions are crucial for all classification, because one must establish a clear difference between things in order to classify them. Faced with different kinds of food, Lévi-Strauss argued (1979), one way of giving them meaning is to start by dividing them into two groups – those which are eaten 'raw' and those eaten 'cooked'. Of course, you can also classify food into 'vegetables' and 'fruit'; or into those which are eaten as 'starters' and those which are eaten as 'desserts'; or those which are served up at dinner and those which are eaten at a sacred feast or the communion table. Here, again, 'difference' is fundamental to cultural meaning.

However, it can also give rise to negative feelings and practices. Mary Douglas argues that what really disturbs cultural order is when things turn up in the wrong category; or when things fail to fit any category – such as a substance like mercury, which is a metal but also a liquid, or a social group like mixed-race *mulattoes* who are neither 'white' nor 'black' but float ambiguously in some unstable, dangerous, hybrid zone of indeterminacy in-between (Stallybrass and White, 1986). Stable cultures require things to stay in their appointed place. Symbolic boundaries keep the categories 'pure', giving cultures their unique meaning and identity. What unsettles culture is 'matter out of place' – the breaking of our unwritten rules and codes. Dirt in the garden is fine, but dirt in one's bedroom is 'matter out of place' – a sign of pollution, of symbolic boundaries being transgressed, of taboos broken. What we do with 'matter out of place' is to sweep it up, throw it out, restore the place to order, bring back the normal state of affairs. The retreat of many cultures towards 'closure' against foreigners, intruders, aliens and 'others' is part of the same process of purification (Kristeva, 1982).

According to this argument, then, *symbolic boundaries are central to all culture. Marking 'difference' leads us, symbolically, to close ranks, shore up culture and to stigmatize and expel anything which is defined as impure, abnormal. However, paradoxically, it also makes 'difference' powerful, strangely attractive precisely because it is forbidden, taboo, threatening to cultural order.* Thus, 'what is socially peripheral is often symbolically centred' (Babcock, 1978, p. 32).

4 The fourth kind of explanation is psychoanalytic and relates to the role of 'difference' in our psychic life. *The argument here is that the 'Other' is fundamental to the constitution of the self, to us as subjects, and to sexual identity.* According to Freud, the consolidation of our definitions of 'self' and of our sexual identities depends on the way we are formed as subjects, especially in relation to that stage of early development which he called the Oedipus complex (after the Oedipus story in Greek myth). A unified sense of oneself as a subject and one's sexual identity – Freud argued – are not fixed in the very young child. However, according to Freud's version of the Oedipus myth, at a certain point the boy develops an unconscious erotic attraction to the Mother, but finds the Father barring his way to 'satisfaction'. However, when he discovers that women do not have a penis, he assumes that his Mother was punished by castration, and that he might be punished in the same way if he persists with his unconscious desire. In fear, he switches his identification to his old 'rival', the Father, thereby taking on the beginnings of an identification with a masculine identity. The girl child identifies the opposite way – with the Father. But she cannot 'be' him, since she lacks the penis. She can only 'win' him by being willing, unconsciously, to bear a man's child – thereby taking up and identifying with the Mother's role, and 'becoming feminine'.

This model of how *sexual 'difference'* begins to be assumed in very young children has been strongly contested. Many people have questioned its speculative character. On the other hand, it has been very influential, as well as extensively amended by later analysts. The French psychoanalyst, Jacques Lacan (1977), for example, went further than Freud, arguing that the child has no sense of itself as a subject separate from its mother until it sees itself in a mirror, or as if mirrored in the way it is looked at by the Mother. Through identification, 'it desires the object of her desire, thus focusing its libido on itself' (see **Segal**, 1997). It is this reflection from outside oneself, or what Lacan calls the 'look from the place of the other', during 'the mirror stage', which allows the child for the first time to recognize itself as a unified subject, relate to the outside world, to the 'Other', develop language and take on a sexual identity. (Lacan actually says, 'mis-recognize itself', since he believes the subject can never be fully unified.) Melanie Klein (1957), on the other hand, argued that the young child copes with this problem of a lack of a stable self by splitting its unconscious image of and identification with the Mother into its 'good' and 'bad' parts, internalizing some aspects, and projecting others on to the outside world. The common element in all these different versions of Freud is the role which is given by these different theorists to the 'Other' in subjective development. Subjectivity can only arise and a sense of 'self' be formed through the symbolic and unconscious relations which the young child forges with a significant 'Other' which is outside – i.e. different from – itself.

At first sight, these psychoanalytic accounts seem to be positive in their implications for 'difference'. Our subjectivities, they argue, depend on our unconscious relations with significant others. However, there are also negative implications. The psychoanalytic perspective assumes that there is no such thing as a given, stable inner core to 'the self' or to identity. Psychically, we are never fully unified as subjects. Our subjectivities are formed through this troubled, never-completed, unconscious dialogue with – this internalization of – the 'Other'. It is formed in relation to something which completes us but which – since it lies outside us – we in some way always lack.

What's more, they say, this troubling split or division within subjectivity can never be fully healed. Some indeed see this as one of the main sources of neurosis in adults. Others see psychic problems arising from the splitting between the 'good' and 'bad' parts of the self – being pursued internally by the 'bad' aspects one has taken into oneself, or alternatively, projecting on to others the 'bad' feelings one cannot deal with. Frantz Fanon (referred to earlier), who used psychoanalytic theory in his explanation of racism, argued (1986/1952) that much racial stereotyping and violence arose from the refusal of the white 'Other' to give recognition 'from the place of the other', to the black person (see Bhabha, 1986b; Hall, 1996).

These debates about 'difference' and the 'Other' have been introduced because the chapter draws selectively on all of them in the course of analysing racial representation. It is not necessary at this stage for you to prefer one explanation of 'difference' over others, or to choose between them. They are not mutually exclusive since they refer to very different levels of analysis – the linguistic, the social, the cultural and the psychic levels respectively. However, there are two general points to note at this stage. First, from many different directions, and within many different disciplines, this question of 'difference' and 'otherness' has come to play an increasingly significant role. Secondly, 'difference' is **ambivalent**. It can be both positive and negative. It is both necessary for the production of meaning, the formation of language and culture, for social identities and a subjective sense of the self as a sexed subject – and at the same time, it is threatening, a site of danger, of negative feelings, of splitting, hostility and aggression towards the 'Other'. In what follows, you should always bear in mind this ambivalent character of 'difference', its divided legacy.

ambivalence

2   Racializing the 'Other'

Holding these theoretical 'tools' of analysis in reserve for a moment, let us now explore further some examples of the repertoires of representation and representational practices which have been used to mark racial difference and signify the racialized 'Other' in western popular culture. How was this archive formed and what were its typical figures and practices?

There are three major moments when the 'West' encountered black people, giving rise to an avalanche of popular representations based on the marking of racial difference. The first began with the sixteenth-century contact between European traders and the West African kingdoms, which provided a source of black slaves for three centuries. Its effects were to be found in slavery and in the post-slave societies of the New World (discussed in section 2.2). The second was the European colonization of Africa and the 'scramble' between the European powers for the control of colonial territory, markets and raw materials in the period of 'high Imperialism' (see below, section 2.1). The third was the post-World War II migrations from the 'Third World' into Europe and North America (examples from this period are discussed in section 2.3). Western ideas about 'race' and images of racial difference were profoundly shaped by those three fateful encounters.

2.1   Commodity racism: empire and the domestic world

We start with how images of racial difference drawn from the imperial encounter flooded British popular culture at the end of the nineteenth century. In the middle ages, the European image of Africa was ambiguous – a mysterious place, but often viewed positively: after all, the Coptic Church was one of the oldest 'overseas' Christian communities; black saints appeared in medieval Christian iconography; and Ethiopia's legendary 'Prester John', was reputed to be one of Christianity's most loyal supporters. Gradually, however, this image changed. Africans were declared to be the descendants of Ham, cursed in *The Bible* to be in perpetuity 'a servant of servants unto his brethren'. Identified with Nature, they symbolized 'the primitive' in contrast with 'the civilized world'. The Enlightenment, which ranked societies along an evolutionary scale from 'barbarism' to 'civilization', thought Africa 'the parent of everything that is monstrous in Nature' (Edward Long, 1774, quoted in McClintock, 1995, p. 22). Curvier dubbed the Negro race a 'monkey tribe'. The philosopher Hegel declared that Africa was 'no historical part of the world … it has no movement or development to exhibit'. By the nineteenth century, when the European exploration and colonization of the African interior began in earnest, Africa was regarded as 'marooned and historically abandoned … a fetish land, inhabited by cannibals, dervishes and witch doctors …' (McClintock, 1995, p. 41).

The exploration and colonization of Africa produced an explosion of popular representations (Mackenzie, 1986). Our example here is the spread of imperial images and themes in Britain through commodity advertising in the closing decades of the nineteenth century.

The progress of the great white explorer–adventurers and the encounters with the black African exotic was charted, recorded and depicted in maps and drawings, etchings and (especially) the new photography, in newspaper illustrations and accounts, diaries, travel writing, learned treatises, official reports and 'boy's-own' adventure novels. Advertising was one means by which the imperial project was given visual form in a popular medium, forging the link between Empire and the domestic imagination. Anne McClintock argues that, through the racializing of advertisements (commodity racism), 'the Victorian middle-class home became a space for the display of imperial spectacle and the reinvention of race, while the colonies – in particular Africa – became a theatre for exhibiting the Victorian cult of domesticity and the reinvention of gender' (1995, p. 34).

Advertising for the objects, gadgets, gee-gaws and bric-a-brac with which the Victorian middle classes filled their homes provided an 'imaginary way of relating to the real world' of commodity production, and after 1890, with the rise of the popular press, from the *Illustrated London News* to the Harmsworth *Daily Mail*, the imagery of mass commodity production entered the world of the working classes via the spectacle of advertising (Richards, 1990). Richards calls it a 'spectacle' because advertising translated *things* into a fantasy visual display of *signs and symbols*. The production of commodities became linked to Empire – the search for markets and raw materials abroad supplanting other motives for imperial expansion.

This two-way traffic forged connections between imperialism and the domestic sphere, public and private. Commodities (and images of English domestic life) flowed outwards to the colonies; raw materials (and images of 'the civilizing mission' in progress) were brought into the home. Henry Stanley, the imperial adventurer, who famously traced Livingstone ('Dr Livingstone, I presume?') in Central Africa in 1871, and was a founder of the infamous Congo Free State, tried to annex Uganda and open up the interior for the East Africa Company. He believed that the spread of commodities would make 'civilization' in Africa inevitable and named his native bearers after the branded goods they carried – Bryant and May, Remington and so on. His exploits became associated with Pears' Soap, Bovril and various brands of tea. The gallery of imperial heroes and their masculine exploits in 'Darkest Africa' were immortalized on matchboxes, needle cases, toothpaste pots, pencil boxes, cigarette packets, board games, paperweights, sheet music. 'Images of colonial conquest were stamped on soap boxes … biscuit tins, whisky bottles, tea tins and chocolate bars … No pre-existing form of organized racism had ever before been able to reach so large and so differentiated a mass of the populace' (McClintock, 1995, p. 209) (Figures 4.6, 4.7 and 4.8).

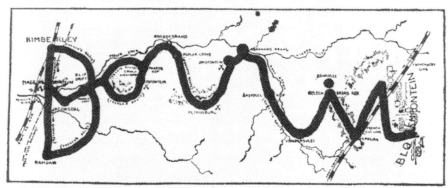

FIGURE 4.6
Bovril advertisement claiming to depict Lord Roberts' historical march from Kimberley to Bloemfontein during the South African (Boer) War, 1900.

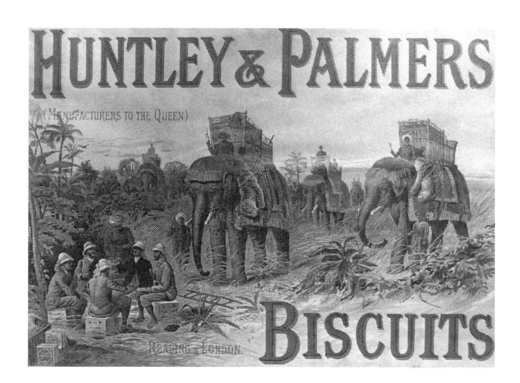

FIGURE 4.7
Huntley and Palmer's biscuit advertisement.

Soap symbolized this 'racializing' of the domestic world and 'domestication' of the colonial world. In its capacity to cleanse and purify, soap acquired, in the fantasy world of imperial advertising, the quality of a fetish-object. It apparently had the power to wash black skin white as well as being capable of washing off the soot, grime and dirt of the industrial slums and their inhabitants – the unwashed poor – at home, while at the same time keeping the imperial body clean and pure in the racially polluted contact zones 'out there' in the Empire. In the process, however, the domestic labour of women was often silently erased.

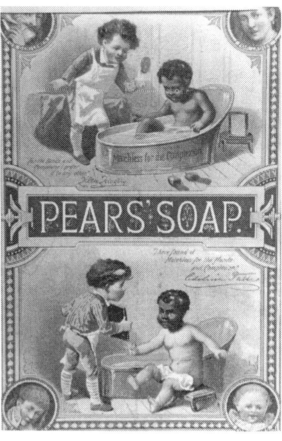

FIGURE 4.8 Nineteenth-century advertisements for Pears' soap.

ACTIVITY 7

Look, now, at the two advertisements for Pears' Soap (Figure 4.8). Before reading further, write down briefly what you think these ads are 'saying'.

READING A

Now read Anne McClintock's analysis of Pears' advertising campaigns, in Reading A: 'Soap and commodity spectacle' at the end of this chapter.

2.2   Meanwhile, down on the plantation …

Our second example is from the period of plantation slavery and its aftermath. It has been argued that, in the USA, a fully fledged racialized ideology did not appear amongst the slave-holding classes (and their supporters in Europe) until slavery was seriously challenged by the Abolitionists in the nineteenth century. Frederickson (1987) sums up the complex and sometimes contradictory set of beliefs about racial difference which took hold in this period:

Heavily emphasized was the historical case against the black man based on his supposed failure to develop a civilized way of life in Africa. As portrayed in pro-slavery writing, Africa was and always had been the scene of unmitigated savagery, cannibalism, devil worship, and licentiousness. Also advanced was an early form of biological argument, based on real or imagined physiological and anatomical differences – especially in cranial characteristics and facial angles – which allegedly explained mental and physical inferiority. Finally there was the appeal to deep-seated white fears of widespread miscegenation [sexual relations and interbreeding between the races], as pro-slavery theorists sought to deepen white anxieties by claiming that the abolition of slavery would lead to inter-marriage and the degeneracy of the race. Although all these arguments had appeared earlier in fugitive or embryonic form, there is something startling about the rapidity with which they were brought together and organized in a rigid polemical pattern, once the defenders of slavery found themselves in a propaganda war with the abolitionists.

(Frederickson, 1987, p. 49)

binary oppositions   This racialized discourse is structured by a set of **binary oppositions**. There is the powerful opposition between 'civilization' (white) and 'savagery' (black). There is the opposition between the biological or bodily characteristics of the 'black' and 'white' 'races', polarized into their extreme opposites – each the signifiers of an absolute difference between human 'types' or species. There are the rich distinctions which cluster around the supposed link, on the one hand, between the white 'races' and intellectual development – refinement, learning and knowledge, a belief in reason, the presence of developed institutions, formal government and law, and a 'civilized restraint' in their emotional, sexual and civil life, all of which are associated with 'Culture'; and on the other hand, the link between the black 'races' and whatever is instinctual – the open expression of emotion and feeling rather than intellect, a lack of 'civilized refinement' in sexual and social life, a reliance on custom and ritual, and the lack of developed civil institutions, all of which are linked to 'Nature'. Finally there is the polarized opposition between racial 'purity' on the one hand, and the 'pollution' which comes from intermarriage, racial hybridity and interbreeding.

The Negro, it was argued, found happiness only when under the tutelage of a white master. His/her essential characteristics were fixed forever – 'eternally' – in Nature. Evidence from slave insurrections and the slave revolt in Haiti (1791) had persuaded whites of the instability of the Negro character. A degree of civilization, they thought, had rubbed off on the 'domesticated' slave, but underneath slaves remained by nature savage brutes; and long buried passions, once loosed, would result in 'the wild frenzy of revenge, and the savage lust for blood' (Frederickson, 1987, p. 54). This view was justified with reference to so-called scientific and ethnological 'evidence', the basis of a new kind of 'scientific racism'. Contrary to Biblical evidence, it was asserted, blacks/whites had been created at different times – according to the theory of 'polygenesis' (many creations).

Racial theory applied the **Culture/Nature** distinction differently to the two racialized groups. Among whites, 'Culture' *was opposed to* 'Nature'. Amongst blacks, it was assumed, 'Culture' *coincided with* 'Nature'. Whereas whites developed 'Culture' to subdue and overcome 'Nature', for blacks, 'Culture' and 'Nature' were interchangeable. David Green discussed this view in relation to anthropology and ethnology, the disciplines which (see Chapter 3) provided much of the 'scientific evidence' for it.

> Though not immune to the 'white man's burden' [approach], anthropology was drawn through the course of the nineteenth century, even more towards causal connections between race and culture. As the position and status of the 'inferior' races became increasingly to be regarded as fixed, so socio-cultural differences came to be regarded as dependent upon hereditary characteristics. Since these were inaccessible to direct observation they had to be inferred from physical and behavioural traits which, in turn, they were intended to explain. Socio-cultural differences among human populations became subsumed within the identity of the individual human body. In the attempt to trace the line of determination between the biological and the social, the body became the totemic object, and its very visibility the evident articulation of nature and culture.
>
> (Green, 1984, pp. 31–2)

Green's argument explains *why* the racialized body and its meanings came to have such resonance in popular representations of difference and 'otherness'. It also highlights the connection between *visual discourse* and *the production of (racialized) knowledge*. The body itself and its differences were visible for all to see, and thus provided 'the incontrovertible evidence' for a naturalization of racial difference. The representation of 'difference' through the body became the discursive site through which much of this 'racialized knowledge' was produced and circulated.

2.3 Signifying racial 'difference'

Popular representations of racial 'difference' during slavery tended to cluster around two main themes. First was the subordinate status and 'innate laziness' of blacks – 'naturally' born to, and fitted only for, servitude but, at the same time, stubbornly unwilling to labour in ways appropriate to their nature and profitable for their masters. Second was their innate 'primitivism', simplicity and lack of culture, which made them genetically incapable of 'civilized' refinements. Whites took inordinate amusement from the slaves' efforts to imitate the manners and customs of so-called 'civilized' white folks. (In fact, slaves often deliberately parodied their masters' behaviour by their exaggerated imitations, laughing at white folks behind their backs and 'sending them up'. The practice – called *signifying* – is now recognized as a well-established part of the black vernacular literary tradition. See, for example, Figure 4.9, reprinted in Gates, 1988).

Culture/Nature

naturalization

Typical of this racialized regime of representation was the practice of reducing the cultures of black people to Nature, or *naturalizing* 'difference'. The logic behind **naturalization** is simple. If the differences between black and white people are 'cultural', then they are open to modification and change. But if they are 'natural' – as the slave-holders believed – then they are beyond history, permanent and fixed. 'Naturalization' is therefore a representational strategy designed to *fix* 'difference', and thus *secure it forever*. It is an attempt to halt the inevitable 'slide' of meaning, to secure discursive or ideological 'closure'.

In the eighteenth and nineteenth centuries popular representations of daily life under slavery, ownership and servitude are shown as so 'natural' that they require *no comment*. It was part of the natural order of things that white men should sit and slaves should stand; that white women rode and slave men ran after them shading them from the Louisiana sun with an umbrella; that white overseers should inspect slave women like prize animals, or punish runaway slaves with casual forms of torture (like branding them or urinating in their mouths), and that fugitives should kneel to receive their punishment (see Figures 4.10, 4.11, 4.12). These images are a form of ritualized degradation. On the other hand, some representations are idealized and sentimentalized rather than degraded, while remaining stereotypical. These are the 'noble savages' to the 'debased servants' of the previous type. For example, the endless representations of the 'good' Christian black slave, like Uncle Tom, in Harriet Beecher Stowe's pro-abolitionist novel, *Uncle Tom's Cabin*, or the ever-faithful and devoted domestic slave, Mammy. A third group occupy an ambiguous middle-ground – tolerated though not admired. These include the 'happy natives' – black entertainers, minstrels and banjo-players who seemed not to have a brain in their head but sang, danced and cracked jokes all day long, to entertain white folks; or the 'tricksters' who were admired for their crafty ways of avoiding hard work, and their tall tales, like Uncle Remus.

For blacks, 'primitivism' (Culture) and 'blackness' (Nature) became interchangeable. This was their 'true nature' and they could not escape it. As has so often happened in the representation of women, their biology *was* their 'destiny'. Not only were blacks represented in terms of their essential characteristics. They were *reduced to their essence*. Laziness, simple fidelity, mindless 'cooning', trickery, childishness belonged to blacks *as a race, as a species*. There was nothing else to the kneeling slave *but* his servitude; nothing to Uncle Tom *except* his Christian forbearing; nothing to Mammy *but* her fidelity to the white household – and what Fanon called her 'sho' nuff good cooking'.

FIGURE 4.9 'A Black Lecture on Phrenology'.

FIGURE 4.10 Slavery: a scene from a planter's life in the West Indies.

FIGURE 4.11 Slavery: a slave auction in the West Indies, c. 1830.

FIGURE 4.12
Slavery: drawing of a Creole lady and black slave in the West Indies.

FIGURE 4.13
A girl and her golliwog: an illustration by Lawson Wood, 1927.

stereotypes

In short, these are **stereotypes**. We will return, in section 4, to examine this concept of *stereotyping* more fully. But for the moment, we note that 'stereotyped' means 'reduced to a few essentials, fixed in Nature by a few, simplified characteristics'. Stereotyping of blacks in popular representation was so common that cartoonists, illustrators and caricaturists could summon up a whole gallery of 'black types' with a few, simple, essentialized strokes of the pen. Black people were reduced to the signifiers of their physical difference – thick lips, fuzzy hair, broad face and nose, and so on. For example, that figure of fun who, as doll and marmalade emblem, has amused little children down the ages: the Golliwog (Figure 4.13). This is only one of the many popular figures which reduces black people to a few simplified, reductive and essentialized features. Every adorable little 'piccaninny' was immortalized for years by his grinning innocence on the covers of the *Little Black Sambo* books. Black waiters served a thousand cocktails on stage, screen and in magazine ads. Black Mammy's chubby countenance smiled away, a century after the abolition of slavery, on every packet of Aunt Jemima's Pancakes.

3 Staging racial 'difference': 'and the melody lingered on …'

The traces of these racial stereotypes – what we may call a 'racialized regime of representation' – have persisted into the late twentieth century (Hall, 1981). Of course, they have always been contested. In the early decades of the nineteenth century, the anti-slavery movement (which led to the abolition of British slavery in 1834) did put into early circulation an alternative imagery of black–white relations and this was taken up by the American abolitionists in the US in the period leading up to the Civil War. In opposition to the stereotypical representations of racialized difference, abolitionists adopted a different slogan about the black slave – 'Are you not a man and brother? Are you not a woman and a sister?' – emphasizing, not difference, but a common humanity. The anniversary coins minted by the anti-slavery societies represented this shift, though not without the marking of 'difference'. Black people are still seen as childish, simple and dependent, though capable of, and on their way to (after a paternalist apprenticeship), something more like equality with whites. They were represented as either supplicants for freedom or full of gratitude for being freed – and consequently still shown kneeling to their white benefactors (Figure 4.14).

This image reminds us that the 'Uncle Tom' of Harriet Beecher Stowe's novel was not only written to appeal to anti-slavery opinion but in the conviction that, 'with their gentleness, their lowly docility of heart – their childlike simplicity of affection and facility of forgiveness', blacks were, if anything, *more* fitted than their white counterparts to 'the highest form of the peculiarly Christian life' (Stowe, quoted in Frederickson, 1987, p. 111). This sentiment counters one set of stereotypes (their savagery) by substituting another (their

eternal goodness). The extreme racialization of the imagery has been modified; but a sentimentalized version of the stereotyping remained active in the discourse of anti-slavery.

After the Civil War, some of the grosser forms of social and economic exploitation, physical and mental degradation associated with plantation slavery were replaced by a different system of racial segregation – legalized in the South, more informally maintained in the North. Did the old, stereotypical 'regime of representation', which had helped to construct the image of black people in the white imaginary, gradually disappear?

That would seem too optimistic. A good test case is the American cinema, *the* popular art form of the first half of the twentieth century, where one would expect to find a very different representational repertoire. However, in critical studies like Leab's *From Sambo to Superspade* (1976), Cripps' *Black Film as Genre* (1978), Patricia Morton's *Disfigured Images* (1991), and Donald Bogle's *Toms, Coons, Mulattos, Mammies and Bucks: an interpretative history of blacks in American films* (1973), the astonishing persistence of the basic racial 'grammar of representation' is documented – of course, with many variations and modifications allowing for differences in time, medium and context.

Bogle's study identifies the five main *stereotypes* which, he argues, made the cross-over: *Toms* – the Good Negroes, always 'chased, harassed, hounded, flogged, enslaved and insulted, they keep the faith, ne'er turn against their white massas, and remain hearty, submissive, stoic, generous, selfless and oh-so-kind' (p. 6). *Coons* – the eye-popping piccanninies, the slapstick entertainers, the spinners of tall tales, the 'no-account "niggers", those unreliable, crazy, lazy, subhuman creatures, good for nothing more than eating watermelons, stealing chickens, shooting crap, or butchering the English language' (pp. 7–8). *The Tragic Mulatto* – the mixed-race woman, cruelly caught between 'a divided racial inheritance' (p. 9), beautiful, sexually attractive and often exotic, the prototype of the smouldering, sexy heroine, whose partly white blood makes her 'acceptable', even attractive, to white men, but whose indelible 'stain' of black blood condemns her to a tragic conclusion. *Mammies* – the prototypical house-servants, usually big, fat, bossy and cantankerous, with their good-for-nothing husbands sleeping it off at home, their utter devotion to the white household and their unquestioned subservience in their workplaces (p. 9). Finally, the *Bad Bucks* – physically big, strong, no-good, violent, renegades, 'on a rampage and full of black rage', 'over-sexed and savage, violent and frenzied as they lust for white flesh' (p. 10). There are many traces of this in contemporary images of black youth – for example, the 'mugger', the 'drug-baron', the 'yardie', the gansta-rap singer, the 'niggas with attitude' bands and more generally black urban youth 'on the rampage'.

The film which introduced these black 'types' to the cinema was one of the most extraordinary and influential movies of all times, D.W. Griffiths' *The Birth of a Nation* (1915), based on a popular novel, *The Clansman*, which had already put some of these racialized images into circulation. Griffiths, a 'founding father' of the cinema introduced many technical and cinematic innovations and virtually single-handedly constructed the 'grammar' of silent feature-film-making. Up to then,

> American movies had been two- or three-reel affairs, shots running no longer than ten or fifteen minutes, crudely and casually filmed. But *Birth of a Nation* was rehearsed for six weeks, filmed in nine, later edited in three months, and finally released as a hundred-thousand dollar spectacle, twelve reels in length and over three hours in running time. It altered the entire course and concept of American movie-making,

developing the close-up, cross-cutting, rapid-fire editing, the iris, the split-screen shot and realistic and impressionistic lighting. Creating sequences and images yet to be seen, the film's magnitude and epic grandeur swept audiences off their feet.

(Bogle, 1987, p. 10)

More astonishingly, it not only marked the 'birth of the cinema', but it told the story of 'the birth of the American nation' – identifying the nation's salvation with the 'birth of the Ku Klux Klan', that secret band of white brothers with their white hoods and burning crosses, 'defenders of white womanhood, white honour and white glory', shown in the film putting the blacks to rout in a magnificent charge, who 'restore(d) to the South everything it has lost including its white supremacy' (p. 12), and who were subsequently responsible for defending white racism in the South by torching black homes, beating up black people and lynching black men.

There have been many twists and turns in the ways in which the black experience was represented in mainstream American cinema. But the repertoire of stereotypical figures drawn from 'slavery days' has never entirely disappeared – a fact you can appreciate even if you are not familiar with many of the examples quoted. For a time, film-makers like Oscar Mischeaux produced a 'segregated' cinema – black films exclusively for black audiences (see Gaines, 1993). In the 1930s black actors principally appeared in mainstream films in the subordinate roles of jesters, simpletons, faithful retainers and servants. Bill 'Bojangles' Robinson faithfully butlered and danced for the child star, Shirley Temple; Louise Beavers steadfastly and cheerfully cooked in a hundred white family-kitchens; while Hattie McDaniel (fat) and Butterfly McQueen (thin) 'mammied' to Scarlet O'Hara's every trick and infidelity in *Gone With The Wind* – a film all about 'race' which failed to mention it (Wallace, 1993). Stepin Fetchit (*step in* and *fetch it*) was made to roll his eyes, spread his dim-witted grin, shuffle his enormous feet and stammer his confused way through twenty-six films – the archetypal 'coon'; and when he retired, many followed in his footsteps. The 1940s was the era of the black musicals – *Cabin in the Sky, Stormy Weather, Porgy and Bess, Carmen Jones* – and black entertainers like Cab Calloway, Fats Waller, Ethel Waters, Pearl Bailey, including two famous, type-cast 'mulatto *femmes fatales*', Lena Horne and Dorothy Dandridge. 'They didn't make me into a maid but they didn't make me anything else either. I became a butterfly pinned to a column singing away in Movieland', was Lena Horne's definitive judgement (quoted in Wallace, 1993, p. 265).

Not until the 1950s did films begin cautiously to broach the subject of 'race' as problem (*Home of the Brave, Lost Boundaries, Pinky*, to mention a few titles) – though largely from a white liberal perspective. A key figure in these films was Sidney Poitier – an extremely talented black actor, whose roles cast him as a 'hero for an integrationist age'. Bogle argues that Poitier, the first black actor to be allowed 'star billing' in mainstream Hollywood films, 'fitted'

FIGURE 4.15 Still from *Charlie McCarthy, Detective.*

FIGURE 4.16 Ann Sheridan and Hattie McDaniel in *George Washington Slept Here, 1942.*

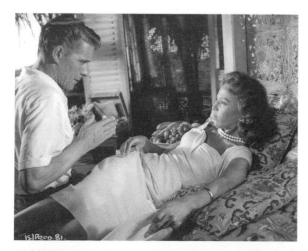

FIGURE 4.17 Dorothy Dandridge, the 1950s definitive tragic mulatto, in *Island in the Sun, 1957.*

because he was cast so rigorously 'against the grain'. He was made to play on screen everything that the stereotyped black figure was *not*: 'educated and intelligent, he spoke proper English, dressed conservatively, and had the best of table manners. For the mass white audience, Sidney Poitier was a black man who met their standards. His characters were tame; never did they act impulsively; nor were they threats to the system. They were amenable and pliant. And finally they were non-funky, almost sexless and sterile. In short they were the perfect dream for white liberals anxious to have a coloured man in for lunch or dinner' (Bogle, 1973, pp. 175–6). Accordingly, in 1967, he actually starred in a film entitled *Guess Who's Coming To Dinner.* Despite outstanding film performances (*The Defiant Ones, To Sir With Love, In the Heat of the Night*), 'There was nothing there', as one critic kindly put it, 'to feed the old but potent fear of the over-endowed Negro' (Cripps, 1978, p. 223).

FIGURE 4.18 Sidney Poitier and Tony Curtis, in *The Defiant Ones, 1958.*

3.1 Heavenly bodies

Did nobody transcend this regime of racialized representation in the American cinema in its heyday up to the 1960s? If anyone could have, that person was Paul Robeson, who was a major black star and performer in the arts between 1924 and 1945, achieving enormous popularity with audiences on both sides of the Atlantic. Richard Dyer, in his full-length study of Robeson in *Heavenly Bodies* (1986), observes that, 'His image insisted on his blackness – musically, in his primary association with Negro folk music, especially spirituals; in the theatre and films, in the recurrence of Africa as a motif; and in general in the way his image is so bound up with the notions of racial character, the nature of black folks, the Negro essence, and so on. Yet he was a star equally popular with black and white audiences.' Dyer asks, 'How did the period permit black stardom? What were the qualities this black person could be taken to embody, that could catch on in a society where there had never been a black star of this magnitude?' (pp. 67, 69). One answer is that in his performances on stage, theatre and screen, Robeson was 'read' differently by black and white audiences. 'Black and white discourses on blackness seem to be valuing the same things – spontaneity, emotion, naturalness – yet giving them a different implication' (ibid., p. 79).

Robeson's is a complex case, shot through with ambivalences. Dyer identifies a number of themes through which Robeson came to embody 'the epitome of what black people are like' (ibid., p. 71). His musical talent, sonorous voice, his intellect, physical presence and stature, coupled with his simplicity, sincerity, charm and authority allowed him to portray the 'male heroes of black culture' in plays like *Toussaint L'Ouverture* and films like *The Emperor Jones* – but also 'the stereotypes of the white imagination' in *Show Boat, Shuffle Along, Voodoo* and *Sanders of the River* (ibid., p. 73) (Figure 4.19). Robeson himself said that 'The white man has made a fetish of intellect and worships the God of thought; the Negro feels rather than thinks, experiences emotions directly rather than interprets them by roundabout and devious abstractions, and apprehends the outside world by means of intuitive perceptions …' (quoted in Dyer, 1986, p. 76). This sentiment, embodied in several of his films, gave his performances a vibrant emotional intensity. But it also played directly into the black/white, emotion/intellect, nature/culture binary oppositions of racial stereotyping.

Something of the same ambivalence can be detected in relation to other themes, Dyer argues, like the representation of blackness

FIGURE 4.19 Paul Robeson in *Sanders of the River*, 1935.

FIGURE 4.20
Paul Robeson
with Wallace
Ford and Henry
Wilcoxon, at the
Giza pyramids in
Egypt, during the
filming of *Jericho*,
1937.

as 'folk' and what he calls 'atavism' (for a definition, see below). The emotional intensity and 'authenticity' of black performers was supposed to give them a genuine feel for the 'folk' traditions of black people – 'folk', here, signifying spontaneity and naturalness as opposed to the 'artificiality' of high art. Robeson's singing epitomized this quality, capturing what was thought to be the essence of the Negro spirituals in, for example, the universally popular and acclaimed song, *Old Man River*. He sang it in a deep, sonorous voice which, to blacks, expressed their long travail and their hope of freedom, but also, to whites, what they had always heard in spirituals and Robeson's voice – 'sorrowing, melancholy, suffering' (Dyer, 1986, p. 87). Robeson gradually altered the words of this song to make it more political – 'to bring out and extend its reference to oppression and to alter its meaning from resignation to struggle' (ibid., p. 105). The line which, in the stage performance of *Show Boat,* went 'Ah'm tired of livin' an' scared of dyin'' was altered in the film to the much more assertive 'I must keep fightin' until I'm dyin'' (ibid., p. 107). On the other hand, Robeson sang black folk songs and spirituals in a 'pure' voice and 'educated' diction, without any of jazz's use of syncopation or delay in phrasing, without any of the 'dirty' notes of black blues, gospel and soul music or the nasal delivery characteristic of 'folk' or the call-and-response structure of African and slave chants.

By 'atavism', Dyer means a return to or 'recovery of qualities that have been carried in the blood from generation to generation … It suggests raw, violent, chaotic and "primitive" emotions' and in the Robeson context, it was closely associated with Africa and the 'return' to 'what black people were supposed to be like deep down' and 'a guarantee of the authentic wildness within of the people who had come from there' (ibid., p. 89). Robeson's 'African' plays and films (*Sanders of the River, Song of Freedom, King Solomon's Mines, Jericho*) were full of 'authentic' African touches, and he researched a great deal into the background of African culture. 'In practice, however,' Dyer observes, 'these are genuine notes inserted into works produced decidedly within American and British discourses on Africa' (ibid., p. 90).

ACTIVITY 8

Look, now, at the photograph of Robeson in a version of African dress (Figure 4.19), taken on the set of *Sanders of the River* (1935). Now, look at the second photograph (Figure 4.20) – Robeson with Wallace Ford and Henry Wilcoxon at the Giza pyramids. What strikes you about these photographs? Write down briefly anything which strikes you about the 'meaning' of these images.

READING B

Now read Richard Dyer's brief analysis of the second of these images (Reading B at the end of this chapter).

Undoubtedly, part of Robeson's immense impact lay in his commanding physical presence. 'His sheer size is emphasized time and again, as is the strength presumed to go with it' (Dyer, p. 134). One can perhaps judge the relevance of this to his representation of blackness from the nude study of Robeson taken by the photographer, Nicholas Muray, which, in Dyer's terms, combines Beauty and Strength with Passivity and Pathos.

ACTIVITY 9

What do you think?

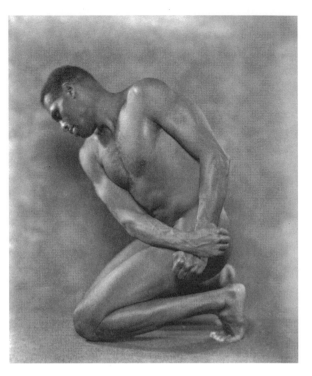

FIGURE 4.21
Paul Robeson, by Nicholas Muray.

Even so outstanding a performer as Paul Robeson, then, could inflect, but could not entirely escape, the representational regime of racial difference which had passed into the mainstream cinema from an earlier era. A more independent representation of black people and black culture in the cinema would have to await the enormous shifts which accompanied the upheavals of the Civil Rights movement in the 1960s and the ending of legal segregation in the South, as well as the huge migration of blacks into the cities and urban centres of the North, which profoundly challenged the 'relations of representation' between racially defined groups in American society.

A second, more ambiguous, 'revolution' followed in the 1980s and 1990s, with the collapse of the 'integrationist' dream of the Civil Rights movement, the expansion of the black ghettos, the growth of the black 'underclass', with its endemic poverty, ill-health and criminalization, and the slide of some black communities into a culture of guns, drugs and intra-black violence. This has, however, been accompanied by the growth of an affirmative self-confidence in, and an insistence on 'respect' for, black cultural identity, as well as a growing 'black separatism' – which features nowhere so visibly as in the massive impact of black music (including 'black rap') on popular music and the visual presence of the music-affiliated 'street-style' scene. These developments have transformed the practices of racial representation, in part because the question of representation itself has become a critical arena of contestation and struggle. Black actors agitated for and got a wider variety of roles in film and television. 'Race' came to be acknowledged as one of the most significant themes of American life and times. In the 1980s and 1990s, blacks themselves entered the American cinema mainstream as independent film-makers, able – like Spike Lee (*Do the Right Thing*), Julie Dash (*Daughters of the Dust*) or John Singleton (*Boys 'n' the Hood*) – to put their own interpretations on the way blacks figure within 'the American experience'. This has broadened the regime of racial representation – the result of a historic 'struggle around the image' – a politics of representation – whose strategies we need to examine more carefully.

4 Stereotyping as a signifying practice

Before we pursue this argument, however, we need to reflect further on how this racialized regime of representation actually works. Essentially, this involves examining more deeply the set of representational practices known as **stereotyping**. So far, we have considered the essentializing, reductionist and naturalizing effects of stereotyping. Stereotyping reduces people to a few, simple, essential characteristics, which are represented as fixed by Nature. Here, we examine four further aspects: (a) the construction of 'otherness' and exclusion; (b) stereotyping and power; (c) the role of fantasy; and (d) fetishism.

stereotyping

Stereotyping as a signifying practice is central to the representation of racial difference. But what is a stereotype? How does it actually work? In his essay on 'Stereotyping', Richard Dyer (1977) makes an important distinction between *typing* and *stereotyping*. He argues that, without the use of *types*, it would be difficult, if not impossible, to make sense of the world. We understand the world by referring individual objects, people or events in our heads to the general classificatory schemes into which – according to our culture – they fit. Thus we 'decode' a flat object on legs on which we place things as a 'table'. We may never have seen that kind of 'table' before, but we have a general concept or category of 'table' in our heads, into which we 'fit' the particular objects we perceive or encounter. In other words, we understand 'the particular' in terms of its 'type'. We deploy what Alfred Schutz called *typifications*. In this sense, 'typing' is essential to the production of meaning (an argument we made earlier in Chapter 1).

Richard Dyer argues that we are always 'making sense' of things in terms of some wider categories. Thus, for example, we come to 'know' something about a person by thinking of the *roles* which he or she performs: is he/she a parent, a child, a worker, a lover, boss, or an old age pensioner? We assign him/her to the *membership* of different groups, according to class, gender, age group, nationality, 'race', linguistic group, sexual preference and so on. We order him/her in terms of *personality type* – is he/she a happy, serious, depressed, scatter-brained, over-active kind of person? Our picture of who the person 'is' is built up out of the information we accumulate from positioning him/her within these different orders of typification. In broad terms, then, 'a *type* is any simple, vivid, memorable, easily grasped and widely recognized characterization in which a few traits are foregrounded and change or "development" is kept to a minimum' (Dyer, 1977, p. 28).

What, then, is the difference between a *type* and a *stereotype*? *Stereotypes* get hold of the few 'simple, vivid, memorable, easily grasped and widely recognized' characteristics about a person, *reduce* everything about the person to those traits, *exaggerate* and *simplify* them, and *fix* them without change or development to eternity. This is the process we described earlier. So the first point is – *stereotyping reduces, essentializes, naturalizes and fixes 'difference'.*

Secondly, *stereotyping deploys a strategy of 'splitting'.* It divides the normal and the acceptable from the abnormal and the unacceptable. It then *excludes* or *expels* everything which does not fit, which is different. Dyer argues that 'a system of social- and stereo-types refers to what is, as it were, within and beyond the pale of normalcy [i.e. behaviour which is accepted as 'normal' in any culture]. Types are instances which indicate those who live by the rules of society (social types) and those who the rules are designed to exclude (stereotypes). For this reason, stereotypes are also more rigid than social types. ... [B]oundaries ... must be clearly delineated and so stereotypes, one of the mechanisms of boundary maintenance, are characteristically fixed, clear-cut, unalterable' (ibid., p. 29). So, *another feature of stereotyping is its practice of 'closure' and exclusion. It symbolically fixes boundaries, and excludes everything which does not belong.*

Stereotyping, in other words, is part of the maintenance of social and symbolic order. It sets up a symbolic frontier between the 'normal' and the 'deviant', the 'normal' and the 'pathological', the 'acceptable' and the 'unacceptable', what 'belongs' and what does not or is 'Other', between 'insiders' and 'outsiders', Us and Them. It facilitates the 'binding' or bonding together of all of Us who are 'normal' into one 'imagined community'; and it sends into symbolic exile all of Them – 'the Others' – who are in some way different – 'beyond the pale'. Mary Douglas (1966), for example, argued that whatever is 'out of place' is considered as polluted, dangerous, taboo. Negative feelings cluster around it. It must be symbolically excluded if the 'purity' of the culture is to be restored. The feminist theorist, Julia Kristeva, calls such expelled or excluded groups, 'abjected' (from the Latin meaning, literally, 'thrown out') (Kristeva, 1982).

The third point is that *stereotyping tends to occur where there are gross inequalities of power.* Power is usually directed against the subordinate or excluded group. One aspect of this power, according to Dyer, is *ethnocentrism* – 'the application of the norms of one's own culture to that of others' (Brown, 1965, p. 183). Again, remember Derrida's argument that, between binary oppositions like Us/Them, 'we are not dealing with ... peaceful coexistence ... but rather with a violent hierarchy. One of the two terms governs ... the other or has the upper hand' (1972, p. 41).

In short, stereotyping is what Foucault called a 'power/knowledge' sort of game. It classifies people according to a norm and constructs the excluded as 'other'. Interestingly, it is also what Gramsci would have called an aspect of the struggle for hegemony. As Dyer observes, 'The establishment of normalcy (i.e. what is accepted as 'normal') through social- and stereo-types is one aspect of the habit of ruling groups … to attempt to fashion the whole of society according to their own world view, value system, sensibility and ideology. So right is this world view for the ruling groups that they make it appear (as it *does* appear to them) as 'natural' and 'inevitable' – and for everyone – and, in so far as they succeed, they establish their hegemony' (Dyer, 1977, p. 30). Hegemony is a form of power based on leadership by a group in many fields of activity at once, so that its ascendancy commands widespread consent and appears natural and inevitable.

4.1   Representation, difference and power

Within stereotyping, then, we have established a connection between representation, difference and power. However, we need to probe the nature of this *power* more fully. We often think of power in terms of direct physical coercion or constraint. However, we have also spoken, for example, of power *in representation*; power to mark, assign and classify; of *symbolic* power; of *ritualized* expulsion. Power, it seems, has to be understood here, not only in terms of economic exploitation and physical coercion, but also in broader cultural or symbolic terms, including the power to represent someone or something in a certain way – within a certain 'regime of representation'. It includes the exercise of *symbolic power* through representational practices. Stereotyping is a key element in this exercise of symbolic violence.

In his study of how Europe constructed a stereotypical image of 'the Orient', Edward Said (1978) argues that, far from simply reflecting what the countries of the Near East were actually like, 'Orientalism' was the *discourse* 'by which European culture was able to manage – and even produce – the Orient politically, sociologically, militarily, ideologically, scientifically and imaginatively during the post-Enlightenment period'. Within the framework of western hegemony over the Orient, he says, there emerged a new object of knowledge – 'a complex Orient suitable for study in the academy, for display in the museum, for reconstruction in the colonial office, for theoretical illustration in anthropological, biological, linguistic, racial and historical theses about mankind and the universe, for instances of economic and sociological theories of development, revolution, cultural personalities, national or religious character' (pp. 7–8). This form of power is closely connected with knowledge, or with the practices of what Foucault called 'power/knowledge'.

FIGURE 4.22   Edwin Long, *The Babylonian Marriage Market*, 1882.

ACTIVITY 10

For an example of Orientalism in visual representation, look at the reproduction of a very popular painting, *The Babylonian Marriage Market* by Edwin Long (Figure 4.22). Not only does the image produce a certain way of knowing the Orient – as 'the mysterious, exotic and eroticized Orient'; but also, the women who are being 'sold' into marriage are arranged, right to left, in ascending order of 'whiteness'. The final figure approximates most closely to the western ideal, the norm; her clear complexion accentuated by the light reflected on her face from a mirror.

Said's discussion of Orientalism closely parallels Foucault's power/ knowledge argument: a *discourse* produces, through different practices of *representation* (scholarship, exhibition, literature, painting, etc.), a form of *racialized knowledge of the Other* (Orientalism) deeply implicated in the operations of *power* (imperialism).

Interestingly, however, Said goes on to define 'power' in ways which emphasize the similarities between Foucault and Gramsci's idea of *hegemony*:

> In any society not totalitarian, then, certain cultural forms predominate over others; the form of this cultural leadership is what Gramsci has identified as *hegemony*, an indispensable concept for any understanding of cultural life in the industrial West. It is hegemony, or rather the result

of cultural hegemony at work, that gives Orientalism its durability and
its strength ... Orientalism is never far from ... the idea of Europe, a
collective notion identifying 'us' Europeans as against all 'those'
non-Europeans, and indeed it can be argued that the major component
in European culture is precisely what made that culture hegemonic
both in and outside Europe: the idea of European identity as a superior
one in comparison with all the non-European peoples and cultures.
There is in addition the hegemony of European ideas about the Orient,
themselves reiterating European superiority over Oriental backwardness,
usually overriding the possibility that a more independent thinker ...
may have had different views on the matter.

(Said, 1978, p. 7)

You should also recall here our earlier discussion in Chapter 1, about
introducing *power* into questions of representation. Power, we recognized
there, always operates in conditions of unequal relations. Gramsci, of course,
would have stressed 'between classes', whereas Foucault always refused to
identify *any* specific subject or subject-group as the source of power, which,
he said, operates at a local, tactical level. These are important differences
between these two theorists of power.

However, there are also some important similarities. For Gramsci, as for
Foucault, power also involves knowledge, representation, ideas, cultural
leadership and authority, as well as economic constraint and physical
coercion. Both would have agreed that power cannot be captured by thinking
exclusively in terms of force or coercion: power also seduces, solicits,
induces, wins consent. It cannot be thought of in terms of one group having a
monopoly of power, simply radiating power *downwards* on a subordinate
group by an exercise of simple domination from above. It includes the
dominant *and* the dominated within its circuits. As Homi Bhabha has
remarked, apropos Said, 'it is difficult to conceive ... subjectification as a
placing *within* Orientalist or colonial discourse for the dominated subject
without the dominant being strategically placed within it too' (Bhabha,
1986a, p. 158). Power not only constrains and prevents: it is also productive.
It produces new discourses, new kinds of knowledge (i.e. Orientalism), new
objects of knowledge (the Orient), it shapes new practices (colonization) and
institutions (colonial government). It operates at a micro-level – Foucault's
'micro-physics of power' – as well as in terms of wider strategies. And, for
both theorists, power is to be found everywhere. As Foucault insists, power
circulates.

The circularity of power is especially important in the context of
representation. The argument is that everyone – the powerful and the
powerless – is caught up, *though not on equal terms*, in power's circulation.
No one – neither its apparent victims nor its agents – can stand wholly
outside its field of operation (think, here, of the Paul Robeson example).

4.2 Power and fantasy

A good example of this 'circularity' of power relates to how black masculinity is represented within a racialized regime of representation. Kobena Mercer and Isaac Julien (1994) argue that the representation of black masculinity 'has been forged in and through the histories of slavery, colonialism and imperialism'.

> As sociologists like Robert Staples (1982) have argued, a central strand of the 'racial' power exercised by the white male slave master was the denial of certain masculine attributes to black male slaves, such as authority, familial responsibility and the ownership of property. Through such collective, historical experiences black men have adopted certain patriarchal values such as physical strength, sexual prowess and being in control as a means of survival against the repressive and violent system of subordination to which they have been subjected.
>
> The incorporation of a code of 'macho' behaviour is thus intelligible as a means of recuperating some degree of power over the condition of powerlessness and dependency in relation to the white master subject. ... The prevailing stereotype (in contemporary Britain) projects an image of black male youth as 'mugger' or 'rioter' ... But this regime of representation is reproduced and maintained in hegemony because black men have had to resort to 'toughness' as a defensive response to the prior aggression and violence that characterizes the way black communities are policed ... This cycle between reality and representation makes the ideological fictions of racism empirically 'true' – or rather, there is a struggle over the definition, understanding and construction of meanings around black masculinity within the dominant regime of truth.
>
> (Mercer and Julien, 1994, pp. 137–8)

During slavery, the white slave master often exercised his authority over the black male slave, by depriving him of all the attributes of responsibility, paternal and familial authority, treating him as a child. This 'infantilization' of difference is a common representational strategy for both men and women. (Women athletes are still widely referred to as 'girls'. And it is only recently that many Southern US whites have ceased referring to grown black men as 'Boy!', while the practice still lingers in South Africa.) Infantilization can also be understood as a way of symbolically 'castrating' the black man (i.e. depriving him of his 'masculinity'); and, as we have seen, whites often fantasized about the excessive sexual appetites and prowess of black men – as they did about the lascivious, over-sexed character of black women – *which they both feared and secretly envied*. Alleged rape was the principal 'justification' advanced for the lynching of black men in the Southern states until the Civil Rights Movement (Jordan, 1968). As Mercer observes, 'The primal fantasy of the big black penis projects the fear of a threat not only to white womanhood, but to civilization itself, as the anxiety of miscegenation, eugenic pollution and racial degeneration is acted out through white male rituals of racial aggression – the historical lynching of black men in the United States routinely involved the literal castration of the Other's "strange fruit"' (1994a, p. 185).

The outcomes were often violent. Yet the example also brings out the circularity of power and the *ambivalence* – the double-sided nature – of representation and stereotyping. For, as Staples, Mercer and Julien remind us, black men sometimes responded to this infantilization by adopting a sort of caricature-in-reverse of the hyper-masculinity and super-sexuality with which they had been stereotyped. Treated as 'childish', some blacks in reaction adopted a 'macho', aggressive–masculine style. But this only served to confirm the fantasy amongst whites of their ungovernable and excessive sexual nature (see Wallace, 1979). Thus, 'victims' can be trapped by the stereotype, unconsciously confirming it by the very terms in which they try to oppose and resist it.

This may seem paradoxical. But it does have its own 'logic'. This logic depends on representation working at two different levels at the same time: a conscious and overt level, and an unconscious or suppressed level. The former often serves as a displaced 'cover' for the latter. The conscious attitude amongst whites – that 'Blacks are not proper men, they are just simple children' – may be a 'cover', or a cover-up, for a deeper, more troubling fantasy – that 'Blacks are really super-men, better endowed than whites, and sexually insatiable'. It would be improper and 'racist' to express the latter sentiment openly; but the fantasy is present, and secretly subscribed to by many, all the same. Thus when blacks act 'macho', they seem to challenge the stereotype (that they are only children) – but in the process, they confirm the fantasy which lies behind or is the 'deep structure' of the stereotype (that they are aggressive, over-sexed and over-endowed). The problem is that blacks are trapped by the *binary structure* of the stereotype, which is split between two extreme opposites – and are obliged to *shuttle endlessly between them*, sometimes being represented as *both of them at the same time*. Thus blacks are both 'childlike' *and* 'oversexed', just as black youth are 'Sambo simpletons' and/or 'wily, dangerous savages'; and older men both 'barbarians' and/or 'noble savages' – Uncle Toms.

The important point is that stereotypes refer as much to what is imagined in fantasy as to what is perceived as 'real'. And, what is visually produced, by the practices of representation, is only half the story. The other half – the deeper meaning – lies in *what is not being said, but is being fantasized, what is implied but cannot be shown*.

So far, we have been arguing that 'stereotyping' has its own *poetics* – its own ways of working – and its *politics* – the ways in which it is invested with power. We have also argued that this is a particular type of power – a *hegemonic* and *discursive* form of power, which operates as much through culture, the production of knowledge, imagery and representation, as through other means. Moreover, it is *circular*: it implicates the 'subjects' of power as well as those who are 'subjected to it'. But the introduction of the sexual dimension takes us to another aspect of 'stereotyping': namely, its basis in *fantasy* and *projection* – and its effects of *splitting* and *ambivalence*.

In 'Orientalism', Said remarked that the 'general idea about who or what was an "Oriental"' emerged according to 'a detailed logic governed' – he insisted – 'not simply by empirical reality but by a battery of desires, repressions, investments and projections' (1978, p. 8). But where does this battery of 'desires, repressions, investments and projections' come from? What role does *fantasy* play in the practices and strategies of racialized representation? If the fantasies which lie behind racialized representations cannot be shown or allowed to 'speak', how do they find expression? How are they 'represented'? This points us in the direction of the representational practice known as *fetishism*.

4.3 Fetishism and disavowal

Let us explore these questions of fantasy and fetishism, summing up the argument about representation and stereotyping, through a concrete example.

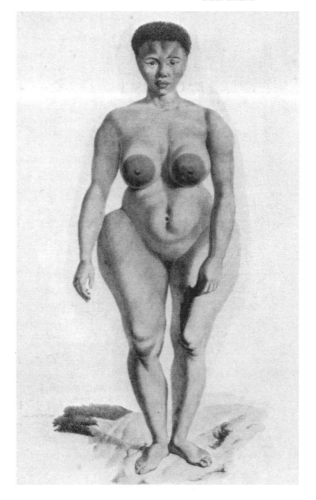

FIGURE 4.23
'The Hottentot Venus' – Saartje Baartman.

> READING C
>
> Read first the short edited extract on 'The deep structure of stereotypes' from *Difference and Pathology* by Sander Gilman (1985), Reading C at the end of this chapter.
>
> Make sure you understand why, according to Gilman, stereotyping always involves what he calls (a) the splitting of the 'good' and 'bad' object; and (b) the projection of anxiety on to the Other.

In a later essay, Gilman refers to the 'case' of the African woman, Saartje (or Sarah) Baartman, known as 'The Hottentot Venus', who was brought to England in 1819 by a Boer farmer from the Cape region of South Africa and a doctor on an African ship, and regularly exhibited over five years in London and Paris (Figure 4.23). In her early 'performances', she was produced on a raised stage like a wild beast, came and went from her cage when ordered, 'more like a bear in a chain than a human being' (quoted from *The Times,* 26 November 1810, in Lindfors, unpublished paper). She created a considerable public stir. She was subsequently baptized in Manchester, married an African and had two children, spoke Dutch and learned some English, and, during a court case in Chancery, taken out to protect her from exploitation, declared herself 'under no restraint' and 'happy to be in England'. She then reappeared in Paris where she had an amazing public impact, until her fatal illness from smallpox in 1815.

Both in London and Paris, she became famous in two quite different circles: amongst the general public as a popular 'spectacle', commemorated in ballads, cartoons, illustrations, in melodramas and newspaper reports; and amongst the naturalists and ethnologists, who measured, observed, drew, wrote learned treatises about, modelled, made waxen moulds and plaster casts, and scrutinized every detail, of her anatomy, dead and alive (Figure 4.24). What attracted both audiences to her was not only her size (she was a diminutive four feet six inches tall) but her *steatopygia* – her protruding buttocks, a feature of Hottentot anatomy – and what was described as her 'Hottentot apron', an enlargement of the labia 'caused by the manipulation of the genitalia and considered beautiful by the Hottentots and Bushmen' (Gilman, 1985, p. 85). As someone crudely remarked, 'she could be said to carry her fortune behind her, for London may never before have seen such a "heavy-arsed heathen"' (quoted in Lindfors, ibid., p. 2).

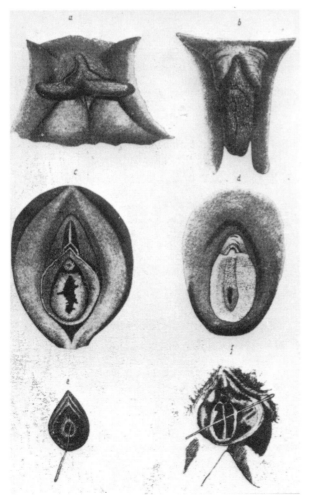

I want to pick out several points from 'The Hottentot Venus' example in relation to questions of stereotyping, fantasy and fetishism.

First, note the preoccupation – one could say the obsession – with *marking 'difference'*. Saartje Baartman became the embodiment of 'difference'. What's more, her difference was 'pathologized': represented as a pathological form of 'otherness'. Symbolically, she did not fit the ethnocentric norm which was applied to European women and, falling outside a western classificatory system of what 'women' are like, she had to be constructed as 'Other'.

Next, observe her reduction to Nature, the signifier of which was her *body*. Her body was 'read', like a text, for the living evidence – the proof, the Truth – which it provided of her absolute 'otherness' and therefore of an irreversible difference between the 'races'.

FIGURE 4.24 ... 'every detail of her anatomy': Sexual anomalies in women, from Cesare Lombroso and Guillaume Ferraro, *La donna deliquente: la prostituta e la donna normale* (Turin, L. Roux, 1893).

Further, she became 'known', represented and observed through a series of polarized, binary oppositions. 'Primitive', not 'civilized', she was assimilated to the Natural order – and therefore compared with wild beasts, like the ape or the orangutan – rather than to the Human Culture. This naturalization of difference was signified, above all, by her sexuality. She was reduced to her body and her body in turn was reduced to her sexual organs. They stood as the essential signifiers of her place in the universal scheme of things. In her, Nature and Culture coincided, and could therefore be substituted for one another, read off against one another. What was seen as her 'primitive' sexual genitalia signified her 'primitive' sexual appetite, and vice versa.

Next, she was subjected to an extreme form of reductionism – a strategy often applied to the representation of women's bodies, of whatever 'race', especially in pornography. The 'bits' of her that were preserved served, in an essentializing and reductionist manner, as 'a pathological summary of the entire individual' (Gilman, 1985, p. 88). In the models and casts of them which were preserved in the Musée De L'Homme, she was literally turned into a set of separate objects, into a thing – 'a collection of sexual parts'. She underwent a kind of symbolic dismantling or *fragmentation* – another technique familiar from both male and female pornography. We are reminded here of Frantz Fanon's description in *Black Skin, White Masks*, of the way he felt disintegrated, as a black man, by the look of the white person: 'the glances of the other fixed me there, in the sense in which a chemical solution is fixed by a dye. I was indignant; I demanded an explanation. Nothing happened. I burst apart. Now the fragments have been put together again by another self' (1986, p. 109). Saartje Baartman did not exist as 'a person'. She had been disassembled into her relevant parts. She was 'fetishized' – turned into an object. This substitution of a *part* for the *whole*, of a *thing* – an object, an organ, a portion of the body – for a *subject*, is the effect of a very important representational practice – *fetishism*.

Fetishism takes us into the realm where fantasy intervenes in representation; to the level where what is shown or seen, in representation, can only be understood in relation to what cannot be seen, what cannot be shown. *Fetishism* involves the substitution of an 'object' for some dangerous and powerful but forbidden force. In anthropology, it refers to the way the powerful and dangerous spirit of a god can be displaced on to an object – a feather, a piece of stick, even a communion wafer – which then becomes charged with the spiritual power of that for which it is a substitute. In Marx's notion of 'commodity fetishism', the living labour of the worker has been displaced and disappears into things – the commodities which workers produce but have to buy back as though they belonged to someone else. In psychoanalysis, 'fetishism' is described as the substitute for the 'absent' phallus – as when the sexual drive becomes displaced to some other part of the body. The substitute then becomes eroticized, invested with the sexual energy, power and desire which cannot find expression in the object to which it is really directed. *Fetishism* in representation borrows from all these

fetishism

FIGURE 4.25
Nuba wrestlers, by
George Rodger.

meanings. It also involves *displacement*. The phallus cannot be represented because it is forbidden, taboo. The sexual energy, desire and danger, all of which are emotions powerfully associated with the phallus, are transferred to another part of the body or another object, which substitutes for it.

An excellent example of this trope is the photograph of the two Nubian wrestlers from a book of photographs by the English documentarist, George Rodger (Figure 4.25). This image was appended in homage to the back cover of her book, *The Last of the Nuba* (1976) by Leni Riefenstahl, the former Nazi film-maker whose reputation was built upon the films she made of Hitler's 1934 Nuremberg rally (*Triumph of the Will*) and the 1936 Berlin Olympics (*Olympiad*).

Gilman (1985) describes a similar example of racial fetishism in the 'The Hottentot Venus'. Here the sexual object of the onlookers' gaze was *displaced* from her genitalia, which is what really obsessed them, to her buttocks. 'Female sexuality is tied to the image of the buttocks and the quintessential buttocks are those of the Hottentot' (p. 91).

disavowal   Fetishism, as we have said, involves **disavowal**. Disavowal is the strategy by means of which a powerful fascination or desire is both *indulged* and at the same time *denied*. It is where what has been tabooed nevertheless manages to find a displaced form of representation. As Homi Bhabha observes, 'It is a non-repressive form of knowledge that allows for the possibility of simultaneously embracing two contradictory beliefs, one official and one secret, one archaic and one progressive, one that allows the myth of origins, the other that articulates difference and division' (1986a, p. 168). Freud, in his remarkable essay on 'Fetishism', wrote:

> ...the fetish is the substitute for the woman's (the mother's) penis that the little boy once believed in and – for reasons familiar to us – does not want to give up. ... It is not true that the [male] child ... has preserved unaltered his belief that women have a phallus. He has retained the belief, but he has also given it up. In the conflict between the weight of the unwelcome perception and the force of his counter-wish, a compromise has been reached ...Yes, in his mind the woman *has* got a penis, in spite of everything; but the penis is no longer the same as it was before. Something else has taken its place, has been appointed its substitute ...

> (1977/1927, p. 353)

(We should note, incidentally, that Freud's tracing of the origin of fetishism back to the castration anxiety of the male child gives this trope the indelible stamp of a male-centred fantasy. The failure of Freud and much of later psychoanalysis to theorize female fetishism has been the subject of extended recent critique (see *inter alia*, McClintock, 1995).)

So, following the general logic of fetishism as a representational strategy, we could say of the Nubian wrestler, 'Though it is forbidden, I *can* look at the wrestler's genitals because they are no longer as they were. Their place has been taken by the head of his wrestling companion.' Thus, of Leni Riefenstahl's use of the Rodger photograph of the Nuba wrestlers, Kobena Mercer observes that 'Riefenstahl admits that her fascination with this East African people did not originate from an interest in their "culture" but from a photograph of two Nubian wrestlers by … George Rodger … In this sense her anthropological alibi for an ethnographic voyeurism is nothing more than the secondary elaboration, and rationalization, of the primal wish to see this lost image again and again' (1994a, p. 187).

Fetishism, then, is a strategy for having-it-both-ways: for both representing and not-representing the tabooed, dangerous or forbidden object of pleasure and desire. It provides us with what Mercer calls an 'alibi', what earlier we called a 'cover' or a 'cover-story'. We have seen how, in the case of 'The Hottentot Venus', not only is the gaze displaced from the genitalia to the buttocks; but also, this allows the observers to *go on looking* while disavowing the sexual nature of their gaze. Ethnology, science, the search for anatomical evidence here play the role as the 'cover', the disavowal, which allows the illicit desire to operate. It allows a double focus to be maintained – looking and not looking – an ambivalent desire to be satisfied. What is declared to be different, hideous, 'primitive', deformed, is at the same time being obsessively enjoyed and lingered over *because* it is strange, 'different', exotic. The scientists can look at, examine and observe Saartje Baartman naked and in public, classify and dissect every detail of her anatomy, on the perfectly acceptable alibi that 'it is all being done in the name of Science, of objective knowledge, ethnological evidence, in the pursuit of Truth'. This is what Foucault meant by knowledge and power creating a 'regime of truth'.

So, finally, fetishism licenses an unregulated *voyeurism*. Few could argue that the 'gaze' of the (largely male) onlookers who observed 'The Hottentot Venus' was disinterested. As Freud (1977/1927) argued, there is often a sexual element in 'looking', an eroticization of the gaze (an argument developed in Chapter 5). Looking is often driven by an unacknowledged search for illicit pleasure and a desire which cannot be fulfilled. 'Visual impressions remain the most frequent pathway along which libidinal excitation is aroused' (ibid., p. 96). We go on looking, even if there is nothing more to see. He called the obsessive force of this pleasure in looking, 'scopophilia'. It becomes perverse, Freud argued, only 'if restricted exclusively to the genitals, connected with the over-riding of disgust … or if, instead of being preparatory to the normal sexual aim, it supplants it' (ibid., p. 80).

Thus voyeurism is perfectly captured in the German caricature of the white gentleman observing 'The Hottentot Venus' through his telescope (Figure 4.26). He can look forever without being seen. But, as Gilman observes, look forever as he may, he 'can see nothing but her buttocks' (p. 91).

FIGURE 4.26 German caricature of man viewing the Hottentot Venus through a telescope, early nineteenth century.

5 Contesting a racialized regime of representation

So far we have analysed some examples from the archive of racialized representation in western popular culture of different periods (sections 1, 2 and 3), and explored the representational practices of difference and 'otherness' (especially section 4). It is time to turn to the final set of questions posed in our opening pages. Can a dominant regime of representation be challenged, contested or changed? What are the counter-strategies which can begin to subvert the representation process? Can 'negative' ways of representing racial difference, which abound in our examples, be reversed by a 'positive' strategy? What effective strategies are there? And what are their theoretical underpinnings?

Let me remind you that, theoretically, the argument which enables us to pose this question at all is the proposition (which we have discussed in several places and in many different ways) that *meaning can never be finally fixed*. If meaning could be fixed by representation, then there would be no change – and so no counter-strategies or interventions. Of course, we *do* make strenuous efforts to fix meaning – that is precisely what the strategies of stereotyping are aspiring to do, often with considerable success, for a time. But ultimately, meaning begins to slip and slide; it begins to drift, or be wrenched, or inflected into new directions. New meanings are grafted on to old ones. Words and images carry connotations over which no one has complete control, and these marginal or submerged meanings come to the surface, allowing different meanings to be constructed, different things to be shown and said. That is why we referred you to the work of Bakhtin and Volosinov in section 1.2. For they have given a powerful impetus to the practice of what has come to be known as **trans-coding**: taking an existing meaning and re-appropriating it for new meanings (e.g. 'Black is Beautiful').

trans-coding

A number of different *trans-coding* strategies have been adopted since the 1960s, when questions of representation and power acquired a centrality in the politics of anti-racist and other social movements. We only have space here to consider three of them.

5.1 Reversing the stereotypes

In the discussion of racial stereotyping in the American cinema, we discussed the ambiguous position of Sidney Poitier and talked about an *integrationist* strategy in US film-making in the 1950s. This strategy, as we said, carried heavy costs. Blacks could gain entry to the mainstream – but only at the cost of adapting to the white image of them and assimilating white norms of style, looks and behaviour. Following the Civil Rights movement, in the 1960s and 70s, there was a much more aggressive affirmation of black cultural identity, a positive attitude towards difference and a struggle over representation.

The first fruit of this counter-revolution was a series of films, beginning with *Sweet Sweetback's Baadasss Song* (Martin Van Peebles, 1971), and Gordon Parks' box-office success, *Shaft*. In *Sweet Sweetback*, Van Peebles values positively all the characteristics which would normally have been negative stereotypes. He made his black hero a professional stud, who successfully evades the police with the help of a succession of black ghetto low-lifers, sets fire to a police car, shafts another with a pool cue, lights out for the Mexican border, making full use of his sexual prowess at every opportunity, and ultimately gets away with it all, to a message scrawled across the screen: 'A BAADASSS NIGGER IS COMING BACK TO COLLECT SOME DUES'. *Shaft* was about a black detective, close to the streets but struggling with the black underworld and a band of black militants as well as the Mafia, who rescues a black racketeer's daughter. What marked *Shaft* out, however, was the detective's absolute lack of deference towards whites. Living in a smart apartment, beautifully turned out in casual but expensive clothes, he was presented in the advertising publicity as a 'lone black Super-spade – a man of flair and flamboyance who has fun at the expense of the white establishment'. He was 'a violent man who lived a violent life, in pursuit of black women, white sex, quick money, easy success, cheap "pot" and other pleasures' (Cripps, 1978, pp. 251–4). When asked by a policeman where he is going, Shaft replies, 'I'm going to get laid. Where are you going?' The instant success of *Shaft* was followed by a succession of films in the same mould, including *Superfly*, also by Parks, in which Priest, a young black cocaine dealer, succeeds in making one last big deal before retirement, survives both a series of violent episodes and vivid sexual encounters to drive off at the end in his Rolls Royce, a rich and happy man. There have been many later films in the same mould (e.g. *New Jack City*) with, at their centre (as the Rap singers would say), 'bad-ass black men, with attitude'.

We can see at once the appeal of these films, especially, though not exclusively, to black audiences. In the ways their heroes deal with whites, there is a remarkable absence, indeed a conscious reversal of, the old deference or childlike dependency. In many ways, these are 'revenge' films – audiences relishing the black heroes' triumphs over 'Whitey', loving the fact that they're getting away with it! What we may call the moral playing-field is levelled. Blacks are neither always worse nor always better than whites. They come in the usual human shapes – good, bad and indifferent. They are no different from the ordinary (white) average American in their tastes, styles, behaviour, morals, motivations. In class terms, they can be as 'cool', affluent and well groomed as their white counterparts. And their 'locations' are the familiar real-life settings of ghetto, street, police station and drug-bust.

At a more complex level, they placed blacks for the first time at the centre of the popular cinematic genres – crime and action films – and thus made them essential to what we may call the 'mythic' life and culture of the American cinema – more important, perhaps, in the end, than their 'realism'. For this is where the collective fantasies of popular life are worked out, and the exclusion of blacks from its confines made them precisely, peculiar, different, placed them 'outside the picture'. It deprived them of the celebrity status, heroic charisma, the glamour and pleasure of identification accorded to the white heroes of *film noir*, the old private eye, crime and police thrillers, the 'romances' of urban low-life and the ghetto. With these films, blacks had arrived in the cultural mainstream – with a vengeance!

These films carried through one counter-strategy with considerable single-mindedness – reversing the evaluation of popular stereotypes. And they proved that this strategy could secure box-office success and audience identification. Black audiences loved them because they cast black actors in glamorous and 'heroic' as well as 'bad' roles; white audiences took to them because they contained all the elements of the popular cinematic genres. Nevertheless, among some critics, the judgement on their success as a representational counter-strategy has become more mixed. They have come to be seen by many as 'blaxploitation' films.

ACTIVITY 11

Can you hazard a guess as to why they have come to be seen in this way?

·To reverse the stereotype is not necessarily to overturn or subvert it. Escaping the grip of one stereotypical extreme (blacks are poor, childish, subservient, always shown as servants, everlastingly 'good', in menial positions, deferential to whites, never the heroes, cut out of the glamour, the pleasure, and the rewards, sexual and financial) may simply mean being trapped in its stereotypical 'other' (blacks are motivated by money, love bossing white people around, perpetrate violence and crime as effectively as the next person, are 'bad', walk off with the goodies, indulge in drugs, crime and promiscuous sex, come on like 'Superspades' and *always get away with it!*). This may be an advance on the former list, and is certainly a welcome change. But it has not escaped the contradictions of the binary structure of racial stereotyping and it has not unlocked what Mercer and Julien call 'the complex dialectics of power and subordination' through which 'black male identities have been historically and culturally constructed' (1994, p. 137). The black critic, Lerone Bennett acknowledged that 'after it [*Sweet Sweetback* …] we can never again see black people in films (noble, suffering, losing) in the same way …' But he also thought it 'neither revolutionary nor black', indeed, a revival of certain 'antiquated white stereotypes', even 'mischievous and reactionary'. As he remarked, 'nobody ever fucked his way to freedom' (quoted in Cripps, 1978, p. 248). This is a critique which has, in retrospect, been delivered about the whole foregrounding of black masculinity during the Civil Rights movement, of which these films were undoubtedly a by-product. Black feminist critics have pointed out how the black resistance to white patriarchal power during the 1960s was often accompanied by the adoption of an exaggerated 'black male macho' style and sexual aggressiveness by black leaders towards black women (Michele Wallace, 1979; Angela Davis, 1983; bell hooks, 1992).

5.2 Positive and negative images

The second strategy for contesting the racialized regime of representation is the attempt to substitute a range of 'positive' images of black people, black life and culture for the 'negative' imagery which continues to dominate popular representation. This approach has the advantage of righting the balance. It is underpinned by an acceptance – indeed, a celebration – of difference. It inverts the binary opposition, privileging the subordinate term, sometimes reading the negative positively: 'Black is Beautiful'. It tries to construct a positive identification with what has been abjected. It greatly expands the *range* of racial representations and the *complexity* of what it

FIGURE 4.27
Photograph by
David A. Bailey.

means to 'be black', thus challenging the reductionism of earlier stereotypes. Much of the work of contemporary black artists and visual practitioners fall into this category. In the photographs specially taken to illustrate David

Bailey's critique of 'positive images' in 'Rethinking black representation' (1988), we see black men looking after children and black women politically organizing in public – giving the conventional meaning of these images a different inflection.

Underlying this approach is an acknowledgement and celebration of diversity and difference in the world. Another kind of example is the 'United Colours of Benneton' advertising series, which uses ethnic models, especially children, from many cultures and celebrates images of racial and ethnic hybridity. But here, again, critical reception has been mixed (Bailey, 1988). Do these images evade the difficult questions, dissolving the harsh realities of racism into a liberal mish-mash of 'difference'? Do these images *appropriate* 'difference' into a spectacle in order to sell a product? Or are they genuinely a political statement about the necessity for everyone to accept and 'live with' difference,

FIGURE 4.28 Photograph by David A. Bailey.

in an increasingly diverse, culturally pluralist world? Sonali Fernando (1992) suggests that this imagery 'cuts both ways: on the one hand suggesting a problematizing of racial identity as a complex dialectic of similarities as well as differences, but on the other ... homogenizing all non-white cultures as other.'

The problem with the positive/negative strategy is that adding positive images to the largely negative repertoire of the dominant regime of representation increases the diversity of the ways in which 'being black' is represented, but does not *necessarily* displace the negative. Since the binaries remain in place, meaning continues to be framed by them. The strategy challenges the binaries – but it does not undermine them. The peace-loving, child-caring Rastafarian can still appear, in the following day's newspaper, as an exotic and violent black stereotype ...

5.3 Through the eye of representation

The third counter-strategy locates itself *within* the complexities and ambivalences of representation itself, and tries to *contest it from within*. It is more concerned with the *forms* of racial representation than with introducing a new *content*. It accepts and works with the shifting, unstable character of meaning, and enters, as it were, into a struggle over representation, while acknowledging that, since meaning can never be finally fixed, there can never be any final victories.

FIGURE 4.29
Still from Isaac Julien's *Looking for Langston*, 1989.

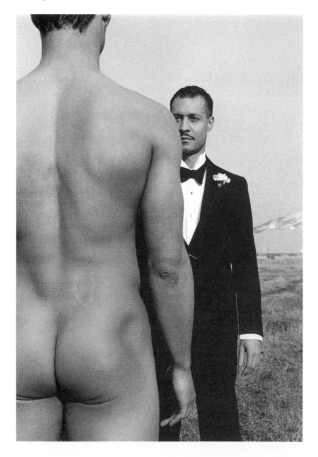

Thus, instead of avoiding the black body, because it has been so caught up in the complexities of power and subordination within representation, this strategy positively takes the body as the principal site of its representational strategies, attempting to make the stereotypes work against themselves. Instead of avoiding the dangerous terrain opened up by the interweaving of 'race', gender and sexuality, it deliberately contests the dominant gendered and sexual definitions of racial difference by *working on* black sexuality. Since black people have so often been fixed, stereotypically, by the racialized gaze, it may have been tempting to refuse the complex emotions associated with 'looking'. However, this strategy makes elaborate play with 'looking', hoping by its very attention, to 'make it strange' – that is, to de-familiarize it, and so make explicit what is often hidden – its erotic dimensions (Figure 4.29). It is not afraid to deploy humour – for example, the comedian, Lenny Henry, forces us by the witty exaggerations of his Afro-Caribbean caricatures, to laugh *with* rather than *at* his characters. Finally, instead of refusing the displaced power and danger of 'fetishism', this strategy attempts to use the desires and ambivalences which tropes of fetishism inevitably awaken.

ACTIVITY 12

Look first at Figure 4.30.

It is by Robert Mapplethorpe, a famous gay, white, American photographer, whose technically brilliant studies of black nude male models have sometimes been accused of fetishism and of fragmenting the black body, in order to appropriate it symbolically for his personal pleasure and desire.

Now look at Figure 4.31. It is by the gay, black, Yoruba photographer, Rotimi Fani-Kayode, who trained in the US and practised in London until his premature death, and whose images consciously deploy the tropes of fetishism, as well as using African and modernist motifs.

1 How far do these images, in your view, bear out the above comments about each photographer?

2 Do they use the tropes of representation in the same way?

3 Is their effect on the viewer – on the way you 'read' the images – the same? If not, what is the difference?

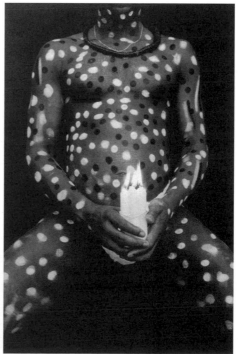

FIGURE 4.30 *Jimmy Freeman,* 1981, by Robert Mapplethorpe (Copyright © 1981 The Estate of Robert Mappelthorpe).

FIGURE 4.31 *Sonponnol,* 1987, by Rotimi Fani-Kayode.

Now read the brief extract from Kobena Mercer's essay 'Reading racial fetishism' (1994), in which he advances the argument against Mapplethorpe summarized above (Reading D at the end of this chapter).

At a later point, in a second part to the same essay, Mercer changed his mind. He argued that Mapplethorpe's aesthetic strategy exploits the ambivalent structure of fetishism (which affirms difference while at the same time denying it). It unsettles the fixity of the stereotypical 'white' gaze at the black body and reverses it:

> Blacks are looked down upon and despised as worthless, ugly and ultimately unhuman. But in the blink of an eye, whites look up to and revere black bodies, lost in awe and envy as the black subject is idealized as the embodiment of its aesthetic ideal.
>
> (Mercer, 1994, p. 201)

Mercer concludes:

> … it becomes necessary to reverse the reading of racial fetishism, not as a repetition of racist fantasies but as a deconstructive strategy, which begins to lay bare the psychic and social relations of ambivalence at play in cultural representations of race and sexuality.
>
> (ibid., p. 199)

ACTIVITY 13

Which of Mercer's two readings of fetishism in Mapplethorpe's work do you find most persuasive?

You won't expect 'correct' answers to my questions, for there are none. They are a matter of interpretation and judgement. I pose them to drive home the point about the complexity and ambivalences of representation as a practice, and to suggest how and why attempting to dismantle or subvert a racialized regime of representation is an extremely difficult exercise, about which – like so much else in representation – there can be no absolute guarantees.

6   Conclusion

In this chapter, we have pushed our analysis of representation as a signifying practice a good deal further, opening up some difficult and complex areas of debate. What we have said about 'race' can in many instances be applied to other dimensions of 'difference'. We have analysed many examples, drawn from different periods of popular culture, of how a racialized regime of representation emerged, and identified some of its characteristic strategies and tropes. In activities, we have tried to get you to *apply* some of these techniques. We have considered several theoretical arguments as to why 'difference' and otherness are of such central importance in cultural studies.

We have thoroughly unpacked *stereotyping as a representational practice*, looking at how it works (essentializing, reductionism, naturalization, binary oppositions), at the ways it is caught up in the play of power (hegemony, power/knowledge), and at some of its deeper, more unconscious effects (fantasy, fetishism, disavowal). Finally, we have considered some of the counter-strategies which have attempted to intervene in representation, *trans-coding* negative images with new meanings. This opens out into a 'politics of representation', a struggle over meaning which continues and is unfinished.

In the next chapter, the theme of *representation* is advanced further, some of the questions introduced here returning to centre stage. They include the relation between representation, sexuality and gender, issues around 'masculinity', the eroticization of 'the look' and questions about power and the subject.

References

BABCOCK, B. (1978) *The Reversible World: symbolic inversion in art and society*, Ithaca, NY, Cornell University Press.

BAILEY, D. (1988) 'Rethinking black representation' in *Ten/8,* No. 31, Birmingham.

BAKHTIN, M. (1981) *The Dialogic Imagination*, Austin, University of Texas. First published 1935.

BARTHES, R. (1977) 'Rhetoric of the image' in *Image–Music–Text*, Glasgow, Fontana.

BHABHA, H. (1986a) 'The Other question' in *Literature, Politics and Theory*, London, Methuen.

BHABHA, H. (1986b) 'Foreword' to Fanon, F. , *Black Skin, White Masks*, London, Pluto Press.

BOGLE, D. (1973) *Toms, Coons, Mulattoes, Mammies and Bucks: an interpretative history of blacks in American films*, New York, Viking Press.

BROWN, R. (1965) *Social Psychology*, London/New York, Macmillan.

CRIPPS , T. (1978) *Black Film as Genre*, Bloomington, IN, Indiana University Press.

DAVIS , A. (1983) *Women, Race and Class*, New York, Random House.

DERRIDA, J. (1972) *Positions*, Chicago, IL, University of Chicago Press.

DIAWARA, M. (ed.) (1993) *Black American Cinema*, New York, Routledge.

DOUGLAS, M. (1966) *Purity and Danger*, London, Routledge & Kegan Paul.

DU GAY, P., HALL, S., JANES, L., MACKAY, H. and NEGUS, K. (1997) *Doing Cultural Studies: the story of the Sony Walkman*, London, Sage/The Open University (Book 1 in this series).

DYER, R. (ed.) (1977) *Gays and Film*, London, British Film Institute.

DYER, R. (1986) *Heavenly Bodies*, Basingstoke, Macmillan/BFI.

FANON, F. (1986) *Black Skin, White Masks*, London, Pluto Press. First published 1952.

FERNANDO, S. (1992) 'Blackened Images' in Bailey, D. A. and Hall, S. (eds) *Critical Decade, Ten/8*, Vol. 2, No. 2, Birmingham.

FREDERICKSON, G. (1987) *The Black Image in the White Mind*, Hanover, NH, Wesleyan University Press.

FREUD, S. (1977) 'Fetishism' in *On Sexualities*, Pelican Freud Library, Vol.7, Harmondsworth, Penguin. First published 1927.

GAINES, J. (1993) 'Fire and desire: race, melodrama and Oscar Mischeaux' in Diawara, M. (ed.).

GATES, H. L. (1988) *The Signifying Monkey*, Oxford, Oxford University Press.

GILMAN, S. (1985) *Difference and Pathology*, Ithaca, NY, Cornell University Press.

GREEN, D. (1984) 'Classified subjects: photography and anthropology – the technology of power', *Ten/8*, No. 14, Birmingham.

HALL, C. (1994) *White, Male and Middle Class*, Cambridge, Polity Press.

HALL, S. (1972) 'Determinations of news photographs' in *Working Papers in Cultural Studies No. 3*, Birmingham, University of Birmingham.

HALL, S. (1981) 'The whites of their eyes' in Brunt, R. (ed.) *Silver Linings*, London, Lawrence and Wishart.

HALL, S. (1996) 'The after-life of Frantz Fanon' in Read, A. (ed.) *The Fact of Blackness: Frantz Fanon and visual representation*, Seattle, WA, Bay Press.

hooks, b. (1992) *Black Looks: race and representation*, Boston, MA, South End Press.

JORDAN, W. (1968) *White Over Black*, Chapel Hill, NC, University of North Carolina Press.

KLEIN, M (1957) *Envy and Gratitude*, New York, Delta.

KRISTEVA, J. (1982) *Powers of Horror*, New York, Columbia University Press.

LACAN, J. (1977) *Écrits*, London, Tavistock.

LEAB, D. (1976) *From Sambo to Superspade*, New York, Houghton Mifflin.

LÉVI-STRAUSS, C. (1970) *The Raw and the Cooked*, London, Cape.

LINDFORS, B. (unpublished) 'The Hottentot Venus and other African attractions'.

LONG, E. (1774) *History of Jamaica*, London, Lowdnes.

MACKENZIE, J. (ed.) (1986) *Imperialism and Popular Culture*, Manchester, Manchester University Press.

McCLINTOCK, A. (1995) *Imperial Leather*, London, Routledge.

MERCER, K. (ed.) (1994) *Welcome to the Jungle*, London, Routledge.

MERCER, K. (1994a) 'Reading racial fetishism' in Mercer, K. (ed.).

MERCER, K. and JULIEN, I. (1994) 'Black masculinity and the politics of race' in Mercer, K. (ed).

MORTON, P. (1991) *Disfigured Images*, New York, Praeger and Greenwood Press.

RICHARDS, T. (1990) *The Commodity Culture of Victorian Britain*, London, Verso.

RIEFENSTAHL, L. (1976) *The Last of the Nuba*, London, Collins.

SAID, E. (1978) *Orientalism*, Harmondsworth, Penguin.

SEGAL, L. (1997) 'Sexualities', Chapter 4 in Woodward, K. (ed.) *Identity and Difference*, London, Sage/The Open University (Book 3 in this series).

STALLYBRASS, P. and WHITE, A. (1986) *The Politics and Poetics of Transgression*, London, Methuen.

STAPLES, R. (1982) *Black Masculinity: the black man's role in American society*, San Fransisco, CA, Black Scholar Press..

WALLACE, M. (1979) *Black Macho*, London, Calder.

WALLACE, M. (1993) 'Race, gender and psychoanalysis in forties films' in Diawara, M. (ed.).

READING A:
Anne McClintock, 'Soap and commodity spectacle'

In 1899, the year that the Anglo-Boer War broke out in South Africa, an advertisement for Pears' Soap in *McClure's Magazine* [Figure 4.8a] announced:

> The first step towards lightening THE WHITE MAN'S BURDEN is through teaching the virtues of cleanliness. PEARS' SOAP is a potent factor in brightening the dark corners of the earth as civilization advances, while amongst the cultured of all nations it holds the highest place – it is the ideal toilet soap.

[...]

The first point about the Pears' advertisement is that it figures imperialism as coming into being through *domesticity*. At the same time, imperial domesticity is a domesticity without women. The commodity fetish, as the central form of the industrial Enlightenment, reveals what liberalism would like to forget: the domestic is political, the political is gendered. What could not be admitted into male rationalist discourse (the economic value of women's domestic labour) is disavowed and projected onto the realm of the 'primitive' and the zone of empire. At the same time, the economic value of colonized cultures is domesticated and projected onto the realm of the 'prehistoric'.

A characteristic feature of the Victorian middle class was its peculiarly intense preoccupation with rigid boundaries. In imperial fiction and commodity kitsch, boundary objects and liminal scenes recur ritualistically. As colonials travelled back and forth across the thresholds of their known world, crisis and boundary confusion were warded off and contained by fetishes, absolution rituals and liminal scenes. Soap and cleaning rituals became central to the demarcation of body boundaries and the policing of social hierarchies. Cleansing and boundary rituals are integral to most cultures; what characterized Victorian cleaning rituals, however, was their peculiarly intense relation to money.

[...]

Soap and commodity spectacle

Before the late nineteenth century, clothes and bedding washing was done in most households only once or twice a year in great, communal binges, usually in public at streams or rivers (Davidoff and Hall, 1992). As for body washing, not much had changed since the days when Queen Elizabeth I was distinguished by the frequency with which she washed: 'regularly every month whether we needed it or not'. By the 1890s, however, soap sales had soared, Victorians were consuming 260,000 tons of soap a year, and advertising had emerged as the central cultural form of commodity capitalism (Lindsey and Bamber, 1965).

[...]

Economic competition with the United States and Germany created the need for a more aggressive promotion of British products and led to the first real innovations in advertising. In 1884, the year of the Berlin Conference, the first wrapped soap was sold under a brand name. This small event signified a major transformation in capitalism, as imperial competition gave rise to the creation of monopolies. Henceforth, items formerly indistinguishable from each other (soap sold simply as soap) would be marketed by their corporate signature (Pears, Monkey Brand, etc.). Soap became one of the first commodities to register the historic shift from myriad small businesses to the great imperial monopolies. In the 1870s, hundreds of small soap companies plied the new trade in hygiene, but by the end of the century, the trade was monopolized by ten large companies.

In order to manage the great soap show, an aggressively entrepreneurial breed of advertisers emerged, dedicated to gracing each homely product with a radiant halo of imperial glamour and radical potency. The advertising agent, like the bureaucrat, played a vital role in the imperial expansion of foreign trade. Advertisers billed themselves as 'empire builders' and flattered themselves with 'the responsibility of the historic imperial mission'. Said one: 'Commerce even more than sentiment binds the ocean sundered portions of empire together. Anyone who increases these commercial interests strengthens the whole fabric of the empire' (quoted in Hindley and Hindley, 1972) Soap was credited not only with bringing moral and economic salvation to Britain's 'great unwashed' but also with magically embodying the spiritual ingredient of the imperial mission itself.

In an ad for Pears, for example, a black and implicitly racialized coal sweeper holds in his hands a glowing, occult object. Luminous with its own inner radiance, the simple soap bar glows like a fetish, pulsating magically with spiritual enlightenment and imperial grandeur, promising to warm the hands and hearts of working people across the globe (Dempsey, 1978). Pears, in particular, became intimately associated with a purified nature magically cleansed of polluting industry (tumbling kittens, faithful dogs, children festooned with flowers) and a purified working class magically cleansed of polluting labour (smiling servants in crisp white aprons, rosy-cheeked match girls and scrubbed scullions) (Bradley, 1991).

Nonetheless, the Victorian obsession with cotton and cleanliness was not simply a mechanical reflex of economic surplus. If imperialism garnered a bounty of cheap cotton and soap oils from coerced colonial labour, the middle class Victorian fascination with clean, white bodies and clean, white clothing stemmed not only from the rampant profiteering of the imperial economy but also from the realms of ritual and fetish.

Soap did not flourish when imperial ebullience was at its peak. It emerged commercially during an era of impending crisis and social calamity, serving to preserve, through fetish ritual, the uncertain boundaries of class, gender and race identity in a social order felt to be threatened by the fetid effluvia of the slums, the belching smoke of industry, social agitation, economic upheaval, imperial competition and anticolonial resistance. Soap offered the promise of spiritual salvation and regeneration through commodity consumption, a regime of domestic hygiene that could restore the threatened potency of the imperial body politic and the race.

The Pears' campaign

In 1789 Andrew Pears, a farmer's son, left his Cornish village of Mevagissey to open a barbershop in London, following the trend of widespread demographic migration from country to city and the economic turn from land to commerce. In his shop, Pears made and sold the powders, creams and dentifrices used by the rich to ensure the fashionable alabaster purity of their complexions. For the elite, a sun-darkened skin stained by outdoor manual work was the visible stigma not only of a class obliged to work under the elements for a living but also of far-off, benighted races marked by God's disfavour. From the outset, soap took shape as a technology of social purification, inextricably entwined with the semiotics of imperial racism and class denigration.

In 1838 Andrew Pears retired and left his firm in the hands of his grandson, Francis. In due course, Francis's daughter, Mary, married Thomas J Barratt, who became Francis' partner and took the gamble of fashioning a middle-class market for the transparent soap. Barratt revolutionized Pears by masterminding a series of dazzling advertising campaigns. Inaugurating a new era of advertising, he won himself lasting fame, in the familiar iconography of male birthing, as the 'father of advertising'. Soap thus found its industrial destiny through the mediation of domestic kinship and that peculiarly Victorian preoccupation with patrimony.

Through a series of gimmicks and innovations that placed Pears at the centre of Britain's emerging commodity culture, Barratt showed a perfect understanding of the fetishism that structures all advertising. Importing a quarter of a million French centime pieces into Britain, Barratt had the name Pears stamped on them and put the coins into circulation – a gesture that marvellously linked exchange value with the corporate brand name. The ploy worked famously, arousing much publicity for Pears and such a public fuss that an Act of Parliament was rushed through to declare all foreign coins illegal tender. The boundaries of the national currency closed around the domestic bar of soap.

Georg Lukács points out that the commodity lies on the threshold of culture and commerce, confusing the supposedly sacrosanct boundaries between aesthetics and economy, money and art. In the mid-1880s, Barratt devised a piece of breathtaking cultural transgression that exemplified Lukács insight and clinched Pears' fame. Barratt bought Sir John Everett Millais' painting 'Bubbles' (originally entitled 'A Child's World') and inserted into the painting a bar of soap stamped with the totemic word *Pears*. At a stroke, he transformed the artwork of the best-known painter in Britain into a mass produced commodity associated in the public mind with Pears. [1] At the same time, by mass reproducing the painting as a poster ad, Barratt took art from the elite realm of private property to the mass realms of commodity spectacle. [2]

In advertising, the axis of possession is shifted to the axis of spectacle, Advertising's chief contribution to the culture of modernity was the discovery that by manipulating the semiotic space around the commodity, the unconscious as a public space could also be manipulated. Barratt's great innovation was to invest huge sums of money in the creation of a visible aesthetic space around the commodity. The development of poster and print technology made possible the mass reproduction of such a space around the image of a commodity (see Wicke, 1988, p.70).

In advertising, that which is disavowed by industrial rationality (ambivalence, sensuality, chance, unpredictable causality, multiple time) is projected onto image space as a repository of the forbidden. Advertising draws on subterranean flows of desire and taboo, manipulating the investment of surplus money. Pears' distinction, swiftly emulated by scores of soap companies including Monkey Brand and Sunlight, as well as countless other advertisers, was to invest the aesthetic space around the domestic commodity with the commercial cult of empire.

Notes

1 Barratt spent £2,200 on Millais' painting and £30,000 on the mass production of millions of individual reproductions of the painting. In the 1880s, Pears was spending between £300,000 and £400,000 on advertising alone.

2 Furious at the pollution of the sacrosanct realm of art with economics, the art world lambasted Millais for trafficking (publicly instead of privately) in the sordid world of trade.

References

BRADLEY, L. (1991) 'From Eden to Empire: John Everett Millais' Cherry Ripe', *Victorian Studies*, Vol. 34, No. 2 (Winter 1991), pp. 179-203.

DAVIDOFF, L. and HALL, C. (1992) *Family Fortunes: Men and Women of the English Middle Class*, London, Routledge.

DEMPSEY, M. (ed.) (1978) *Bubbles: early advertising art from A. & F.Pears Ltd.*, London, Fontana.

HINDLEY, D. and HINDLEY, G. (1972) *Advertising in Victorian England, 1837-1901*, London, Wayland.

LINDSEY, D.T.A. and BAMBER, G.C. (1965) *Soap-making, Past and Present*, 1876-1976, Nottingham, Gerard Brothers Ltd.

WICKE, J. (1988) *Advertising Fiction: Literature, Advertisement and Social Reading,* New York, Columbia University Press.

Source: McClintock, 1995, pp. 32–33 and 210–213.

READING B:
Richard Dyer, 'Africa'

An initial problem was that of knowing what Africa was like. There is an emphasis in much of the work Robeson is associated with on being authentic. The tendency is to assume that if you have an actual African doing something, or use actual African languages or dance movements, you will capture the truly African. In the African dream section of *Taboo* (1922), the first professional stage play Robeson was in, there was 'an African dance done by C. Kamba Simargo, a native' (Johnson, 1968/ 1930, p. 192); for *Basalik* (1935), 'real' African dancers were employed (Schlosser, 1970, p. 156). The titles for *The Emperor Jones* (1933) tell us that the tom-toms have been 'anthropologically recorded', and several of the films use ethnographic props and footage – *Sanders of the River* (1934, conical huts, kraals, canoes, shields, calabashes and spears, cf. Schlosser, 1970, p. 234), *Song of Freedom* (1936, Devil Dancers of Sierra Leone, cf. ibid., p. 256) and *King Solomon's Mines* (1936). Princess Gaza in *Jericho* (1937) is played by the real life African princess Kouka of Sudan. Robeson was also widely known to have researched a great deal into African culture; his concerts often included brief lectures demonstrating the similarity between the structures of African folk song and that of other, both Western and Eastern, cultures (see Schlosser, 1970, p. 332). However, this authentication of the African elements in his work is beset with problems. In practice, these are genuine notes inserted into works produced decidedly within American and British discourses on Africa. These moments of song, dance, speech and stage presence are either inflected by the containing discourses as Savage Africa or else remain opaque, folkloric, touristic. No doubt the ethnographic footage of dances in the British films records complex ritual meanings, but the films give us no idea what these are and so they remain mysterious savagery. Moreover, as is discussed later, Robeson himself is for the most part distinguished from these elements rather than identified with them; they remain 'other'. This authentication enterprise also falls foul of being only empirically authentic – it lacks a concern with the paradigms through which one observes any empirical phenomenon. Not only are the 'real' African elements left undefended from their immediate theatrical or filmic context, they have already been perceived through discourses on Africa that have labelled them primitive, often with a flattering intention.

This is not just a question of white, racist views of Africa. It springs from the problem, as Marion Berghahn (1977) notes, that black American knowledge of Africa also comes largely through white sources. It has to come to terms with the image of Africa in those sources, and very often in picking out for rejection the obvious racism there is a tendency to assume that what is left over is a residue of transparent knowledge about Africa. To put the problem more directly, and with an echo of DuBois' notion of the 'twoness' of the black American – when confronting Africa, the black Westerner has to cope with the fact that she or he is of the West. The problem, and its sometimes bitter ironies, is illustrated in two publicity photos from Robeson films. The first, from the later film *Jericho*, shows Robeson with Wallace Ford and Henry Wilcoxon during the filming in 1937 [Figure 4.20]. It is a classic tourist photo, friends snapped before a famous landmark. Robeson is dressed in Western clothes, and grouped between the two white men; they are even, by chance no doubt, grouped at a break in the row of palm trees behind them. They are not part of the landscape, they are visiting it.

References

BERGHAHN, M. (1977) *Images of Africa in Black American Literature*, Totawa NJ, Rowman and Littlefield.

JOHNSON, J. W. (1968) *Black Manhattan*, New York, Atheneum. First published 1930.

POLHEMUS, T. and PROCTOR, L. (1978) *Fashion and Anti-Fashion*, London, Thames and Hudson.

SCHLOSSER, A.I. (1970) 'Paul Robeson, his career in the theatre, in motion pictures, and on the concert stage', unpublished PhD dissertation, New York University.

Source: Dyer, 1986, pp. 89–91.

READING C:
Sander Gilman, 'The deep structure of stereotypes'

Everyone creates stereotypes. We cannot function in the world without them (see, for example, Levin, 1975). They buffer us against our most urgent fears by extending them, making it possible for us to act as though their source were beyond our control.

The creation of stereotypes is a concomitant of the process by which all human beings become individuals. Its beginnings lie in the earliest stages of our development. The infant's movement from a state of being in which everything is perceived as an extension of the self to a growing sense of a separate identity takes place between the ages of a few weeks and about five months.[1] During that stage, the new sense of 'difference' is directly acquired by the denial of the child's demands on the world. We all begin not only by demanding food, warmth, and comfort, but by assuming that those demands will be met. The world is felt to be a mere extension of the self. It is that part of the self which provides food, warmth, and comfort. As the child comes to distinguish more and more between the world and self, anxiety arises from a perceived loss of control over the world. But very soon the child begins to combat anxieties associated with the failure to control the world by adjusting his mental picture of people and objects so that they can appear 'good' even when their behaviour is perceived as 'bad' (Kohut, 1971).

But even more, the sense of the self is shaped to fit this pattern. The child's sense of self itself splits into a 'good' self, which, as the self mirroring the earlier stage of the complete control of the world, is free from anxiety, and the 'bad' self, which is unable to control the environment and is thus exposed to anxieties. This split is but a single stage in the development of the normal personality. In it lies, however, the root of all stereotypical perceptions. For in the normal course of development the child's understanding of the world becomes seemingly ever more sophisticated. The child is able to distinguish ever finer gradations of 'goodness' and 'badness', so that by the later oedipal stage an illusion of verisimilitude is cast over the inherent (and irrational) distinction between the 'good' and 'bad' world and self,

between control and loss of control, between acquiescence and denial.

With the split of both the self and the world into 'good' and 'bad' objects, the 'bad' self is distanced and identified with the mental representation of the 'bad' object. This act of projection saves the self from any confrontation with the contradictions present in the necessary integration of 'bad' and 'good' aspects of the self. The deep structure of our own sense of self and the world is built upon the illusionary image of the world divided into two camps, 'us' and 'them'. 'They' are either 'good' or 'bad'. Yet it is clear that this is a very primitive distinction which, in most individuals, is replaced early in development by the illusion of integration.

Stereotypes are a crude set of mental representations of the world. They are palimpsests on which the initial bipolar representations are still vaguely legible. They perpetuate a needed sense of difference between the 'self' and the 'object', which becomes the 'Other'. Because there is no real line between self and the Other, an imaginary line must be drawn; and so that the illusion of an absolute difference between self and Other is never troubled, this line is as dynamic in its ability to alter itself as is the self. This can be observed in the shifting relationship of antithetical stereotypes that parallel the existence of 'bad' and 'good' representations of self and Other. But the line between 'good' and 'bad' responds to stresses occurring within the psyche. Thus paradigm shifts in our mental representations of the world can and do occur. We can move from fearing to glorifying the Other. We can move from loving to hating. The most negative stereotype always has an overtly positive counterweight. As any image is shifted, all stereotypes shift. Thus stereotypes are inherently protean rather than rigid.

Although this activity seems to take place outside the self, in the world of the object, of the Other, it is in fact only a reflection of an internal process, which draws upon repressed mental representations for its structure. Stereotypes arise when self-integration is threatened. They are therefore part of our way of dealing with the instabilities of our perception of the world. This is not to say that they are good, only that they are necessary. We can and must make the distinction between pathological stereotyping and the stereotyping all of us need to do to preserve our illusion of control over the self and the world. Our Manichean perception of the world as 'good' and 'bad' is triggered by a recurrence of the type of insecurity that induced our initial division of the world into 'good' and 'bad'. For the pathological personality every confrontation sets up this echo. Stereotypes can and often do exist parallel to the ability to create sophisticated rational categories that transcend the crude line of difference present in the stereotype. We retain our ability to distinguish the 'individual' from the stereotyped class into which the object might automatically be placed. The pathological personality does not develop this ability and sees the entire world in terms of the rigid line of difference. The pathological personality's mental representation of the world supports the need for the line of difference, whereas for the non-pathological individual the stereotype is a momentary coping mechanism, one that can be used and then discarded once anxiety is overcome. The former is consistently aggressive toward the real people and objects to which the stereotypical representations correspond; the latter is able to repress the aggression and deal with people as individuals.

Notes

1 I am indebted to Otto Kernberg's work for this discussion.

References

KERNBERG, O. (1980) *Internal World and External Reality: Object Relations Theory Applied*, New York, Jason Aronson.

KERNBERG, O. (1984) *Severe Personality Disorders: Psychotherapeutic Strategies*, New Haven, Conn., Yale University Press.

KOHUT, H. (1971) *The Analysis of Self,* New York, International Universities Press.

LEVIN, J. (1975) *The Functions of Prejudice*, New York, Harper and Row.

Source: Gilman, 1985, pp. 16–18.

READING D:
Kobena Mercer, 'Reading racial fetishism'

Mapplethorpe first made his name in the world of art photography with his portraits of patrons and protagonists in the post-Warhol New York avant-garde milieu of the 1970s. In turn he [became] something of a star himself, as the discourse of journalists, critics, curators and collectors [wove] a mystique around his persona, creating a public image of the artist as author of 'prints of darkness'. As he [...] extended his repertoire across flowers, bodies and faces, the conservatism of Mapplethorpe's aesthetic [became] all too apparent: a reworking of the old modernist tactic of 'shock the bourgeoisie' (and make them pay), given a new aura by his characteristic signature, the pursuit of perfection in photographic technique. The vaguely transgressive quality of his subject matter – gay S/M ritual, lady bodybuilders, black men – is given heightened allure by his evident mastery of photographic technology.

In as much as the image-making technology of the camera is based on the mechanical reproduction of unilinear perspective, photographs primarily represent a 'look'. I therefore want to talk about Mapplethorpe's *Black Males* not as the product of the personal intentions of the individual behind the lens, but as a cultural artifact that says something about certain ways in which white people 'look' at black people and how, in this way of looking, black male sexuality is perceived as something different, excessive, Other. Certainly this particular work must be set in the context of Mapplethorpe's oeuvre as a whole: through his cool and deadly gaze each found object – 'flowers, S/M, blacks' – is brought under the clinical precision of his master vision, his complete control of photo-technique, and thus aestheticized to the abject status of thinghood. However, once we consider the author of these images as no more than the 'projection, in terms more or less psychological, of our way of handling texts' (Foucault, 1977, p. 127), then what is interesting about work such as *The Black Book* is the way the text facilitates the imaginary projection of certain racial and sexual fantasies about the black male body. Whatever his personal motivations or creative pretensions, Mapplethorpe's camera-eye opens an aperture onto aspects of stereotypes – a fixed way of seeing that freezes the flux of experience – which govern the circulation of images of black men across a range of surfaces from newspapers, television and cinema to advertising, sport and pornography.

Approached as a textual system, both *Black Males* (1983) and *The Black Book* (1986) catalogue a series of perspectives, vantage points and 'takes' on the black male body. The first thing to notice – so obvious it goes without saying – is that all the men are *nude*. Each of the camera's points of view lead to a unitary vanishing point: an erotic/aesthetic objectification of black male bodies into the idealized form of a homogenous type thoroughly saturated with a totality of sexual predicates. We look through a sequence of individual, personally named, Afro-American men, but what we *see* is only their *sex* as the essential sum total of the meanings signified around blackness and maleness. It is as if, according to Mapplethorpe's line of sight: Black + Male = Erotic/Aesthetic Object. Regardless of the sexual preferences of the spectator, the connotation is that the 'essence' of black male identity lies in the domain of sexuality. Whereas the photographs of gay male S/M rituals invoke a subcultural sexuality that consists of *doing* something, black men are confined and defined in their very *being* as sexual and nothing but sexual, hence hypersexual. In pictures like 'Man in a Polyester Suit,' apart from his hands, it is the penis and the penis alone that identifies the model in the picture as a black man.

This ontological reduction is accomplished through the specific visual codes brought to bear on the construction of pictorial space. Sculpted and shaped through the conventions of the fine art nude, the image of the black male body presents the spectator with a source of erotic pleasure in the act of looking. As a generic code established across fine art traditions in Western art history, the conventional subject of the nude is the (white) female body. Substituting the socially inferior black male subject, Mapplethorpe nevertheless draws on the codes of the genre to frame his way of seeing black male bodies as abstract, beautiful 'things'. The aesthetic, and thus erotic, objectification is totalizing in effect, as all references to a social, historical or political context are ruled out of the frame. This visual codification abstracts and essentializes the black man's body

into the realm of a transcendental aesthetic ideal. In this sense, the text reveals more about the desires of the hidden and invisible white male subject behind the camera and what 'he' wants-to-see, than it does about the anonymous black men whose beautiful bodies we see depicted.

Within the dominant tradition of the female nude, patriarchal power relations are symbolized by the binary relation in which, to put it crudely, men assume the active role of the looking subject while women are passive objects to be looked at. Laura Mulvey's (1989 [1975]) contribution to feminist film theory revealed the normative power and privilege of the male gaze in dominant systems of visual representation. The image of the female nude can thus be understood not so much as a representation of (hetero)sexual desire, but as a form of objectification which articulates masculine hegemony and dominance over the very apparatus of representation itself. Paintings abound with self-serving scenarios of phallocentric fantasy in which male artists paint themselves painting naked women, which, like depictions of feminine narcissism, constructs a mirror image of what the male subject wants-to-see. The fetishistic logic of mimetic representation, which makes present for the subject what is absent in the real, can thus be characterized in terms of a masculine fantasy of mastery and control over the 'objects' depicted and represented in the visual field, the fantasy of an omnipotent eye/I who sees but who is never seen.

In Mapplethorpe's case, however, the fact that both subject and object of the gaze are male sets up a tension between the active role of looking and the passive role of being looked at. This *frisson* of (homo)sexual sameness transfers erotic investment in the fantasy of mastery from gender to racial difference. Traces of this metaphorical transfer underline the highly charged libidinal investment of Mapplethorpe's gaze as it bears down on the most visible signifier of racial difference – black skin. In his analysis of the male pinup, Richard Dyer (1982) suggests that when male subjects assume the passive, 'feminized' position of being looked at, the threat or risk to traditional definitions of masculinity is counteracted by the role of certain codes and conventions, such as taut, rigid or straining bodily posture, character types and narrativized plots, all of which aim to stabilize the gender-based dichotomy of seeing/being seen.

Here Mapplethorpe appropriates elements of commonplace racial stereotypes in order to regulate, organize, prop up and *fix* the process of erotic/aesthetic objectification in which the black man's flesh becomes burdened with the task of symbolizing the transgressive fantasies and desires of the white gay male subject. The glossy, shining, fetishized surface of black skin thus serves and services a white male desire to look and to enjoy the fantasy of mastery precisely through the scopic intensity that the pictures solicit.

As Homi Bhabha has suggested, 'an important feature of colonial discourse is its dependence on the concept of "fixity" in the ideological construction of otherness' (Bhabha, 1983, p. 18). Mass-media stereotypes of black men – as criminals, athletes, entertainers – bear witness to the contemporary repetition of such *colonial fantasy*, in that the rigid and limited grid of representations through which black male subjects become publicly visible continues to reproduce certain *idées fixes,* ideological fictions and psychic fixations, about the nature of black sexuality and the 'otherness' it is constructed to embody. As an artist, Mapplethorpe engineers a fantasy of absolute authority over the image of the black male body by appropriating the function of the stereotype to stabilize the erotic objectification of racial otherness and thereby affirm his own identity as the sovereign I/eye empowered with mastery over the abject thinghood of the Other: as if the pictures implied, Eye have the power to turn you, base and worthless creature, into a work of art. Like Medusa's look, each camera angle and photographic shot turns black male flesh to stone, fixed and frozen in space and time: enslaved as an icon in the representational space of the white male imaginary, historically at the centre of colonial fantasy.

There are two important aspects of fetishization at play here. The erasure of any social interference in the spectator's erotic enjoyment of the image not only reifies bodies but effaces the material process involved in the production of the image, thus masking the social relations of racial power entailed by the unequal and potentially exploitative exchange between the well-known, author-named artist and the unknown, interchangeable, black models. In the same way that labor is said to be 'alienated' in commodity fetishism, something

similar is put into operation in the way that the proper name of each black model is taken from a person and given to a thing, as the title or caption of the photograph, an art object which is property of the artist, the owner and author of the look. And as items of exchange-value, Mapplethorpe prints fetch exorbitant prices on the international market in art photography.

The fantasmatic emphasis on mastery also underpins the specifically sexual fetishization of the Other that is evident in the visual isolation effect whereby it is only ever *one* black man who appears in the field of vision at any one time. As an imprint of a narcissistic, ego-centred, sexualizing fantasy, this is a crucial component in the process of erotic objectification, not only because it forecloses the possible representation of a collective or contextualized black male body, but because the solo frame is the precondition for a voyeuristic fantasy of unmediated and unilateral control over the other which is the function it performs precisely in gay and straight pornography. Aestheticized as a trap for the gaze, providing pabulum on which the appetite of the imperial eye may feed, each image thus nourishes the racialized and sexualized fantasy of appropriating the Other's body as virgin territory to be penetrated and possessed by an all-powerful desire, 'to probe and explore an alien body'.

Superimposing two ways of seeing – the nude which eroticizes the act of looking, and the stereotype which imposes fixity – we see in Mapplethorpe's gaze a reinscription of the fundamental *ambivalence* of colonial fantasy, oscillating between sexual idealization of the racial other and anxiety in defence of the identity of the white male ego. Stuart Hall (1982) has underlined this splitting in the 'imperial eye' by suggesting that for every threatening image of the black subject as a marauding native, menacing savage or rebellious slave, there is the comforting image of the black as docile servant, amusing clown and happy entertainer. Commenting on this bifurcation in racial representations, Hall describes it as the expression of

> both a nostalgia for an innocence lost forever to the civilized, and the threat of civilization being over-run or undermined by the recurrence of savagery, which is always lurking just below the

surface; or by an untutored sexuality threatening to 'break out'.

(Hall, 1982, p. 41)

In Mapplethorpe, we may discern three discrete camera codes through which this fundamental ambivalence is reinscribed through the process of a sexual and racial fantasy which aestheticizes the stereotype into a work of art.

The first of these, which is most self-consciously acknowledged, could be called the *sculptural* code, as it is a subset of the generic fine art nude. [In the photograph of the model, Phillip, pretending to put the shot], the idealized physique of a classical Greek male statue is superimposed on that most commonplace of stereotypes, the black man as sports hero, mythologically endowed with a 'naturally' muscular physique and an essential capacity for strength, grace and machinelike perfection: well hard. As a major public arena, sport is a key site of white male ambivalence, fear and fantasy. The spectacle of black bodies triumphant in rituals of masculine competition reinforces the fixed idea that black men are 'all brawn and no brains', and yet, because the white man is beaten at his own game — football, boxing, cricket, athletics — the Other is idolized to the point of envy. This schism is played out daily in the popular tabloid press. On the front page headlines, black males become highly visible as a threat to white society, as muggers, rapists, terrorists and guerrillas: their bodies become the imago of a savage and unstoppable capacity for destruction and violence. But turn to the back pages, the sports pages, and the black man's body is heroized and lionized; any hint of antagonism is contained by the paternalistic infantilization of Frank Bruno and Daley Thompson to the status of national mascots and adopted pets — they're not Other, they're OK because they're 'our boys'. The national shame of Englands' demise and defeat in Test Cricket at the hands of the West Indies is accompanied by the slavish admiration of Viv Richards's awesome physique — the high-speed West Indian bowler is both a threat and a winner. The ambivalence cuts deep into the recess of the white male imaginary — recall those newsreel images of Hitler's reluctant handshake with Jesse Owens at the 1936 Olympics.

If Mapplethorpe's gaze is momentarily lost in admiration, it reasserts control by also 'feminizing'

the black male body into a passive, decorative *objet d'art*. When Phillip is placed on a pedestal he literally becomes putty in the hands of the white male artist — like others in this code, his body becomes raw material, mere plastic matter, to be molded, sculpted and shaped into the aesthetic idealism of inert abstraction [...]. Commenting on the differences between moving and motionless pictures, Christian Metz suggests (1985, p.85) an association linking photography, silence and death as photographs invoke a residual death effect such that, 'the person who has been photographed is dead... dead for having been seen'. Under the intense scrutiny of Mapplethorpe's cool, detached gaze it is as if each black model is made to die, if only to reincarnate their alienated essence as idealized, aesthetic objects. We are not invited to imagine what their lives, histories or experiences are like, as they are silenced as subjects in their own right, and in a sense sacrificed on the pedestal of an aesthetic ideal in order to affirm the omnipotence of the master subject, whose gaze has the power of light and death.

In counterpoint there is a supplementary code of *portraiture* which 'humanizes' the hard phallic lines of pure abstraction and focuses on the face — the 'window of the soul' — to introduce an element of realism into the scene. But any connotation of humanist expression is denied by the direct look which does not so much assert the existence of an autonomous subjectivity, but rather, like the remote, aloof, expressions of fashion models in glossy magazines, emphasizes instead maximum distance between the spectator and the unattainable object of desire. Look, but don't touch. The models' direct look to camera does not challenge the gaze of the white male artist, although it plays on the active/passive tension of seeing/being seen, because any potential disruption is contained by the subtextual work of the stereotype. Thus in one portrait the 'primitive' nature of the Negro is invoked by the profile: the face becomes an after-image of a stereotypically 'African' tribal mask, high cheekbones and matted dreadlocks further connote wildness, danger, exotica. In another, the chiseled contours of a shaved head, honed by rivulets of sweat, summon up the criminal mug shot from the forensic files of police photography. This also recalls the anthropometric uses of photography in the colonial scene, measuring the cranium of the colonized so as to show, by the documentary evidence of photography, the inherent 'inferiority' of the Other. This is overlaid with deeper ambivalence in the portrait of Terrel, whose grotesque grimace calls up the happy/sad mask of the nigger minstrel: humanized by racial pathos, the Sambo stereotype haunts the scene, evoking the black man's supposedly childlike dependency on ole Massa, which in turn fixes his social, legal and existential 'emasculation' at the hands of the white master.

Finally, two codes together – of *cropping* and *lighting* – interpenetrate the flesh and mortify it into a racial sex fetish, a juju doll from the dark side of the white man's imaginary. The body-whole is fragmented into microscopic details – chest, arms, torso, buttocks, penis – inviting a scopophilic dissection of the parts that make up the whole. Indeed, like a talisman, each part is invested with the power to evoke the 'mystique' of black male sexuality with more perfection than any empirically unified whole. The camera cuts away, like a knife, allowing the spectator to inspect the 'goods'. In such fetishistic attention to detail, tiny scars and blemishes on the surface of black skin serve only to heighten the technical perfectionism of the photographic print. The cropping and fragmentation of bodies – often decapitated, so to speak – is a salient feature of pornography, and has been seen from certain feminist positions as a form of male violence, a literal inscription of a sadistic impulse in the male gaze, whose pleasure thus consists of cutting up women's bodies into visual bits and pieces. Whether or not this view is tenable, the effect of the technique here is to suggest aggression in the act of looking, but not as racial violence or racism-as-hate; on the contrary, aggression as the frustration of the ego who finds the object of his desires out of reach, inaccessible. The cropping is analogous to striptease in this sense, as the exposure of successive body parts distances the erotogenic object, making it untouchable so as to tantalize the drive to look, which reaches its aim in the denouement by which the woman's sex is unveiled. Except here the unveiling that reduces the woman from angel to whore is substituted by the unconcealing of the black man's private parts, with the penis as the forbidden totem of colonial fantasy.

As each fragment seduces the eye into ever more intense fascination, we glimpse the dilation of a libidinal way of looking that spreads itself across the surface of black skin. Harsh contrasts of shadow and light draw the eye to focus and fix attention on the texture of the black man's skin. According to Bhabha, unlike the sexual fetish *per se,* whose meanings are usually hidden as a hermeneutic secret, skin color functions as '*the most visible of fetishes*' (Bahbha, 1983, p. 30). Whether it is devalorized in the signifying chain of 'negrophobia' or hypervalorized as a desirable attribute in 'negrophilia', the fetish of skin color in the codes of racial discourse constitutes the most visible element in the articulation of what Stuart Hall (1977) calls 'the ethnic signifier'. The shining surface of black skin serves several functions in its representation: it suggests the physical exertion of powerful bodies, as black boxers always glisten like bronze in the illuminated square of the boxing ring; or, in pornography, it suggests intense sexual activity 'just before' the photograph was taken, a metonymic stimulus to arouse spectatorial participation in the imagined *mise-en-scène*. In Mapplethorpe's pictures the specular brilliance of black skin is bound in a double articulation as a fixing agent for the fetishistic structure of the photographs. There is a subtle slippage between representer and represented, as the shiny, polished, sheen of black skin becomes consubstantial with the luxurious allure of the high-quality photographic print. As Victor Burgin has remarked (1980, p. 100), sexual fetishism dovetails with commodity-fetishism to inflate the economic value of the print in art photography as much as in fashion photography, the 'glossies'. Here, black skin and print surface are bound together to enhance the pleasure of the white spectator as much as the profitability of these art-world commodities exchanged among the artist and his dealers, collectors and curators.

In everyday discourse *fetishism* probably connotes deviant or 'kinky' sexuality, and calls up images of leather and rubberwear as signs of sexual perversity. This is not a fortuitous example, as leather fashion has a sensuous appeal as a kind of 'second skin'. When one considers that such clothes are invariably black, rather than any other color, such fashion-fetishism suggests a desire to simulate or imitate black skin. On the other hand, Freud's theorization of fetishism as a clinical phenomenon of sexual pathology and perversion is problematic in many ways, but the central notion of the fetish as a metaphorical substitute for the absent phallus enables understanding of the psychic structure of disavowal, and the splitting of levels of conscious and unconscious belief, that is relevant to the ambiguous axis upon which negrophilia and negrophobia intertwine.

For Freud (1977 [1927], pp. 351-7), the little boy who is shocked to see the absence of the penis in the little girl or his mother, which he believes has either been lost or castrated, encounters the recognition of sexual or genital difference with an accompanying experience of anxiety which is nevertheless denied or disavowed by the existence of a metaphorical substitute, on which the adult fetishist depends for his access to sexual pleasure. Hence, in terms of a linguistic formula: I *know* (the woman has no penis), *but* (nevertheless, she does, through the fetish).

Such splitting is captured precisely in 'Man in a Polyester Suit', as the central focus on the black penis emerging from the unzipped trouser fly simultaneously affirms and denies that most fixed of racial myths in the white male imaginary, namely the belief that every black man has a monstrously large willy. The scale of the photograph foregrounds the size of the black dick which thus signifies a threat, not the threat of racial difference as such, but the fear that the Other is more sexually potent than his white master. As a phobic object, the big black prick is a 'bad object', a fixed point in the paranoid fantasies of the negrophobe which Fanon found in the pathologies of his white psychiatric patients as much as in the normalized cultural artefacts of his time. Then as now, in front of this picture, 'one is no longer aware of the Negro, but only of a penis; the Negro is eclipsed. He is turned into a penis. He *is* a penis' (Fanon, 1970, p. 120). The primal fantasy of the big black penis projects the fear of a threat not only to white womanhood, but to civilization itself, as the anxiety of miscegenation, eugenic pollution and racial degeneration is acted out through white male rituals of racial aggression – the historical lynching of black men in the United States routinely involved the literal castration of the Other's strange fruit. The myth of penis size – a 'primal fantasy' in the mythology of white supremacy in the sense that it is shared and collective in nature – has been the target of enlightened liberal demystification as the modern science of sexology repeatedly embarked

on the task of measuring empirical pricks to demonstrate its untruth. In post-Civil Rights, post-Black Power America, where liberal orthodoxy provides no available legitimation for such folk myths, Mapplethorpe enacts a disavowal of this ideological 'truth': I *know* (it's not true that all black guys have huge willies) *but* (nevertheless, in my photographs, they do).

References

BHABHA, H.K. (1983) 'The other question: the stereotype and colonial discourse', *Screen*, Vol. 24, No. 4.

BURGIN, V. (1980) 'Photography, fantasy, fiction', *Screen*, Vol. 21, No. 1.

DYER, R. (1982) 'Don't look now – the male pin-up', *Screen*, Vol. 23, Nos 3/4.

FANON, F. (1970) *Black Skin, White Masks*, London, Paladin.

FOUCAULT, M. (1977) 'What is an author?' in *Language, Counter-Memory, Practice*, Oxford, Basil Blackwell.

FREUD, S. (1977 [1927]) 'Fetishism', *Pelican Freud Library*, 7, 'On Sexuality', Harmondsworth, Pelican.

HALL, S. (1977) 'Pluralism, race and class in Caribbean society', in *Race and Class in Post-Colonial Society*, New York, UNESCO.

HALL, S. (1982) 'The whites of their eyes: racist ideologies and the media', in Bridges, G. and Brunt, R. (eds) *Silver Linings: some strategies for the eighties*, London, Lawrence and Wishart.

MAPPLETHORPE, R. (1983) *Black Males,* Amsterdam, Gallerie Jurka.

MAPPLETHORPE, R. (1986) *The Black Book*, Munich, Schirmer/Mosel.

METZ, C. (1985) 'Photography and fetish', *October*, Vol. 34 (Fall).

MULVEY, L. (1989) *Visual and Other Pleasures*, London, Macmillan. First published 1975.

Source: Mercer, 1994a, pp. 173–85.

EXHIBITING MASCULINITY

Sean Nixon

Contents

292

1 Introduction

Writing in the advertising trade magazine *Campaign* in July 1986, the critic George Melly offered a brief review of a group of adverts (see Figure 5.1). In the review he pondered on the emergence of what he saw as a new use of 'sex' in the process of selling: the use, as he put it, of 'men as passive sex objects' (Melly, 1986, p. 41). Commenting on the television adverts for the jeans manufacturer Levi-Strauss's recently relaunched 501 jeans, Melly noted:

> Jeans have always carried a heavy erotic charge, but the young man who gets up, slips into a pair and then slides into a bath (the water seeps over him in a most suggestive manner) is really pushing it ... there is no question that this method of presenting beefcake is strongly voyeuristic.

> (Melly, 1986, p. 41)

Writing from within academic cultural studies in 1988, Frank Mort was also struck by the visual presentation of the male body within the same Levis adverts. He emphasized what he saw as the sexualization of the male body produced through the presentation of the jeans, arguing:

> ... the sexual meanings in play [in the adverts] are less to do with macho images of strength and virility (though these are certainly still present) than with the fetished and narcissistic display – a visual erotica. These are bodies to be looked at (by oneself and other men?) through fashion codes and the culture of style.

> (Mort, 1988, p. 201)

(a) 'Launderette'

(b) 'Bath'

FIGURE 5.1 Television advertisements for Levi 501 jeans, 1985–6, Bartle Bogle Hegarty.

By fetishizing, he meant the intense focusing on objects like belt and button-fly as Nick Kamen and James Mardle (the models) undressed in the adverts. By narcissism, he meant the foregrounding of the pleasures associated with the dressing and grooming of the body.

It is these new visual codings of masculinity identified by Melly and Mort which this chapter sets out to explore. There is good reason for such an enquiry. The adverts these authors cite were not isolated images. Rather, the Levis adverts formed part of a phenomenon. From the mid-1980s there has been a proliferation of images of this sort, and 1986 was a particularly rich year in this process. Along with the broadcasting of the Levis adverts, the advertising agency Tony Hodges and Partners put together a press campaign for Shulton GB's new prestige male fragrance 'Grey Flannel' in August. Appearing in 'style magazines' like *The Face*, the advert

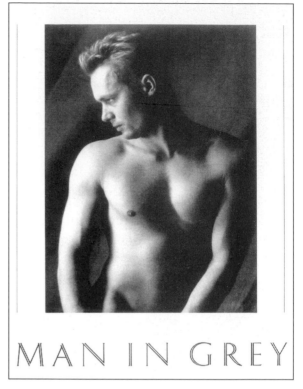

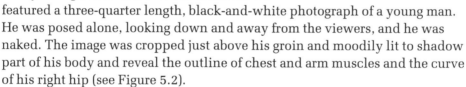

FIGURE 5.2
'Man in Grey', magazine advert, 1986–7, Tony Hodges & Partners agency.

featured a three-quarter length, black-and-white photograph of a young man. He was posed alone, looking down and away from the viewers, and he was naked. The image was cropped just above his groin and moodily lit to shadow part of his body and reveal the outline of chest and arm muscles and the curve of his right hip (see Figure 5.2).

A foregrounding of similar physical characteristics (the developed arm and chest muscles), together with highly groomed hair and skin, also figured in the range of male pin-ups featured on posters, postcards and greetings cards sold by the Athena chain. The best-selling image from 1986 featured a young man cradling a small baby in his muscular arms. Again, reproduced in black and white, the image gave a close-up view of the surface of the male body (see Figure 5.3). The summer of 1986 also saw the launch of a press and poster campaign by Grey Advertising for Beecham's Brylcreem. The campaign featured a range of masculine images, all playing on the 'look' of early 1960s' neat and respectable masculinity (itself associated with Brylcreem adverts from this period). The images were subtly updated, however, displaying the highly groomed hair and skin of the models and – in the case of two of the images – their developed arm and upper-body muscles.

This explosion of new imagery had direct connections to changes in consumer markets. By far the biggest slice of it was associated with developments in three men's markets: menswear, grooming products and toiletries, and consumer magazines. In each of these markets, new products were produced (like new ranges of fragrances or new magazines) or the marketing of existing

FIGURE 5.3
This image featured on posters, postcards and greetings cards sold by the Athena chain

products was reworked (through new packaging or advertising) so as to appeal to what producers and service-providers identified as new groups of male consumers. The emergence of new designs in menswear was particularly significant in this process. It was the innovations in menswear design – for example, broader shouldered suits, more flamboyant coloured ties, shirts and knitwear, figure-hugging sportswear lines – which established the key terms for the coding of the 'new man' as a distinctive new version of masculinity. It was through the presentation of these menswear designs in popular representations that the 'new man' was often coded. One important site where this presentation occurred was within menswear shops and I want to come back to these shops later (in section 6). In this chapter, then, I want to reflect on the cultural significance of the 'new man' images which were linked to these men's markets and consider the meaning of these images in relation to established notions of masculinity and masculine culture. In other words, I want to ask what do these images mean? What do they tell us about the changing meaning of masculinity in the 1980s and 1990s? And what are the consequences of these shifts in the way masculinity is being represented for gender relations as a whole?

In setting about this task, I will focus on the images found in the fashion pages of men's 'style' and 'lifestyle' magazines. There are two reasons for privileging these magazines. First, it was within magazine fashion photography that these images initially emerged. Secondly, it was within this form that the images were most extensively elaborated. In developing a reading of these fashion images, I also want to advance a more general argument about the representation process itself, its centrality to the formation of cultural identities (in this case masculinities), and to reflect on the role of spectatorship and looking in this process. The aims of the chapter can be summarized as follows:

- To develop the argument that gender identities are not unitary and fixed, but rather are subject to social and historical variation.

- To analyse the role of systems of representation in shaping the attributes and characteristics of masculinity as they are lived by men.

- To develop the usefulness of Michel Foucault's conceptualization of discourse in analysing visual representations.

● To offer a reading of the significance of the versions of masculinity coded within the 'new man' imagery.

● To explore the debate between Foucauldian and psychoanalytically informed approaches to conceptualizing the impact of these visual representations on the consumers of them.

● To locate historically the forms of looking or spectatorship associated with the 'new man' imagery.

2   Conceptualizing masculinity

Getting to grips with the 'new man' imagery in ways which focus critically upon its relationship to masculinity and masculine culture requires a more general conceptualization of masculinity. In this section, I want to offer you what I think are some key precepts for this task by drawing upon an expanding body of literature on masculinity (much of it now written by men). The starting-point for this body of work remains the critique which feminists have advanced over the past twenty years. Central to these injunctions has been an analysis of men's power and from this a problematizing of the dominant and exclusive forms of masculinity which were seen to underpin it. What these injunctions have emphasized, then, has been the negative effects of dominant definitions of masculinity on women's relationships with men in both the public and private worlds.

This critique by feminists established the terms on which the early writing by men on masculinity attempted to piece together conceptually a picture of the attributes and characteristics which made up this problematic category of masculinity. The earliest of this work, influenced by the sexual politics of the 1970s, was strongly associated with the men's anti-sexist movement. This was a grouping of usually middle-class men living within urban centres (like Birmingham and London in the UK, San Francisco in the USA), generally associated with radical or communitarian politics and typically connected to feminism through partners and friends. The counter-culture and an interest in therapy were also recurrent influences on the men involved in the men's anti-sexist movement.

What emerged from this early writing was a particular account of masculinity. In books like *The Sexuality of Men* (Metcalf and Humphries, 1985), published in 1985 and representing the most nuanced strand of this body of writing on masculinity, the authors described a masculinity characterized by aggression, competitiveness, emotional ineptitude and coldness, and dependent upon an overriding and exclusive emphasis on penetrative sex. In addition, however, for the authors in *The Sexuality of Men*, what also emerged, as men began to reflect critically on masculinity, was a sense of the fears, anxieties and pain expressed by these men in relation to established scripts of masculinity: anxieties about sexual performance, estrangement from emotions, and poor relations with fathers.

A contradictory picture of masculinity was produced in books such as *The Sexuality of Men*. On the one hand, a singular or unitary conception of masculinity was advanced: one that was effectively seen as synonymous with men's dominance over women; while, on the other hand, the burden of masculinity for men was also emphasized.

2.1 Plural masculinities

It is both this unitary conception of masculinity and the confessional emphasis on the burden of masculinity for men which more recent work on masculinity has challenged. The central claim of this more recent work has been an insistence on the plural forms of masculinity against the reductive conception found in works like *The Sexuality of Men*. A concern to speak about masculinities in the plural has become an important starting-point for this recent work. Some historical writings have proved illuminating in this regard. Jeffrey Weeks has charted historically the formation of a range of (largely masculine) sexual identities from the late eighteenth century onwards. These accounts – particularly in *Sex, Politics and Society*, and *Sexuality and its Discontents* (Weeks, 1981, 1985) – emphasized the impact of what Weeks called the sexual tradition in setting the big terms for the shaping of contemporary sexualities. As Weeks shows, the interventions of the sexologists and medical men (discussed at length by **Segal**, 1997) in categorizing the sexually perverse – and especially homosexuality towards the end of the nineteenth century – were part and parcel of the general tightening of definitions and norms of masculinities during the Victorian period. In the process, any signs of homosexuality in men were assumed to preclude the full acquisition of a 'true' masculinity. Homosexuality placed its subject in a position of inversion and effeminacy or, at least, of belonging to a 'third sex'.

Weeks's accounts underline the need for historical specificity in conceptualizing masculinities. The best examples of contemporary work take this demonstration of specificity further, emphasizing not only the determinants of historical period and sexuality on shaping masculinity, but also those of class, 'race', ethnicity and generation. What emerges from this work is a conception of masculinities produced as the result of the articulation or interweaving of particular attributes of masculinity with other social variables. There is an emphasis, then, on the way in which the gendering of identity is always already interwoven with other factors. For example, Catherine Hall, in her essay 'Missionary stories: gender and ethnicity in England in the 1830s and 1840s' (1992), makes a strong case for the way a particular kind of ethnicity and 'racial' characteristics – that of white Englishness – was central to the sense of manliness as it was lived by missionary men working in the Caribbean in the period after 1830. In Hall's view, it is impossible to isolate the elements which make up the masculinity of these men without recognizing their dependence upon ethnicity – Englishness – and 'race' – whiteness. Developing a sense of this articulation of masculinity with other social variables is important to the account of the 'new man' which I advance later in this chapter. As you will see, what looms large is the centrality of generation, ethnicity and 'race' to the distinctiveness of the kinds of masculinity that emerged around the figure of the 'new man' in the 1980s.

2.2 Thinking relationally

Insisting upon the differentiation between versions of masculinity does not in itself, however, produce an adequate conceptualization of masculinity. A second key strand of contemporary writing on masculinity is the insistence that particular versions of masculinity are not only constituted in their difference from other versions of masculinity but are also defined in relation to femininity. This suggests, then, that an adequate understanding of masculinity requires our locating it within the wider field of gender relations as a whole; that is, in relation to the contemporary formations of femininity. An example drawn from Davidoff and Hall's *Family Fortunes* (1987) demonstrates the importance of doing this.

Family Fortunes charts the formation of the English middle class from 1780 to 1850, largely through the personal writings of middle-class men and women. In the book, Davidoff and Hall emphasize not only the way emergent forms of middle-class masculinity in this period were defined against both working-class and aristocratic forms of masculinity, but also that a hardening of gender differences – the attributes and characteristics of men and women – within middle-class culture itself – was also central to middle-class men's specific sense of masculinity.

The professionalization of middle-class work that grew apace in the period they cover is important to the formation of middle-class masculinity in Davidoff and Hall's account. Middle-class men's involvement in production, design, building, accountancy and insurance involved quite specific forms of knowledge and skill. The mastery of these procedures – of assessing risk, of accountancy methods, of dealing with capital and investment – represented a set of practices and symbolic forms through which a middle-class manliness was staked out. These competences, as quintessentially manly tasks and skills, were counterposed, not only to the repertoire of skills and competencies associated with aristocratic masculinity (such as the valuing of gambling, sport and sexual prowess) and to the craft skills of artisanal masculinity, but also to the characteristics of middle-class femininity.

Davidoff and Hall also argue that the competences of middle-class manhood were consolidated through a range of formal and informal institutions (such as scientific and professional societies, gatherings at men's clubs). These represented public spaces where the contours of middle-class masculinity were reaffirmed. The chapel was also an important public place where this masculinity was shaped. Practising Christianity, and the rituals associated with communion, forged these men's masculinity as a Christian manhood. As Davidoff and Hall suggest, religious observance shaped and dignified middle-class work through its extension of established Protestant notions of the religious calling and 'doing God's duty in the world' (ibid., p. 111). Enterprise and business acumen were worldly solutions to the service of God.

Doing God's work in a broader sense – the work of winning souls for salvation – also fostered what Davidoff and Hall call 'a stress on moral earnestness, the belief in the power of love and a sensitivity to the weak and the helpless' (ibid., p. 110). These moral dispositions and emotional languages amounted to a specific repertoire of conduct that set middle-class men apart from, again, aristocratic masculinity. The validation of piety and forms of manly emotion went together with an increasing sobriety of dress amongst middle-class men. These dress codes confirmed the different cultural space occupied by middle-class and aristocratic men, and set clear boundaries between masculine and feminine appearance amongst the middle class. The 'gorgeous plumage' of eighteenth-century men's attire fell foul of what J. C. Flugel called the 'great masculine renunciation': in came 'stiff, dark, heavy materials, shapeless nether garments, and narrow black ties … the ubiquitous trousers and coat' (ibid., p. 142).

The creation of the middle-class home in the late eighteenth and early nineteenth centuries formed another determinant of the attributes and characteristics of middle-class manliness. Davidoff and Hall devote a long chapter to the factors that shaped the development of a distinctive middle-class version of the household and 'home': the production of 'my own private fireside'. A central element in its production was the robust demarcation of the public and private worlds. The home became the site of the distinctive 'elementary community of which larger communities and ultimately the nation are constituted' (ibid., p. 321), and also a place removed from the world (particularly of work) – separated literally by gates, hedges, walls. The suburban villa stood as the epitome of this new middle-class 'home'; safely distanced from the urban context and its proximity of classes, and offering a flavour of the rustic. It was women, as Davidoff and Hall suggest, who were mainly responsible for creating and servicing the home. And in the demarcation of the public and private, a gendering of the two spheres was increasingly produced: acting in the world through business and social reform, middle-class men staked out key parts of their masculinity in a public sphere that was more and more associated with their masculinity; while the private, domestic realm became the limit of middle-class women's sphere of action. This domestic space, however, as Davidoff and Hall argue, played an important role in middle-class men's masculinity as they moved between the world of the home and the world of public life. These men operated with a powerful investment in domestic harmony as the reward for enterprise as well as the basis of public virtue (ibid., p. 18).

The centrality of being able to provide for a household of dependants – in particular a wife – manifested a fierce independence that was important to these middle-class men. This masculine independence was increasingly characterized from the 1830s, as Catherine Hall suggests, by the way it was articulated through a specific English ethnicity. The authority of middle-class men was defined through their power over a range of dependants in the territories of Empire, as well as at home (Hall, 1992).

Always thinking relationally about masculinity – both in terms of the relations between masculinities and in terms of the relations between masculinity and femininity – forces us to consider the power relations operating in and through these relations. Clearly – as contemporary sexual politics has insisted – the field of gender relations is not a powerless universe. It is possible to see in Davidoff and Hall's work that middle-class men's masculinity was not only different from middle-class femininity but was also defined in a position of dominance over it. For some writers, the power relations which mediate gender relations – the relations between masculinity and femininity – point to a recognizable system of patriarchy (Alexander and Taylor, 1994; Walby, 1986). I do not want to explore the concept of patriarchy in this chapter, but I do want to signal a few problems with it as they relate to my arguments about the 'new man'. One central problem concerns the way in which it advances a universal model of the power relations between the genders – one that is weak on the historical specificity of the categories of gender and variations in the relations between them in different periods. In particular, the concept of patriarchy is weak at explaining the relations of power between different masculinities. I think that an adequate account of the field of gender relations, in addition to analysing the relations between masculinity and femininity, also needs to explore the relations of domination and subordination operating between different formations of masculinity. Rather than mobilize the concept of patriarchy, then, I want to suggest that we need to move away from a picture of the field of gender relations as always divided in the same way around the poles of masculine domination and feminine subordination. Rather, a more plural model of power relations is needed – one which grasps the multiple lines of power which position different masculinities and femininities in relation to each other at different times. An important pay-off from this conceptualization is that it allows us to consider dominant, subordinate and oppositional forms of masculinity. This is important because, as John Tosh and Michael Roper (1992) have argued, the field of gender relations has historically included forms of resistance to (as well as collusion with) prevailing notions of gender, on the part of groups of men. Such a conception, of course, allows us to situate the groups of men associated with, for example, contemporary sexual politics; men (like those of the men's anti-sexist movement, with whom I begin this section) who form a part of the biggest contemporary challenge to the established alignment of gender relations.

2.3 Invented categories

I want to make a further point about conceptualizing masculinity, which draws this section to a close and leads us into the next one. Underpinning all these arguments about masculinity drawn from recent sociological, historical and cultural analysis is the assertion that masculinity is not a fixed and unitary category. In other words, it is argued that there is no true essence of masculinity guaranteed by God or nature which we could appeal to in analysing men's gender identities. Rather, like all identities, masculinities are, to borrow Jeffrey Weeks's phrase, **invented categories** (Weeks, 1991). They are the product of the cultural meanings attached to certain attributes, capacities, dispositions and forms of conduct at given historical moments. Asserting their invented status, however, is not to diminish the force of these categories over us. To argue that masculinities are invented or constructed and therefore lack the guarantee of a foundation (which the idea of rooting masculinity in biology or divinity clearly offers) is not to argue that they are insubstantial. Quite the reverse. Identities are *necessary constructions* or *necessary fictions* (to deploy another phrase from Weeks). We need them to operate in the world, to locate ourselves in relation to others and to organize a sense of who we are. Emphasizing the invented character of identities, however, does direct us towards the processes through which identities are forged or fictioned. Such an enterprise leads us to the cultural or symbolic work involved in this process. It is my central contention that a large part of the symbolic work through which the meanings historically associated with masculinity are produced takes place within particular cultural languages. In other words, I am emphasizing the constitutive role of representation in the formation of the attributes and characteristics of masculinity through which real historical men come to live out their identities as gendered individuals. Cultural languages or systems of representation, then, are not a reflection of a pre-given masculinity fixed outside of representation. Rather, they actively construct the cultural meanings we give to masculinities. It is to how we might understand the dynamics of these images and the wider system of cultural languages of which they form a part that the next section is devoted. Before I do that, though, let me summarize the key implications of this section for our analysis of the 'new man' imagery.

(margin note: invented categories)

2.4 Summary of section 2

1   I have argued that there is more than one version of masculinity, which means that we have to attend to the specificity of the 'new man' version of masculinity – that is, how the attributes and characteristics associated with it differ from other versions of masculinity which have existed at different periods.

2   I have insisted that relations of power operate both between masculinity and femininity and between different masculinities. This means that we need to consider how the 'new man' version of masculinity fits into the established ranking of masculinities. Does it reinforce dominant scripts of masculinity or does it disturb these dominant scripts?

3   I have argued for the need to locate particular versions of masculinity within the wider field of gender relations. This means being sensitive to the positioning of the 'new man' in relation to femininity. Does the 'new man' version of masculinity reproduce masculine privileges?

3 Discourse and representation

A persistent theme running through this volume is that forms of representation are not best understood within the terms of what we have called reflective or mimetic theories of representation (see Chapter 1). The key influence here has been post-Saussurian theories of language. You will recall that the central contribution of this body of work is its insistence on the active, productive work of language or representation. Language does not simply reflect or passively transmit meanings fixed or established elsewhere – whether in the intention of a speaking or writing individual or in a stable external reality. Rather, what is emphasized is the way in which language is a structured system through which meaning is produced. Pre-eminent in this formulation is Saussure's attention to rules which govern the production of meaning within the structured system which makes up language. These rules – the rules of signification – point to the mechanism through which language generates meaning. It is this necessary submission of meaning production to the rules of signification which is the key to Saussure's conception of language. This general argument about the constitutive role of representation was a major influence on Roland Barthes. As you saw in Chapter 1, Barthes took up Saussure's ambition to extend semiology from written and spoken language to a wider field of cultural languages.

Barthes's work has proved influential on the cultural analysis of visual representations. However, as you saw in Chapters 1 and 3, as we move from Barthes to Foucault we encounter an author who (while he shares the general position of Saussure and Barthes on the constitutive role of representation) breaks in important ways with the semiotic approach to analysing representations. You may already feel comfortable with Foucault's formulations. However, I want to rehearse again briefly the pertinent elements of his arguments as they inform the reading of the 'new man' which I advance in this chapter. Later in the chapter (in section 5.5), I want to return to Foucault's work and open out the way he theorizes the process of subjection or subjectivization to discourse. In doing this, I will be developing a thread in Foucault's work only briefly considered so far in this volume.

3.1 Discourse, power/knowledge and the subject

You will recall from Chapter 1 that Foucault's understanding of discourse shifts attention away from the formal analysis of the universal workings of language proposed by Saussure (and developed by Barthes) towards an analysis of the rules and practices which shape and govern what is sayable and knowable in any given historical moment. In this sense, Foucault uses discourse or discursive formations to refer to groups of statements which provide a way of representing a particular topic, concern or object. These statements might be produced across a number of different texts and appear at more than one institutional site, but are connected by a regularity or underlying unity. In Foucault's later work, this attention to the way discourses make possible certain kinds of representation and knowledge was tied in with a greater attention to the apparatuses and institutions through which discursive formations operated. You will recall that Stuart Hall suggested in Chapter 1 that this new focus in Foucault's work marked his increased interest in exploring the way specific social practices – what individuals did – were regulated by discourse. Central to this focus in Foucault's work was an attention to the way knowledge about certain issues or topics was inextricably linked with the workings of power. Thus, knowledge for Foucault – especially that associated with the growth of the human sciences – was connected with a concern amongst experts and professionals to regulate and control the habits and actions of the wider population and particular groups of individuals. In Chapter 1, you saw how this concern with regulation worked in positive or productive ways by generating new kinds of knowledge and representations. In addition, you also saw how the body emerged in Foucault's work as the privileged point of articulation of modern regulatory forms of power.

Foucault's conception of discourse also offers a particular account of the place of the subject in relation to discourse. In common with the work of Saussure and Barthes, Foucault problematized traditional notions of the subject which see it as the source and guarantee of meaning in relation to language, representation and knowledge. Rather, as Stuart Hall discusses in his analysis of Velasquez' painting *Las Meninas* in Chapter 1, Foucault emphasized the way the subject was itself produced in discourse. This was a central insistence for Foucault. He argued that there was no possibility of a secret, essential form of subjectivity outside of discourse. Rather, discourses themselves were the bearers of various subject-positions: that is, specific positions of agency and identity in relation to particular forms of knowledge and practice.

The consequences of these aspects of Foucault's conception of discourse or discursive formations for our analysis of the 'new man' can be summarized in five points:

1   Foucault's arguments about discursive formations invite us to focus not on one or two privileged images of the 'new man', but to grasp the regularities which linked the different manifestations of the 'new man' imagery together across different sites of representation. Thus, we need to be alert to the way the 'new man' surfaced not just in television adverts, but in shop interiors, magazine spreads, postcards and posters.

2   Foucault's arguments about discursive specificity remind us of the need to be attentive to the specific discursive codes and conventions through which masculinity is signified within magazine publishing, retail design and advertising. These are centrally codes to do with the body, appearance and individual consumption and they will colour the kinds of masculinity it is possible to represent.

3   Foucault's insistence on the operation of power through discursive regimes opens up the possibility of analysing the power relations which function in the construction of these images. Power will be productive in the constitution of masculinity through specific visual codes, marking out

certain visual pleasures and forms of looking. It will also fix the boundaries between the normal and abnormal, the healthy and the sick, the attractive and the unattractive, and so on.

4 Foucault's emphasis on the institutional dimension of discourses directs us towards the way the 'new man' images were rooted within specific institutional practices (within menswear retailing, magazine publishing, advertising) and forces us to be alert to the particular forms of knowledge and expertise which are associated with the representations at each of these sites.

5 Foucault's contention about the discursive production of subjectivity allows us to think of the emergence of the 'new man' as, precisely, a new subject-position opened up within the contemporary visual discourse of fashion, style and individual consumption. It is to a reflection on the novelty of the visual codes associated with the regime of 'new man' representations that I now want to turn.

4   Visual codes of masculinity

I began this chapter by citing the television adverts for Levi-Strauss's 501 jeans. As we saw, for both George Melly and Frank Mort, these adverts threw up a distinctively new set of codings of masculinity within the domain of popular culture. In introducing the 'new man' imagery through these examples, we got a preliminary sense of the novelty of these codings. What stood out, as Melly and Mort suggested, was a new framing of the surface of men's bodies; one that emphasized not so much the assertive power of a muscular masculine physique as its passive sexualization. In Mort's phrase, these were men's bodies openly inviting a desiring look. In this section, I want to explore in more detail the novelty of the 'new man' codings and the forms of spectatorship associated with them; specifically, the forms of spectatorship staged between the men in the images and the groups of men at whom the images were principally targeted. In doing so I want to focus not on television adverts nor on the images deployed in menswear shops, but rather on the images of the 'new man' found within the fashion pages of 'style' and 'lifestyle' magazines for men.

As a way of organizing my reading of these images, I want to begin by delimiting the scope of what I have to say. One of the significant characteristics of the magazine fashion photography produced over the last decade is the range of new codings of masculinity. In other words, we do not find only one version of the 'new man' represented across these fashion images. This is an important finding in itself. It suggests that we need to think about a range of new codings which share a loose family resemblance. In part because of this range of codings, I want to focus on what I think are three important 'looks' produced across these 'new man' images. These are:

1   The 'street style' version.

2   The 'Italian-American' version.

3   The 'conservative Englishness' version.

I want to begin with the 'street style' version. This is because it was principally through these fashion images that a recognizable version of the 'new man' first emerged.

4.1 'Street style'

Let us start with the code of casting (see Figures 5.4 and 5.5). This is a very important code in fashion photography. It relates to the selection of certain physical characteristics in the choice of the model, the connotations of his particular physical 'look'. In Figure 5.4, the model chosen is young, with strong, well-defined features. Together these elements produce a mixture of boyish softness – connoted through the clear skin (and re-connoted by the hat pushed back on his head) – and an assertive masculinity – connoted through the hard edge of his features and the facial tattoo. This combination of 'boyishness' and 'hardness' represents one of a number of contradictory elements of masculinity held together in images associated with 'street style' codings of this sort. This combination of 'soft and hard' is reinforced by the casting of a light-black model. This casting is important and is repeated in Figure 5.5 (in fact, it is the same model, Simon de Montford). In terms of the signification of masculinity, it brings into play two connotations: an equivalence of 'light-black' with sensuality, and of 'black masculinity' with hypermasculinity.

What do I mean by this? This use of black masculinity to signify hypermasculinity has a long history, shaped by a pathologizing of blackness, and has been the site historically of pronounced fantasies about black men's sexuality and physical prowess (Mercer and Julien, 1988; see also Chapter 4 of this volume, section 4.3). These connotations of black masculinity operate as an important trace within the signification of the light-black male; they impart to it the connotations of an assertive masculinity. However, 'light-black' has a partially separate set of connotations. The light-black model makes acceptable or sanctions this otherwise threatening black masculine sensuality. It does this through the indices of skin tone and features. The casting of the light-black model makes possible the playing off of 'soft' and 'hard'.

In the selection of the clothes, Figures 5.4 and 5.5 bring together elements of workwear (the white T-shirt worn under a shirt in Figure 5.4) and strong outerwear (the wool jacket and heavy-duty boots in Figure 5.5). In both figures, the styling of the 'look' is completed with the natty hats worn by the model. This both works to signify the highly stylized nature of the 'look' and draws strongly on the idioms of black street style. This connection to black style is clearly underlined by the title given to Figure 5.5 ('Yard Style Easy Skanking'). The selection and styling of these clothes are typical of the

FIGURE 5.4 'Hard are the looks', *The Face*, March 1985.

FIGURE 5.5 'Ragamuffin hand me down my walking cane', *Arena*, spring 1987.

WOOL JACKET BY
MARK LAWRENCE AT
SITE, 84 BERWICK ST,
LONDON W1; COTTON
TROUSERS BY ISSEY
MIYAKE FROM
PLANTATION, 311
BROMPTON RD,
LONDON SW1;
LEATHER CAP FROM
HATATTACK, 253
PORTOBELLO RD,
LONDON W11; BOOTS
SECONDHAND FROM
CAMDEN TOWN
MARKET. MODEL
SIMON DE MONTFORD
(LARAINE ASHTON
AGENCY)

YARD STYLE
EASY SKANKING

resolutely, stylishly masculine 'look' associated with 'street style' in the magazines. The urban connotations of 'street style' are underlined by the location setting in Figure 5.5: a piece of derelict wasteland within the city.

The posing and model's expressions are the next elements in this coding that I want to consider. In Figure 5.4, the conventions of modelling were knowingly drawn upon in order to attain the perfect pout and that moody stare. The use of these conventions of modelling was often particularly marked in stylings of this sort. Figure 5.5 exemplifies this in that the posing of the model plays on the distinctive stylized walk associated with particular forms of black subcultural masculinity (what the title of the whole fashion story calls 'ragamuffin'). The postures and forms of expression mobilized in these figures give a distinctive gloss to what I would call the romantic individuality of male youth. These are street-wise, pretty, hard boys. These romantic masculine identities offered resources for a 'tough', stylish masculinity – men who carried their maleness with a self-contained poise. A certain pre-permissive feel was important in accenting this masculine romanticism. By this I mean, the images draw on masculine codes which predate the shifts in masculinity associated with the late 1960s. This masculine romanticism is signified in Figure 5.4 by the selection of a seamless, glossy, black-and-white reproduction of the image. This alludes to the choice of film stock and lighting of 1940s' and 1950s' star portraits (particularly those associated with the Kobal collection).

Another coded feature of these images is the strongly narcissistic absorption or self-containment of the models. This is most clear in Figure 5.4. Posed alone, the gaze of the model is focused downwards and sideways out of frame, registering self-reflection and a hint of melancholy. Part of this relates to the way the image accents the codes of male romanticism and individualism that register the restrictions on young men in 1980s' 'hard times' culture (reduced life-chances, lack of money, the authoritarian shifts in social life) (Winship, 1986). More significantly, however, the conventions of posing and expression established in the spreads invite the viewer into complicity or identification with the model's narcissistic absorption in his 'look' or self-presentation; complicity with the ways in which he carries his 'looks' and appearance. This is underscored by the manner in which the photograph is cut or cropped and set on the page in Figure 5.4 which produces an intensity in the image: the model is brought close up to the viewer. What is important for my argument is the way this invited complicity between the viewer of the image and the model in relation to his (the model's) narcissism is focused upon men's bodies that are at once highly masculine and openly sensual. Two aspects are crucial here. First, the attention focused upon the model's appearance and the pleasures this establishes (in the quality and styling of the clothes, in his grooming, his 'looks', in the lighting and quality of the paper) are not directed towards an imagined feminine spectator who would mediate the relationship between the male model and the imagined male viewer. In other words, there is no woman in the representation or implicitly addressed by the image at whom these qualities might be addressed. The masculine–masculine look staged by this image is not coded within the norms of heterosexuality; his 'look' is not aimed at attracting an approving feminine look. Secondly, the choice of the model and some of the elements of clothing in the stylings allude to a tradition of representation of masculinity aimed at and taken up by gay men. What I mean here, specifically, is the valorizing of a 'tough' masculinity. In addition, Figure 5.4 draws upon an older tradition of representing male homosexuality associated with the beautiful, but melancholic young man (see Dyer, 1993).

I am not suggesting, however, that Figures 5.4 and 5.5 are gay male codings; or, rather, that they are straightforwardly that. There is a limited displaying of the surface of the body in the fashion spreads, and the choice of models breaks with the tighter generic figures of some more explicitly sexualized gay representations (such as the denim-clad boy or the cop). These images are instead strongly rooted in the stylistic community that they both invoked and simultaneously represented (London 'street style') and this was not strictly defined in terms of sexuality. What is pivotal, however, is the way the styling organizes a masculine–masculine look that draws upon a gay accent without either pathologizing that accent or re-inscribing a binary coding of gay or straight.

4.2 'Italian-American'

In commenting on Figures 5.6, 5.7 and 5.8, I want to draw attention to the role of ethnicity as a key element in the coding of these 'new man' versions of masculinity. By this I mean the way a signification of 'Italian-American-ness' is central to the coding of masculinity in these images. Casting is, again, a central code. It is through the casting of the models that 'Italian-American-ness' is principally signified. To make sure we get this message, Figure 5.8 belongs within a fashion story titled 'Wiseguys, goodfellas and godfathers show off their brand new suits'. A dark white skin tone, strong features and a marked sensuality (the lips, in particular, are pronounced) are prominent among the models chosen. As with the 'street style' images, these physical features signify both sensuality and hardness, or a mixture of both 'soft' and 'hard'. Thus, the sensuality connoted by the dark skin, eyes and full lips intersects with both strong chins and noses and the connotations of the bravado and swagger of an Italian-American 'macho'. The casting of these models, then, works to produce a set of connotations of masculinity similar to those signified by the casting of light-black models.

The location setting chosen in Figure 5.7 is also important in the signification of 'Italian-American-ness'. The backdrop of buildings and the general invocation of the public space of the city (New York?) grounds the 'look' of the models in this metropolitan landscape. These are men at home in this sophisticated milieu. Figure 5.7 also emphasizes the male camaraderie of being 'out on the town'. This is given greater resonance by the garments worn by the models (naval attire) and the explicit reference to shore leave given in the copy which accompanies the whole fashion story (the reference is to the 1949 movie, *On The Town*).

FIGURE 5.6 'The last detail: On The Town navy style in P-coats and caps', *Arena*, summer/autumn 1991.

FIGURE 5.7 'The last detail: On The Town navy style in P-coats and caps', *Arena*, summer/autumn 1991

FIGURE 5.8 'Wiseguys, goodfellas and godfathers show off their brand new suits', *Arena*, spring 1991.

The selection and styling of garments, which draw upon naval apparel, helps to produce a strongly masculine 'look' through the codes of dress. The caps, wool jacket and heavy-duty canvas coats are resolutely masculine garments which emphasize – in the case of the coats – a solid masculine frame. This emphasis on a broad-shouldered look is equally clear in Figure 5.8 – through the cut of the suit. The accessories worn by the model in this image – the bracelet and the chunky ring – signify a brash, showy masculinity.

The selection of film stock and lighting is very important in these images. The grey-sepia tones signal a 1940s' America and, in a similar way to the glossy black-and-white film stock used in Figure 5.4, connote an era of more fixed and conservative gender identities (and, specifically, masculinities). In addition, the selection of this film stock and the glossy reproduction further emphasize the gloss of skin, eyes and hair, together with the texture of the clothing.

Finally, if we turn to the codes of posture and expression, Figure 5.6 mobilizes a similar code of expression to that deployed in Figure 5.4. Here the model's gaze is focused sideways and away from the imagined spectator and is accompanied by his melancholic expression. Again, this stages a sexually ambivalent masculine–masculine look. In Figure 5.8, the model looks moodily towards the camera, looking through the position of the spectator without engaging it.

4.3 'Conservative Englishness'

The casting of the models was key to producing the 'conservative Englishness look' (see Figures 5.9 and 5.10). The models both have pale white skin, with lighter hair and softer features than the Italian-American-looking models and the light-black model. The styling of the hair, however, is particularly important to the coding of the 'conservative Englishness look'. It is cropped at the sides and back, but left long enough on top to be pushed back. Although slightly dressed with hair-oil, the hair on top has been cut so that it can flop forward. This combines the romantic associations of long hair with the connotations of the masculine discipline and civilized neatness of the 'short back and sides'.

The repertoire of clothing worn is also key to signifying 'conservative Englishness'. In Figures 5.9 and 5.10, the models wear a version of classic English menswear in the form of three-piece suits. The garments are made of cotton (the shirts) and a wool-mixture (the suits) – materials which signify quality and tradition. These values are also connoted in Figure 5.11, where we see a desk littered with the paraphernalia of the office: a Filofax, leatherbound cases and fountain pens. The selection of these objects and their styling imprecisely evoke an inter-war England.

A sense of tradition, however, is not the only factor at play here in accenting the design codes of classic English menswear. Looming large in Figure 5.9 is the contemporary glossing of these codes of menswear by the addition of the

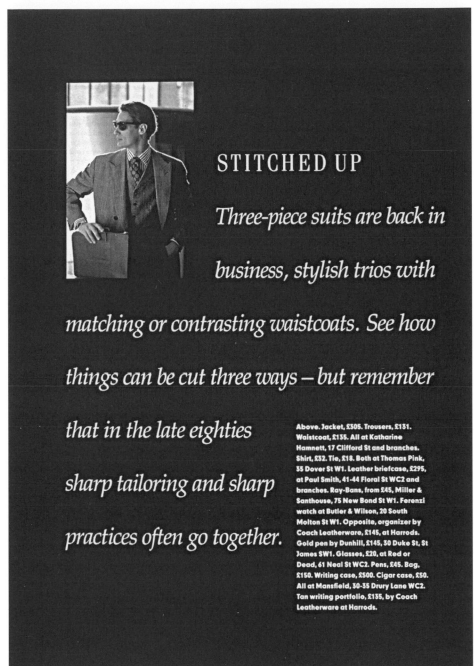

STITCHED UP

Three-piece suits are back in business, stylish trios with matching or contrasting waistcoats. See how things can be cut three ways — but remember that in the late eighties sharp tailoring and sharp practices often go together.

Above. Jacket, £305. Trousers, £131. Waistcoat, £135. All at Katharine Hamnett, 17 Clifford St and branches. Shirt, £32. Tie, £18. Both at Thomas Pink, 35 Dover St W1. Leather briefcase, £295, at Paul Smith, 41-44 Floral St WC2 and branches. Ray-Bans, from £45, Miller & Santhouse, 75 New Bond St W1. Ferenzi watch at Butler & Wilson, 20 South Molton St W1. Opposite, organizer by Coach Leatherware, £145, at Harrods. Gold pen by Dunhill, £145, 30 Duke St, St James SW1. Glasses, £20, at Red or Dead, 61 Neal St WC2. Pens, £45. Bag, £150. Writing case, £500. Cigar case, £50. All at Mansfield, 30-35 Drury Lane WC2. Tan writing portfolio, £135, by Coach Leatherware at Harrods.

FIGURE 5.9
'Stitched up', GQ, February/March 1989, photograph by Tim Brett-Webb, © The Condé Nast Publications Ltd/GQ.

bright tie and sunglasses. These contemporary elements work to signify the entrepreneurial codes of business indicated by the reference to 'sharp practices' in the written copy which accompanies the fashion story. The aggressive masculinity associated with these codes of business is reinforced by the posture and expression of the model in Figure 5.9: his pose and expression signify confident manliness and independence. In Figure 5.10, the posture and expression of the model are less aggressive, more open to the viewer. He openly solicits our look at him.

...Two's company, three's a deal

Above and opposite right. Puppy tooth
check suit, £580. Waistcoat, £100. Blue
striped shirt with white collar, £65.
Paisley bow-tie, from £18. All at Polo
Ralph Lauren, 143 New Bond St W1.
Pocket chain, from £200, at Thomas
Kettle, 53a Neal St WC2. Dark leather
portfolio case with zipper by Coach
Leatherware, £135, at Harrods.
Meisterstuck Mont Blanc pen, in
pocket, £160, at Harrods; Selfridges;
Liberty; W H Smith.
Opposite left. Windowpane check pure
wool suit, £969. Self stripe cotton shirt,
£150. Both at Gianni Versace, 92
Brompton Rd SW5; 18 New Bond St W1.
Polka dot tie, £18, at Thomas Pink, 35
Dover St W1.

FIGURE 5.10
'Stitched up', *GQ*,
February/March
1989, photograph
by Tim Brett-Webb,
© The Condé Nast
Publications Ltd/GQ.

The version of masculinity coded within Figures 5.9 and 5.10, then, is
strongly marked by the interplay between, on the one hand, the assertive
masculinity associated with a dominant version of Englishness and
entrepreneurial codes of business and, on the other, the romantic connotations
of narcissistic young manhood. These spreads code a spectatorial look in
which identification with the models (especially in terms of the power of their
imagined Englishness) sits alongside the sanctioning of visual pleasures in the
cut of clothes, lighting and the 'look' of the models themselves.

FIGURE 5.11
'Stitched up', *GQ*,
February/March
1989, photograph
by Tim Brett-Webb,
© The Condé Nast
Publications Ltd/GQ.

4.4 Summary of section 4

Let me take stock of what my reading of these three 'looks' has produced. I have argued that, across these three 'looks':

1   The casting of the models (especially in the 'street style' and 'Italian-American' images) codes an ambivalent masculinity which combines both boyish softness and a harder, assertive masculinity. This sanctions the display of masculine sensuality.

2   The clothes worn by the models are assertively masculine and often emphasize a broad-shouldered and solid body shape.

3   The models display highly masculine forms of posture and expression – notably, connoting masculine independence and assurance – as well as the coding of narcissistic self-absorption.

4   The choice of lighting and film stock emphasizes the surface qualities of skin, hair and eyes and the texture of clothing.

5   The cropping of the images works to produce an intensity in many of the images.

In addition, I suggested that these visual codes work to produce a spectatorial look for the imagined spectator. In my reading of the images, I invoked three aspects of this look. First, I commented upon its gendering and emphasized the way the imagined viewer of the images is assumed to be male. This establishes forms of masculine–masculine looking. Secondly, I reflected on its organization of identification; that is, on the way the images invite an imagined male viewer to invest himself in the 'look' being presented by the model. Thirdly, I referred to its organization of a pleasure in looking at an external object or 'other'. My attention to the gendering of the look was important. It directed us towards the way the visual pleasures coded in the representations are connected to wider gender scripts and sexual identities – in other words, who looks at whom and in what way. The coding of the look across the images as a masculine–masculine one frames the visual pleasures signified in the images. What figures prominently in this respect is the organization of identification in the look. It is clear that the imagined male spectator is literally invited to buy into the 'look' of the model; that is, to identify with his 'look'.

Visual pleasures associated with the display of menswear are also in play in the representations. In this sense, the images walk a fine line between inciting identification with the 'look' displayed and the marking of visual pleasures around the model so that he himself becomes the object of a desiring look. This interplay between identification with and pleasure in the models is strongly incited by the coding of masculine sensuality across the images and by the way some of the images draw on forms of looking which were historically the prerogative of gay men – without pathologizing that look. Emphasizing these visual pleasures and the forms of spectatorship or looking associated with them directs us towards a set of arguments about the impact of these images on their readers or viewers. In the next section, I want to open out some of the terms which have been introduced in this section and consider more explicitly how we might theorize the articulation of these images with the readers of them.

5   Spectatorship and subjectivization

We saw, from the discussion of Foucault's conception of discourse in section 3, that he emphasizes the way discourses are the bearers of various historically specific positions of agency and identity for individuals. It is these subject-positions which provide the conditions for individuals to act or know in relation to particular social practices. This conception of subject-positions was key to my reading of the 'new man'. I suggested that we could see the coding of the 'new man' within popular representations as marking the formation of a new subject-position for men in relation to the practices of fashion, style and individual consumption. What is absent from our discussions so far, however, is some sense of how the subject-positions formally produced within representation come to be inhabited by groups of men. In other words, how do we conceptualize the articulation of the 'new man' images with the masculinity of individual men. Embedded in Foucault's conceptualization of subjectivity – notably in his writings in the 1970s – is a particular understanding of the process by which individuals come to inhabit subjectivization particular discursive subject-positions. It is this question of **subjectivization** which I want to consider in sections 5 and 6 where I pick up a thread in Foucault's work not yet discussed in this volume.

As we've already seen, Foucault's account of subjectivity is strongly accented towards a delimiting of the formal, discursive production of subject-positions. This is writ large in the concerns of his historical surveys. He is interested in the emergence of modern forms of individuality through the growth of new bodies of knowledge and networks of power. The central mechanism which Foucault posits to understand the process whereby historical individuals are subjected to these discursive positions is the operation of power within discourse. Foucault is most explicit on the workings of this process in an interview in *Power/Knowledge* (1980) and in the essay 'The subject and power' (1982). In 'The subject and power', he talks about the way power subjects individuals through the government of conduct. By this, Foucault means the prescribing and shaping of conduct according to certain norms which set limits on individuals but also make possible certain forms of agency and individuality. In the interview in *Power/Knowledge*, Foucault goes even further in describing the moment of subjectivization or subjection. Power is again the central mechanism. He says:

> … power relations can materially penetrate the body in depth without depending on the mediation of the subject's own representations. If power takes hold of the body, this isn't through it having first to be interiorized in people's consciousness.

> (Foucault, 1980, p. 186)

Individuals are positioned within particular discourses, then, as an effect of power upon them. This might work, for example, through the intensification of the pleasures of the body, its posture and movements and the solidifying of certain practices. This is a productive relation, with power constituting the fabric of the individual and the individual's conduct.

In these comments, then, Foucault emphasizes the way subjectivization does not require individuals to be interpellated through mechanisms of identification to secure the workings of power/knowledge over them. Bodily attributes and capacities (such as dressing, walking, looking) are acquired through the 'brute outcome' of imitation and doing (Hunter, 1993, p. 128). In other words, specific discourse can work upon you – can subject you – without necessarily winning you over in your head.

Despite the richness of these formulations, however, Foucault's attention to the government of conduct and the workings of power upon the body is not without its problems for our purposes. Most importantly, these formulations are extremely vulnerable to the charge that Foucault overemphasizes the effectiveness of specific power-plays upon individuals and pays insufficient attention to the ways in which individuals might resist them. Foucault also, more straightforwardly, overlooks the possible failure of specific attempts to regulate or govern conduct. The mechanism or process of subjectivization is, in a certain sense, perfunctory in these conceptualizations. The emphasis in Foucault's work at this point is to see the identities inhabited by historical individuals as simply the mirror-image of the subject-positions produced within particular discursive regimes. For me, this aspect of Foucault's approach has been unhelpful. It has led me in two directions: first, towards an alternative account of the articulation of representations with individuals found in the appropriation of psychoanalysis within cultural theory; and, secondly, towards a more useful account of subjectivization found in Foucault's late writings.

5.1 Psychoanalysis and subjectivity

Psychoanalysis has provided a rich source of arguments for cultural critics concerned to understand the impact of systems of representations upon real historical individuals. In this section, I want to focus upon three concepts drawn from psychoanalysis which offer a way of conceptualizing the relationship between the 'new man' images and the spectators or consumers of these images. These are the concepts of identification, scopophilia and narcissism. As I hope you will see, these concepts are particularly suggestive for our purposes in that they foreground the organization of gender identities within representation and play up the acts of looking and spectatorship which shape this process.

Identification is the central of the three concepts and carries precise meanings in Freud's writing. In his essay 'Group psychology and the analysis of the ego' (Freud, 1977/1921), for example, he explicitly distinguishes between two kinds of relationship which individuals enter into with the external world of objects around them. On the one hand, he says, there is a relationship with the object which involves the focusing of libidinal investments (the sexual drives) upon, usually, another person. On the other hand, there is identification which involves some projection based on a similarity between the individual and an external person and, from that, the moulding of the ego after that person. Freud summarizes this distinction as a distinction between two kinds of desire: a desire to *have* the other person (which he calls **object cathexis**) and a desire to *be* the other person (**identification**) (ibid., p. 135).

object cathexis

identification

What is striking about Freud's comments on these processes is the possessive or proprietorial dimension of object cathexis and the destructive, assimilating tendency in identification. These possessive and aggressive undercurrents of object cathexis and identification emerge very clearly in Freud's account of the **Oedipus Complex**. The Oedipus Complex represented a defining moment in the development of the child for Freud; it was the moment at which gender identity and sexuality (or sexual object choice) were fixed. It is, in addition, a moment which also reveals the importance of two other concepts which, as you will see, are important for the psychoanalytic understanding of identification. These are the concepts of scopophilia and narcissism.

Oedipus Complex

In 'Three essays on the theory of sexuality' (1984/1905), Freud claimed that a pleasure in looking was a component part of human sexuality (you may recall the discussion of scopophilia in Chapter 4, section 4.4). This pleasure in looking or **scopophilia** could be channelled along different routes for Freud. One of these was a fascination with the human form. Freud labelled this fascination **narcissism** and it provided him with the mechanism of identification. Centrally, for Freud, the narcissistic pull of identification was largely unconscious, secured beyond the individual's conscious awareness.

scopophilia

narcissism

Identification, for Freud, organized not only the narcissistic components of the scopophilic drive; it also involved a process of splitting, and we can use Freud's account of the Oedipal drama, which has already been briefly introduced in Chapter 4, section 1.2, to illustrate this. The developmental moment of the Oedipus crisis and its successful dissolution involved – for Freud – a 'boy' child taking up a masculine identification with the father and in the process displacing earlier aggressive fantasies towards the father. It also entailed the stabilizing of a heterosexual object choice. This masculine identification, however, precluded the 'boy' from taking up a feminine identification with the mother, while the stabilizing of heterosexual object choice precluded other kinds of object choice. In the Oedipal scenario, then, Freud posits the formation of sexual difference and sexual identity in a moment of splitting – between the identification that is made (in the case of the 'boy', masculine) and the identification that is refused (feminine). The identification that is refused, Freud argues, has to be actively negated or repressed, and continues to haunt the individual. In this psychoanalytical sense, then, a fixed sexual identity and sexual difference are always unstable and never completely achieved. The subject remains divided, with a precarious sense of coherence (Rose, 1986).

Freud's conceptualization of the process of splitting in the moment of identification forms a central component of the French theorist and psychoanalyst Jacques Lacan's theorizing of identification and the early moments of subject formation. In what is, in large degree, a rigorous reworking of Freud's writings on narcissism, Lacan (in 'The mirror phase as formative of the function of the I', 1968) defines the infant's first sense of itself (its first self-identification) as coming through its imaginary positioning by its own mirror image: that is, by looking at its own reflection, or being literally reflected in its mother's eyes. Lacan argues that the infant misrecognizes itself as its mirror image. Lacan describes this as a moment of primary narcissistic identification, and it is for him the basis and prototype of all future identifications.

5.2 Spectatorship

What is significant in Freud's and Lacan's accounts of identification – including the theorizings on narcissism and scopophilia – is the visual character of the structures of identification they describe. It was within film theory in the 1970s that writers most assertively developed the implications of these aspects of Freud's and Lacan's accounts and laid claim to this lineage of psychoanalysis as offering a privileged way into the analysis of cinematic representations. This work – most notably developed in the journal *Screen* – is instructive for my account of the impact of representations upon individuals in a number of ways. Pivotally, it addressed the power of the visual for the consumers of visual culture, and offered a gendered account of the processes of looking and identification. This filled out the psychoanalytic account of the process of subjectivization.

Laura Mulvey's 1975 *Screen* essay, 'Visual pleasure and narrative cinema', illustrated particularly clearly what a psychoanalytic-informed account could deliver regarding the theorizing of the power of representation (reprinted in Mulvey, 1989). The analysis of the look – and the organization of the pleasure in looking – is most interesting in Mulvey's essay. Drawing on Freud in particular, Mulvey detailed the way narrative cinema mobilized both the narcissistic aspects of the scopophilic instinct (ego libido) and its voyeuristic and fetishistic components (object-cathexis) – essentially those forms of active scopophilia. For Mulvey, however, the mobilization of these pleasures in looking was far from innocent. She asserted a very specific organization of **spectatorship** in relation to the scopophilic drives. For Mulvey, in her famous conceptualization, the 'pleasure in looking has been split between active/male and passive/female' (ibid., p. 19). She distinguished between three kinds of look: the look from camera to event or scene; the look from the spectator to the screen action; and the looks between characters in the film story. For Mulvey, the interplay between these looks was organized to produce the split in looking characteristic of Hollywood cinema. On the one hand, the male characters were positioned as the bearer of the look (the active eye) in the film story, with the feminine coded as visual spectacle (passive object to be looked at). On the other hand, the look of the spectator was aligned with that of the

spectatorship

male character. In these formulations, Mulvey suggests that one important element of this gender imbalance in looking is the careful coding and positioning in the storyline of the film of the male figures. For Mulvey, there is a marked displacement of any erotic, 'spectacular' significations in relation to men in narrative film which maintains the power relations between men and women; between the active masculine control of the look and the passive feminine object of the look.

Mulvey's development of Freudian concepts provides a suggestive way of conceptualizing the moment of articulation between individuals and representational forms. It suggests that the positioning of the individual within the subject-positions established by a particular representation is achieved through the organization of scopophilic drives and the channelling of unconscious identifications. This is also a process that can (depending upon representational conventions) reproduce the positions of sexual difference or gender.

Mulvey's arguments are a major influence on Steve Neale in his essay 'Masculinity as spectacle' (Neale, 1983). Neale's essay is useful for my account in this chapter because it takes up Mulvey's basic argument about the cinematic gaze, but also extends the theorizing of both the representational conventions of masculinity within narrative cinema and of the positioning of the male spectator in relation to these conventions.

> READING A
>
> Now read Reading A, 'Masculinity as spectacle', by Steve Neale, which you will find at the end of this chapter. Consider the following questions as you read the extract:
>
> 1 What is a central characteristic of the genres of film which Neale focuses on?
> 2 How do these films undercut the possibility of an erotic look at the male body?
> 3 What qualities of masculinity do they privilege?

5.3 The spectacle of masculinity

Does Neale's analysis offer any specific pointers to conceptualizing the moment of articulation between a masculine subject in a text (in this case a film) and historical men? Neale's essay focuses on male genres – such as the western – in which masculinity is necessarily the object of considerable visual attention and visual spectacle. Neale argues, however, that the narrative structure and shot organization of these films work to undercut the potential of an erotic look at the male figures (principally for the male spectator in the auditorium). He argues that the films do this through representing sadism or aggression – that is, by in some way wounding or injuring the male body – as a way of circumventing eroticization. In addition, the codings of masculinity in these films privilege the attributes of toughness, hardness and being in control. These are codings which do not allow the display of ambiguities, uncertainties or weaknesses and therefore, for the male spectator, offer a fantasy of control and power. In other words, they foreground the possibility of a narcissistic identification with the protagonists.

Neale's argument corroborates Mulvey's claims that the representational conventions of narrative cinema and its organization of spectatorship reproduce the terms of sexual difference and the power relations between men and women. A number of objections, however, have been raised to this kind of appropriation of Freud by other writers working within this tradition of film theory. In particular, in line with much psychoanalytically informed work, both Mulvey and Neale foreground questions of sexual difference – differences between masculinity and femininity – and play down differences within these categories. The inability to consider differences between masculinities leads to their failure to consider the organization of other forms of sexual desire in the cinema. The long tradition of eroticizing the figure of the cowboy amongst gay men suggests an immediate problem with this omission. You will recall, from Chapter 4, that Stuart Hall also develops some of these criticisms in his reflection on Robert Mapplethorpe's photographs of black male models. There are some further, more general objections to both Neale's and Mulvey's arguments which I want to raise by way of drawing this section to a close.

5.4   The problem with psychoanalysis and film theory

I began this section by suggesting that the appropriation of a particular tradition of psychoanalysis within cultural theory (and, in particular, film theory) appeared to offer a more dynamic conceptualization of subjectivization than that found in Foucault's work. This was a conceptualization which was not only sensitive to the gendering of identities, but could also account for the way visual representation worked on individuals through its emphasis on the interlocking of deep-rooted psychic processes with the codes and conventions of cinema. The problems begin, I think, when it comes to thinking about how we might apply Neale's or Mulvey's work to analysing the 'new man' images. Looming large here is the problem of moving from an account of spectatorship and the positioning of viewers developed in relation to narrative cinema to an account of these same processes in relation to very different kinds of visual representation: magazine fashion images, television adverts, shop displays. The first difficulty concerns the staging of the spectatorial look. In Mulvey and Neale's work, the look is conceived of as a fixed gaze within the environment of the cinema auditorium. The conditions for this staging of the look are clearly not met in relation to the visual representations which concern us here. This immediately forces us to rethink questions of spectatorship – including the way in which the look is gendered at these other sites. Secondly, and more seriously, the account of spectatorship developed in this section rests upon a particular account of identity, drawn from psychoanalysis. This psychoanalytic account of identity is fundamentally at odds with the Foucauldian account which I set out in section 3, with – in my view – its very proper emphasis on the historical character of identities. Let me explain why I think it is extremely difficult to square the differences between a psychoanalytic and a Foucauldian account of identity.

Lacan and Freud are both explicitly concerned with the primary processes that constitute identity; that is, those processes that forge (in Juliet Mitchell's phrase) 'the human in culture' (Mitchell, 1984, p. 237). These processes are, for psychoanalysis, universal – that is, they have a transhistorical status. In addition, they follow a developmental pattern involving a number of phases; they are secured unconsciously and are fixed by the parameters of Oedipal order – the underlying universal structuring of human relations which Freud and Lacan posit.

It is this universal account of the formation of identity, however, that is so problematic in relation to Foucault's deeply historical emphasis. The psychosexual structures of the Oedipal order are given the privileged position in accounting for (almost) all there is to say about the formation of identity. The arguments of Mulvey and Neale do attempt, certainly, to moderate this universal account of identity. In considering the interplay between psychic structures and historically specific forms of representation (Hollywood cinema), they do suggest that these representations can carry real force. However, in describing the articulation of the social/historical with psychic structures, the psychic is privileged as providing the fundamental parameters of identity. In analysis of the look and the gendered positioning of individuals, there is a search for the positions of looking given by particular visual texts in terms of the fundamental tropes of sexual difference – active/passive; masculine/feminine; mother/son; father/daughter. Subjectivization, then, is conceptualized in these accounts as being secured through the reactivation of the fundamental positions of identity which Freud posits – ultimately, always in the terms of the Oedipal order. Historical and social factors which determine identity are – in the end – reduced to the calculus of psychosexual structures. In addition, the emphasis on psychosexual structures produces a reductive account of identity conceived fundamentally in terms of sexual difference. In other words, psychoanalysis privileges the acquisition of gender and sexual identity as the bedrock of identity. Other determinants upon identity (such as class) are effectively sidelined.

While psychoanalysis can give a clear account of the articulation of individuals with fields of representation, and certainly poses some important questions about the unconscious and about desire and the look, this is in the end too ahistorical and totalizing. It pitches 'secondary' processes of identification only at the level of primary processes and sees identity only in terms of sexual difference (Morley, 1980). Where, then, does this leave our account of subjectivization? The attention to the organization of spectatorship as a way of conceptualizing subjectivization does point to important processes. I want to hold on to this concern with spectatorship, but not in its psychoanalytically understood sense. Foucault's late writings both help to re-situate an account of looking and offer considerable conceptual reach in terms of theorizing subjectivization.

5.5   Techniques of the self

In his late work and in interviews published shortly before his death, Foucault made reference to his interest in what he called practices or **techniques of the self**. He maintained that:

techniques of the self

> ... it is not enough to say that the subject is constituted in a symbolic system. It is not just in the play of symbols that the subject is constituted. It is constituted in real practices. There is a technology of the constitution of the self which cuts across symbolic systems while using them.
>
> (interview in Rabinow, 1984, p. 369)

Foucault elaborates further in his essay 'Technologies of the self' (1988). Commenting on four major types of technologies (those of production, sign systems, power and the self), he suggests that **technologies of the self**:

technologies of the self

> ... permit individuals to effect by their own means or with the help of others a certain number of operations on their own bodies and souls, thoughts, conduct and way of being, so as to transform themselves in order to attain a certain state of happiness, purity, wisdom, perfection or immortality.
>
> (Foucault, 1988, p. 18)

Technologies or techniques of the self, in other words, are specific techniques or practices through which subject-positions are inhabited by individuals. Foucault, in his brief comments on these techniques, emphasized his interest in forms of writing such as private diaries or other 'narratives of the self'. These represented, for him, characteristically modern forms of 'practices of the self'.

What is so useful about these assertions is the way they get Foucault away from his earlier exclusive emphasis on how historical identities are produced as the effect of discourses. This represents a shift from an attention to the regulating and disciplining of the subject to a more expanded formulation of agency. 'Techniques of the self' are still – it is important to underline – conducted within fields of power-knowledge and within the domains of a discrete number of discourses. They suggest, though, the putting into practice of discursive subject-positions in ways which emphasize the dynamic nature of this process. More than that, they underline again the important attention Foucault gives to the non-ideational elements of subjectivization; that is, the way in which the body and mental capacities are the product of practices and not (necessarily) of forms of self-representation in either consciousness or the unconscious.

Foucault's comments on 'practices of the self' make it possible to conceptualize the articulation of concrete individuals to particular representations as a performance based upon the citing and reiteration of discursive norms; a performance in which the formal positions of subjectivity are inhabited through specific practices or techniques (Butler, 1993). This lays the basis for an account of subjectivization that is historical in nature and circumvents the deployment of the full psychoanalytic connotations of identification in order to theorize in a dynamic way the process of subjectivization.

In thinking about how we might conceptualize the way the formal subjectivities inscribed within the regime of 'new man' representations might have been inhabited by historical men, Foucault's comments, then, direct us towards a specific set of practices or techniques of the self. A number of techniques of care, consumption and leisure seem to me pivotal in this respect. The practices of grooming and dressing and the activity of shopping represent practices through which the attributes and characteristics of masculinity coded in relation to the 'new man' imagery might be operationalized or performed as a historical identity. At the heart of these techniques or practices of the self, I want to suggest, are specific techniques of looking. By this I mean the acquired acts of looking which cite and reiterate the ways of looking formally coded in advertising images, shop display photographs, and magazine fashion photography. It is these codes and techniques of looking on which I want to reflect in the next section.

6 Consumption and spectatorship

In the previous section, I suggested that psychoanalysis offered a number of suggestive terms – identification, scopophilia, narcissism – through which we could conceptualize the impact of visual representations upon the consumers of them. Looming large in this, as we saw, was the positioning of the consumer in relation to the image through the codes of spectatorship. I also raised some significant reservations about the wider psychoanalytic conception of identity which underpinned the theories of identification, scopophilia and narcissism as they were developed within cultural criticism. I suggested that Foucault's ideas offered an alternative way of approaching the question of consumers' relationship to visual representations through his comments on 'techniques of the self' and their historically varied performances. In emphasizing the usefulness of Foucault, however, I also suggested that I wanted to retain the attention to the coding of spectatorship. A central part of this reassessment of theories of spectatorship is a concern to chart historically the formation of the codes of looking available to contemporary consumers of the 'new man' imagery. In rethinking spectatorship, I want to offer you an account of how we might understand the forms of looking established between the 'new man' images – in magazine spreads, in shop windows, in television advertising – and the groups of men at whom they were principally aimed.

6.1 Sites of representation

In getting to grips with the codes and techniques of looking associated with the 'new man' imagery, we can usefully begin with the role of shop interiors in the staging of these looks. Shop interiors direct us towards both the establishment of codes of looking and the interweaving of techniques of looking with other practices – handling the garments, trying on clothes, interacting with shop staff – which are integral to the activity of shopping. The interior space of shops and their windows thus represent one of the privileged places for the performance of techniques of the self by individual men in relation to the 'new man' imagery.

In order to explore these issues, however, I need to preface them with some more explicit comments concerning the representation of the 'new man' within shops. How is the 'new man' represented at the point of sale? I want to suggest that there are two distinct moments to this encoding: the first is produced through the design codes of menswear and the second through the design and display techniques of retailing.

The design codes of menswear are easiest to deal with. As cultural forms, menswear garments (like all clothes) carry particular cultural meanings. The choices made by designers in terms of the selection and design of garments, choice of fabrics and colours work to signify, most importantly, particular masculine identities through the menswear. Think of how tweed jacket and brogues signify a certain version of English upper-class masculinity. In the case of the 'new man', then, it was innovations in menswear design which shaped a new version of masculinity.

The forging of these new versions of masculinity through the design codes of menswear, however, was also dependent upon other practices of representation to help fix these meanings around the garments. This is where the design and display techniques used in menswear retailing come into play. Through the presentation of the garments on mannequins or display stands in the shop window and around the shop, through the use of display boards with photographs of the clothes being worn by models, and through techniques like lighting and interior decoration, shop design and display attempt to fix a series of cultural values and meanings around the garments – values centrally to do, in this case, with masculinity. It was through these techniques that the 'new man' was signified within menswear shops as a particular version or type of masculinity.

What was so striking about the design and display techniques deployed by menswear retailers up and down the High Street in recent years was the way they addressed their target male customers in highly visual terms. The selection of high quality materials in the fitting out of the shops, the use of lighting and display boards and the placing of mirrors in the shops offered a particular kind of visual spectacle in which the selling of the clothes took part.

One of the best examples of these new trends in menswear retailing is offered by Next for Men. Central to the design of the Next menswear interiors (including the point-of-sale materials and packaging) was the use of space and materials. The frontage of the stores gave the first indication of this: a large window set in a dark matt grey frame beneath the trademark signage 'Next', in lowercase lettering. The window displays – framed by this frontage – were similarly uncluttered. A combination of garments was displayed on abstract mannequins, backed, often, by large display or show cards that gave written accounts of the merchandise range. The display cards – featuring details of the clothes being worn as well as the accompanying copy – played off the themes of space, colour and line in the shop through their layout and lettering. Inside the shops, the lighting, colouring and organization of space were distinctive. Here were the features that formed a coherent design vocabulary: bleached wooden pigeon-holes and dresser units; downlighting spotlights; gently spiralling staircases with matt black banisters. The 'edited' collection of clothes were displayed in a range of ways. Around the sides of the shop, slatted wooden units displayed a few folded jumpers next to hangers with three jackets; socks were folded in pigeon-holes or individual shoes perched on bleached wood units. A dresser unit commanded the central space of the shop, standing upon a classic woven carpet. Such features acted as centripetal counterpoints to the displays of clothes that were set against the walls and encouraged customers to circulate around the shop. The design of the shop interiors, then, combined a number of distinctive stylistic borrowings to produce a shop space in which the assertively modern idioms of cruise-line aesthetics sat alongside the warmer English colourings of dark wood and brass detailing (Nixon, 1996).

What is important for my argument in this chapter is that Next's retail design established a set of ways of visually apprehending the shop environment and the clothes within it through the design and display techniques. In other words – if we put this in slightly different terms – the design and display techniques established particular forms of spectatorship for men at the point of sale; forms of spectatorship directed at the 'new man' masculinity represented through the design, selection and presentation of the garments. As a way of getting to grips with these forms of spectatorship, I want to turn to a body of work devoted to the emergence of consumer culture from the mid-nineteenth century. There is a good reason for such an exercise. I want to suggest that the essential characteristics of the forms of spectatorship associated with menswear shops like Next for Men have their origins in this earlier period.

6.2 Just looking

Rachel Bowlby has offered some useful pointers to the emergence of contemporary consumer culture and its visual characteristics in her book *Just Looking* (1985). Drawing upon the writings of a group of naturalist writers (Emile Zola, George Gissing and Theodore Dreisser) and their responses to the expansion of consumer culture around the turn of the century, Bowlby identifies two related tendencies within the new cultures of consumption. On the one hand, she argues that the latter half of the nineteenth century witnessed the rationalization and systematic organization of selling. Citing the development of the department store, she argues they represented 'factories for selling'. Looming large in this was the rationalizing of selling techniques. This ranged from the establishment of fixed pricing to the organization of sales staff and supervisors. On the other hand, Bowlby also noted that selling itself was transformed by a new emphasis on arranging the goods in displays both in the shop window and inside the store. As she puts it: 'The grand magasins ... appear as places of culture, fantasy, divertissement, which the customer visits more for pleasure than necessity' (Bowlby, 1985, p. 6).

What figured prominently in this organization of consumer pleasure, for Bowlby, was the pleasure of – in her phrase – **just looking**; that is, taking in the visual spectacle of the displayed goods. Bowlby's emphasis on the visual pleasures staged by the new consumer culture owes much to the work of the German cultural critic Walter Benjamin. In his extensive study of nineteenth-century Paris – generally known as the 'Arcades Project' – written during the inter-war years but first published in English in 1973, Benjamin offered a celebrated account of the spectacular qualities of consumer culture in the nineteenth century.

just looking

READING B

Turn now to Reading B entitled 'Technologies of looking: retailing and the visual', which you will find at the end of this chapter. When you are reading this extract, consider the following questions:

1   How did the arcades establish a new style of consumption?

2   What did the allegorical figure of the *flâneur* principally represent for Benjamin?

3   What kind of cultural identities were privileged in the emergent consumer culture?

4   What role did print culture play in shaping the new styles of consumption described by Benjamin?

6.3 Spectatorship, consumption and the 'new man'

Let me underline the key points from Reading B. It argues that Benjamin's commentary on the *flâneur* pointed us towards the staging of specific ways of looking. These were shaped by the new techniques of consumer display concentrated within the new retail and leisure-based districts of the large metropolitan cities like London and Paris and by the representation of the city and consumption in visual terms within print cultural forms like periodicals. At the heart of this new kind of looking was a new consumer subject who looked. This spectatorial subjectivity was allegorically represented in Benjamin's description of the *flâneur*. In addition, the reading suggested that these ways of looking were dominated by an interrupted series of looks, rather than a fixed gaze. Within these looks, forms of self-visualization by consumers were also important. In other words, they opened up the narcissistic dimensions of spectatorship.

What can we draw out from this argument about the forms of spectatorship coded in relation to the 'new man' imagery within retailing? I have argued that the forms of spectatorship associated with contemporary menswear retailing (such as Next for Men) reproduced ways of looking associated with the emergence of characteristically modern forms of consumption. Contemporary forms of consumer spectatorship, then, belong within this longer historical formation. In addition, reflecting on the work on nineteenth-century developments in consumer culture reveals that the forms of looking staged within and around shops form part of a larger regime of looking; a regime of looking constructed as much within cultural forms associated with this consumption – be that periodicals, consumer guides or catalogues – as at the point of sale. If we think about the contemporary 'new man' images, it is clear that press and television advertising and consumer magazines played an important role in helping to construct this regime of looking. It is in this sense that we can consider the forms of looking which I detailed in section 4 as being part of a series of looks which crossed from the magazines to the spaces of menswear shops.

7 Conclusion

I began this chapter by citing an image drawn from television advertising and have, in the course of the chapter, considered in some detail a range of images drawn from magazine fashion photography. A central argument of the chapter has been about the need to grasp the way this imagery signified across these sites, as well as across (notably) menswear shops. Michel Foucault's arguments about discursive regimes have been critical in this respect, allowing me to reflect on the 'new man' images as a regime of representation. In addition, they have pointed me towards the regime of looking or spectatorship which was also produced across the various sites at which the imagery signified. This was a regime of looking, then, which linked a series of looks formally staged within shop interiors, television advertising and magazine fashion photography.

In considering the impact of this new regime of representation on the groups of men at whom it was principally targeted, I suggested that spectatorship played an important role. I proposed that we could identify the specific techniques of looking associated with the formal codes of spectatorship produced across the regime of 'new man' imagery, together with the other practices of the self (the multiple activities included in shopping, the routines of grooming and dressing), as the means for operationalizing the 'new man' images as historical identities.

Foucault's work not only informed my insistence on grasping the 'new man' imagery as a regime of representation and my understanding of the process of subjectivization through techniques of the self; it also alerted me to the institutional underpinnings of the new imagery. Implicit in the account I set out in this chapter, then, was an argument about the way developments within the consumer institutions of advertising, menswear retailing and magazine publishing set the terms for the formation of this new regime of representation.

Getting to grips with the cultural significance of the 'new man' imagery, however, has been the overriding concern of this chapter. I argued that the images were distinctive in sanctioning the display of masculine sensuality and, from this, opening up the possibility of an ambivalent masculine sexual identity; one that blurred fixed distinctions between gay- and straight-identified men. In this sense, much of the significance of this imagery related to the way it redrew relations between groups of men through the codes of style and consumer spectatorship. Much harder to read is its significance for relations between men and women. Women were effectively absent from the space of representation which I detailed. To develop a fuller account of the cultural significance of these images, however, we do need to locate them in relation to the wider field of gender relations. In this regard, it is worth noting that the moment of the emergence of the 'new man' in the mid–late 1980s was also the moment when shifts were occurring in popular representations of femininity. One of the most important in relation to representations of young femininity was the emergence of what Janice Winship (1985) termed a 'street-wise' femininity. This drew upon a set of 'street style' dress codes analogous to those I commented on earlier. These dress codes – which mixed feminine items like mini-skirts with thick black tights and Doc Martens boots or shoes, cropped hair and bright lipstick – played around with the conventions of gender and dress. For Winship, these new visual representations of femininity were most strongly developed within young women's magazines like *Just Seventeen* and *Mizz*. In the magazines, these new visual codes were articulated to appropriations of certain feminist arguments and offered young women a more assertive and confident sense of independent femininity.

In order to grasp fully the cultural significance of the opening up of new consumer pleasures for men through the figure of the 'new man', then, we need to locate it in relation to these contemporary shifts in femininity and also in relation to more recent shifts in popular representations of gender and sexual identity (like the 'new lad' and the 'lipstick lesbian'). By doing this, it is possible to see the 'new man' as part of this wider realignment of gender and sexual relations which is registered within popular representations. Although we would need more evidence to see how these images are transforming gender and sexual identities amongst groups of men and women, the value of attending to the 'new man' images is that they direct us towards the possibility of a shift in these identities and relations. This is a shift in which the images I have focused on in this chapter do not simply reflect changing masculinities being lived by groups of men, but play an active role in the process of change.

There is a final important point to make about the reading of the 'new man' images which I have advanced. Any assessment of their cultural impact needs to be clear on the limits of what a purely formal textual analysis can deliver. This means giving due regard to the processes of articulation between these images and their consumers in order to understand the way in which the images might have transformed the masculinity of particular groups of men. Getting at this process requires moving away from the moment of representation towards a different moment in the circuit of culture: the moment of consumption.

References

ALEXANDER, S. and TAYLOR, B. (1994) 'In defence of patriarchy' in Alexander, S. (ed.) *Becoming a Woman, and Other Essays in Nineteenth and Twentieth Century Feminist History*, London, Virago.

BENJAMIN, W. (1973) *Charles Baudelaire: a lyric poet in the era of high capitalism*, London, New Left Books.

BOWLBY, R. (1985) *Just Looking*, Basingstoke, Macmillan.

BUTLER, J. (1993) *Bodies that Matter*, London, Routledge.

DAVIDOFF, L. and HALL, C. (1987) *Family Fortunes: men and women of the English middle class 1780–1850*, London, Hutchinson.

DYER, R. (1993) 'Coming out as going in: the image of the homosexual as a sad young man' in *The Matter of Images: essays on representation*, London, Routledge.

FOUCAULT, M. (1980) *Power/Knowledge: selected interviews and other writings 1972–7* (ed. Gordon, C.), Hemel Hempstead, Harvester Wheatsheaf.

FOUCAULT, M. (1982) 'The subject and power' in Rabinow, P. and Dreyfus, H. (eds) *Michel Foucault: beyond structuralism and hermeneutics*, Hemel Hempstead, Harvester Wheatsheaf.

FOUCAULT, M. (1988) 'Technologies of the self' in Martin, L., Gutman, H. and Hutton, P. (eds) *Technologies of the Self: a seminar with Michel Foucault*, Amherst, MA, University of Massachussetts Press.

FREUD, S. (1977) 'Group psychology and the analysis of the ego' in *Pelican Freud Library, Volume 12*, Harmondsworth, Penguin (first published 1921).

FREUD, S. (1984) 'The dissolution of the Oedipus complex' in *Pelican Freud Library, Volume 8*, Harmondsworth, Penguin (first published 1924).

FREUD, S. (1984) 'Three essays on the theory of sexuality' in *Pelican Freud Library, Volume 8*, Harmondsworth, Penguin (first published 1905).

HALL, C. (1992) 'Missionary stories: gender and ethnicity in England in the 1830s and 1840s' in Grossberg, L., Nelson, C. and Triechler, P. (eds) *Cultural Studies*, London, Routledge.

LACAN, J. (1968) 'The mirror phase as formative of the function of the I', *New Left Review*, No. 51, pp. 71–7.

MELLY, G. (1986) 'Why the tables have turned on macho males', *Campaign*, 18 July, pp. 40–1.

MERCER, K. and JULIEN, I. (1988) 'Territories of the body' in Rutherford, J. and Chapman, R. (eds) *Male Order*, London, Lawrence & Wishart.

METCALF, A. and HUMPHRIES, M. (eds) (1985) *The Sexuality of Men*, London, Pluto Press.

MITCHELL, J. (1984) 'Psychoanalysis: a humanist humanity or a linguistic science?' in *Women: the longest revolution*, Harmondsworth, Penguin.

MORLEY, D. (1980) 'Texts, readers, and subjects' in Hall, S., Hobson, D., Lowe, A. and Willis, P. (eds) *Culture, Media, Language*, London, Hutchinson.

MORT, F. (1988) 'Boy's own? Masculinity, style and popular culture' in Rutherford, J. and Chapman, R. (eds) *Male Order*, London, Lawrence & Wishart.

MULVEY, L. (1989) *The Visual and Other Pleasures*, Basingstoke, Macmillan.

NEALE, S. (1983) 'Masculinity as spectacle', *Screen*, Vol. 24, No. 6, pp. 2–16.

NIXON, S. (1996) *Hard Looks: masculinities, spectatorship and contemporary consumption*, London, UCL Press.

RABINOW, P. (ed.) (1984) *The Foucault Reader*, Harmondsworth, Penguin.

ROSE, J. (1986) *Sexuality in the Field of Vision*, London, Verso.

SEGAL, L. (1997) 'Sexualities' in Woodward, K. (ed.) *Identity and Difference*, London, Sage/The Open University (Book 3 in this series).

TOSH, J. and ROPER, M. (eds) (1992) *Manful Assertions*, London, Routledge.

WALBY, S. (1986) *Patriarchy at Work*, Cambridge, Cambridge University Press.

WEEKS, J. (1981) *Sex, Politics and Society*, Harlow, Longman.

WEEKS, J. (1985) *Sexuality and its Discontents*, London, Routledge.

WEEKS, J. (1991) *Against Nature: essays on sexuality, history and identity*, London, Rivers Oram Press.

WINSHIP, J. (1985) 'A girl needs to get "street-wise"', *Feminist Review*, No. 21, pp. 25–46.

WINSHIP, J. (1986) 'Back to the future', *New Socialist*, September, pp. 5–6.

READING A:
Steve Neale, 'Masculinity as spectacle'

I want to turn to Mulvey's remarks about the glamorous male movie star below. But first it is worth extending and illustrating her point about the male protagonist and the extent to which his image is dependent upon narcissistic phantasies, phantasies of the 'more perfect, more complete, more powerful ideal ego'.

It is easy enough to find examples of films in which these phantasies are heavily prevalent, in which the male hero is powerful and omnipotent to an extraordinary degree: the Clint Eastwood character in *A Fistful of Dollars*, *For a Few Dollars More* and *The Good, the Bad and the Ugly*, the Tom Mix westerns, Charlton Heston in *El Cid*, the *Mad Max* films, the Steve Reeves epics, *Superman*, *Flash Gordon* and so on. There is generally, of course, a drama in which that power and omnipotence are tested and qualified (*Superman 2* is a particularly interesting example as are Howard Hawks's westerns and adventure films), but the Leone trilogy, for example, is marked by the extent to which the hero's powers are rendered almost godlike, hardly qualified at all. Hence, perhaps, the extent to which they are built around ritualized scenes which in many ways are devoid of genuine suspense. […]

[…]

In discussing these two types of looking [voyeuristic looking and fetishistic looking], both fundamental to the cinema, Mulvey locates them solely in relation to a structure of activity/passivity in which the look is male and active and the object of the look female and passive. Both are considered as distinct and variant means by which male castration anxieties may be played out and allayed.

Voyeuristic looking is marked by the extent to which there is a distance between spectator and spectacle, a gulf between the seer and the seen. This structure is one which allows the spectator a degree of power over what is seen. It hence tends constantly to involve sado-masochistic phantasies and themes. Here is Mulvey's description:

> voyeurism … has associations with sadism: pleasure lies in ascertaining guilt (immediately associated with castration), asserting control and

subjecting the guilty person through punishment and forgiveness. This sadistic side fits in well with narrative. Sadism demands a story, depends on making something happen, forcing a change in another person, a battle of will and strength, victory and defeat, all occurring in a linear time with a beginning and an end. (Mulvey, 1975)

Mulvey goes on to discuss these characteristics of voyeuristic looking in terms of the *film noir* and of Hitchcock's movies, where the hero is the bearer of the voyeuristic look, engaged in a narrative in which the woman is the object of its sadistic components. However, if we take some of the terms used in her description – 'making something happen', 'forcing a change in another person', 'a battle of will and strength', 'victory and defeat' – they can immediately be applied to 'male' genres, to films concerned largely or solely with the depiction of relations between men, to any film, for example, in which there is a struggle between a hero and a male villain. War films, westerns and gangster movies, for instance, are all marked by 'action', by 'making something happen'. Battles, fights and duels of all kinds are concerned with struggles of 'will and strength', 'victory and defeat', between individual men and/or groups of men. All of which implies that male figures on the screen are subject to voyeuristic looking, both on the part of the spectator and on the part of other male characters.

Paul Willemen's thesis on the films of Anthony Mann is clearly relevant here. The repression of any explicit avowal of eroticism in the act of looking at the male seems structurally linked to a narrative content marked by sado-masochistic phantasies and scenes. Hence both forms of voyeuristic looking, intra- and extra-diegetic, are especially evident in those moments of contest and combat referred to above, in those moments at which a narrative outcome is determined through a fight or gun-battle, at which male struggle becomes pure spectacle. Perhaps the most extreme examples are to be found in Leone's westerns, where the exchange of aggressive looks marking most western gun-duels is taken to the point of fetishistic parody through the use of extreme and repetitive close-ups. At which point the look begins to oscillate between voyeurism and fetishism as the narrative starts to freeze and spectacle takes over. The anxious 'aspects' of the look at the male to which Willemen refers are here both embodied and allayed not just by playing out the sadism inherent in voyeurism through scenes of violence and combat, but also by drawing upon the structures and processes of fetishistic looking, by stopping the narrative in order to recognise the pleasure of display, but displacing it from the male body as such and locating it more generally in the overall components of a highly ritualised scene.

John Ellis has characterised fetishistic looking in the following terms:

> where voyeurism maintains (depends upon) a separation between the seer and the object seen, fetishism tries to abolish the gulf. ... This process implies a different position and attitude of the spectator to the image. It represents the opposite tendency to that of voyeurism. ... Fetishistic looking implies the direct acknowledgement and participation of the object viewed ... with the fetishistic attitude, the look of the character towards the viewer ... is a central feature. ... The voyeuristic look is curious, inquiring, demanding to know. The fetishistic gaze is captivated by what it sees, does not wish to inquire further, to see more, to find out. ... The fetishistic look has much to do with display and the spectacular. (Ellis, 1982)

Mulvey again centrally discusses this form of looking in relation to the female as object: 'This second avenue, fetishistic scopophilia, builds up the physical beauty of the object, transforming it into something satisfying in itself' (Mulvey, 1975, p. 14). 'Physical beauty' is interpreted solely in terms of the female body. It is specified through the example of the films of Sternberg:

> While Hitchcock goes into the investigative side of voyeurism, Sternberg produces the ultimate fetish, taking it to the point where the powerful look of the male protagonist is broken in favour of the image in direct erotic rapport with the spectator. The beauty of the woman as object and the screen space coalesce; she is no longer the bearer of guilt but a perfect product, whose body, stylised and fragmented by close-ups, is the content of the film and the direct recipient of the spectator's look. (ibid.)

If we return to Leone's shoot-outs, we can see that some elements of the fetishistic look as here described are present, others not. We are offered the spectacle of male bodies, but bodies unmarked as objects of erotic display. There is no trace of an acknowledgement or recognition of those bodies as displayed solely for the gaze of the spectator. They are on display, certainly, but there is no cultural or cinematic convention which would allow the male body to be presented in the way that Dietrich so often is in Sternberg's films. We see male bodies stylised and fragmented by close-ups, but our look is not direct, it is heavily mediated by the looks of the characters involved. And those looks are marked not by desire, but rather by fear, or hatred, or aggression. The shoot-outs are moments of spectacle, points at which the narrative hesitates, comes to a momentary halt, but they are also points at which the drama is finally resolved, a suspense in the culmination of the narrative drive. They thus involve an imbrication of *both* forms of looking, their intertwining designed to minimise and displace the eroticism they each tend to involve, to disavow any explicitly erotic look at the male body.

There are other instances of male combat which seem to function in this way. Aside from the western, one could point to the epic as a genre, to the gladiatorial combat in S*partacus*, to the fight between Christopher Plummer and Stephen Boyd at the end of *The Fall of the Roman Empire*, to the chariot race in *Ben Hur*. More direct displays of the male body can be found, though they tend either to be fairly brief or else to occupy the screen during credit sequences and the like (in which case the display is mediated by another textual function). Examples of the former would include the extraordinary shot of Gary Cooper lying under the hut toward the end of *Man of the West*, his body momentarily filling the Cinemascope screen. Or some of the images of Lee Marvin in *Point Blank*, his body draped over a railing or framed in a doorway. Examples of the latter would include the credit sequence of *Man of the West* again (an example to which Willemen refers), and *Junior Bonner*.

The presentation of Rock Hudson in Sirk's melodramas is a particularly interesting case. There are constantly moments in these films in which Hudson is presented quite explicitly as the object of an erotic look. The look is usually marked as female. But Hudson's body is *feminised* in those moments, an indication of the strength of those conventions which dictate that only women can function as the objects of an explicitly erotic gaze. Such instances of 'feminisation' tend also to occur in the musical, the only genre in which the male body has been unashamedly put on display in mainstream cinema in any consistent way. (A particularly clear and interesting example would be the presentation of John Travolta in *Saturday Night Fever*.)

It is a refusal to acknowledge or make explicit an eroticism that marks all three of the psychic functions and processes discussed here in relation to images of men: identification, voyeuristic looking and fetishistic looking. It is this that tends above all to differentiate the cinematic representation of images of men and women. Although I have sought to open up a space within Laura Mulvey's arguments and theses, to argue that the elements she considers in relation to images of women can and should also be considered in relation to images of men, I would certainly concur with her basic premise that the spectatorial look in mainstream cinema is implicitly male: it is one of the fundamental reasons why the erotic elements involved in the relations between the spectator and the male image have constantly to be repressed and disavowed. Were this not the case, mainstream cinema would have openly to come to terms with the male homosexuality it so assiduously seeks either to denigrate or deny. As it is, male homosexuality is constantly present as an undercurrent, as a potentially troubling aspect of many films and genres, but one that is dealt with obliquely, symptomatically, and that has to be repressed. While mainstream cinema, in its assumption of a male norm, perspective and look, can constantly take women and the female image as its object of investigation, it has rarely investigated men and the male image in the same kind of way: women are a problem, a source of anxiety, of obsessive enquiry; men are not. Where women are investigated, men are tested. Masculinity, as an ideal, at least, is implicitly known. Femininity is, by contrast, a mystery. This is one of the reasons why the representation of masculinity, both inside and outside the cinema, has been so rarely discussed.

References

ELLIS, J. (1982) *Visible Fictions: cinema, television, video,* London, Routledge.

MULVEY, L. (1975) 'Visual pleasure and narrative cinema', *Screen*, Vol. 16, No. 3, pp.6–18.

Source: Neale, 1983, pp. 5–6; 11–16.

READING B:
Sean Nixon, 'Technologies of looking: retailing and the visual'

It was the *flâneur*, the male stroller in the city, who, above all, condensed the quintessentially new in modern life for Benjamin. Significantly, it was through his proximity to the new signs of modern consumption that the modernity of the *flâneur* was shaped. As Benjamin put it:

> he [the *flâneur*] is as much at home among the façades of houses as a citizen is in his four walls. To him the shiny, enamelled signs of businesses are at least as good a wall ornament as an oil painting is to a bourgeois in his salon. The walls are the desks against which he presses his notebooks; news-stands are his libraries and the terraces of cafés are the balconies from which he looks down on his household after his work is done. (Benjamin, 1973, p. 37)

In particular it was in the arcades that the *flâneur* was at home. They provided the perfect space for strolling and looking. Benjamin quotes from a contemporary illustrated guide to Paris in invoking the arcades:

> The arcades […] are glass-covered, marble-panelled passageways through entire complexes of houses whose proprietors have combined for such speculations. Both sides of these passageways, which are lighted from above, are lined with the most elegant shops, so that such an arcade is a city, even a world, in miniature. (Benjamin, 1973, pp. 36–7)

This is a gushing advertisement for the arcades. Nevertheless, it testifies to both their spectacular qualities and gives us a clue to their importance in establishing the basis for a new style of consumption. Underlying the development of the arcades were new production technologies and materials: advances in plate-glass manufacture, iron-working techniques, gas lighting, bitumen and later electricity. These made possible features such as the smooth street surfaces for promenading and the display windows and interiors of the arcades. These technologies also underpinned the development of the department store and consumer spectacles like the Grandeville or world exhibitions in Paris and the Great Exhibition of 1851 in London.

Benjamin saw in these retail spectacles (the arcades, the department stores, the World exhibitions) a new staging of the commodity, and in the *flâneur* an allegorical representation of the new relationship between the display of commodities and consumers. The way Benjamin conceptualised this new commodity culture is significant for my account. Centrally, Benjamin's description of the *flâneur* suggested the construction of a new spectatorial consumer subjectivity in relation (initially) to the arcades and their window displays of deluxe goods and expensive trifles. In other words, it suggests the formation of a distinct way of looking at 'beautiful and expensive things' (Benjamin, 1973, p. 55). In addition, Benjamin emphasised the way this consumer subjectivity not only established a series of looks at the displays of goods and the detail of the shop interiors, but also invited the consumer to look at themselves amidst this spectacle – often literally, through catching sight of their reflection in a mirror or shop window. A self-monitoring look was implicit, then, in these ways of looking. The self-consciousness of the *flâneur* in Benjamin's account underlined this.

Benjamin's account of the *flâneur* also hints at other determinants on the spectatorial consumer subjectivity. Together with the display techniques used in the arcades, the immediate context of the city – and in particular the crowds which filled a city like Paris – shaped specific ways of looking in Benjamin's account. What was produced were a series of interrupted looks or glances. Baudelaire's description of the *flâneur* captured this way of looking well:

> For the perfect *flâneur*, for the passionate spectator, it is an immense joy to set up house in the heart of the multitude, amid the ebb and flow of movement, in the midst of the fugitive and the infinite. To be away from home and yet to feel oneself everywhere at home; to see the world, to be a centre of the world, and yet to remain hidden to the world. The spectator is a prince who everywhere rejoices in his incognito. (Frisby, 1985, p. 17)

Modern life for the *flâneur* – the life of the arcades and the crowds of Paris – is here visually apprehended through such 'transitory, fugitive elements, whose metamorphoses are so rapid' (Frisby, 1985, p. 18).

Baudelaire's sonnet, 'To A Passer-by', which Benjamin comments on, further underlines the formation of new ways of looking conditioned by the urban environment. In the sonnet, the male narrator catches sight of, and is fascinated by, a woman who passes by in the crowd. In the moment of his desire being aroused, however, the woman is already lost again in the crowd. For Benjamin this representation of masculine desire in the city is significant. It is, he suggests, a representation 'not so much of love at first sight, as love at last sight'. In other words, the desire experienced by the narrator in seeing the woman is the product of the fleeting quality of his look and the transitory nature of the encounter. It is a representation of the frisson of the passing stranger.

II

Benjamin's commentary on the *flâneur* points us towards the formation of specific ways of looking that were shaped by the new techniques of consumer display and the increasingly differentiated space of the wider city context (such as the distinctions between industrial districts and largely retail and leisure-based areas) (Green, 1990, pp. 23–42). The sonnet, 'To A Passer-by', also alerts us to a further dimension of these ways of looking. That is, the way in which these ways of looking were implicated in a set of gendered power relations of looking.

Janet Wolff and Griselda Pollock, as Elizabeth Wilson has shown, have emphasised in quite similar terms the dominance of specifically masculine pleasures in looking associated with modern city space and its consumer display. Wolff goes so far as to suggest that:

> the possibility of unmolested strolling and observation first seen by Baudelaire, and then analysed by Walter Benjamin were entirely the experiences of men. (Wolff, quoted in Wilson, 1992, p. 99)

Pollock cites the career of the painter Berthe Morisot and her focus on domestic scenes and interiors, to make the same point. Thus for Pollock:

> the gaze of the *flâneur* articulates and produces a masculine sexuality which in the modern sexual economy enjoys the freedom to look, appraise and possess. (Pollock, quoted in Wilson, 1992, p. 101)

This was a look, importantly, in which women shoppers were as much the object of masculine visual enquiry as the shop displays. Quite deliberate slippages were often made, in fact, in consumerist commentaries between decorative consumer trifles and women's appearances. Rachel Bowlby quotes an emphatic representation of these relations of looking. The illustration from *La Vie de Londres* (1890), titled, 'Shopping dans Regent Street', put it succinctly: '"Shopping is checking out the stores – for ladies; for gentlemen, it's checking out the lady shoppers! *Shop qui peut!*"' (Bowlby, 1985, pp. 80–1).

This latter commentary, however, also hints at a more complex picture of the gender ascribed to forms of consumer spectatorship in the nineteenth century than the totalising conceptualisation advocated by Pollock and Wolff. Elizabeth Wilson, in her essay, 'The invisible *flâneur*' takes to task Wolff and Pollock for underestimating the ability of groups of women to actively participate in the new consumer subjectivity and its associated forms of spectatorship. Noting the growth of white-collar occupations for women towards the end of the nineteenth century, Wilson argues that this constituency of women were explicitly courted by commercial entrepreneurs and also participated in the pleasures of 'just looking' associated with consumption. As she says:

> the number of eating establishments grew rapidly, with railway station buffets, refreshment rooms at exhibitions, ladies-only dining rooms, and the opening of West End establishments such as the Criterion (1874), which specifically catered for women. At the end of the century Lyons, the ABC tearooms, Fullers tearooms … the rest rooms and refreshment rooms in department stores had all transformed the middle- and lower-middle class woman's experience of public life. (Wilson, 1992, p. 101)

Nicholas Green also argues that certain groups of women were visible as promenaders and active shopping *voyeurs* around the emergent sites of consumption. An important constituent in this respect were what he calls 'fashionable women' (Green, 1990, p. 41); namely, wealthy women often involved in fashion or part of the new breed of society hostesses. These women had the necessary economic power to consume and were able to

negotiate, Green suggests, the uninvited looks of men in the pursuit of the visual and material pleasures of consumption. These women had a privileged and respectable place in the fashionable boulevards of Paris, quite different from the other femininities which also moved across the urban topography. These were 'immoral' women like street prostitutes, lorettes and courtesans, themselves part of the modern phantasmagoria of the city and part of another arena of masculine consumption.

Green's and Wilson's accounts suggest that women of all classes were a much more significant presence within the modern city and around its new sites of consumption than either Wolff or Pollock suggest, and, more than that, were able to enjoy the pleasures of shopping spectacle – albeit within more tightly controlled boundaries than leisured men. It is also important to reassert – in contradistinction to Pollock – that these ways of looking were shaped by the predominance of an interrupted or broken series of looks (including those which involved forms of self-visualisation) rather than by a fixed gaze. What remains clear from these accounts, however, is the specific link which was forged in the formative periods of consumer culture between certain public masculine identities (and the *flâneur* is, of course, exemplary) and the new modes of spectatorial consumer subjectivity.

III

The modes of leisurely looking – at the spectacle of displayed goods and the visual delights of other shoppers – through which the spectatorial subjectivity of the *flâneur* was produced, were determined by more, though, than the spatial configuration of shop display and the built form of the city. My argument is that these ways of looking formed part of a larger 'technology of looking' associated with consumption and leisure. The forms of representation associated with a new style of journalism linked to the expansion of the popular press and popular periodicals, and subsequently (and critically) the circulation of photographic images through these same forms, were the other key components of this technology of looking. Benjamin, again, provides some pointers to these processes and their cultural significance.

A whole popular literature devoted to representing the culture of the metropolis and the new delights of consumption was associated with the development of modern forms of consumption. Benjamin singled out the genre of popular publications called 'physiologies', pocket-sized volumes which detailed Paris and the figures who populated the new districts. These were immensely popular publications, with, as Benjamin details, seventy-six new physiologies appearing in 1841. In addition, other styles of brochure and pamphlet appeared that detailed salon culture and were often tied in with the expansion of art dealing and the trade in contemporary pictures and other *objects de luxe*. What is important for my argument is that these publications represented the city and the new forms of consumption in highly visual terms. In Benjamin's memorable phrase, 'the leisurely quality of these descriptions [of Paris life in the physiologies] fits the style of the *flâneur* who goes botanizing on the asphalt' (Benjamin, 1973, p. 36). I think this can be put more firmly. The spectatorial subjectivity of the *flâneur* had conditions of existence in the visual apprehension of the city represented in these literatures; the *flâneur*'s ways of looking were shaped by the organisation of particular looks or ways of seeing within popular publications. The widespread circulation of photographic images of the city and consumer goods which followed the introduction of half-tone plates in the 1880s extended this process through another representational form. Half-tone plates made possible the cheap reproduction of photographic images in newspapers, periodicals, in books and advertisements (Tagg, 1988, pp. 55–56). In practical terms this massively extended what John Tagg calls the 'democracy of the image', undercutting the previous luxury status of the photograph and turning it into an everyday, throw-away object.

Culturally, this photography set the terms for new forms of perception. For Benjamin, at the heart of this process were techniques like the close-up and juxtaposition. The practices of photography associated with the new 'democracy of the image', then, visually represented modern life in new and distinctive ways. As such, they formed an important part of the 'technology of looking' that structured the experience of consumption in the period around the turn of the century. This was a technology of looking whose precepts went back, as we have seen, as early perhaps as the 1770s and which linked an intertextual set of looks from the interiors of retail environments and the surrounding streets to the

written and pictorial representations of city life and consumption in paperbacks, magazines and newspapers. The spectatorial consumer subjectivity associated with the characteristically modern forms of consumption was produced across these constructions of ways of looking or seeing.

References

BENJAMIN, W. (1973) *Charles Baudelaire: a lyric poet in the era of high capitalism*, London, New Left Books.

BOWLBY, R. (1985) *Just Looking: consumer culture in Dreiser, Gissing and Zola*, Basingstoke, Macmillan.

FRISBY (1985) *Fragments of Modernity*, London, Polity.

GREEN, N. (1990) *The Spectacle of Nature: landscape and bourgeois culture in nineteenth century France*, Manchester, Manchester University Press.

TAGG, J. (1988) *The Burden of Representation: essays on photographies and histories*, London, Macmillan.

WILSON, E. (1992) 'The invisible flâneur', *New Left Review*, Jan./Feb., pp. 90–110.

Source: Nixon, 1996, pp. 63–9.

GENRE AND GENDER: THE CASE OF SOAP OPERA

Christine Gledhill

Contents

1   Introduction

Earlier chapters in this book have examined a wide range of representations and identities which circulate through different signifying practices: constructions of Frenchness, produced and circulated through photojournalism; images of cultural differences constructed in the museum; images of the Other, as portrayed in the media; alternative masculinities emerging in the 'new man' of shop window displays and fashion photography. As cultural constructions, such representations address us in the practices of everyday life even while calling on our subjective sense of self and our fantasies: what being French means, how we relate to those who are in some way 'different', how to be a certain kind of man. What these chapters stress is that all social practices – whether reading newspapers and magazines, visiting museums, shopping for clothes – take place within representation and are saturated with meanings and values which contribute to our sense of who we are – our culturally constructed identities.

This chapter continues with these concerns, but narrows the focus to that signifying practice which we might think of as specializing in the production of cultural representations: the mass production of *fiction*, of stories – novels, films, radio and television dramas and serials. While many of the issues raised in this chapter are relevant across the range of popular culture, I will focus on the specific example of television *soap opera* to explore how popular fictions participate in the production and circulation of cultural meanings, especially in relation to gender. 'Soap opera' is a particular type or *genre* of popular fiction first devised for female audiences in the 1930s by American radio broadcasters, which has since spread to television around the world.

In section 2, we look at the pervasiveness of soap opera and the role of narrative fiction in popular culture. In section 3, we will consider the impact of gender on mass cultural forms, while section 4 introduces concepts from *genre theory* in order to explore how soap opera works as a signifying practice. The impact of gender on the form of soap opera as a type of programme which seeks to address a female audience is discussed in section 5, where we will encounter feminist debates about *representation* and the *construction of female subject-positions*. But soap opera's extraordinary shift in recent years from the female-dominated daytime to the family primetime schedule – when, research suggests, household viewing choices are more likely to be in the control of men – raises more general questions (dealt with particularly in section 6) about the *gendering of popular genres* and the way in which the soap opera form participates in changing definitions of masculinity and femininity.

This chapter, then, will be asking you to give as much time as you can to watching soap operas aired on television this week, to looking at the way soap operas are presented in television magazines and listings, noting any references to soap opera that may turn up in newscasts, newspapers and magazines.

The key questions to be explored are:

- How does soap opera as an example of mass-produced popular entertainment contribute to the field of cultural representations, and in particular to definitions of gender?

- How does popular fiction contribute to the production and circulation of gendered identities?

- How does the nature of soap opera as a *genre* affect the cultural struggle over representations, meanings and identities?

- In what way can it be said that soap opera is a female genre?

- What do changes in the content and style of soap operas suggest about gender struggles and changing definitions of masculinity and femininity?

2 Representations and media fictions

2.1 Fiction and everyday life

The term *fiction* suggests a separation from real life. In common-sense terms sitting down with a novel, going to the cinema, or watching a TV drama is to enter an imaginary world which offers a qualitatively different experience from the activities of everyday life and from those media forms which claim to deal with the real world – such as the news or photojournalism. And in some senses, which this chapter will deal with, this is true. Stories are by definition only stories: they are not real life. This often leads to the dismissal of popular fictions as 'only' or 'harmless' entertainment, or worse, time-wasting money-spinners made by the profit-driven entertainment industries. But granted that popular fictions *are* entertainment and *do* have to be profitable, are they for these reasons either irrelevant to *lived experience* or without *significance*? Just consider for a moment some statistics offered by Robert Allen about perhaps the most notorious example of fictional consumption, soap opera:

> Since the early 1930s nearly 100,000 hours of daytime dramatic serials – soap operas – have been broadcast on radio and television in the United States. These hours represent the unfolding of nearly 200 different fictive worlds, many of them over the course of decades. Within 9 years after the debut of the first network radio soap opera in 1932, the soap opera form constituted 90 per cent of all sponsored network radio programming broadcast during the daylight hours. With but a brief hiatus in the mid-1940s, *Guiding Light* has been heard and, since 1952, seen continuously, 260 days each year, making it the longest story ever told.
>
> (Allen, 1985, p. 3)

Such statistics demonstrate the *pervasiveness* of soap opera as *a fact of life*. The twice-, thrice-weekly and often daily broadcasting of soap opera serials offers a fictional experience which audiences encounter as part of a routine in which fiction and everyday life intertwine – to such a degree in fact that major events in soap opera characters' lives become national news, as happened in Spring 1995 with the *Brookside* trial of Mandy and Beth Jordash for the murder of a violent and abusive husband and father, a trial moreover which coincided with the real-life campaign and appeal on behalf of Sara Thornton, imprisoned like Mandy for the murder of her violent husband.

ACTIVITY 1

Over the next week keep a media consumption diary and note the different kinds of fiction you (and perhaps other members of your family) encounter:

1   How much of what you read/listen to/view is fiction of one kind or another?

2   On average how many hours a day or week do you each spend in a fictional world?

3   List the different kinds of fiction you encounter: e.g. serials, soap operas, novels, romances, TV dramas, feature films, etc.

4   Does one kind of fiction predominate in your experience over another?

5   What is your immediate reaction to these observations?

Robert Allen's soap opera statistics establish the *centrality of fiction to everyday life* and perhaps your own experience recorded in your media consumption diary will back this up. Ien Ang, in a study of the American soap *Dallas* and its female audience, argues that '... only through the imagination, which is always subjective, is "objective reality" assimilated: a life without imagination does not exist' (Ang, 1985, p. 83). The calculated 'staging' of Mandy Jordash's trial by the British soap *Brookside* and the news media is worth considering in the light of this claim. In this case, a special two-hour episode of *Brookside* devoted to the trial was given extensive advance publicity, as was the (fictional) event itself in the news media. And connections were made in the press – although denied by legal bodies – between this national event of the imagination and the winning of Sara Thornton's appeal.

Clearly in this instance the fictional imagination of what it is like to be driven to murder, to conceal the crime (under the patio, in an echo of a topical real-life case, the notorious West murders), and to face life imprisonment, became an integral part of public debate about marriage, wife-battering, child abuse and the degree to which women may be justified or not in resorting to violence against abusive husbands. This is not to say anything about what *Brookside* contributed to the debate, nor about its contradictory representations of women and, by implication, feminism, to which we will return later. The point here is that there is a circulation between the events we learn about from one media form – the news – into another – soap opera – and back again. Public debates about child abuse, domestic violence, the administration of the law, become material – signifiers and signs – for the construction of an imaginary world which works over the social and gender contradictions of such events and returns them to public discourse.

2.2 Fiction as entertainment

What this chapter is concerned with, then, are the processes involved in this interchange between fiction and the social world it references. We will need to take account of the specific *signifying practices* involved in producing fictions; in particular *how the social world enters fictional discourse* and what happens to it once there; how particular genres *address different audiences* and *invite participation;* the gendered *representations* and *meanings* they construct and – an important, and often neglected factor – *pleasure.* It is important that we do not lose sight of this last consideration, difficult though it is to find concepts to analyse such an intangible thing. Box 6.1 will help to illustrate the problem of analysing pleasure.

BOX 6.1

In the omnibus edition of *EastEnders* shown on 28 July 1995, a mixture of high farce and melodrama was going on, with two brothers (the aggressive, hard-nosed Grant Mitchell smarting from his ex-wife's emotional revenge; and the softer, more considerate Philip) losing their way between Seville and Torremolinos. They were in a race against time to protect the honour of their errant sister, Samantha, who, despite Phil's reassurances that she could look after herself, the belligerent Grant presumed was destined to be picked up by some 'dirty old man' on a package holiday from the North of England. And she was indeed about to be picked up, not by some Northern male rogue, but by their own travelling companion, the ladykilling David Wicks.

FIGURE 6.1 *EastEnders:* Grant (Ross Kemp) and Phil (Steve McFadden) in the bar, head to head and heart to heart

While, true to the tradition of British bedroom farce, three of the holidaying couples seeking a moment alone coincide in the apartment upstairs, Phil and Grant, having just missed meeting their sister, get drunk in the bar below. Suddenly the farcical tone shifts, as a series of tight reverse-shots focus an exchange of intense looks between the two brothers, for a moment lifting the story into a different register altogether. Under the influence of drink, their bickering subsides, as Phil, having probed Grant for the underlying reasons for his pursuit of

Samantha, declares his unconditional love and support for him.

Everything else that has been going on in this episode has been comically predictable – much of its pleasure, in fact, lying in the fulfilment of our expectations. But for this moment we encounter the unexpected as camera and dialogue switch from hysterical farce into a personal drama of inexplicable emotions with far-reaching resonances.

Using *content analysis* to catalogue character roles and plot types in search of a 'message' about the world generated by fiction, may yield information about male, female and ethnic stereotypes and conclude perhaps that *EastEnders* is reproducing outdated gender ideologies about family honour, the virtue of younger sisters and the taciturnity of men. And indeed this particular episode *does* play with such ideas. But if we restrict ourselves to content analysis, we ignore the pleasurable feelings with which we may respond to its cocktail of farce and melodrama, or register the intensity of the reverse-shot eye-contact between two normally antagonistic brothers. For me at least, this produced a dramatic frisson. Moreover, we have to remember that the continuous serial form of soap opera requires that the ending of one episode is the beginning of the next, so that the meaning of events is never easily pinned down: the following week's edition of *What's on TV* (5–12 August, 1995) featured David and Samantha on its cover as a loving couple under the question, 'Is This Love?'

If you remember this episode you may well want to argue with me about some of the meanings and emotional affects I am attributing to it. But this for the moment is not the point. We need to take care in using the concept of representation, that we do not use it in a limiting way to refer only to the representation of discourses, figures and events of the social world, and neglect the purpose of fiction in producing the pleasures of drama, comedy, melodrama, as well as the pleasures of recognizing situations we know from lived experience.

Alongside the naming of certain ideological values and stereotypes, I have in these comments made a number of references to features which are to do with the *form* of the programmes:

1   their nature as a particular broadcast *genre*, the soap opera;

2   the *narrative structure* both of this particular episode and of soap opera as a continuous serial;

3   the *organization of shots* – through *visual composition* and *editing structures;*

4   *character types;*

5   *modes* of expression such as melodrama, comedy and realism; and

6   our reception of audio-visual dramatized fiction as *aesthetic and affective experiences*, in which the pacing and ordering of plots, visual organization, pitch of the voice, and the dramatically charged encounters between protagonists register on our senses and our emotions.

My argument is that *if we want to know how fictions gain hold of our imaginations so that they effectively become a central part of our 'real' lives on a day-to-day basis we have to pay attention to these properties of aesthetic form and emotional affect.* For these effects produce or imply meanings which we may well find at odds with the ostensible 'messages' we might arrive at through counting stereotypes, themes or plot outcomes.

This means that our study of soap opera will be concerned with questions of representation at the level of story *form*: including different kinds of story type or *genre*, questions of *narrative organization* (the way the story unfolds), and *modes of expression* such as realism and melodrama, all factors which bear on the pleasure-producing, representational and signifying work of fictional forms and the subject-positions they create.

2.3   But is it good for you?

In moving from consideration of consumer goods as culture in the previous chapters to analysis of popular fictions in this one, we enter a sphere of activity which is devoted not only to cultural production in general (e.g. of texts, stories, images) but to the production of *Culture* as a general category, which is comparable in status to *Art*. Since production of artistic objects serves as a measure of a society's 'civilization', they are subject to a type of evaluation not generally accorded to the production of consumer goods such as the Sony Walkman or men's toiletries. As a central feature of any society, *fiction* has been an object of public discussion almost since its production began. In our school experiences we have all undergone some kind of training, however rudimentary, in the analysis of stories and characters in classes on 'English Literature', and we all encounter at some level critical discourse about books, films, TV programmes. Indeed there is a whole industry – educational, journalistic, academic – devoted to the critical assessment and evaluation of dramas, novels, films and television programmes. We do not, then, start out innocently to explore the question of how to understand the phenomenon of soap opera.

> ### ACTIVITY 2
>
> Pause for a moment to take stock of your own starting point by registering your immediate reaction to the idea of taking soap opera as a subject for academic study!

If your reaction is a decided negative, don't be surprised. Nor should those of you who registered a positive response be surprised if in some way you find yourself qualifying your pleasure: 'I like watching soap operas, but ...'. Charlotte Brunsdon, a feminist cultural analyst, speaks of how soap opera is popularly used as a measure of 'the truly awful'. However, what I want to emphasize here is that the *practice of critical assessment* is itself a type of cultural production: it defines those works of fiction (novels, plays, films, paintings) which are considered touchstones of a society's culture against which the rest are ranked. This, however, is not a neutral process: it is a way of policing the boundaries of official culture in order to ensure which cultural meanings and possibilities are privileged within a society – witness, for example, political arguments in the mid-1990s about the place of Shakespeare and the English 'classics' in the National Curriculum.

3   Mass culture and gendered culture

In this section we take up a number of issues concerning the place of popular narrative in mass culture.

3.1   Women's culture and men's culture

An apparently anomalous feature of mass culture, often noted by feminists, is the provision of a cultural space designated explicitly as 'women's' – the woman's page in daily newspapers, women's magazines, the woman's film, *Woman's Hour*, etc., while a corresponding category for men hardly exists. There is, for example, no 'man's page' in the daily newspapers, nor 'man's film' amongst Hollywood genres. Feminists argue this is because in western society the norm of what counts as human is provided by the masculine and only women's culture needs to be marked as specifically gendered – much in the same way that 'man' is said to stand for men *and* women, or 'his' incorporates 'hers', etc. The gendering of culture therefore is not straightforwardly visible. The central, established values claim universal status and are taken to be gender-free.

Gender only becomes an issue if women as a specific category are in question, when they become discussible as a deviation from the norm. Feminists, for example, have had to fight a gender-blind academic and critical establishment to get forms such as romance fiction or soap opera on to the agenda as worthy of serious study. Given soap opera's association with the female audience, its relegation to the domain of 'the truly awful' suggests a gendered standard that aligns core cultural values with the masculine, which then needs protection from the feminizing deviations of mass culture. We can observe this unconscious gendering of cultural value at work even in feminist and Marxist analysis. For example, feminist film journalist, Molly Haskell described the Hollywood woman's film as 'emotional porn for frustrated housewives' (Haskell, 1974); Marxist critic David Margolies attacked Mills and Boon romances for encouraging their female readers to 'sink into feeling' (Margolies, 1982/3); Marxist analyst, Michele Mattelart consigns Latin American soap operas to 'the oppressive order of the heart' (Mattelart, 1985). This identification of *feeling* with female cultural forms is perhaps one reason why men often dislike acknowledging their place in the soap opera audience. Clearly the realms of the domestic and of feeling are felt to be beyond serious consideration. We may, then, have to revise some of our assumptions about critical value if we are to get at the heart of the cultural significance of soap opera's popularity.

The questions posed for this book, then, are not only *how is gender constructed in representation?* but *how does gender impact on the cultural forms that do the constructing?* and *on the way they are perceived in our culture? How,* in particular, *does the space designated 'woman's' differ from the masculine norm?*

3.2 Images of women vs. real women

Early feminist approaches to the media were concerned with the role of the dominant media images of women in circulating and maintaining established beliefs about the nature of the feminine and the masculine and the proper roles to be played by women and men, wives and husbands, mothers and fathers. They attacked such images for not representing women as they really are or really could or should be – for being **stereotypes**, rather than positive images, psychologically rounded characters, or real women. In other words, the critique pitted one form of representation against another in terms of their presumed realism: the *stereotype*, because obviously constructed, was assumed to be 'false', while the **psychologically rounded character** was assumed to guarantee truth to human nature. The problem with this analysis is not the rejection of media distortions, but the supposed remedy. What is required, according to this view, is simply a readjustment of the lens, a refocusing of the programme maker's perspective, in order to produce accurate reflections.

stereotypes

psychologically rounded character

But is it as simple as this? The 'mimetic' assumptions which underlie this view were challenged by Stuart Hall in Chapter 1: we encounter very practical problems in appealing to 'reality' as a means of assessing the constructive work of representations. For the category 'women' does not refer to a homogeneous social grouping in which all women will recognize themselves. For a start, gender intersects with other social identities during the practice of daily life – worker, student, tax-payer, etc. And being 'a woman' will be experienced differently according to one's age, class, ethnicity, sexual orientation and so on. The notion that representation can or should reflect 'real women' therefore stalls on the questions:

- whose reality?
- what reality? (the oppression of women? women as victims? positive heroines?)
- according to whom?

In opposition to this mimetic approach, the 'constructionist' view of representation outlined by Stuart Hall implies that even the terms 'man' and 'woman' – whether word or image – which touch on what appears most personal to us – our sex and gender – are in fact cultural signifiers which construct rather than reflect gender definitions, meanings and identities. However 'natural' their reference may seem, these terms are not simply a means of symbolic representation of pre-given male and female 'essences'. The psychologically rounded character, so often appealed to as a kind of gold standard in human representation, is as much a work of construction as the stereotype; it is produced by the discourses of popular psychology, sociology, medicine, education and so on, which, as Sean Nixon suggests in Chapter 5, contribute in their own turn dominant notions of what constitutes feminine and masculine identity. Thus stereotypes and psychologically rounded characters are different kinds of mechanisms by which the protagonists of fiction 'articulate with reality'; the 'stereotype' functioning as a short-hand reference to specific cultural perceptions (as discussed by Stuart Hall in Chapter 4), the 'psychologically rounded character' constructing a more complex illusion from the popular currency of sociological or psychological ideas. Their *cultural significance*, however, cannot be measured in any direct comparison with the real world, but, as we shall see in the following sections, depends on how they are called on within the particular genres or narrative forms which use them, as well as on the circumstances of their production and reception, and on the social context of their audiences.

3.3 Entertainment as a capitalist industry

The higher value placed on the 'character' over the 'stereotype' stems in part from the function which the latter play in the mass-produced formulae of the entertainment and consumer industries. This perception returns us to the question of power. For example, in her investigation of the female audience for *Dallas*, Ien Ang found, amongst those declaring a dislike of the programme, both a rejection of the profit motive at work in the production of the serial and an implicit sense of the power imbalance between the money makers and the mass audience:

> It really makes me more and more angry. The aim is simply to rake in money, loads of money and people try to do that by means of all these things – sex, beautiful people, wealth and you always have people who fall for it. To get high viewing figures.
>
> (quoted in Ang, 1985, p. 91)

Many of the *Dallas* haters make an explicit equation between the 'commercial' aims and traditional gender roles validated in the programme. The problem with this critique, however, is that the brunt of the criticism falls on the 'people who fall for it'. The audience so represented never includes the critic, but consists of 'those others, out there'. In other words 'I' and the 'you' whom I address are not among 'those' people. Nor does this critique acknowledge that money is a necessity for any cultural work whether mass or minority (starving in a garret for the sake of art may be very high minded but not very practical!). Typically, within what Ien Ang terms 'the ideology of mass culture', it is 'money' *and* the 'mass audience' which are attacked rather than the power relations in play between the media and their audiences.

3.4 Dominant ideology, hegemony and cultural negotiation

What emerges in these perceptions of media manipulation is the question of the link between social and cultural domination. This was initially approached through the early Marxist concept of *ideology*. According to Marx those groups who own the means of production thereby control the means of producing and circulating a society's ideas. Through their ownership of publishing houses, newspapers and latterly the electronic media, the dominant classes subject the masses to ideologies which make the social relations of domination and oppression appear natural and so mystify the 'real' conditions of existence. The return to Marx in the 1960s and 1970s, after a period in which it appeared that the traditional working class had been 'bought off' by the growing affluence and consumer culture of the 1950s, put the issue of the link between the mass media and dominant ideology at the centre of the agenda of those struggling for social change. For feminists, as for Marxists, the media have figured as a major instrument of **ideological domination**.

ideological domination

The problem with this notion of ideological domination by the media is that it makes it difficult to conceptualize a position from which to resist or challenge it, except through the values or ideas of the dominant elite which necessarily exclude the mystified masses. A way of moving beyond this impasse was offered in the thinking of the Italian Marxist, Antonio Gramsci, discussed in Chapter 4, which permitted a decisive reformulation of the concept of ideology, displacing the notion of domination by that of **hegemony**. According to Gramsci, since power in a bourgeois democracy is as much a matter of persuasion and consent as of force, it is never secured once and for all. Any dominant group has to a greater or lesser degree to acknowledge the existence of those whom it dominates by winning the consent of competing or marginalized groups in society. Unlike the fixed grip over society implied by 'domination', 'hegemony' is won in the to-and-fro of **negotiation** between competing social, political and ideological forces through which power is contested, shifted or reformed. *Representation* is a key site in such struggle, since the power of definition is a major source of hegemony. In Chapter 4, for example, Stuart Hall points to the way the slogan 'Black is Beautiful' contributed to decisive changes in the meanings of ethnicity and hence the possibilities for changing race-relations in America and the UK. Thus in the process of negotiating hegemony, ideologies may shift their ground, the central consensus may be changed, and 'the real' reconstructed.

hegemony

negotiation

The concepts of hegemony and negotiation enable us to rethink the real and representation in a way which avoids the model of a fixed reality or fixed sets of codes for representing it. And they enable us to conceptualize the production of definitions and identities by the media industries in a way that acknowledges both the unequal power relations involved in the struggle and at the same time the space for negotiation and resistance from subordinated groups. Thus the 'real' is, as it were, an on-going production, in constant process of transformation, and subject to struggle and contest through equally dynamic processes of signification. Within this framework, ideologies are not simply imposed by governments, business interests or the media as their agents – although this possibility always remains an institutional option through mechanisms of direct control such as censorship. Rather, media forms and representations constitute major sites for conflict and negotiation, a central goal of which is the definition of what is to be taken as 'real', and the struggle to name and win support for certain kinds of cultural value and identity over others. 'Realism', then, is a crucial value claimed by different parties to the contest.

3.5 The gendering of cultural forms: high culture vs. mass culture

If we now return to the question of the gendering of cultural forms, what becomes clear is that ranking what counts as culturally significant is 'gendered', and thus the privileging of certain cultural forms or characteristics must also be seen as part of a struggle within patriarchal culture to define 'reality'. We can schematize this struggle like this:

Mass culture/entertainment	High culture/art
Popular genre conventions	Realism
Romanticized stereotypes	Rounded psychological characterization
Glamour	Severity
Emotions	Thought
Expressive performance	Underplaying, understatement
Talk about feelings	Taciturnity, decisive action
Fantasy	Real problems
Escapism	Coming to terms
Private domesticity	The public world
Pleasure	Difficulty
Soap opera	The western
Femininity	**Masculinity**

Such cultural oppositions proliferate and no doubt you could extend the list. I want to draw this section to a close by highlighting two aspects of this chart. First, from the perspective of high culture, all mass entertainment is inferior, and is associated with qualities that are inherently feminizing, while the cultural gold standard of realism is drawn into an alignment with values characterized as masculine. This is not to say that female cultural producers or characters do not operate within high culture; only that when they do, they tend to function on masculinized territory and must abandon or suppress those features characterized as feminizing. Secondly, within a model of hegemonic struggle, the chart represents not a set of rigidly fixed oppositions but values that exist in tension, in constantly shifting relation to each other. For example, the chart may suggest to you why it is that, of all the popular genres, the western has most easily crossed over into the camp of the culturally respectable and worthy (for example, Clint Eastwood's long sought Oscar for *Unforgiven)* while soap opera is still popularly the butt of journalistic humour.

Finally, I want to glance at a term you may have expected to find in the chart and which it would not be surprising to find among your 'gut responses' to soap opera in Activity 1, namely *melodramatic.* The term 'melodramatic' is often applied to soap opera to describe its emphasis on the heightened drama of family relationships and personal feelings, as opposed to the focus on public action in 'male' genres. But melodrama's long and complicated history demonstrates perfectly the shifting intersections between realism and gender in struggles for cultural definition and control. In the nineteenth century, melodrama constituted a pervasive mode of dramatic and fictional production, with broad class and gender appeal. Cape and sword melodramas, nautical melodramas, frontier melodramas, and so on, were action genres and certainly not aimed at women alone. Nor were such melodramas perceived as antithetical to realism. Rather they were conceived as viewing reality in moral and emotional terms and were judged in terms of their authenticity and labour-intensive technical realization on stage. However, in the twentieth century, melodramatic forms, such as the so-called 'women's picture' or 'weepies' which Hollywood produced in the 1930s, '40s and '50s, and the emotionally intense TV drama series and serials, such as soap opera, have become identified as feminine *genres*.

This alerts us to the fact that, like the codes for representing reality, the gendering of genres is not fixed once and for all. Rather, shifts in the gendering of genres may well indicate struggles over defining what counts as masculine and feminine in the construction of social reality. This is important for our investigation of the cultural work of soap opera. For in recent times soap operas have hit primetime television, and appear, like nineteenth-century melodrama, to be making appeals to broader and cross-gendered audiences – for example, *Dallas* (USA) or *Brookside* (UK). Moreover many 'action' based serials, conventionally understood as 'male' genres, are incorporating elements of soap opera – such as *The Bill, London's Burning* (UK). *Do such shifts imply changes in the forms of 'male' and 'female' genres? Or changes in what counts as 'masculine' and 'feminine' themes and characteristics? Or both?* Whatever conclusion we come to, it behoves us not to take the gendering of *genres* as fixed, but to explore what each genre contributes to changing definitions of the masculine and feminine within and around popular fictions in the 1990s.

The next section turns to genre theory for concepts which can both clarify the signifying work of popular fictional forms and the way they may participate in the contest and negotiation for hegemony within representation.

4   Genre, representation and soap opera

In this section I want to turn to the question of soap opera as a signifying practice. In other words, *how does soap opera produce its meanings?* What are the institutional, discursive and formal mechanisms which enable soap opera and other popular fictional TV programmes to function as sites for the negotiation of meanings and identities, sites of cultural struggle over representation, sites for the construction of the real, and for the production of popular pleasures? Finally, how is gender caught up in this textual work?

4.1 The genre system

To answer these questions we need concepts which can deal with the work of soap opera as a mass-produced form of entertainment; concepts that can handle the work of its conventions and stereotypes in relation to the social world of the audience, without presuming either a fixed reality or a fixed set of codes for representing that reality. And we need a model of the discursive work of soap opera which can address questions of power and hegemony and the processes of cultural negotiation taking place in popular culture.

As one of a range of popular fictional types or genres, soap opera belongs to the overarching *genre system* which governs the division of mass-produced print and audio-visual fictions into distinct kinds: romantic novels, detective stories, westerns, thrillers, sitcoms, as well as soap operas. I shall, therefore, be turning to **genre theory** – especially as it has been applied to film and television fiction – for a number of concepts which together offer a productive approach to the work of soap opera within the context of the media industries. For it is within the working of the genre system that economic and production mechanisms, particular textual forms, and audiences or readers interconnect and struggles for hegemony takes place.

genre theory

4.1.1 The genre product

First, what does the term 'genre' imply about the product to which it is applied? A particular genre category refers to the way the individual fictions which belong to it can be grouped together in terms of similar plots, stereotypes, settings, themes, style, emotional affects and so on. Just naming these different popular genres – the detective story, soap opera, etc.– will probably invoke for you certain expectations about the kind of stories and affects they offer, even if you rarely read or watch them. Indeed such categories function as important guides to our viewing choices and practices.

These expectations mean that we already know roughly what *kind* of story we will be watching by, for example, tuning in to television programmes such as *Taggart* or *Home and Away*, or going to the cinema to see *Unforgiven* or *Aliens 3*. Such expectations arise from our familiarity with the *conventions* of each genre – the police series, the soap opera, the western or science fiction. These conventions represent a body of rules or codes, signifiers and signs, and the potential combinations of, and relations between, signs which together constitute the genre.

ACTIVITY 3

Pause for a moment to note down anything you *know* about soap opera as a *genre*, whether or not you are a fan. Use the following headings:

- format and medium
- subject matter
- setting and locations

- narrative pattern
- character types
- plots

Amongst other things you have probably listed some of the following:

Format and medium   Radio or television continuous serial (i.e not series nor serialization, see section 5.1.5 below), broadcast once or more per week, usually in 30-minute slots.

Subject matter   Ups and downs of family or community life and personal relationships.

Setting and locations   Home interiors and public places where lots of people can meet, e.g. pubs, launderettes, corner shops, offices, street corners, hospitals, sometimes the workplace.

Narrative pattern   Multiple and interweaving story lines; we probably don't remember or never saw the beginning; no end in sight.

Character types   Multiple and diverse characters across the social spectrum; many female roles, including older women, widows and divorcees.

Plots   Fallings out between family and community members; jealousies, infidelities, dirty dealings, hidden secrets and their exposure, social problems, e.g. illegitimacy, abortion; sometimes work problems, e.g. redundancy.

These are the conventions which define soap opera as a genre. They are shared by the makers and audiences of a genre product and *to a degree* have to be followed if we are to recognize what genre a particular film or television programme belongs to. The fact that you are probably familiar with the conventions I have listed for soap opera even though you may not watch them, indicates the way popular genres circulate as part of widespread public cultural knowledge.

ACTIVITY 4

As a further test of the pervasiveness of genre knowledge you could pay special attention to an evening's television advertisements or go through one or two weekend newspaper supplements to find how many references to popular genres you can pick up.

4.1.2 Genre and mass-produced fiction

One aspect of the genre product, then, is that it is recognizable by its *similarity* to other products of its kind. It is this that leads to the frequent complaint of predictability. Given an initial clue, we can fill in the rest. Within the ideology of mass culture this use of 'convention' is often associated with industrial mass production as a source of plot formulae, stereotypes and clichés. In this respect, *convention* takes on an inherently conservative connotation, its main function being to reinforce normative meanings and values. Genre theory was developed as a means of countering this deterministic conception by seeking to understand the productive work of convention in the context of three interconnected but distinct 'moments' or 'stages' in the cultural work of the media industries:

1   **Production and distribution**: financiers, studios, TV companies, producers and controllers, censors, script-writers, directors, stars, festivals and awards, advertising and publicity, trade press, etc.

2   **The product or text:** genres and programme formats, conventions, narrative structures, styles, iconography, performances, stars, etc.

3   **Reception**: going to the cinema, the TV schedule, 'girls' night out', the family audience, the kitchen TV, the gaze at the cinema screen, the glance at the TV screen, pin-ups, reviews and reviewers, etc.

The approach from the perspective of 'media domination' argues that it is the iron control of stage 1 – Production – over the processes going on in stages 2 and 3 which produces formulaic conventions and stereotypes as part of a cultural assembly line and as a means of maintaining dominant ideologies. However, the variety of procedures and practices involved in the production and consumption of genre fiction undertaken at each stage suggests the complexity of the relations between production, product and reception or 'consumption' and thus the difficulty of imposing economic, ideological and cultural control, even at the level of production.

The alternative approach, developed by genre theory, is useful because it enables us to define the relationship between these three stages, not as the imposition of 'media domination' but rather as a struggle over which meanings, which definitions of reality, will win the consent of the audience and thus establish themselves as the privileged reading of an episode (hegemony). Hegemony is established *and* contested in the interaction and negotiation between : (1) industrial production, (2) the semiotic work of the text, and (3) audience reception. Moreover, each stage contains within itself potential tensions and contradictions between the different economic, professional, aesthetic and personal practices and cultural traditions involved.

4.2 Genre as standardization and differentiation

First let us examine the genre system at the level of production, focusing on the *repeatability* of genre conventions as a key to the *mass production* of fictions. The economic rationale for genre production is, perhaps, most vividly illustrated by the Hollywood studio system. As is frequently asserted, film-making is a hugely costly affair requiring capital investment both in plant – studio buildings, technological hardware, laboratories, cinemas – and in individual productions. Economies of scale require **standardization of production** and the emergence of popular genres – which began with the growth of nineteenth-century mass fiction and syndicated theatrical entertainments – served this need. The elaborate sets, costume

standardization of
production

designs, and props of one genre film can be re-utilized with a modicum of alteration in the next production; writers familiar with the conventions of plotting and dialogue appropriate to a particular genre can move from script to script in assembly-line fashion; bit-part actors and stars can be groomed to produce the gestural mannerisms, style of delivery and overall 'image' appropriate to the protagonists of a particular genre; studio technicians, cameramen (rarely women), editors and directors become increasingly efficient in the design, lighting and cinematography required to produce the particular visual world and mode of narration of the given genre. *Genre becomes a means of standardizing production.*

ACTIVITY 5

Stop at this point and note down:

1   how investment in a soap opera might contribute to economies of scale, standardization and efficiency, and

2   what special problems the soap opera format might present for this need for standardization.

In looking at soap opera from this perspective you may have noted that the form offers production companies the advantage of extended use of sets and properties over time. This made it economically worthwhile, for example, for Granada to build a permanent set for *Coronation Street,* and for Brookside Productions Ltd to invest not in a set, but in a real close of modern houses. The longevity of soap opera, however, plays havoc with continuity of personnel and story-line. For example, changes of writers can produce terrible mistakes out of ignorance of past relationships or events, to the point that *Coronation Street* employs a serial historian in order to avoid embarrassing slips! This demonstrates an important tension between the pressures for economy at the production stage through standardization and the 'rules' which govern a fictional world, which once brought into being, take on a certain life of their own, not least in the memories of listeners and viewers who ring studios to tell producers when they get things wrong.

This example also shows that genre not only standardizes the production process, it serves *to stabilize an audience.* What we buy with our cinema ticket, television licence or cable subscription is the promise of a certain type of experience – entry to a fictional world as a means of being entertained. This, however, is a state of being, the conditions for which are notoriously difficult to predict or control! By offering familiar tried and tested worlds with familiar appeals and pleasures, genres serve not only to standardize production but to predict markets and stabilize audiences. For the film studio or television company, genres become a means of reaching an audience and hopefully of developing a bond with that audience – inducing a kind of 'brand loyalty'.

ACTIVITY 6

Pause for a moment, and note down what aspects of soap opera might contribute to 'brand loyalty'.

Genre production, however, is not just about standardization – about fixing conventions and audiences. If all soap operas were exactly like one another, they would soon lose their audiences because they would become too predictable and repetitive. So genre production is equally about **differentiation** – managing product differentiation to maximize, and appeal to, different audiences and to keep tabs on changing audiences. This manifests itself in two ways: the production of a *variety of genres* for different audiences, and *variation within genres* between one example and the next. Thus, for example, one western will in some respects be much like another, but it will differ in well-known ways from a gangster film or a family melodrama. Similarly, the soap opera is defined partly in its difference from the police series, for example. Equally, a new western will differ from past westerns, and a new soap opera will try to open up different territory from its rivals – for instance, the BBC's attempt to vary the traditional working-class 'world' of *EastEnders* with the (unsuccessful) *El Dorado* about middle-class expatriates in Spain.

differentiation

Such differentiation is vital, ensuring both the pleasure of recognition, along with the frisson of the new. For while we may stick to our favourite brands of soap or washing powder, we don't on the whole want to see the same film or television programme over and over again. On the other hand we may have a particular liking for some genres over others and experience pleasure in revisiting that 'world' again and again. Thus the genre system offers the possibility of variety, enabling film studios and TV companies to offer choice and acknowledge differences among audiences, while retaining the advantage of standardized production procedures with its attendant rewards. For audiences, then, the question that brings us back to our favourite genre is less *what* is going to happen, which as detractors point out we can probably predict, but *how*. The popular audience, far from being the *passive consumers* constructed within the ideology of mass culture, are required to be *expert readers* in order to appreciate the twists and innovations within the familiar which are the pleasures of the genre system.

4.3 The genre product as text

I want now to consider more precisely the work of the genre text as a semiotic site for the production and negotiation of representations, meanings and identities.

What does it mean to define a popular genre as a 'signifying practice'? In Chapter 1 of this book (p. 36), Stuart Hall introduced the work of Claude Lévi-Strauss, the French anthropologist, who:

> … studied the customs, rituals, totemic objects, designs, myths and folk-tales of so-called 'primitive' peoples…, not by analysing how these things were produced and used …, but in terms of what they were trying to 'say', what messages about the culture they communicated. He analysed their meaning, not by interpreting their content, but by looking at the underlying rules and codes through which such objects or practices produced meaning …

I have suggested that any given genre provides just such a system of underlying rules and codes by which films or TV programmes are produced and understood. At its most basic level the genre system orchestrates signifiers which determine the attributes of different fictional worlds: for example, *settings* (e.g. the American West, an East End community); *locations* (e.g. a saloon bar, a launderette); *character types* (e.g. the outlaw, the manageress of the motel); *iconography* (e.g. a smoking Winchester 73, three flying ducks on a living-room wall), *plots* (e.g. a new sheriff arrives to establish law and order by driving out corrupt business interests, the community social worker finds out that her underage daughter is pregnant by her ex-lover). At first sight, generic codes consist of rules of inclusion and exclusion governing what can and cannot appear or happen within particular generic worlds. We would, for instance, be startled if not downright confused to see the three flying ducks – which are perfectly acceptable on the Ogdens' living-room wall in *Coronation Street* – adorning the Deadwood saloon; or, conversely, a Winchester 73 hung over the washing machines in *EastEnders*' launderette! These settings, character types and images become *signs* for a particular kind of fictional world.

However, it is unwise to assert too confidently that particular attributes *cannot* appear or happen in a particular genre, because sooner or later you will be proved wrong. The rules or codes establish limits but they are not eternally fixed. In the early days of analysis of soap opera, it was said, first, that you would never see inside a factory in a soap opera and, later, when Mike Baldwin opened up his clothing factory in *Coronation Street* , that you'd never have a strike in a soap opera. Within a year the Baldwin factory was closed down while the female workforce came out on strike. This is because the semiotic principles of signification determine that generic signs produce meanings through relationships of similarity *and difference.* Of course, repetition and similarity are necessary to establish familiarity with the codes which bind signifier to signified, but meaning is produced only in the difference between signs. For example, the code that matches the iconography of a white hat and horse/black hat and horse with the upright Westerner and the outlaw, plays on a binary colour coding to mark the difference, and it is that which produces the meaning of the character types. But there are several different combinations that can be made with even these few elements. Switch hats and character types and the new combination produces new meanings through the difference – about, for instance, the moral complexity of the law, or the ambivalent position of the outsider. In other words, rather than inert counters with already assigned, fixed and predictable meanings – white hat and horse means upright westerner, black hat and horse means outlaw – generic conventions *produce* meanings through a process of constantly shifting combination and differentiation.

4.3.1 Genres and binary differences

This has led some critics to analyse genres in terms of a shifting series of binary differences or oppositions. For example, Jim Kitzes (1969) explores the western in terms of a series of structuring differences or 'antimonies' which he traces back to the core opposition, Wilderness versus Civilization. Together these represent a 'philosophical dialectic, an ambiguous cluster of meanings and attitudes that provide the traditional/thematic structure of the genre'. Within this flexible set of shifting antinomies the opposition masculinity/femininity constitutes one of the ideological tensions played out. Typically in the western, masculinity is identified with the Wilderness/ the Individual/Freedom and femininity with Civilization/Community/ Restriction, but this poses the problem of how to include the gunslinging westerner in the genre's representation of social order which concludes the film. The main point I want to make here, however, is that any given genre film produces its meanings from a shifting pattern of visual, thematic and ideological differences and that gender is a key signifying difference in this orchestration.

ACTIVITY 7

Stop now to consider what you have so far noted as the conventions of soap opera. How far can these be grouped in a series of oppositions or binary differences?

Christine Geraghty (1991) suggests that the opposition 'men/women' is a core organizing difference. How far can you group the differences you have so far noted around this opposition?

Drawing up such lists of oppositions can illuminate what is at stake in the conflicts orchestrated by a particular genre. However, the point of the exercise is not to fix signifiers in permanent opposition, but to uncover a pattern, the terms of which can be shifted to produce a different meaning. It is the shifting of ideological and cultural values across the terms of the oppositions that enables us to pursue the processes of and struggles over meaning.

4.3.2   Genre boundaries

So far I have argued that it is not possible to fix the meaning of particular generic signifiers. Neither is it possible to define genres through a fixed set of attributes unique to themselves. So, for example, guns are key to both the western and the gangster film, and weddings are important to both romantic comedies and soap operas. What defines the genre is not the specific convention itself but its placing in a particular relationship with other elements – a relationship which generates different meanings and narrative possibilities according to the genre: for example, the gun wielded against the wilderness in the western, or against society in the gangster film; the wedding as a concluding integration of warring parties in the romantic comedy or the wedding as the start of marriage problems in soap opera.

Given such overlaps, the boundaries between genres are not fixed either: rather we find a sliding of conventions from one genre to another according to changes in production and audiences. This sliding of conventions is a prime source of generic evolution. So, for example, when soap opera left the daytime women's television audience for primetime, with the appearance of *Dallas,* echoes of the western evoked by the Southfork ranch, its landscape and its menfolk extended soap opera's domestic terrain as part of an attempt to produce a more inclusive gendered address for the evening audience. This has led to arguments as to whether, given these western elements, strong male roles, and business intrigues, it is correct to identify *Dallas* as a soap opera. But this effort to fix genre boundaries ignores the dynamic and interdependent processes of signification and media production, where new meanings and generic innovation are produced by breaking rules, pushing at boundaries and redefining difference. The point is less whether *Dallas* is a soap opera or not, but rather what meanings are produced when signifiers from different genres intersect, and in this case when differently gendered genres are involved. As we shall see in section 6, the sliding of meaning as signifiers shift across the boundaries that demarcate one genre from another produces negotiations around gender difference which are highly significant for our study of the media and representation.

ACTIVITY 8

Pause here and consider examples of current popular fictional series on television (like *London's Burning, Casualty* or *The Bill)* which are not classified as soap opera.

1   What genre would you say these belong to?

2   Have they shifted in any significant way from the genre to which they belong?

3   Why might we want either to distinguish them from or relate them to soap operas?

4   What does thinking of these series as soap opera bring to light about the way they work?

The problems that you may have encountered in identifying the genres to which these programmes belong suggests that the definition of genre as a system of inclusion and exclusion with which I started has to be modified.

To sum up so far: despite a grounding in repetition and similarity, difference is key to the work of genre. Our knowledge of any generic system can only be provisional. Genre is a system or framework of conventions, expectations and possibilities, or, to put it in the semiotic terms introduced in Chapter 1, the *genre* conventions function as the deep-structure or *langue,* whilst individual programmes, which realize these underlying rules, function as *paroles.* Moreover, as the French literary structuralist Tzvetan Todorov argues (1976), each new manifestation of a genre work changes the possibilities of future works, extending the genre's horizon of expectations and changing what can and cannot be said within the framework of a particular generic world. Steve Neale (1981) insists that generic production, like any system for producing meaning, must be considered not as a fixed and static body of conventions but as a *process.*

FIGURE 6.2
(a) *London's Burning,* (b) *The Bill: male action series or soap opera?*
(Figure 6.2(b) photograph copyright Carlton UK Televsion 1996. Reproduced with permission from Thames Television.)

4.4 Signification and reference

To this point we have considered the work of genre convention as internal to the genre system. Now I want to turn to the question of the relation between the production of genre fictions and social reference, which is central to our consideration of genre's work of cultural negotiation. In Chapter 1, Stuart Hall, describing the three basic elements in the production of meaning – signifier, signified (a mental concept) and the referent – stressed the arbitrary relation between signifier and signified, which produces a sign that refers to, represents, but does not reflect the real world. However, the signs and signifiers of the genre code take signs from our social and cultural world not simply to represent that world but to produce another, fictional, one. In this case we are considering highly specialized signs, produced within and for the genre system. But what exactly is the relation between the signifiers of the generic world and the social? How does genre production engage in reference to the social world while in the process of constructing a fictional one?

4.4.1 Cultural verisimilitude, generic verisimilitude and realism

Steve Neale, in his article on genre (1981), makes two useful distinctions which are helpful in understanding the work of the referent in genre films. First he distinguishes between *verisimilitude* and *realism*. These terms refer in significantly different ways to the work of the referent. *Realism* is today the more familiar term through which we judge whether a fiction constructs a world we recognize as like our own; but, as we have seen, realism is a highly problematic category. Steve Neale, therefore, revives a concept from literary history, to underline the fact that, in fiction, 'reality' is always constructed. *Verisimilitude*, he argues, refers not to what may or may not *actually* be the case but rather to what the dominant culture *believes* to be the case, to what is generally accepted as credible, suitable, proper. Neale then distinguishes between **cultural verisimilitude** and **generic verisimilitude**. In order to be recognized as a film belonging to a particular genre – a western, a musical, a horror film – it must comply with the rules of that genre: in other words, genre conventions produce a second order verisimilitude – what ought to happen in a western or soap opera – by which the credibility or truth of the fictional world we associate with a particular genre is guaranteed. Whereas generic verisimilitude allows for considerable play with fantasy *inside* the bounds of generic credibility (e.g. singing about your problems in the musical; the power of garlic in gothic horror movies), cultural verisimilitude refers us to the norms, mores, and common sense of the social world *outside* the fiction.

cultural verisimilitude
generic verisimilitude

Different genres produce different relationships between generic and cultural verisimilitude. For example, the generic verisimilitude of the gangster film in the 1930s drew heavily on cultural verisimilitude – what audiences then knew about actual bootlegging and gang warfare in the streets, if not from first-hand experience, then from other cultural sources such as the press – whereas the horror film has greater licence to transgress cultural verisimilitude in the construction of a generic world full of supernatural or impossible beings and events.

ACTIVITY 9

Think about recent episodes of a soap opera you have seen and note the way the form establishes its generic verisimilitude – the norms and common sense of its fictional reality. Then consider how soap opera relates to cultural verisimilitude.

We can now return to the distinction between *verisimilitude* and *realism*. Although these two concepts cannot in practice be cleanly separated, the distinction is useful because it suggests how and why *realism* is always a matter of contest. For the demand for realism won't go away, however problematic the notion. And while the concept of verisimilitude refers to normative perceptions of reality – what is generally accepted to be so – the demand for a 'new' realism from oppositional or emerging groups opens up the contest over the definition of the real and forces changes in the codes of verisimilitude. For conventions of cultural verisimilitude get in the way of pressures for social change – newly emerging social groups or practices demand changes in the conventions of representation. Thus *realism* becomes a polemic in an assault on *cultural verisimilitude*: it demands representation of what has not been seen before, what has been unthinkable because unrepresentable. But the new signifiers of the real in their turn solidify into the established codes of cultural verisimilitude and become open to further challenge. The Women's Movement saw this happen in the 1970s, when the dress codes and body language which signified 'women's liberation' circulated into the pages of fashion magazines and advertising – for example, the frequently attacked Virginia Slims adverts which tried to identify liberation with smoking. However, what this demonstrates is that 'cultural verisimilitude' is not monolithic, but fractured by the different signifying practices and discourses through which different social groups stake out their identities and claims on the real.

ACTIVITY 10

Turn back to your notes on the generic and cultural verisimilitude of soap opera and consider whether and how it has been pressured to engage with social change, either by taking on board new kinds of social issues or incorporating characters from previously marginalized groups. Can you identify specifically gendered narrative, thematic or ideological tensions at work in this process?

4.5 Media production and struggles for hegemony

The tension between *realism* and *cultural* and *generic verisimilitude* enables us to link the industrial production of genre fiction to the conceptions of hegemony and cultural struggle introduced in section 3, suggesting how and why the media industries participate in contests over the construction of the real.

We have seen that both the competition for markets and the semiotic conditions of genre production entail a search for difference, for innovation. A genre such as soap opera – a daily 'story of everyday life', itself incorporated into the daily routines of listeners and viewers – is heavily invested in *cultural verisimilitude*. Since, as I have argued, the conventions of cultural verisimilitude are constantly mutating under pressure from shifting cultural discourses and newly emerging social groups, soap operas are driven to engage in some way with social change, if they are not to fall by the wayside as 'old fashioned'. The need to maintain the recognition of existing audiences and attract newly emerging ones, together with the constant need for new story material and the need for an edge over competitors, makes topicality, being up-to-date, controversy, all vital factors in the form's continuance. Christine Geraghty comments on the changing British soap opera scene in the 1980s:

A number of factors ... in the early 1980s provided the impetus for change. The launching of a new national channel on British television, Channel 4, gave an opportunity to Phil Redmond who had been experimenting with a different audience for soaps, particularly in the successful school serial, *Grange Hill.* Redmond had a track record of using social issues to generate a greater sense of realism and such an approach tied in with the new channel's overt commitment to appeal to groups not represented on the other three channels. Channel 4 made a long-term commitment to *Brookside* which enabled it to survive a rocky start and set up a challenge to its staider rivals. At the other end of the spectrum, the US primetime soaps were demonstrating that it was possible to get away with a greater degree of explicitness on sexual issues and a speedier and more dramatic approach to plotting. *EastEnders* took on the *Brookside* commitment to realism through the dramatization of social issues and combined it with US-style paciness. In their various ways, the new serials were thus looking to be marked as different from existing soaps and issues around sexuality, race and class gave them material which would both stand out as different but could be dealt with through the narrative and aesthetic experience already established by soaps. If there were groups in society who were not represented in soaps in the late 1970s, it is also true that soaps with their rapid consumption of material and their continual demand for story lines were particularly receptive to new material.

(Geraghty, 1991, p. 134)

These multiple pressures towards innovation and renewal mean that popular genres not only engage with social change but become key sites for the emerging articulation of and contest over change. So the discourses and imagery of new social movements – for example, the women's, gay, or black liberation movements – which circulate into public consciousness through campaign groups, parliamentary and social policy debates, new and popular journalism, and other media representations, provide popular genres with material for new story lines and the pleasures of dramatic enactment. It is important, though, not to let this suggest a linear model of representation – social change followed by its representation in the media. Rather, what we seek to locate is the circulation of images, representations, and discourses from one area of social practice to another.

How, exactly, does this process take place within the production process? Christine Geraghty's reference to Phil Redmond's role in the development of *Grange Hill* and *Brookside* reminds us of the variety of vested and conflicting interests caught up in the process of media production. Company executives, advertisers, producers, writers, directors and actors, also have different professional and personal stakes in the process of generic innovation and social change.

While such struggles can be viewed on the ground as conflicts between business executives and creative personnel, or between men and women, the acts and decisions of these 'agents' of conflict take place within the movement of cultural discourses discussed by Stuart Hall in Chapter 1 of this book. Julie

FIGURE 6.3
Cagney and Lacey:
Christine Cagney
(Sharon Gless)
and Mary Beth
Lacey (Tyne Daly)
– female buddies
inside the police
series.
(Photograph
copyright
Orion Pictures
Corporation.)

D'Acci (1994), for example, in her study of the American television police series, *Cagney and Lacey*, beloved by female audiences for its substitution of a female for a male police partnership, suggests that the series would not have originated without the public spread of ideas circulated by the Women's Movement. For the writing/producing trio (two women friends and a husband) were inspired by the feminist journalist, Molly Haskell's critique of the buddy movie, centring on the bonding of two male heroes, for its displacement of good women's roles in the late 1960s and 1970s. For the executives and advertisers at CBS the constant search for new and contemporary ideas meant that the innovation of a female buddy pairing in a cop show seemed like a good idea – at the time, that is. Despite successful ratings and an Emmy award, the series came under frequent threat of cancellation from CBS, who were fearful for their advertising revenue, in large part, D'Acci argues, because of the problematic definitions of 'woman' and female sexuality that it invokes. Particularly problematic was the unmarried Christine Cagney, whose fierce independence and intense friendship with Mary Beth Lacey led to two changes of actress in an effort to bring the series under control and reduce the implication of lesbianism – something such strategies singularly failed to do. The fact that the show survived for three series was in part to do with a concerted campaign by an audience of white, middle-class women who used the networks of the Women's Movement to counter-threaten CBS's advertisers with supermarket boycotts and so on. While the arguments were not mounted specifically around lesbianism, and the British female fan club refuses the identification 'feminist', nevertheless contradictory discourses of sexuality and gender can be seen at work mobilizing and shaping the conflict.

If, for the executives at CBS, gender reversal seemed like a commercially good prospect, for the writers putting a female buddy pairing in *Cagney and Lacey* was an assault on the cultural verisimilitude of the police series in the name of the reality of changing gender roles in society. But the attempt to adapt to changing codes of recognition – women are in fact on career routes within the police force; they do try to juggle the demands of paid work and homemaking – had an inevitable impact on the codes of generic recognition: on what until then had been the norm for the police series. The production of a female partnership had to draw on a different set of generic codes and stereotypes – for example, the woman's film, soap opera, the independent or liberated woman.

Moreover, such a partnership could be convincingly constructed only by drawing on the subcultural codes of women's social discourse and culture. Inside a soap opera those codes are taken for granted as part of its cultural as well as generic verisimilitude. Inside a police series, however, they have a range of consequences for both genre and ideology. When female protagonists, for example, have to function as law enforcers and confront criminal behaviour – both associated with male authority and action – gendered conflict inevitably follows. In the search for credibility with the American female middle-class professional audiences which the series sought, this meant drawing on discourses about sexism put into public circulation by the Women's Movement. Such discourses become in their turn a new source of drama and ideological explanation. The plotting of *Cagney and Lacey*, then, is itself made out of a series of negotiations around definitions of gender roles and sexuality, definitions of heterosexual relations and female friendships, as well as around the nature of law and policing.

4.6 Summary

To sum up so far: popular genres represent patterns of repetition and difference, in which difference is crucial to the continuing industrial and semiotic existence of the genre. Far from endless mechanical repetition, the media industries are constantly on the look-out for a new angle, making genre categories remarkably flexible. Genres produce fictional worlds which function according to a structuring set of rules or conventions, thereby ensuring recognition through their conformity to generic verisimilitude. However, they also draw on events and discourses in the social world both as a source of topical story material and as a means of commanding the recognition of audiences through conformity to cultural verisimilitude. The conventions of cultural verisimilitude are under constant pressure for change as social practices and mores change and newly emerging social groups (and potential audiences) put pressure on representation. This highlights the need to consider the changing historical circumstances of fictional production and consumption. These changing circumstances determine that genres cannot exist by mere repetition and recycling past models, but have to engage with difference and change, in a process of negotiation and contest over representation, meaning and pleasure.

In the next section we will shift from the broad question of how the internal signifying processes of popular genres intersect with social discourses circulating outside the text, in order to focus on the intersection of a particular genre – soap opera – with discourses of gender.

5   Genres for women: the case of soap opera

5.1   Genre, soap opera and gender

In what sense can soap opera be said to be a women's form? It is, after all –
feminists argue – produced within male-dominated, multinational media
conglomerates and within discursive practices which construct the masculine as
the norm. This provokes questions such as:

- How do the media construct a female space?
- What are the generic conventions which contribute to creating soap opera
  as a world gendered in the feminine?
- How do soap operas attempt to construct a gendered cultural
  verisimilitude?
- How far and in what ways do these conventions construct feminine
  subject-positions?
- How do soap operas address their increasingly cross-gendered audiences?

First I want to examine certain of soap opera's conventions for their impact on
the representation of gender. Secondly, I will introduce some key concepts
used by feminists to analyse how soap opera addresses the female audience
or constructs positions of viewing which imply a female (or feminized)
spectator.

5.1.1   The invention of soap opera

I will begin by considering the origins of soap opera as an example of how
two mass media – American commercial radio and advertising industries –
combined in the 1930s to produce a form aimed as a fictionalized product
pitch to the daytime female audience of homebound housewives. According
to Robert Allen, soap opera was devised as a more effective alternative to the
radio magazine/advice column format because of the greater power of serial
fiction to capture audiences for the advertising message – which might be
given direct from sponsor to audience as part of the credits, or embedded in
the fiction.

If the motive for the production of mass media forms aimed at a female
market lay in the need of advertisers to attract women as consumers, the
problem remained how to reach this audience. In the 1930s, the radio and
advertising industries turned to previous formats through which women's
cultural concerns have circulated – material often produced by women or out
of traditions associated with female writing. For example, the idea of using
the serial format came from women's magazines, according to Frank
Hummert, who, with his wife, Anne, was a major pioneer of soap opera on
American radio (Buckman, 1984).

5.1.2 Women's culture

In what sense, then, can these forms be thought to belong to women's culture? First, the term *women's culture* requires some caution. This book has insisted that the language of culture is not neutral but carries social values. If the 'masculine' functions as a cultural norm, mainstream media will privilege a masculinist perspective which must impact on those forms developed for the female market: the woman's page, the woman's film, soap opera. The notion of 'women's culture', then, is not intended to suggest some pure feminine space where women speak freely to each other outside of social constraint. Nor, as I have already suggested, can the category 'women' be taken unproblematically, since, as this book contends, gendered and sexual identities are social constructs to which representation contributes. 'Women's culture', then, refers to those spaces on the margins of the dominant culture where women's different positioning in society is acknowledged and allowed a degree of expression. This space may narrow or broaden at different points in social history, but here I am using 'culture' in its widest sense to refer to how women live their daily lives in the home and in the workplace – either in women's jobs or in competition with men; to the social forms and discourses through which women interact with each other – mother and toddler groups, townswomen's guilds, women's campaign groups, health groups, and so on; as well as to the women-addressed forms of cultural expression which women use among others – the domestic novel, novelettes, magazine serials, romances, diaries, confessions, letter pages, advice columns, fashion pages, and so on.

In turning to women's cultural forms, then, programme makers sought to attract women to soap opera listening as a prelude to product purchase by constructing a fictional world which they (1) would recognize as relating to them, (2) would find pleasurable, and (3) could access while doing housework or caring for children.

> ACTIVITY 11
>
> To begin with, take a few moments to note down your thoughts about
>
> 1 how soap opera differs from other genres,
>
> 2 how it might be thought to appeal especially to women, and
>
> 3 any problems you perceive with this idea.

5.1.3 Soap opera as women's genre

Probably the feature of soap opera that most strongly suggests a women's cultural form is its *subject matter* : family and community, relationships and personal life – all social arenas in which women exercise a socially mandated expertise and special concern. But we can say little about the meanings produced by this subject matter without considering the impact on it of the textual conventions and discursive strategies of soap opera as a generic form. To what extent do such conventions and discursive strategies have implications for gender representation? As an immediate consequence of soap opera's domestic and community subject matter, for example, we find a greater number of female protagonists than is usual in other types of TV fiction. The construction of soap opera's fictional world out of the extended family, as in *Dallas* or *Dynasty,* or a neighbourhood community, as in *Coronation Street* or *EastEnders,* entails a variety of female figures representing a cross-section of social or family types. This is reinforced by soap opera's serial format which needs a multiplicity of characters to fuel the continuous generation of story lines, providing many and diverse entry points for identification and recognition – or, importantly as we shall see below, rejection.

> ### ACTIVITY 12
> What is the impact of a greater number of female characters on the kind of fictional world produced by soap opera and on the kinds of narrative action and outcome that can take place in it?

5.1.4 Soap opera's binary oppositions

As we have seen (section 4.3.1), one way of approaching such questions is to explore the structure of *oppositions and differences* which characterize soap opera's fictional world. In the course of her analysis of the representation of women in soap opera, for example, Christine Geraghty suggests a series of oppositions that produce a world constructed between the poles of gendered difference:

women	men
personal	public
home	work
talk	action
community	individualism

(Geraghty, 1991)

As soap opera's wide range of female figures work out their life patterns in this world, this structure of oppositions provides considerable scope both for narrative complications and for shifting negotiations and struggles around gender. However, in tracing the shifting play of such oppositions within the world of soap opera, the impact of the peculiarities of its narrative format is crucial. Key here is its defining feature, **continuous serialization** – the source, in Robert Allen's words, of 'the longest story ever told'.

continuous
serialization

5.1.5 Serial form and gender representation

We can perceive more clearly how the continuous serial works if we compare it to the series and the serial. The *serial* refers to a fiction which is divided into a sequence of parts, so that a strong sense of linear progression is maintained across episodes as the plot unfolds from beginning, through a middle, to the end – for example, the three-part *Taggart* serials, or the serialization of a classic novel. The *series* – for example, *Cagney and Lacey* or

The Bill – bases its sense of continuity on the stability of its central characters to whom different stories happen each week. In this respect, there is a strong sense of beginning, middle and end constructed within each episode. The *continuous serial*, on the other hand, promises a 'never-ending story'.

One of the many interesting features of this type of narrative is its running of several story lines simultaneously. This is not a matter of sub-plots as adjuncts to a central action but the intertwining of different characters' lives. This clearly helps to keep the serial going, so that as one story line runs out, another is coming to the boil. Secondly, the endlessness of soap opera contravenes the 'classic' structure of the majority of popular fictions based on the beginning/ middle/end formula. The pleasure of such a structure is regularly described in terms of an abstract three-part movement: equilibrium, disruption, equilibrium restored.

Steve Neale (1990) has argued that different genres can be distinguished by the different ways they disrupt and restore equilibrium, and the different relationship they produce between initial and closing stable states. For example, western and gangster films work towards driving out a corrupt old order and establishing a new, while romantic comedy aims to integrate disrupting elements into a reformed order, and family melodrama reinstates the old order after what Neale terms 'an in-house rearrangement': despite the evident impossible contradictions and pain of family relations, a new family is established at the drama's end, though significantly often a non-biological family. These differences of narrative resolution produce not only formal or psychological pleasures, but also forms of ideological movement and negotiation in their different organizations of social order.

So what can we say about the impact of continuous serialization on soap opera's shifting structure of gendered oppositions and the negotiations around femininity and masculinity this entails?

ACTIVITY 13

Take a few minutes to consider:

1   the consequences for the narrative and ideological form of soap opera of never being able to end, and

2   what this might mean for the form's construction of its female characters' stories.

Since no end is in sight and we have probably long forgotten the beginning, soap opera has been called the narrative of the 'extended middle'. Christine Geraghty has argued that the form is 'based on the premise of continuous disruption' (1991, p. 15). Compared to the model of the self-contained narrative as a movement from equilibrium through disequilibrium to equilibrium restored, often signalled by a heterosexual kiss or the expulsion of a disruptive woman, 'the premise of continuous disruption' is ideologically significant, for any attempt to *conclude* a story line must, sooner rather than later, shift into reverse gear. While death is a possibility in soap opera, it cannot be overused without bringing the fiction to an end! As for weddings, Terry Lovell comments:

FIGURE 6.4
Coronation Street:
Len and Rita
Fairclough's
wedding (Peter
Adamson and
Barbara Knox) –
a utopian interlude
in the Street's
norm of broken
marriages.

Bill Podmore, the current producer of …
[*Coronation Street*] … has remarked in
connection with Rita's marriage to Len
Fairclough, that marriage easily diminishes a
character, and it was no surprise to find,
eighteen short months later, that Len and Rita's
marriage was under threat, and Rita had left
home. However such a 'disturbance' will be
resolved, whether by Rita (temporarily)
returning to Len or, alternatively, to the
marriage market for a lover or husband, the
acknowledgement of the difficulty of
maintaining the norms of romantic love and
marriage still stands, and is reaffirmed again
and again in the serial. In this particular case
indeed it is difficult to know what constitutes
order and what disturbance. In a sense, the
conventions of the genre are such that the normal order of things in
Coronation Street is precisely that of broken marriages, temporary
liaisons, availability for 'lasting' romantic love which in fact never lasts.
This order, the reverse of the patriarchal norm, is in a sense interrupted by
the marriages and 'happy family' interludes, rather than vice versa. The
breakdown of Rita and Len's marriage, if it occurs, will be a resolution of
the problem which Podmore has created in marrying them in the first
place.

(Lovell, 1981, p. 50)

Thus the combination of subject matter, multiple story lines and never-
resolving narrative impacts on the *type* of female protagonist who inhabits
soap opera. Narrative disruption disposes of husbands and lovers and
longevity of narrative leads to an unusual number of older, widowed,
divorced and independent female figures. Such figures play an important
role in the negotiations around gender that come increasingly to the centre of
soap opera as it gives greater space to male characters, an issue to which we
will return below.

5.2   Soap opera's address to the female audience

So far we have considered the impact of soap opera's generic conventions on
its construction of gender representations which we might assume make it a
pleasurable form for female viewers. I now want to turn to the way these
conventions are deployed as a means of speaking to – addressing – the social
audience of women listeners and viewers. The concept of **address** is
important in considering how a genre might be said to be gendered. As the
history of the invention of soap opera indicates, writers, programme makers
and advertisers produce their products *for* someone. Who they imagine you
are affects the way the product is constructed, the way it speaks to you, or
solicits your attention – just as our sense of who the doctor, or boss, or naughty

address

child is affects the way we speak to them. The way we address someone incorporates a position for that person within the construction of our statement or question (subject-position). For example, the familiar joke, 'Have you stopped beating your wife?', plays on the power of address to position the addressee – in this case as wife-beater. Cross-examination in the law courts develops this feature of language to a fine art. In the 1970s the feminist slogan, 'Who does this ad think you are?' pasted across street advertisements, sought to expose the hidden power of address to position women as subordinate.

In this respect it is noteworthy that the serial fiction format was developed as a more effective way of 'hooking' women listeners and viewers than the advice programme.

ACTIVITY 14

Pause for a moment to consider why the continuous serial might prove more effective than a daily advice programme as a listening hook for female audiences.

The advice format, as with many advertisements, incorporates almost by definition, an address from a position of authority to one who is in some way lacking, in need of advice, information, exhortation. How is authority represented in western culture? Much advice to women is given by male experts. But even if proffered by women, advice-giving will generally be authorized by the voice, personage, dress, and language of white, middle-class officialdom. One of the advantages of audio-visual fiction for the advertiser is that the source and mode of address is indirect. It generally appears 'unauthored'. For example, soap operas are announced as if they are already in progress: 'now, over to *Coronation Street*, where …'; they simply 'appear' on our screens, cued in by their signature tunes and opening credits which *invite us* into a fictional world materialized for us by maps, aerial shots, closer location shots, and perhaps close-ups of the chief players. So we need to consider the different positions constructed for an audience by the different forms of address – advice and invitation. Secondly, to invite women to become involved in a fictional world as women requires positions of identification within the fictional world attuned to a female perspective. One advantage of the serialization of everyday life within the domestic context over the advice format was that it appears to address women on a more equal footing. As we shall see, the degree to which this is simply a question of disguising the male source of address is a matter of debate amongst feminist analysts.

ACTIVITY 15

Before moving on, you might find it useful to watch ten minutes or so of a soap opera with the following questions in mind:

1   How is this fiction speaking to me?

2   Who does it assume I am?

3   What does it assume my interests are?

4   What does it assume about my interest in these characters?

5   Does my gender count in my responses to what I am watching?

6   Do I feel that I am being asked to take a 'male' or 'female' point of view on the events and characters?

7   Am I being involved in this fiction in a different way from watching, say, a crime or detective series, like *Taggart* or *Prime Suspect*?

5.2.1 Talk vs. action

To begin answering such questions, a good place to start is with what perhaps is a defining feature of soap opera: its predilection for *talk*. This is not simply a matter of the dependency of radio on dialogue – for dialogue clearly can be used to signify action, as in radio thrillers or science fiction. Moreover the shift to television has not detracted from this. Try fast-forwarding an episode of *EastEnders* and it becomes clear that its characteristic camera set-up is a 'close-up two shot', producing a drama of talking heads in intimate exchanges or altercation. However, while antipathetic to the criteria of plot development and narrative progression associated with high cultural aesthetics, talk offers a different mode of *social action*: conversation, gossip, dissection of personal and moral issues, and, at crisis points, rows. Talk, in these forms, however, is culturally defined as feminine, involving the exercise of skills and methods of understanding developed by women in the particular socio-historical circumstances in which they live. It is, therefore, a key to establishing a *female cultural verisimilitude*, as opposed to the investment of male-oriented genres in action. In this respect, soap opera's talk is a major factor in its negotiation of gender, a point that we will return to in concluding this section.

5.2.2 Soap opera's serial world

We started thinking about the way soap opera addresses its audience by considering what kind of viewer is presupposed by *continuous serialization*. What kind of invitation is made by the regular listening or viewing slot at particular times during the week or even on a daily basis? Clearly we are being invited to form a habit, often termed by hostile critics as an 'addiction' which is considered to work in the interests of advertisers, shareholders and dominant ideology. But the more interesting question is, exactly what is it we are addicted to? And what is the meaning of this habit to the female audience? Christine Geraghty has identified as a major effect of serialization its production of a sense of 'unchronicled growth' – the sense that while we are not watching or listening, the lives of the characters in the fictional world are continuing in parallel with ours. Combined with a focus on 'everyday, ordinary life', this sense of unchronicled growth enables the soap opera to function as a 'neighbouring' world – its characters exist, quite literally for the Australian soap of that name, as 'neighbours'.

Is there a gendered dimension in this address to us as a neighbour, soliciting our interest and concern for the daily goings-on in the street, the close, the neighbourhood, the community? Traditionally – if less so in a period of high unemployment – it is women who have formed and held together neighbourhood and community networks of social intercourse: in the shops and supermarkets, play groups and nurseries, launderettes, health clinics and schools. Moreover the housewife has depended on the neighbourhood for social contact outside the home. The female soap opera viewer, then, is invited to become involved in another community, a fictional one indeed, but one which parallels her own with characters who share many recognizable problems and dilemmas: who, moreover, experience the same passage of time as the listener or viewer, who age with her, go through many of the same 'stages' and crises of life, experience a similar pattern of achievements, frustrations, reversals and disappointments.

Lastly, serialization addresses in a more literal sense the material conditions under which women in the domestic context can listen or view television. Regularity enables the episodes to be built into a domestic routine, often with a considerable degree of planning and timetabling. Fragmentation of the multiple narratives that intertwine to create the soap opera world accommodate the fragmented, semi-distracted state in which many women combine media listening or viewing with other domestic tasks. Continuousness, overlap of segments within and between episodes, and repeated recounting of events between different characters, all help to combat the fragmented viewing situation and the missed episode. It is possible to drop in and out of the soap opera world without losing the narrative thread.

5.3 Textual address and the construction of subjects

I hope by now to have established some of the ways in which soap opera can be said to speak to a female audience by incorporating in its method of storytelling some of the forms usually associated with women's culture. But what does this say about the **subject-position** which soap opera constructs for its viewer? What of the potential power relations implied in the operation of address and the evident inequality between producers and receivers of mass media entertainments? What happens to the audience once they accept the invitation to enter soap opera's serial world? Does soap opera's female address simply reposition its audience in subordination or can we argue that for women to be offered a female position at all in popular fiction is potentially empowering?

I want now to introduce three different ways in which feminist analysts have conceived the text–audience relations of soap opera, which ask in particular how soap opera's conventions of narration and address construct a female subject-position and with what ideological effects.

subject-position

5.3.1   The ideal spectator

The first approach I want to look at is offered by Tania Modleski (1982), author of an influential analysis of American soap opera: 'The search for tomorrow in today's soap operas'. Her starting point is an argument developed within film theory which concerns the structure of looking in the cinema which has already been touched on in Chapter 5 by Sean Nixon. Because classic Hollywood narrative offers so central a place in its narrative for the glamourized image of woman as object of the male hero's search or investigation, his reward or his downfall, feminist film theorists have argued that the organization of camera and narrative in mainstream cinema is predicated on a masculine spectator. Laura Mulvey (1989/1975), quoted by Sean Nixon in Chapter 5, analysed the cinematic spectacle in terms of a relay of looks *at* the woman – the spectator looks with the camera which looks at the hero who looks at the woman – and, drawing on psychoanalytic theory, argues that the narrative and visual form of Hollywood films has been developed according to the Oedipal fantasies and anxieties of the male unconscious. The gaze in the cinema, Mulvey and others have argued, is constructed as a masculinized gaze; in other words the subject-position offered by cinema's mode of address is masculine. To gaze at, and take pleasure in, the female image is to occupy a male position, one that is set up for us not only in the visual control the male hero has in the organization of the image, which leaves him free to move in and out of frame while the female is frequently trapped at its centre, but also in the narrative agency given to the hero, who drives the plot, makes things happen, and generally gains control of the woman. This argument has had an enormous impact on thinking about the relation between fictional production, gender, and sexual identity.

- What, then, does the argument mean for the female cinema audience?

- What does it mean for those filmic genres (e.g. the woman's film, romantic comedy) that attempt to address that audience directly?

- Can this theory of the masculinized gaze be transferred to television?

ideal spectator

social audience

Such questions focus attention on a potential disjuncture between patriarchal text and female audience and a crucial distinction between the **ideal spectator** or *subject-position created by the text*, which can be found through textual analysis, and the **social audience** at a given point in time. It is important to note that in this debate the 'spectator in the text', the spectator for whom the text is made, which the text needs in order for its constructed meanings and pleasures to be fully realized, is different from the common-sense use of the term 'spectator' as a synonym for the individual viewer or audience member. For this reason you will find that critical theories which deal with these questions tend to use the term 'spectator' to refer to the textual spectator or subject-position, which is distinguished from the 'social audience' who buy tickets to see films, watch TV or rent video tapes for home viewing. As we will see, however, it is often difficult to keep these two meanings of 'spectator' apart.

It is against the background of these debates in feminist film theory that Tania Modleski first posed the question of the kind of spectator which soap opera constructs in its attempt to address female audiences. She begins by noting that unlike the ninety-minute feature film, soap opera does not centre on an individual hero, nor, through his gaze, on the spectacle of the glamourized woman who is his inspiration or downfall. In fact, as Robert Allen points out, soap opera has difficulty in centring at all. Rather, the narrative structuring of soap opera involves fragmentation, interruption, false endings, reversals and new beginnings. The question Modleski explores is what kind of spectator position does this fragmented, constantly interrupted story line offer to us?

READING A

After giving this question some thought, go on to read the extract from Modleski's article, provided as Reading A at the end of this chapter.

How does Modleski's 'ideal spectator' for soap opera differ from Mulvey's 'ideal spectator' for the Hollywood movie?

According to Modleski, we find in fact two quite different 'spectators' constructed by the two different forms: in the classic Hollywood movie, the filmic spectator is constructed as the voyeuristic male, taking control of events and the female image; in soap opera, the spectator is constructed as the idealized mother, passively responsive to events and endlessly identifying with the needs of a range of conflicting characters. These positions which the viewer is invited to occupy, irrespective of her or his actual sex, in the process of following the story are clearly gendered according to dominant conceptions of male and female identity. And Modleski's analysis of the spectatorial position as ideal mother suggests the power of textual address to reinforce the social construction of female identity, in so far as the female viewer occupies this subject-position which confirms passivity and long-suffering as the woman's lot.

However, this method of analysis poses some very important questions:

● Does a fiction construct only one, fixed position for the spectator, so that our choice is either to occupy that position or switch channels?

● Is the viewer – the social audience member – in total thrall to the subject position constructed in the text?

● Can the viewer find – or construct – *other* positions within the text, which coincide more closely with her own particular social experience and outlook, and which may be at variance with dominant gender ideologies?

5.3.2   Female reading competence

You will probably have noticed that, in analysing the spectator of soap opera, Modleski moves between, on the one hand, a strictly textual construction based on its narrative organization and, on the other, a construction based on women's social experience. Thus her interpretation of soap opera's textual spectator as 'ideal mother' is derived from her own knowledge of the social conditions of motherhood, and arises in part because she wants to produce a model of the spectator which, unlike Mulvey's, *could* be occupied by soap opera's female audience. It is, though, only by reference to the social experience and practices of mothering that Modleski is able to bring this gendered perspective to bear on the narrative structure of soap opera.

Nevertheless, Tania Modleski's model of soap opera's address is of an unconscious operation which calls *all* women into a subject-position they are socially and psychologically conditioned to occupy. The match Modleski assumes between the ideological position of the passively forbearing mother who suffers on behalf of all her troublesome children and the woman in the audience leaves little space for the viewer to resist or otherwise engage with soap opera. There is, however, a more dynamic way of approaching the relation of text and audience through the idea of **reading competence**, a semiotic concept referring to the learned interpretative frameworks and reading skills employed by different social groups or 'readerships' to decode signs and representations.

reading competence

From this perspective our capacity to use codes in order to communicate is embedded in the *specific interpretative frameworks and social practices of given groups* and constitutes a form of 'competence' which accounts for *differences in cultural usage*. 'Competence' here does not mean efficiency or correctness but refers to the common-sense knowledge and perspectives shared by a particular readership. Within the specific cultural competencies exercised by given social groups, the signs of verbal or visual language will take on meanings that may be opaque to those outside. Take the familiar icon of three flying ducks which used to adorn the wall of Hilda Ogden's terraced house in *Coronation Street*. What exactly these plastercast ducks signify will depend on the 'competence' of any given reader to decode them. For the set-designers who constructed this working-class living room, three ducks flying diagonally across the wall are signs which mean perhaps: 'this is the sort of thing people like the Ogdens would have on their walls' – a touch of authenticity, an easy cliché, perhaps a patronizing smile. But what do those ducks mean to the viewers? According to class and cultural frameworks, the ducks could evoke fond recognition or a sign of bad taste. Things become even more complicated if we think of those ducks in the form of a brooch worn by a London art student, or on the wall of a Cultural Studies lecturer's Kentish Town flat. I leave it to you to think about what the ducks signify in these situations! But my point is that the cultural meaning of the ducks is radically transformed by social context and the reading competence shared by the owner and his or her milieux.

FIGURE 6.5
Plastercast ducks in flight – a mobile signifier.

A further point to make is that some readings of the ducks have more cultural prestige and social power than others. Some people, through class, ethnic or gender position, education, professional experience, have access to more cultural competences than others. The art student who wears the ducks as a badge is dipping into the cultural competence of one group in order to make another statement within the competence of her or his own and different group. This has led the French cultural sociologist, Pierre Bourdieu, to develop the notion of *cultural capital* in an analogy with financial capital as a source of social division. Just as access to financial capital gives a person economic security and status, so – Bourdieu argued – we use cultural capital to give us knowledge, 'know-how' about the world, practical competences which underpin our status and position, and help us to differentiate ourselves from those who are less well 'culturally endowed' (Bourdieu, 1984). A while back, *Coronation Street*, in an episode that must have been made with Cultural Studies lecturers in mind, made a humorous drama out of this theory in an argument about stone-cladding at The Rover's Return. Curly, defending his 'puce' shirt as a 'keep off' message to the world, declares to the mystified Jack that 'in the empire of signs', his and Vera's stone-cladding similarly says something about them, although it would take a 'trained semiotician' to tell them what. Jack is dumbfounded and Curly can get no further, but the situation is saved when ex-grammar school boy, Ken Barlow, walks in and bluffs his way through an explanation by putting two and two together!

5.3.3 Cultural competence and the implied reader of the text

Soap opera's address to the socially mandated concerns of women – the family, the domestic arena, personal relationships as they work out both in the family and at work – has led Charlotte Brunsdon (1982) to discuss the gendering of this particular genre in terms of **female cultural competence**. Soap operas utilize, and need to be read according to, the cultural codes and reading competences employed by women. This is not to suggest that they cannot be understood by males; rather that soap operas employ a range of knowledges, perspectives and nuances that emerge out of female cultural experience and can be fully activated only within this framework.

female cultural competence

> READING B
>
> Now turn to Reading B at the end of this chapter. In what ways is the notion of the feminine 'implied reader' used by Charlotte Brunsdon different from Modleski's 'ideal spectator'?

The first important difference to note is that whereas the ideal spectator is a *textual construction* into which viewers fit or not, with the implied reader the text has to employ the codes which belong to the cultural competence of an actual *particular readership*. Although we are still analysing codes activated by and through the programme, we are being asked to look for a frame of reading reference *outside* the text, the one used by a particular *social audience*. The second difference is the dynamic relation this implies between audience and programme text. Whereas the textual spectator calls us into and fixes us in a subject-position for which we are already conditioned by unconscious and social structures, the implication of a social reader invites readers to deploy the cultural competence derived from their lived experience in their engagement with the text. As has been suggested, the discursive strategies of soap opera narration – talk, gossip, chewing over events, deciding what is likely to or should happen – are all part of the repertoire of female cultural competence. Moreover, as Charlotte Brunsdon notes, the fragmentation of the soap opera text requires considerable extra-textual work to keep track of events. In other words, pleasure comes not from the text alone, but from the extension of the text into the thinking, communicating activity and skills of the viewer.

5.3.4 The social audience

Thus we are passed from *textual spectator*, through the *implied reader*, into the practices of the historically situated *social audience*. Feminist readings of the work of soap opera such as those made by Tania Modleski and Charlotte Brunsdon emerge from the serious attention devoted by the Women's Movement to the practices, competences and meanings involved in women's engagement in domestic and community life and in personal and family relationships. It is this cultural knowledge that enables Brunsdon to interpret the dramatic dynamic of a ringing telephone in *Crossroads* for an implied female reader. But it is one thing to know that the textual spectator or the implied reader is gendered. It is another to know what the activity of viewing or reading contributes to, or draws from, the gendering of audience identity. The next logical step is to investigate that audience itself.

Ien Ang's work on *Dallas* threw an illuminating spotlight on the audience for soap opera, demonstrating the power of both the mental frameworks and social conditions within which viewing takes place to shape reception. Her analysis of letters written to her by *Dallas* fans showed how, as they described their pleasurable responses to the programme, they also, as it were, viewed their own viewing from within the critical perspectives of the ideology of mass culture:

> In fact it's a flight from reality. I myself am a realistic person and I know that reality is different. Sometimes too I really enjoy having a good old cry with them. And why not? In this way my other bottled-up emotions find an outlet.
>
> (quoted in Ang, 1985, p. 105)

Ien Ang in this study and elsewhere has insisted on viewing as a social practice which differs according to media form and social context. Going to the cinema, switching on the television, bringing home a video are different social practices which have their own specific meanings even before the encounter with a particular film, TV programme or video takes place. In fact several commentators have noted the difficulty of defining or capturing the television 'text' which, as the phrase 'wall-to-wall *Dallas*' suggests, exists as part of the living-room furniture and has to compete for the viewer's attention along with other household and familial activities. The fact that the television is on does not mean that it is being watched and certainly not that it is being given undivided attention. This poses the following sort of questions:

- How, then, do women watch TV?

- What is a woman saying to her family when she leaves the kitchen, sits down in front of the television, and is deaf to requests for the whereabouts of clean socks, the salt or the TV guide?

- What is the difference between a woman watching *Emmerdale* or *Coronation Street* with the whole family, with a daughter, with friends, alone, with a husband or boyfriend?

- How do gender, class, age, ethnicity in general affect the patterns and conditions of viewing?

- What are the knock-on effects of such variable conditions for the meanings produced during that viewing?

A recent ethnographic study conducted by Ellen Seiter, Hans Borchers, Gabriele Kreutzner and Eva-Maria Warth with a group of female viewers of soap opera in Oregon, USA, has begun to probe the impact of the social context of viewing on the relations of particular audiences to their favourite soaps. The study was based on a series of interview/discussions in all-women groups of friends and neighbours. It found that the sociality of television viewing encouraged these viewers to exercise the female competences implied in soap opera's narrative structure as a means of engaging with but also extending the text as part of their own social interaction. In some cases friends plugged into the telephone system in order to 'talk about everything as it's happening'. In this respect the researchers suggest,

> ... soap opera texts are the products not of individual and isolated readings but of collective constructions – collaborative readings, as it were, of small social groups such as families, friends, and neighbours, or people sharing an apartment.
>
> (Seiter et al., 1989, p. 233)

Their preliminary interpretation of their findings takes us further into the distinction between the textual spectator and social audience, identifying a process of negotiation with or even resistance to the viewing position of 'ideal mother' which Modleski argues is constructed by soap opera's narrative structure. Against her view that the female viewer is unconsciously conditioned to occupy this position as 'an egoless receptacle for the suffering of others', the research group argue:

Modleski offers no possibility for *conscious* resistance to the soap opera text; the spectator position is conceived of in terms of a perfectly 'successful' gender socialization entirely in keeping with a middle-class (and white) feminine ideal … While this position was partially taken up by some of our middle-class, college-educated informants, it was consciously resisted and vehemently rejected by most of the women we interviewed, especially by working-class women. The relationship between the viewer and character more typically involved hostility – in the case of some of the presumably sympathetic characters – as well as fond admiration – for the supposedly despised villainesses …

(ibid.)

6   In conclusion

The last section outlined some of the main features through which soap opera was developed as a woman's form seeking to address a female audience. In the process we have seen how certain strategies – for example, daily serialization – produced unlooked-for consequences for the representation of women, most notably the need to extend the woman's story beyond marriage. Another unlooked-for consequence has been the longevity of soaps and circulation into a culture beyond that initially envisaged – first, from women at home to American college students and eventually into the primetime audience. We now need to pick up some of the themes concerning the nature of genre identity and the increasing evolution of genres across gender boundaries which were raised in section 4 in order to answer our initial question: how does soap opera function as a site of contest of gendered meanings and representations?

6.1   Soap opera: a woman's form no more?

It used to be relatively safe to identify soap opera as a women's form, since its daytime or early evening scheduling was more likely to net women listeners and viewers than men. But mass unemployment, which means men are as likely to be daytime viewers as women, and the gradual development of primetime soaps for mixed audiences, have meant that soap opera, despite the frequent denials men make of watching it, can no longer belong exclusively to women. Two changes in particular have struck recent commentators: first, the increasing centrality of male characters and, second, the increasing intrusion into soap opera of features from male-oriented genres. Thus *Dallas* incorporates elements of the western in its representation of the Southfork ranch, while both *Brookside* and *EastEnders* have drawn on elements of the crime drama for stories involving male characters – e.g. Barry Grant (*Brookside*) and Dirty Den (*EastEnders*). This has resulted in fast action sequences and goal-driven plotting to a degree uncharacteristic of traditional soap opera.

Such changes have led Christine Geraghty to conclude her study, *Women and Soap Opera* (1991), with the question, 'Soap opera: a woman's form no more?', while Charlotte Brunsdon speaks of the 'corruption' of women's genres by the incursion of characters, story lines and conventions of male genres. Well, perhaps. But equally interesting is an opposite movement, whereby the strategies and conventions of soap opera are increasingly deployed by what are traditionally thought of as male genres such as police or law series – e.g. *Hill Street Blues, The Bill, LA Law*. We might even be led to conclude of male-oriented series like *London's Burning* or *Soldier, Soldier* that we have male soap opera! Is this breaking down and intersection of genre boundaries evidence of the reassertion of male cultural dominance – the so-called feminist backlash? Or perhaps a sign of gender negotiation and contest taking place through the interaction of differently gendered genre conventions? In particular we need to consider how the traditional investment of 'male' genres in action and the public sphere negotiates with the conventions of soap opera which foreground the realm of the personal and feelings, and which deploy talk – gossip – as its major narrational strategy. What, then, is going on when in the constant shifting of genre boundaries men's genres and women's genres interact?

6.2   Dissolving genre boundaries and gendered negotiations

The increasing number of soap operas, their shift into the mainstream, and influence on male-oriented forms, suggest that soap opera has generated a far more extensive potential than its early progenitors ever envisaged, becoming itself a cultural resource to other genres. The question is, what kind of resource? First, as a form aimed at women, soap opera developed in the margins of popular culture as a space for the cultural representation of an undervalued area of experience – personal and emotional life. This fact frequently leads to the confusion of soap opera with melodrama. But such an equation fails to take account of the central role of talk in soap opera which cuts across melodrama's projection of emotion into expressive action and spectacle. In fact, drawing on melodrama's history, I have argued elsewhere (Gledhill, 1994) that it is the so-called male genres of action and adventure – genres in which monosyllabic heroes and villains project their antagonisms into violent conflict rather than intimate discussion – which are more properly termed 'melodramatic'. Women's genres such as women's fiction and soap opera draw on a tradition of domestic realism in which a set of highly articulate discursive forms – talk, the confessional heart-to-heart, gossip – work through psychic and social contradictions which melodrama must externalize through expressive action. Far from representing an 'excess' of emotion which displaces action, talk in soap opera *is* its action, while action in masculine genres more often than not represents unexpressed and often unexpressible male emotion, which needs a melodramatic climax to break out.

In this context, then, we can consider what negotiations are set going by the entry of more central male characters and actions into the soap operatic world. If this world makes greater space for female characters and the female perspective, then power over speech features as a major weapon in the struggles of female characters with their menfolk. Whereas in the majority of genres narrative events are controlled by male characters, in traditional soap operas the greater number of female protagonists exercising authority in the practices of domestic, personal and community life circumscribes and delimits the male characters. This, Christine Geraghty argues, has framed the spectator position within a female perspective, offering a viewpoint which would otherwise be unheard or heard only to be marginalized or mocked. The space given to this female point of view, from which male discourses are perceived and judged, is threatened, she argues, by the increasing number of male characters and actions in contemporary soap operas.

However, as we have seen, of all the genres soap opera is perhaps the most difficult to fix into particular meanings and effects. Cutting across the impact of male dominance in any given episode are the consequences of the still equal if not greater number of roles for female characters, of narrative inconclusiveness and reversal, of the role of audiences in extending the fiction beyond the bounds of the text, and the primacy, both textual and extra-textual, in this process of the feminine competence of talk. So, for example, in *Brookside* in 1995 a big public event or a high drama action – such as the Mandy Jordash appeal or the siege at Mike's flat – were relayed through the discussions and gossip taking place between the serial's characters gathered as bystanders in the street at some remove from events, discussions in which, in the case of the Jordash appeal, the general public was invited to join. Or we find, as in the example from *EastEnders* given at the start of this chapter, the diagnostic techniques of soap opera leading the most traditionally masculine of characters into unexpected confessional and introspective moments. This breakthrough to articulacy and intimacy for male protagonists is now penetrating action series such as *The Bill, NYPD Blue* or *London's Burning,* so that episodes are as likely to consist of exchanges in the men's washroom as of crime and fire-fighting.

FIGURE 6.6
Soldier, Soldier: Garvey and Tucker (Robson Green and Jerome Flynn) – male bonding.

This is not to suggest that talk as a culturally feminized activity is more ideologically acceptable than 'masculine' action, but, rather, that the submission of one to the other in the increasing intermingling of genres produces intersections of gendered modes and values which offer the potential for negotiations around gender definition and sexual identities. Male protagonists enter the confessional sphere of soap opera, but equally female protagonists imbue action with the values of the personal and domestic in, for example, traditionally masculinized genres such as the police series – e.g. *Cagney and Lacey* – or action movies – e.g. *Terminator 2* or *Aliens*. The question of what ideological work is performed by the tensions and contradictions set going between such intersecting gendered discourses depends on how they are viewed by different audiences operating within different reading frameworks.

Finally, I want to offer one last summarizing example from *Brookside* and the Mandy Jordash appeal to suggest how, as cultural media analysts, we might approach the intersection of the shifting conventions of soap opera – at their different levels of production, text, reception – with the social circulation of gender discourses. The staging of the appeal over several episodes drew on representations and discourses circulating in society belonging to, or representing, women's action groups, extremists, family violence, lesbians, which interwove with the generic conventions of soap opera and of the trial melodrama, producing through its formal and ideological organization the possibility of contradictory readings for different audience members. The courtroom has long served as a prime site for dramatizing the intersection of public with private life and, moreover, facilitates the stronger male roles favoured by *Brookside*. The public spaces appear to be dominated by male protagonists: in the courtroom itself by male judge and barristers, in the street outside by Sinbad, Mandy's new partner, railing against the women's protest group whose violence has caused the court's doors to be locked. Mandy and her female counsel speak only in the privacy of the anteroom behind the court. Moreover, the women's protest group shouting slogans outside the court are put down as disruptive intruders and lesbians by Sinbad and Mandy's neighbourhood women friends.

But in fact public and private, talk and action, domestic realism and melodrama, intersect to produce tensions that suggest an ideological cross-over between spheres and genders for those in the audience with sympathies to respond. Sinbad is a soap opera protagonist and acts not for the public interest, but on the contrary claims that the case on trial – one highly charged for feminist politics – is purely personal, family matter. On the other hand, the formal enactment of the courtroom melodrama brings the personal tragedy witnessed behind the scenes in a private sisterly space between Mandy and her female counsel into full public glare, providing evidence of the opposite contention, that the personal is in fact political. For as the circumstances surrounding Mandy and Beth's life with an abusive husband and father are argued in verbal interchange between male barristers, intercut with close-ups of the silent face of Mandy Jordash, framed behind the railings of courtroom furniture – a woman without a voice in a drama fought out between male protagonists – the pathos of her situation, caught between forces not of her making, becomes a potent symbol of women's oppression. For those among the female audience who find a certain resonance in the idea of disposing of an abusive husband and feel the parallels with the similar real-life case of Sara Thornton or other such cases, the possibility is offered of extending a

FIGURE 6.7 *Brookside:* Beth and Mandy Jordash (Anna Friel and Sandra Maitland) in the dock, July–August 1995.

FIGURE 6.8 Sara Thornton, on her release from prison, 29 July 1995.

gendered solidarity with Mandy of the kind represented by the women protesters outside the court but ostensibly put down as extremism. It is, then, as if there is a kind of contest going on between characters, generic and aesthetic forms, ideologies and potential readers as to the ownership of the trial and appeal, and whose interests it is to represent.

Included in such a contest, of course, will be polemical critiques of the programme's mobilization of stereotypes of the woman protester or lesbian, or personal identifications with the situation of a fictional protagonist that leads to the opening of a help-line after broadcasting. Indeed, part of the cultural work of soap opera is precisely this extension of debate into the public arena beyond the fiction. But as cultural media analysts we must avoid both fixing meanings and deciding the ideological effects of representations on the evidence of the textual product alone. Rather, primed with an awareness of the semiotic and social possibilities of a film or television programme, what we can do is establish conditions and possibilities of gendered (or other) readings and open up the negotiations of the text in order to understand the state of the contest.

References

ALLEN, R. (1985) *Speaking of Soap Opera*, Chapel Hill, NC, University of North Carolina Press.

ANG, I. (1985) *Watching Dallas: soap opera and the melodramatic imagination*, New York, Methuen.

BOURDIEU, P. (1984) *Distinction*, (tr. R. Nice), London, Routledge.

BRUNSDON, C. (1982) '*Crossroads*: notes on soap opera' in *Screen*, Vol. 22, No. 4, Spring, Society for Education in Film and Television Ltd.

BRUNSDON, C. (1984) 'Writing about soap opera' in Masterman, L. (ed.) *Television Mythologies*, London, Comedia/MK Press.

BUCKMAN, P. (1984) *All For Love: a study in soap opera*, London, Secker and Warburg.

D'ACCI, J. (1994) *Defining Women: television and the case of Cagney and Lacey*, London and Chapel Hill, NC, University of North Carolina Press.

DU GAY, P., HALL, S., JANES, L., MACKAY, H. and NEGUS, K. (1997) *Doing Cultural Studies: the case of the Sony Walkman*, London, Sage/The Open University (Book 1 in this series).

GERAGHTY, C. (1991) *Women and Soap Opera: a study of prime time soaps*, Cambridge, Polity Press.

GLEDHILL, C. (1994) 'Speculations on the relationship between melodrama and soap opera' in Browne, N. (ed.) *American Television: economies, sexualities, forms*, New York, Harwood Academic Publishers.

HASKELL, M. (1974) *From Reverence to Rape*, Harmondsworth, Penguin,.

KITZES, J. (1969) *Horizons West*, London, Thames and Hudson/BFI.

LOVELL, T. (1981) 'Coronation Street and ideology' in Dyer, R. et al., *Coronation Street*, Television Monograph 13, London, BFI.

MARGOLIES, D. (1982/3) 'Mills and Boon: guilt without sex', *Red Letters*, No.14.

MATTELART, M. (1985) 'From soap to serial' in *Women, Media and Crisis*, London, Comedia.

MODLESKI, T. (1982) 'The search for tomorrow in today's soap operas' in *Loving with a Vengeance*, New York, Methuen.

MULVEY, L. (1989) 'Visual pleasure and narrative cinema' in *Visual and Other Pleasures*, Basingstoke, Macmillan.

NEALE, S. (1981) *Genre*, London, BFI.

NEALE, S. (1990) 'Questions of genre', *Screen*, Vol.31, No.1.

SEITER, E., BORCHERS, H., KREUTZNER, G. and WARTH, E.-M. (1989) '"Don't treat us like we're so stupid and naive": toward an ethnography of soap opera viewers' in Seiter, E. et al. (eds) *Remote Control: television, audiences and cultural power*, London, Routledge.

TODOROV, T. (1976) 'The origin of genres', *New Literary History*, Vol. 8, No. 1 (Autumn).

READING A:
Tania Modleski, 'The search for tomorrow in today's soap operas'

[T]he classic (male) narrative film is, as Laura Mulvey points out, structured 'around a main controlling figure with whom the spectator can identify' (Mulvey, 1977, p. 420). Soap operas continually insist on the insignificance of the individual life. A viewer might at one moment be asked to identify with a woman finally reunited with her lover, only to have that identification broken in a moment of intensity and attention focused on the sufferings of the woman's rival.

If, as Mulvey claims, the identification of the spectator with 'a main male protagonist' results in the spectator's becoming 'the representative of power' (p. 420), the multiple identification which occurs in soap opera results in the spectator's being divested of power. For the spectator is never permitted to identify with a character completing an entire action. Instead of giving us one 'powerful ideal ego ... who can make things happen and control events better than the subject/spectator can' (p.420), soap operas present us with numerous limited egos, each in conflict with the others, and continually thwarted in its attempts to control events because of inadequate knowledge of other peoples' plans, motivations, and schemes. Sometimes, indeed, the spectator, frustrated by the sense of powerlessness induced by soap operas, will, like an interfering mother, try to control events directly:

> Thousands and thousands of letters [from soap fans to actors] give advice, warn the heroine of impending doom, caution the innocent to beware of the nasties ('Can't you see that your brother-in-law is up to no good?'), inform one character of another's doings, or reprimand a character for unseemly behavior.

> (Edmondson and Rounds, 1976, p. 193)

Presumably, this intervention is ineffectual, and feminine powerlessness is reinforced on yet another level.

The subject/spectator of soap operas, it could be said, is constituted as a sort of ideal mother: a person who possesses greater wisdom than all her children, whose sympathy is large enough to encompass the conflicting claims of her family (she identifies with them all) , and who has no demands or claims of her own (she identifies with no one character exclusively). [...]

[...]

It is important to recognize that soap operas serve to affirm the primacy of the family not by presenting an ideal family, but by portraying a family in a constant turmoil and appealing to the spectator to be understanding and tolerant of the many evils which go on within that family. The spectator/mother, identifying with each character in turn, is made to see 'the larger picture' and extend her sympathy to both the sinner and the victim. She is thus in a position to forgive all. As a rule, only those issues which can be tolerated and ultimately pardoned are introduced on soap operas. The list includes careers for women, abortions, premarital and extramarital sex, alcoholism, divorce, mental and even physical cruelty. An issue like homosexuality, which could explode the family structure rather than temporarily disrupt it, is simply ignored. Soap operas, contrary to many people's conception of them, are not conservative but liberal, and the mother is the liberal par excellence. By constantly presenting her with the many-sidedness of any question, by never reaching a permanent conclusion, soap operas undermine her capacity to form unambiguous judgments.

References

EDMONDSON, M. and ROUNDS, D. (1976) *From Mary Noble to Mary Hartman: the complete soap opera book*, New York, Stein and Day.

MULVEY, L. (1977) 'Visual pleasure and narrative cinema' in Kay, K. and Peary, G. (eds) *Women and the Cinema,* New York, E.P. Dutton.

Source: Modleski, 1982, pp. 91–3.

READING B:
Charlotte Brunsdon, 'Crossroads: notes on soap opera'

I will consider the [...] question of the type of cultural competence that *Crossroads* as soap-opera narrative(s) demands of its social reader.

Just as a Godard film requires the possession of certain forms of cultural capital on the part of its audience to 'make sense' – an extra-textual familiarity with certain artistic, linguistic, political and cinematic discourses – so too does *Crossroads/* soap opera. The particular competences demanded by soap opera fall into three categories:

1   Generic knowledge – familiarity with the conventions of soap opera as a genre. For example, expecting discontinuous and cliff-hanging narrative structures.

2   Serial-specific knowledge – knowledge of past narratives and of characters (in particular, who belongs to who).

3   Cultural knowledge of the socially acceptable codes and conventions for the conduct of personal life.

I will only comment on the third category here. The argument is that the narrative strategies and concerns of *Crossroads* call on the traditionally feminine competencies associated with the responsibility for 'managing' the sphere of personal life. It is the culturally constructed skills of femininity – sensitivity, perception, intuition and the necessary privileging of the concerns of personal life – which are both called on and practised in the genre. The fact that these skills and competencies, this type of cultural capital, is ideologically constructed as natural, does not mean, as many feminists have shown, that they are the *natural* attributes of femininity. However, under present cultural and political arrangements, it is more likely that female viewers will possess this repertoire of both sexual and maternal femininities which is called on to fill out the range of narrative possibilities when, for example, the phone rings. That is, when Jill is talking to her mother about her marriage (17 January 1979), and the phone rings, the viewer needs to know not only that it is likely to be Stan (her nearly ex-husband) calling about custody of their daughter Sarah-Jane (serial-specific knowledge) and that

we're unlikely to hear the content of the phone-call in that segment (generic knowledge) but also that the mother's 'right' to her children is no longer automatically assumed. These knowledges only have narrative resonance in relation to discourses of maternal femininity which are elaborated elsewhere, already in circulation and brought to the programme by the viewer. In the enigma that is then posed – will Jill or Stan get Sarah-Jane? – questions are also raised about who, generally and particularly *should* get custody. The question of what *should* happen is rarely posed 'openly' – in this instance it was quite clear that 'right' lay with Jill. But it is precisely the terms of the question, the way in which it relates to other already circulating discourses, if you like, the degree of its closure, which form the site of the construction of moral consensus, a construction which 'demands', seeks to implicate, a skilled viewer.

I am thus arguing that *Crossroads* textually implies a feminine viewer to the extent that its textual discontinuities require a viewer competent within the ideological and moral frameworks, the rules of romance, marriage and family life, to make sense of it.

Against critics who complain of the redundancy of soap opera, I would suggest that the radical discontinuities of the text require extensive, albeit interrupted, engagement on the part of the audience, before it becomes pleasurable. This is not to designate *Crossroads* 'progressive' but to suggest that the skills and discourses mobilized by its despised popularity have partly been overlooked because of their legitimation as natural (feminine).

Source: Brunsdon, 1982, pp. 36-7.

Acknowledgements

Grateful acknowledgement is made to the following sources for permission to reproduce material in this book:

Chapter 1

Text

Reading A: Looking at the Overlooked: Four Essays on Still Life Painting first published in English by Reaktion Books 1990 © Reaktion Books 1990; *Readings B and C:* Barthes, R. (1972) *Mythologies*, Random House (UK) Ltd. Reprinted by permission of Hil and Wang, a division of Farrar, Straus & Giraux, Inc.: Excerpts from 'The world of wrestling' and 'Myth today' from *Mythologies* by Roland Barthes, translated by Annette Lavers. Translation copyright © 1972 by Jonathan Cape Ltd; *Reading D:* Barthes, R. (1977) *Image – Music – Text*, HarperCollins Publishers Ltd; *Reading E:* Laclau, E. and Mouffe, C. (1990) *New Reflections on the Revolution of Time*, Verso; *Reading F:* From *The Female Malady* by Elaine Showalter, Copyright © 1985 by Elaine Showalter. Reprinted by permission of Pantheon Books, a division of Random House, Inc. Also by permission of Little Brown and Company (UK); *Table 1.1:* courtesy of the library, Scott Polar Research Institute, Cambridge.

Figures

Figure 1.1: Copyright Tate Gallery, London; *Figure 1.2:* Courtesy White Cube Gallery; *Figure 1.3:* San Diego Museum of Art (Gift of Anne R. and Amy Putnam); *Figure 1.4:* Colorsport; *Figure 1.5:* Courtesy of Gucci/Mario Testino; *Figure 1.6:* Panzani Frères; *Figure 1.7:* Jaguar Cars Ltd/J. Walter Thompson, London; *Figure 1.8:* Photo: Jean Loup Charmet; *Figure 1.9:* Madrid, Prado/ Photo: Giraudon; *Figure 1.10:* Photo: P. Regnard, from *Iconographie photographique de la Salpêtrière*, 1878.

Chapter 2

Text

From *Eyes of Time* by Marianne Fulton. Copyright © 1989 by the International Museum of Photography at George Eastman House. By permission of Little, Brown and Company.

Figures

Figures 2.1a, 2.2, 2.5, 2.7, 2.9, 2.10, 2.16, 2.17, 2.18, 2.19, 2.20, 2.23, 2.24: Robert Doisneau/Network/Rapho; *Figure 2.3:* Photo: A. Kertész. Copyright Ministère de la Culture, France; *Figures 2.4, 2.8, 2.11, 2.14, 2.15, 2.22, 2.26, 2.27, 2.29, 2.30:* Willy Ronis/Network/Rapho; *Figures 2.6, 2.12, 2.13, 2.21, 2.31:* Henri Cartier-Bresson/Magnum; *Figures 2.25, 2.28:* Jean-Phillipe Charbonnier/Network/Rapho; *Figure 2.32:* Copyright William Klein.

Chapter 3

Text

Reading B: Lawrence, E.A. (1991) 'His very silence speaks: the horse who survived Custer's Last Stand', in Browne, R.B. and Browne, P. (eds) *Digging into Popular Culture, Theories and Methodologies in Archeology, Anthropology and Other Fields*, Copyright © 1991 by Bowling Green State University Popular Press; *Reading C:* O'Hanlon, M. (1993) *Paradise Portraying the New Guinea Highlands*, British Museum Press; *Reading D:* Clifford, J. (1995) 'Paradise', *Visual Anthropology Review*, 11 (1), American Anthropology Association; *Reading E:* Coombes, A. (1994) *Reinventing Africa*, Yale University Press. Copyright © 1994 by Annie E.S. Coombes.

Figures

Figure 3.1: Ashmolean Museum, Oxford; *Figure 3.2:* Stock Montage, Inc; *Figures 3.3, 3.5:* Pitt Rivers Museum, Oxford; *Figures 3.4, 3.7:* Copyright British Museum; *Figures 3.6 a,b:* Ancient Art and Architecture Collection; *Figure 3.8:* Missouri Historical Society, St Louis; *Plates 3.I–3.XV:* Photographs provided courtesy of the Trustees of the British Museum.

Chapter 4

Text

Reading A: McClintock, A. (1995) *Imperial Leather*, Routledge; *Reading B:* Dyer, R. (1986) *Heavenly Bodies*, Macmillan Press Ltd, also by permission of St Martin's Press, Inc.; *Reading C:* Gilman, S. (1985) *Difference and Pathology*, used by permission of the publisher, Cornell University Press; *Reading D:* Mercer, K. (1994) *Welcome to the Jungle*, Routledge.

Figures

Figure 4.1: Photo component of cover – Stewart Fraser/Copyright Colorsport; *Figure 4.2:* © World copyright ALLSPORT; *Figure 4.3:* Copyright 1996 Kenneth Jarecke/CONTACT Press Images/Colorific!; *Figure 4.4:* Copyright 1989 Jose Azel/AURORA/Colorific!; *Figure 4.5:* Courtesy of Pirelli Tyres Limited. Carl Lewis is a member of the Santa Monica Track Club; *Figure 4.7:* Huntley & Palmers Biscuits; *Figure 4.8a:* British Library; *Figure 4.8b:* A. & F. Pears Ltd; *Figure 4.9:* Courtesy of the Print Collection, Lewis Walpole Library, Yale University; *Figures 4.10, 4.11, 4.12, 4.14:* Copyright pictures: Felix de Rooy, Negrophilia Foundation Amsterdam. Photographer: Pierre Verhoeff; *Figure 4.13:* Mary Evans Picture Library; *Figures 4.15, 4.16, 4.17, 4.18:* Ronald Grant Archive;. *Figure 4.19:* Culver Pictures; *Figure 4.20:* Source unknown. Reproduced from Richard Dyer (1987) *Heavenly Bodies*, London, Macmillan; *Figure 4.21:* Courtesy of George Eastman House; *Figure 4.22:* Edwin Long (1829–91) *The Marriage Market, Babylon*. Royal Holloway and Bedford New College, Surrey. The Bridgeman Art Library, London; *Figure 4.23:* Reproduced from: S. Gilman (1985) *Difference and Pathology*, Cornell University Press; *Figure 4.24:* Reproduced from: Cesare Lombroso and Guillaume Ferraro (1893) *La donna delinquente: la prostituta e la donna normale*, L. Roux; *Figure 4.25:* George Rodger/Magnum; *Figure 4.26:* Reproduced from: John Grand-Carteret

(1909) *Die Erotik in der französchen Karikatur*, Vienna, C.W. Stern; *Figures 4.27, 4.28:* Copyright David Bailey/Autograph; *Figure 4.29:* Photo from *Looking for Langston*. Copyright Sunil Gupta, *Looking for Langston*, Director: Isaac Julien/Sankofa; *Figure 4.30:* Jimmy Freeman, 1981. Copyright © 1981 The Estate of Robert Mapplethorpe; *Figure 4.31:* Copyright 1987 (The Estate of) Rotimi Fani-Kayode/Courtesy: Autograph.

Chapter 5

Text

Reading A: Neale, S. (1983) 'Masculinity as spectacle', *Screen,* 24, (6), Oxford University Press; *Reading B:* Nixon, S. (1996) *Hard Looks*, UCL Press.

Figures

Figure 5.1a: Reproduced by kind permission of Nick Kamen. Photo: Shilland and Co; *Figure 5.1b:* Reproduced by kind permission of Select Men. Photo: Bartle Bogle Hegarty; *Figure 5.2:* Reproduced from *The Face*, August 1986/ Tony Hodges and Partners Advertising Agency; *Figure 5.3:* Spencer Rowell 'L'Enfant'. Reproduced by kind permission of the artist and Cartel International Limited; *Figure 5.4:* Reproduced from *The Face*, March 1985. Without prejudice. All attempts to trace the photographer, Jamie Morgan and the model, Simon de Montford (*sic*) having failed we wish to acknowledge their rights in this image; *Figure 5.5: Arena,* Spring 1987. Photo: Martin Brading. By permission of Smile Agency; *Figures 5.6, 5.7: Arena,* Summer/ Autumn 1991. Photo: Randall Mesdun. By permission of Camilla Arthur Representation Europe; *Figure 5.8: Arena,* Spring 1991. Photo: Robert Erdmann; *Figures 5.9, 5.10, 5.11: GQ,* February/March 1989, Photographs by Tim Brett-Webb, © The Condé Nast Publications Ltd/GQ.

Chapter 6

Text

Reading A: Modleski, T. (1982) *Loving with a Vengeance: mass-produced fantasies for women*, Methuen, Inc., Copyright © 1982 by Tania Modleski. All rights reserved; *Reading B:* Brunsdon, C. (1981) *'Crossroads* – notes on soap opera', *Screen,* 22 (4), Oxford University Press.

Figures

Figure 6.1: Copyright BBC; *Figure 6.2a:* Copyright LWT Productions Ltd 1993; *Figure 6.2b:* Photograph copyright Carlton UK Television 1996. Reproduced with permission from Thames Television; *Figure 6.3:* Artwork copyright Orion Pictures Corporation; *Figure 6.4:* Granada Television Ltd; *Figure 6.5:* Last Resort Picture Library; *Figure 6.6:* Photograph copyright Carlton UK Television 1996; *Figure 6.7:* Copyright Mersey Television Company; *Figure 6.8:* Martin Argles/The Guardian.

Every effort has been made to trace all copyright owners, but if any have been inadvertently overlooked, the publishers will be pleased to make the necessary arrangements at the first opportunity.

Index